SACRED AND SECULAR

Seminal thinkers of the nineteenth century – Auguste Comte, Herbert Spencer, Émile Durkheim, Max Weber, Karl Marx, and Sigmund Freud – all predicted that religion would gradually fade in importance and cease to be significant with the emergence of industrial society. The belief that religion was dying became the conventional wisdom in the social sciences during most of the twentieth century. During the last decade, however, the secularization thesis has experienced the most sustained challenge in its long history.

The traditional secularization thesis needs updating. Religion has not disappeared and is unlikely to do so. Nevertheless, the concept of secularization captures an important part of what is going on. This book develops a theory of secularization and existential security and compares it against survey evidence from almost 80 societies worldwide.

Sacred and Secular is essential reading for anyone interested in comparative religion, sociology, public opinion, political behavior, political development, social psychology, international relations, and cultural change.

Pippa Norris is the McGuire Lecturer in Comparative Politics at the John F. Kennedy School of Government, Harvard University. Her work compares elections and public opinion, gender politics, and political communications. Companion volumes by this author, also published by Cambridge University Press, include *A Virtuous Circle* (2000), *Digital Divide* (2001), *Democratic Phoenix* (2002), *Rising Tide* (2003, with Ronald Inglehart), and *Electoral Engineering* (2004).

Ronald Inglehart is professor of political science and program director at the Institute for Social Research at the University of Michigan. His research deals with changing belief systems and their impact on social and political change. He helped found the Euro-Barometer Surveys and directs the World Values Surveys. Related books include *Modernization and Postmodernization: Cultural, Economic and Political Change in 43 Societies* (1997), *Rising Tide* (2003, with Pippa Norris), and *Modernization, Cultural Change and Democracy* (forthcoming, with Christian Welzel).

Cambridge Studies in Social Theory, Religion, and Politics

Editors

David C. Leege *University of Notre Dame*
Kenneth D. Wald *University of Florida, Gainesville*

The most enduring and illuminating bodies of late-nineteenth-century social theory – by Marx, Weber, Durkheim, and others – emphasized the integration of religion, polity, and economy through time and place. Once a staple of classic social theory, however, religion gradually lost the interest of many social scientists during the twentieth century. The recent emergence of phenomena such as Solidarity in Poland; the dissolution of the Soviet empire; various South American, Southern African, and South Asian liberation movements; the Christian Right in the United States; and Al-Qaeda have reawakened scholarly interest in religiously based political conflict. At the same time, fundamental questions are once again being asked about the role of religion in stable political regimes, public policies, and constitutional orders. The series Cambridge Studies in Social Theory, Religion, and Politics will produce volumes that study religion and politics by drawing on classic social theory and more recent social scientific research traditions. Books in the series offer theoretically grounded, comparative, empirical studies that raise "big" questions about a timely subject that has long engaged the best minds in social science.

Sacred and Secular

RELIGION AND POLITICS WORLDWIDE

Pippa Norris
Harvard University

Ronald Inglehart
University of Michigan

CAMBRIDGE
UNIVERSITY PRESS

CAMBRIDGE UNIVERSITY PRESS
Cambridge, New York, Melbourne, Madrid, Cape Town, Singapore, São Paulo

Cambridge University Press
40 West 20th Street, New York, NY 10011–4211, USA

www.cambridge.org
Information on this title:www.cambridge.org/9780521839846

First published 2004
Reprinted 2005 (twice), 2006

Printed in the United States of America

A catalogue record for this book is available from the British Library.

Library of Congress Cataloguing in Publication Data
Norris, Pippa.
Sacred and secular ; religion and politics worldwide / Pippa Norris and Ronald Inglehart.
p.   cm. — (Cambridge studies in social theory, religion, and politics)
Includes bibliographical references and index.
ISBN 0-521-83984-X — ISBN 0-521-54872-1 (pbk.)
1. Religion and politics. I. Inglehart, Ronald. II. Title. III. Series.
BL65.P7N67   2004
306.6—dc22   2004045119

ISBN-13   978-0-521-83984-6 hardback
ISBN-10   0-521-83984-X hardback

ISBN-13   978-0-521-54872-4 paperback
ISBN-10   0-521-54872-1 paperback

Contents

CONCLUSIONS

Tables

Figures

Preface and Acknowledgments

The events of 9/11 and their aftermath in Afghanistan and Iraq have shaken scholarly assumptions about "the end of history" and the post–Cold War peace dividend – and the study of religion has suddenly emerged into the glare of public attention. Is religious conflict now the central issue? Were the prophecies of a new "clash of civilizations" being realized? Speculation about these matters was fed by a rapidly expanding literature on everything from the causes of terrorism to divisions in the Atlantic alliance, the prospects for democracy in the Middle East, and the nature of Islamic beliefs.

Social scientists are divided concerning whether the process of secularization is reducing the role of religion in everyday life – or whether the world's major religious faiths are experiencing a strong resurgence. Fortunately, a massive body of new evidence about the underlying factors driving religiosity around the globe has recently become available. This book uses this evidence to reexamine the classic questions about the nature of religion. Building on ideas Weber and Durkheim developed a century ago, it develops a new theoretical framework for understanding how the experience of existential security drives the process of secularization. We test this theory against evidence from the Values Surveys 1981–2001, which have carried out representative national surveys in eighty societies around the globe, covering all the world's major faiths. This analysis builds on our previous book, *Rising Tide: Gender Equality and Cultural Change Around the World* (2003), which examined the role of religiosity in explaining egalitarian or traditional attitudes toward the roles of women and men. We hope that this study will contribute to informing the debate about the role of religion in the contemporary world.

This book owes multiple debts to many friends and colleagues. The analysis draws on a unique database – the World Values Survey (WVS) and the European Values Survey (EVS). These surveys provide data from countries containing more than 85% of the world's population and covering the full range of variation, from societies with per capita incomes as low as $300 per year to societies with per capita incomes one hundred times that high; and from long-established democracies with market economies to authoritarian states and ex-socialist states. We owe a large debt of gratitude to the following WVS and EVS participants for creating and sharing this invaluable dataset: Abdel-Hamid Abdel-Latif, Anthony M. Abela, Q. K. Ahmad, Rasa Alishauskene, Helmut Anheier, Jose Arocena, W. A. Arts, Soo Young Auh, Taghi Azadarmaki, Ljiljana Bacevic, Olga Balakireva, Josip Balobn, Miguel Basanez, Elena Bashkirova, Abdallah Bedaida, Jorge Benitez, Jaak Billiet, Alan Black, Ammar Boukhedir, Rahma Bourquia, Fares al Braizat, Pavel Campeanu, Augustin Canzani, Marita Carballo, Henrique Carlos de O. de Castro, Pi-Chao Chen, Pradeep Chhibber, Mark F. Chingono, Hei-yuan Chiu, Margit Cleveland, Andrew P. Davidson, Jaime Diez Medrano, Herman De Dijn, Juan Diez Nicolas, Karel Dobbelaere, Peter J. D. Drenth, Javier Elzo, Yilmaz Esmer, P. Estgen, T. Fahey, Nadjematul Faizah, Georgy Fotev, James Georgas, C. Geppaart, Renzo Gubert, Linda Luz Guerrero, Peter Gundelach, Jacques Hagenaars, Loek Halman, Mustafa Hamarneh, Sang-Jin Han, Stephen Harding, Mari Harris, Bernadette C. Hayes, Camilo Herrera, Virginia Hodgkinson, Nadra Muhammed Hosen, Kenji Iijima, Ljubov Ishimova, Wolfgang Jagodzinski, Aleksandra Jasinska-Kania, Fridrik Jonsson, Stanislovas Juknevicius, Jan Kerkhofs SJ, Johann Kinghorn, Zuzana Kusá, M. Legrand, Ola Listhaug, Hans-Dieter Klingemann, Hennie Kotze, Marta Lagos, Bernard Lategan, Carlos Lemoine, Noah Lewin-Epstein, Jin-yun Liu, Brina Malnar, Mahar Mangahas, Felipe Miranda, Mario Marinov, Carlos Matheus, Robert Mattes, Mansoor Moaddel, Jose Molina, Rafael Mendizabal, Alejandro Moreno, Gaspar K. Munishi, Elone Nwabuzor, Neil Nevitte, F. A. Orizo, Dragomir Pantic, Juhani Pehkonen, Paul Perry, Thorleif Pettersson, Pham Minh Hac, Pham Thanh Nghi, Gevork Pogosian, Bi Puranen, Ladislav Rabusic, Angel Rivera-Ortiz, Catalina Romero, David Rotman,

Rajab Sattarov, Seiko Yamazaki, Sandeep Shastri, Shen Mingming, Renata
Siemienska, John Sudarsky, Tan Ern Ser, Farooq Tanwir, Jean-Francois
Tchernia, Kareem Tejumola, Larissa Titarenko, Miklos Tomka, Alfredo
Torres, Toru Takahashi, Niko Tos, Jorge Vala, Andrei Vardomatskii,
Malina Voicu, Alan Webster, Friedrich Welsch, Christian Welzel, Ephraim
Yuchtman-Yaar, Josefina Zaiter, Brigita Zepa, and Paul Zulehner.
Most of these surveys were supported by sources within the given coun-
try, but assistance for surveys where such funding was not available and for
central coordination was provided by the National Science Foundation, the
Bank of Sweden Tercentenary Foundation, the Swedish Agency for Inter-
national Development, the Volkswagen Foundation, and the BBVA Foun-
dation. For more information about the World Values Survey, see the WVS
websites: http://wvs.isr.umich.edu/ and http://www.worldvaluessurvey.org.
The European surveys used here were gathered by the European Values
Survey group (EVS). For details of EVS findings, see Loek Halman, *The
European Values Study: A Sourcebook Based on the 1999/2000 European Values Study Surveys*. Tilburg: EVS, Tilburg University Press, 2001. For more
information, see the EVS website, http://evs.kub.nl.
Some preliminary ideas were first sketched out in articles published in
Foreign Policy and *Comparative Sociology*. The theme of the book received
encouragement in conversations over the years with many colleagues including David Appel, William Inglehart, Swanee Hunt, Richard Parker,
Larry Diamond, Ivor Crewe, Mark Franklin, and Sam Huntington. We
also are most grateful to all those who went out of their way to provide
feedback on initial ideas or to read through draft chapters and provide
comments. The support of Cambridge University Press has been invalu-
able, particularly the efficient assistance and continuous enthusiasm of our
editor, Lew Bateman, and his assistant, Sarah Gentile, as have the comments
of the anonymous reviewers and of David C. Leege, co-editor of the series Cambridge Studies in Social Theory, Religion, and Politics. We thank
Karen Long and Zhengxu Wang for assistance in cleaning and coding the
WVS, and Roopal Thaker and Jose Chicoma at the Kennedy School for
research assistance in the collection of datasets and literature. Lastly, this
book would not have been possible without the encouragement and stimulation provided by many colleagues and students at the John F. Kennedy
School of Government, Harvard University, and the Department of Political Science and the Institute for Social Research at the University of
Michigan.

– Cambridge, Massachusetts, and Ann Arbor, Michigan

SACRED AND SECULAR

PART I

Understanding Secularization

The Secularization Debate

THE SEMINAL SOCIAL thinkers of the nineteenth century – Auguste Comte, Herbert Spencer, Émile Durkheim, Max Weber, Karl Marx, and Sigmund Freud – all believed that religion would gradually fade in importance and cease to be significant with the advent of industrial society.[1] They were far from alone; ever since the Age of the Enlightenment, leading figures in philosophy, anthropology, and psychology have postulated that theological superstitions, symbolic liturgical rituals, and sacred practices are the product of the past that will be outgrown in the modern era. The death of religion was the conventional wisdom in the social sciences during most of the twentieth century; indeed it has been regarded as *the* master model of sociological inquiry, where secularization was ranked with bureaucratization, rationalization, and urbanization as the key historical revolutions transforming medieval agrarian societies into modern industrial nations. As C. Wright Mills summarized this process: "*Once the world was filled with the sacred – in thought, practice, and institutional form. After the Reformation and the Renaissance, the forces of modernization swept across the globe and secularization, a corollary historical process, loosened the dominance of the sacred. In due course, the sacred shall disappear altogether except, possibly, in the private realm.*"[2]

During the last decade, however, this thesis of the slow and steady death of religion has come under growing criticism; indeed, secularization theory is currently experiencing the most sustained challenge in its long history.

Critics point to multiple indicators of religious health and vitality today, ranging from the continued popularity of churchgoing in the United States to the emergence of New Age spirituality in Western Europe, the growth in fundamentalist movements and religious parties in the Muslim world, the evangelical revival sweeping through Latin America, and the upsurge of ethno-religious conflict in international affairs.[3] After reviewing these developments, Peter L. Berger, one of the foremost advocates of secularization during the 1960s, recanted his earlier claims: *"The world today, with some exceptions . . . is as furiously religious as it ever was, and in some places more so than ever. This means that a whole body of literature by historians and social scientists loosely labeled 'secularization theory' is essentially mistaken."* [4] In a fierce and sustained critique, Rodney Stark and Roger Finke suggest it is time to bury the secularization thesis: *"After nearly three centuries of utterly failed prophesies and misrepresentations of both present and past, it seems time to carry the secularization doctrine to the graveyard of failed theories, and there to whisper 'requiescat in pace.'"* [5]

Were Comte, Durkheim, Weber, and Marx completely misled in their beliefs about religious decline in industrialized societies? Was the predominant sociological view during the twentieth century totally misguided? Has the debate been settled? We think not. Talk of burying the secularization theory is premature. The critique relies too heavily on selected anomalies and focuses too heavily on the United States (which happens to be a striking deviant case) rather than comparing systematic evidence across a broad range of rich and poor societies.[6] We need to move beyond studies of Catholic and Protestant church attendance in Europe (where attendance is falling) and the United States (where attendance remains stable) if we are to understand broader trends in religious vitality in churches, mosques, shrines, synagogues, and temples around the globe.

There is no question that the traditional secularization thesis needs updating. It is obvious that religion has not disappeared from the world, nor does it seem likely to do so. Nevertheless, the concept of secularization captures an important part of what is going on. This book develops a revised version of secularization theory that emphasizes the extent to which people have a sense of existential security – that is, the feeling that survival is secure enough that it can be taken for granted. We build on key elements of traditional sociological accounts while revising others. We believe that the importance of religiosity persists most strongly among vulnerable populations, especially those living in poorer nations, facing personal survival-threatening risks. We argue that feelings of vulnerability to physical, societal, and personal risks are a key factor driving religiosity and we demonstrate that the process of secularization – a systematic erosion of religious practices, values, and beliefs – has occurred most clearly among the most prosperous social sectors living in affluent and secure postindustrial nations.

Secularization is a tendency, not an iron law. One can easily think of striking exceptions, such as Osama bin Laden, who is (or was) extremely rich and fanatically religious. But when we go beyond anecdotal evidence such as this, we find that the overwhelming bulk of evidence points in the opposite direction: people who experience ego-tropic risks during their formative years (posing direct threats to themselves and their families) or socio-tropic risks (threatening their community) tend to be far more religious than those who grow up under safer, comfortable, and more predictable conditions. In relatively secure societies, the remnants of religion have not died away; in surveys most Europeans still express formal belief in God, or identify themselves as Protestants or Catholics on official forms. But in these societies the importance and vitality of religion, its ever-present influence on how people live their daily lives, has gradually eroded.

The most persuasive evidence about secularization in rich nations concerns values and behavior: the critical test is what people say is important to their lives and what they actually *do*. As this book will document, during the twentieth century in nearly all postindustrial nations – ranging from Canada and Sweden to France, Britain, and Australia – official church records report that where once the public flocked to Sabbath worship services, the pews are now almost deserted. The surveys monitoring European churchgoing during the last fifty years confirm this phenomenon. The United States remains exceptional in this regard, for reasons explained in detail later in Chapter 4.

Despite trends in secularization occurring in rich nations, this does not mean that the world as a whole has become less religious. As this book will demonstrate:

1. The publics of virtually all advanced industrial societies have been moving toward more secular orientations during the past fifty years. Nevertheless,

2. The world as a whole now has more people with traditional religious views than ever before – and they constitute a growing proportion of the world's population.

Though these two propositions may initially seem contradictory, they are not. As we will show, the fact that the first proposition is true helps account for the second – because secularization and human development have a powerful negative impact on human fertility rates. Practically all of the countries in which secularization is most advanced show fertility rates far below the replacement level – while societies with traditional religious orientations have fertility rates that are two or three times the replacement level. They contain a growing share of the world's population. The expanding gap between sacred and secular around the globe has important consequences for cultural change, society, and world politics.

Part I uses this theoretical framework to develop and test a series of propositions, demonstrating how religiosity is systematically related to (i) levels of societal modernization, human security, and economic inequality; (ii) the predominant type of religious culture in any nation; (iii) generational shifts in values; (iv) different social sectors; and (v) patterns of demography, fertility rates, and population change. Part II analyzes detailed regional case studies comparing religiosity in the United States and Western Europe, the Muslim world, and post-Communist Europe. Part III then examines the social and political consequences of secularization, and its ramifications for cultural and moral values, religious organizations and social capital, and voting support for religious parties. The conclusion summarizes the key findings and highlights the demographic patterns generating the widening gap over religion around the world.

This study draws on a massive base of new evidence generated by the four waves of the World Values Survey executed from 1981 to 2001. The World Values Survey has carried out representative national surveys in almost eighty societies, covering all of the world's major faiths. We also examine other evidence concerning religiosity from multiple sources, including Gallup International polls, the International Social Survey Program, and Eurobarometer surveys. At one level, there is nothing novel or startling about our claims. A mainstream tradition in sociology, anthropology, history, and social psychology has long theorized that cross-cultural differences in religiosity exist in many societies worldwide. But traditional secularization theory has come under powerful and sustained criticism from many influential scholars during the past decade. Systematic survey evidence comparing cultural attitudes toward religion across many developing nations remains scattered and inconclusive, with most studies limited to a handful of affluent postindustrial societies and established democracies in Western Europe and North America. As well as reconceptualizing and refining secularization theory, our study examines the wealth of survey evidence for religiosity from a broader perspective and in a wider range of countries than ever before.

Traditional Theories of Secularization

The most influential strands of thought shaping the debate over secularization can be broadly subdivided into two perspectives. On the one hand, *demand-side* theories, which focus "bottom up" on the mass public, suggest that as societies industrialize, almost regardless of what religious leaders and organizations attempt, religious habits will gradually erode, and the public will become indifferent to spiritual appeals. By contrast, the *supply-side* theory, which focuses "top-down" on religious organizations, emphasizes that the public demand for religion is constant and any cross-national variations in the vitality of spiritual life are the product of its supply in religious markets.[7] Supply-siders argue that religious organizations and leaders play a strategic role in aggressively building and maintaining congregations, essentially suggesting that "if you build a church, people will come." After outlining these alternative accounts, we conclude that, although the original theory of secularization was flawed in certain regards, it was correct in the demand-side perspective. We then summarize our alternative theory of secularization, based on conditions of existential security, which is developed fully throughout this study.

The Rational Weltanschauung: The Loss of Faith

The idea that the rise of a rational worldview has undermined the foundations of faith in the supernatural, the mysterious, and the magical predated the thought of Max Weber, but it was strongly influenced by his work in *The Protestant Ethic and the Spirit of Capitalism* (1904) and in *Economics and Society* (1933).[8] Many leading sociologists advanced the rationalist argument farther during the 1960s and 1970s, foremost among them Peter Berger, David Martin, and Brian Wilson.[9]

In this perspective, the era of the Enlightenment generated a rational view of the world based on empirical standards of proof, scientific knowledge of natural phenomena, and technological mastery of the universe. Rationalism was thought to have rendered the central claims of the Church implausible in modern societies, blowing away the vestiges of superstitious dogma in Western Europe. The loss of faith was thought to cause religion to unravel, eroding habitual churchgoing practices and observance of ceremonial rituals, eviscerating the social meaning of denominational identities, and undermining active engagement in faith-based organizations and support for religious parties in civic society.

Science and religion could confront each other directly in a zero-sum game where scientific explanations undermined the literal interpretation of Biblical teachings from Genesis 1 and 2, exemplified by the Darwinian theory of evolution that challenged ideas of special creation by God.[10] Even more importantly, scientific knowledge, its applications through technology and engineering, and the expansion of mass education could have a broader and more diffuse social impact by ushering in a new cultural era. Following the European enlightenment, rational calculation was thought to have gradually undercut the foundations of core metaphysical beliefs. The idea of the mysterious was regarded by Weber as something to be conquered by human reason and mastered by the products of technology, subject to logical explanations found in physics, biology, and chemistry rather than to divine forces outside this world. The dazzling achievements of medicine, engineering, and mathematics – as well as the material products generated by the rise of modern capitalism, technology, and manufacturing industry during the nineteenth century – emphasized and reinforced the idea of mankind's control of nature.[11] Personal catastrophes, contagious diseases, disastrous floods, and international wars, once attributed to supernatural forces, primitive magic, and divine intervention, or to blind fate, came to be regarded as the outcome of predictable and preventable causes. Priests, ministers, popes, rabbis, and mullahs appealing to divine authority became only one source of knowledge in modern societies, and not necessarily the most important or trusted one in many dimensions of life, when competing with the specialized expertise, certified training, and practical skills of professional economists, physicists, physicians, or engineers.[12] The division of church and state, and the rise of secular-rational bureaucratic states and representative governments, displaced the rule of spiritual leaders, ecclesiastical institutions, and hereditary rulers claiming authority from God. As Bruce summarized this argument:

> Industrialization brought with it a series of social changes – the fragmentation of the life-world, the decline of community, the rise of bureaucracy, technological consciousness – that together made religion less arresting and less plausible than it had been in pre-modern societies. That is the conclusion of most social scientists, historians, and church leaders in the Western world.[13]

The core Weberian thesis concerns the impact of the Reformation and the Industrial Revolution occurring many centuries earlier, so it remains difficult to scrutinize systematically with any contemporary empirical evidence. But if a rational worldview generates widespread skepticism about the existence of God and belief in the metaphysical, then those societies that express most confidence in science might be expected to prove least religious; in fact, as documented in Chapter 3, we find the reverse.

Functional Evolution: The Loss of Purpose

A related explanation is offered by theories of functional differentiation in industrialized societies, predicting the loss of the central role of religious institutions in society. This argument originated from the seminal work of Émile Durkheim in *The Elementary Forms of the Religious Life* (1912), and by the 1950s the functionalist perspective had become the predominant sociological view.[14] Contemporary theorists who developed this account further include Steve Bruce, Thomas Luckman, and Karel Dobbelaere.[15]

Functionalists emphasize that religion is not simply a system of beliefs and ideas (as Weber suggests); it is also a system of actions involving formal rituals and symbolic ceremonies to mark the major passages of birth, marriage, and death, as well as the regular seasonal celebrations. These rituals played an essential function for society as a whole, Durkheim suggested, by sustaining social solidarity and cohesion, maintaining order and stability, thereby generating collective benefits. Durkheim argued that industrialized societies are characterized by functional differentiation, where specialized professionals and organizations, dedicated to healthcare, education, social control, politics, and welfare, replaced most of the tasks once carried out exclusively in Western Europe by monasteries, priests, and parish churches. Faith-based voluntary and charitable organizations in the medieval era – the alms-house, the seminary, and the hospice – were displaced in Europe by the expansion of the welfare state during the mid-nineteenth and early twentieth centuries. The growth of the state created publicly funded schools, healthcare, and welfare safety nets to care for the unemployed, the elderly, and the destitute. Stripped of their core social purposes, Durkheim predicted that the residual spiritual and moral roles of religious institutions would gradually waste away in industrial societies, beyond the traditional formal rites of births, marriages, and death, and the observance of special holidays.

The theory of evolutionary functionalism became the popular orthodoxy in the sociology of religion during the postwar decades. Jagodzinski and Dobbelaere, for example, proposed such an explanation to account for the shrinking church-going congregations in Western Europe: *"All the empirical evidence in this chapter is compatible with the assumption that functional rationalization related to functional differentiation, detraditionalization, and ensuring individualization have a cumulative impact on the decline of church involvement, especially among the post-war generation.*"[16] If this thesis is correct, one implication is that church congregations should have fallen further and fastest in affluent societies that have developed extensive welfare states, such as in Sweden, the Netherlands, and France – and indeed much of the evidence is consistent with this account.[17]

Yet in recent decades growing numbers of critics have expressed reservations about the core claims of the functionalist version of societal development. An erosion of the *social* purpose of the church through functional differentiation does not necessarily mean that the core moral and spiritual roles of religious institutions are diminished or lost – indeed, they could become more important. Functionalist theory, which dominated the literature on social development during the 1950s and 1960s, gradually fell out of intellectual fashion; the idea that all societies progress along a single deterministic pathway of socioeconomic development toward a common end-point – the modern secular democratic state – came under increasing challenge in anthropology, comparative sociology, and comparative politics from a multicultural perspective emphasizing that communities, societies, and states experience diverse forms of change.[18] Rather than an inevitable and steady loss of spiritual faith or purpose as societies modernize, critics argue that more complex historical and cross-country patterns are evident, where religion rises and falls in popularity at different periods in different societies, fueled by specific factors, such as the charisma of particular spiritual leaders, the impact of contingent events, or the mobilization of faith-based movements. To support this argument, observers point to a resurgence of religiosity evident in the success of Islamic parties in Pakistan, the popularity of Evangelicalism in Latin America, outbreaks of ethno-religious bloodshed in Nigeria, and international conflict in Afghanistan and Iraq in the aftermath of the events of 9/11.[19] At the same time, elsewhere religious faith may flounder, and the church may experience a crisis of mass support, due to contingent events and local circumstances, such as the American public's reaction toward sex abuse scandals among the Roman Catholic clergy, or deep divisions within the international Anglican Church leadership over the issue of homosexuality. Hence Andrew Greeley argues that diverse patterns of religiosity exist today, even among affluent European nations, rather than observing any consistent and steady conversion toward atheism or agnosticism, or any loss of faith in God.[20]

The demand-side accounts of secularization initiated by the work of Weber and Durkheim have been subjected to massive intellectual battering during the last decade. After reviewing the historical evidence of church-going in Europe, Rodney Stark concludes that secularization is a pervasive myth, based on failed prophecies and ideological polemic, unsupported by systematic data: *"The evidence is clear that claims about a major decline in religious participation [in Europe] are based in part on very exaggerated perceptions of past religiousness. Participation may be very low today in many nations, but not because of modernization; therefore the secularization thesis is irrelevant."*[21] For Jeffrey Hadden, the assumptions within secularization constitute a doctrine or dogma more than a well-tested rigorous theory: *"a taken-for-granted ideology rather than a systematic set of interrelated propositions."*[22] He argues that benign neglect, rather than confirming evidence, kept the claims of secularization intact for so long. The idea that religion would shrink and eventually vanish was a product of the social and cultural milieu of its time, fitting the evolutionary functional model of modernization. The emergence of new spiritual movements, and the way that religion remains entangled in politics, suggests, Hadden believes, that secularization is not happening as predicted. He argues that those who claim that secularization has occurred have exaggerated and romanticized the depth of religious practices in the European past and also simultaneously underestimated the power and popularity of religious movements in the present era, exemplified by an evangelical revival in Latin America and New Age spirituality in Western Europe. The body of scholarship that arose during the last decade has generated a vigorous debate about the contemporary vitality of religious life, raising important questions about the links that were assumed to connect the process of modernization with secularization.

The Theory of Religious Markets: The Loss of Competition

Traditional secularization theory is now widely challenged, but no single theoretical framework has yet won general acceptance to replace it. The supply-side school of rational choice theorists that emerged in the early 1990s, although remaining controversial, provides the most popular alternative. Indeed, Warner claims that this represents a "new paradigm," as the model has stimulated numerous studies during the last decade.[23] The religious market model disregards the public's "demand" for religion, which is assumed to be constant, but focuses instead on how conditions of religious freedom, and the work of competing religious institutions, actively generate its "supply." The principal proponents include, among others, Roger

Finke, Rodney Stark, Lawrence R. Iannaccone, William Sims Bainbridge, and R. Stephen Warner.[24]

The earlier prevailing view was that pluralism *eroded* religious faith. The Protestant Reformation led to the fragmentation of Western Christendom, with diverse sects and denominations emphasizing alternative beliefs and doctrines. For Durkheim this process destroyed the hegemonic power of a single pervasive theological faith, sowing the seeds of skepticism and doubt.[25] Drawing heavily upon the analogy of firms struggling for customers in the economic market, supply-side theory assumes the exact opposite. The core proposition in the religious market approach is the notion that vigorous competition between religious denominations has a *positive* effect on religious involvement. The explanation why religion flourishes in some places while languishing in others rests upon the energies and activities of religious leaders and organizations. The more churches, denominations, creeds, and sects compete in a local community, the theory assumes, the harder rival leaders need to strive to maintain their congregations. Proponents argue that the continued vitality of religious beliefs and practices in the United States can plausibly be explained by the sheer diversity of American faith-based organizations, strong pluralistic competition among religious institutions, freedom of religion, and the constitutional division of church and state.[26] Older mainstream denominations in America, such as Catholics, Episcopalians, and Lutherans, have been challenged by rival evangelical churches which demand more time and energies, but also offer a more vigorous religious experience.[27]

By contrast, communities where a single religious organization predominates through government regulation and subsidies, for example establishment churches, are conditions thought to encourage a complacent clergy and moribund congregations, stultifying ecclesiastical life in the same way that state-owned industries, corporate monopolies, and business cartels are believed to generate inefficiencies, structural rigidities, and lack of innovation in the economic market. Stark and Finke suggest that Northern Europe is dominated by "socialized religion," where state regulations favor established churches, through fiscal subsidies or restrictions on rival churches. This process, they suggest, reinforces religious monopolies, and complacent and apathetic clergy, leading to indifferent publics and the half-empty pews evident in Scandinavia.[28]

Yet, after more than a decade of debate and study, the supply-side claim that religious pluralism fosters religious participation remains in dispute (as discussed more fully in Chapter 4). Critics suggest that some of the comparative evidence is inconsistent with the theory, for example this account has trouble explaining the continuing strength of congregations in many countries in Southern Europe, despite the monopolistic role of the Catholic Church.[29] One of the most common empirical measures of religious pluralism used to support this account was subsequently discovered to be flawed and statistically contaminated.[30] A thorough meta-review of the series of more than two dozen empirical studies published in the academic literature on the sociology of religion, conducted by Chaves and Gorski, concluded with harsh criticism of the theory:

> The claim that religious pluralism and religious participation are generally and positively associated with one another – the core empirical hypothesis of the market approach to the study of religion – is not supported, and attempts to discredit countervailing evidence on methodological grounds must be rejected. A positive relationship between religious pluralism and religious participation can be found only in a limited number of contexts, while the concepts themselves translate poorly to non-modern settings.[31]

The contemporary debate has therefore thrown considerable doubt on the traditional Weberian and Durkheimian versions of the secularization thesis, but the grounds for accepting religious market theory are based on faith more than fact. The supply-side account has not yet won general acceptance in the social sciences.

The Thesis of Secularization Based on Existential Security

The classic version of secularization theory clearly needs to be updated; but to simply reject it entirely would be a major mistake, for it is correct in some major respects. Stark and Finke conclude: *"What is needed is not a simple-minded theory of inevitable religious decline, but a theory to explain variation."*[32] We agree. Our theory of secularization based on existential security rests on two simple axioms or premises that prove extremely powerful in accounting for most of the variations in religious practices found around the world. The core axioms and hypotheses are illustrated schematically in Figure 1.1. What is the underlying logic of our argument?

The Security Axiom

The first basic building block of our theory is the assumption that rich and poor nations around the globe differ sharply in their levels of sustainable human development and socioeconomic inequality, and thus also in the basic living conditions of human security and vulnerability to risks. The idea of human security has emerged in recent years as an important objective of international development, although the concept is complex and multiple definitions exist in the literature.[33] At its simplest, the core idea of security denotes freedom from various risks and dangers.[34] The traditional view focused upon using military strength to ensure the territorial integrity and security of nation states. During the last decade this view was revised as analysts began to recognize that this definition was excessively narrow, with many other risks also contributing to human security, ranging from environmental degradation to natural and manmade disasters such as floods, earthquakes, tornadoes, and droughts, as well as the threat of disease epidemics, violations of human rights, humanitarian crisis, and poverty. The wide range of dangers means that the concept of human security can become so broad and overloaded that it can lose all coherence and practical utility, as well as becoming difficult or even impossible to gauge with a single composite measure. Nevertheless, the core idea of human security, irrespective of the specific nature of the risks, is one that is widely recognized as important to well-being, and we regard the absence of human security as critical for religiosity.

The inhabitants of poor nations remain highly susceptible to premature death – above all from hunger and hunger-related diseases. They also face sudden disasters from drought or flood, or weather-related emergencies. Poor nations have limited access to the basic conditions of survival, including the provision of uncontaminated water and adequate food, access to effective public services offering basic healthcare, literacy, and schooling, and an adequate income. These countries also often face endemic problems of pollution from environmental degradation, conditions of widespread gender inequality, and a legacy of deep-rooted ethnic conflict. Lack of capacity to overcome these difficulties arises from corruption in government, an ineffective public sector, and political instability. Poor nations often have weak defenses against external invasion, threats of internal coup d'etat, and, in extreme cases, state failure.

Where poorer agrarian economies develop into moderate industrial societies, and then progress further to becoming more affluent postindustrial societies, this process brings broadly similar trajectories generally improving the basic conditions of human security. The process of industrialization and human development helps lift developing countries out of extreme poverty, greatly reducing the uncertainty and daily risks to survival that people face, as documented in the extensive literature on development published by the United National Development Program and the World Bank.[35] The

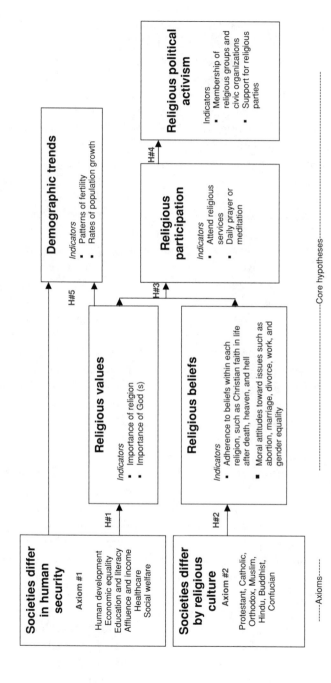

Figure 1.1. Schematic Model Explaining Religiosity

move from subsistence rural farming to moderate-income manufacturing generally helps to lift the most vulnerable population out of dire poverty and commonly improves standards of living, bringing urbanization, better nutrition, sanitation, and access to clean water. More developed societies also usually have better hospitals, trained healthcare professionals, access to basic drugs and medicine, and public services reducing infant and child mortality, immunization programs, family planning, and more adequate prevention and treatment against the ravages of HIV/AIDS. Schooling, and the essential literacy and numeric skills, become more widely available for boys *and* girls. This development, combined with the diffusion of mass communications, gradually creates a more informed and politically aware public. The expansion of the professional and managerial service sectors brings middle-class employees access to health insurance, pensions, and greater material assets. Meanwhile, the growth of the welfare safety net, and more effective delivery of government services as societies develop, ensures the less well-off against the worst risks of ill health and old age, penury and destitution. For all these reasons, the first stage of societal modernization transforms the living conditions for many people, reducing their vulnerability to sudden, unpredictable risks.

Yet economic development is a necessary, but not sufficient, condition to create human security. In many developing nations, pockets of deep-rooted poverty often remain among the least well-off sectors. In Mexico, Colombia, or Brazil, for example, extreme poverty exists among residents in urban favelas, shantytowns, and isolated rural villages, along with a growing bourgeoisie. Conditions of socioeconomic inequality are critical for widespread conditions of human security; otherwise growth only enriches the affluent elite and the governing classes, a common pattern in many mineral and oil-rich nations such as Nigeria, Venezuela, and Saudi Arabia.

Moreover, there is an important distinction to be drawn between our account and some simpler and more mechanical versions of modernization theory. Although we believe that human development and conditions of economic equality usually generate growing levels of security, this generalization should be understood as probabilistic, *not* deterministic; situation-specific factors make it impossible to predict exactly what will happen in any given society. We believe that the public generally gains conditions of greater security during the process of modern development, but this process can always be momentarily halted or temporarily reversed, even in rich countries, by particular dramatic events such as major natural disasters, experience of wars, or severe recessions. Even the most affluent postindustrial nations may experience a sudden widespread resurgence of insecurity; for example, fears of terrorism arose sharply in the United States, especially for residents on the East Coast, immediately after the events of September 11, 2001.[36] Another example is the recent experience of Argentina, a country rich in agricultural and natural resources, with a well-educated workforce, a democratic political system, and one of South America's largest economies. But economic growth experienced a sudden crisis; a deep recession was the prelude to economic collapse in 2001, leaving more than half the population living in poverty. The country struggled with record debt defaults, a ruined banking system, deep cynicism about politics, and currency devaluation. Formerly middle-class professionals who lost their savings and their jobs – teachers, office workers, and civil servants – suddenly became dependent upon soup kitchens, bartering, and garbage collections to feed their children. Through modernization, we believe that rising levels of security become increasingly likely to occur. But these changes are not mechanical or deterministic; specific events and leaders can hinder or advance the pace of human development in a society.

The Cultural Traditions Axiom

The second building block for our theory assumes that the distinctive worldviews that were originally linked with religious traditions have shaped the cultures of each nation in an enduring fashion; today, these distinctive values are transmitted to the citizens even if they never set foot in a church, temple, or mosque. Thus, although only about 5% of the Swedish public attends church weekly, the Swedish public as a whole manifests a distinctive Protestant value system that they hold in common with the citizens of other historically Protestant societies such as Norway, Denmark, Iceland, Finland, Germany, and the Netherlands. Today, these values are not transmitted primarily by the church, but by the educational system and the mass media, with the result that although the value systems of historically Protestant countries differ markedly and consistently from those of historically Catholic countries – the value systems of Dutch Catholics are much more similar to those of Dutch Protestants than to those of French, Italian, or Spanish Catholics. Even in highly secular societies, the historical legacy of given religions continues to shape worldviews and to define cultural zones. As a distinguished Estonian colleague put it, in explaining the difference between the worldviews of Estonians and Russians, "We are all atheists; but I am a Lutheran atheist, and they are Orthodox atheists." Thus we assume that the values and norms in Catholic and Protestant societies, for example orientations toward the work ethic, sexual liberalization, and democracy, will vary systematically based on past historical traditions, as well as varying in Hindu, Buddhist, Confucian, Orthodox, and Muslim societies, even among people living in these societies who do not adhere to these faiths or feel that they belong to any church, temple, or mosque.

Hypotheses

If we can accept these two basic axioms as reasonable and relatively uncontroversial, they suggest a series of propositions or hypotheses that are tested throughout this book to see if they stand up to scrutiny against the empirical evidence.

1. The Religious Values Hypothesis

Religious market theorists assume that demand is constant, so that variance in religiosity must be generated by supply. We start from very different premises since we believe that the experience of living under conditions of human security during a person's formative years will shape the demand for religion and therefore the priority that people give to religious values. In particular, we hypothesize that, all things being equal, *the experiences of growing up in less secure societies will heighten the importance of religious values*, while conversely *experience of more secure conditions will lessen it*.

Modernization theories suggest that economic and political changes go together with cultural developments in coherent and consistent ways. We demonstrate later that the process of human development has significant consequences for religiosity; as societies transition from agrarian to industrial economies, and then develop into postindustrial societies, the conditions of growing security that usually accompany this process tends to reduce the importance of religious values. The main reason, we believe, is that the need for religious reassurance becomes less pressing under conditions of greater security. These effects operate at both the societal level (socio-tropic) and the personal level (ego-tropic), although we suspect that the former is more important. Greater protection and control, longevity, and health found in postindustrial nations mean that fewer people in these societies regard traditional spiritual values, beliefs, and practices as vital to their lives, or to the lives of their community. This does not imply that all forms of religion necessarily disappear as societies develop; residual and symbolic elements often remain, such as formal adherence to religious identities, even when their substantive meaning has faded away. But we expect that people living in advanced industrial societies will often grow increasingly indifferent to traditional religious leaders and institutions, and become less willing to engage in spiritual activities. Contrary to the religious markets school, we assume that the "demand" for spirituality is far from constant; instead, striking variations are evident due to experience of the basic living conditions found in rich and poor nations.

Virtually all of the world's major religious cultures provide reassurance that, even though the individual alone can't understand or predict what lies ahead, a higher power will ensure that things work out. Both religion and secular ideologies assure people that the universe follows a plan, which guarantees that if you follow the rules, everything will turn out well, in this world or the next. This belief reduces stress, enabling people to shut out anxiety and focus on coping with their immediate problems. Without such a belief system, extreme stress tends to produce withdrawal reactions. Under conditions of insecurity, people have a powerful need to see authority as both strong and benevolent – even in the face of evidence to the contrary.

Individuals experiencing stress have a need for rigid, predictable rules. They need to be sure of what is going to happen because they are in danger – their margin for error is slender and they need maximum predictability. Conversely, people raised under conditions of relative security can tolerate more ambiguity and have less need for the absolute and rigidly predictable rules that religious sanctions provide. People with relatively high levels of existential security can more readily accept deviations from familiar patterns than people who feel anxiety concerning their basic existential needs. In economically secure industrial societies, with an established basic safety net safeguarding against the risks of absolute poverty and a relatively egalitarian distribution of household incomes, an increasing sense of safety brings a diminishing need for absolute rules, which contributes to the decline of traditional religious norms.

In agrarian societies, humanity remains at the mercy of inscrutable and uncontrollable natural forces. Because their causes were dimly understood, people tended to attribute whatever happened to anthropomorphic spirits or gods. The vast majority of the population made their living from agriculture, and were largely dependent on things that came from heaven, like the sun and rain. Farmers prayed for good weather, for relief from disease, or from plagues of insects.

Industrialization brings a cognitive mismatch between traditional normative systems and the world most people know from their first-hand experience. The symbols and worldview of the established religions are no longer as persuasive or compelling as they were in their original setting. In industrial society, production moved indoors into a manmade environment. Workers did not passively wait for the sun to rise and the seasons to change. When it got dark, people turned on the lights; when it got cold, people turned up the heating. Factory workers did not pray for good crops – manufacturing production depended on machines created by human ingenuity. With the discovery of germs and antibiotics, even disease ceased to be seen as a divine visitation; it became a problem within human control.

Such profound changes in people's daily experience led to changes in the prevailing cosmology. In industrial society, where the factory was the center of production, a mechanistic view of the universe seemed natural. Initially, this gave rise to the concept of God as a great watchmaker who had constructed the universe and then left it to run largely on its own. But as human control of the environment increased, the role ascribed to God dwindled. Materialistic ideologies arose that proposed secular interpretations of history and secular utopias to be attained by human engineering. As people moved into a knowledge society, the mechanical world of the factory became less pervasive. People's life experiences dealt more with ideas than with material things. In the knowledge society, productivity depends less on material constraints than on information, innovation, and imagination. But under the conditions of existential insecurity that have dominated the lives of most of humanity throughout most of history, the great theological questions concerned a relatively narrow constituency; the vast majority of the population was most strongly concerned with the need for reassurance in the face of a world where survival was uncertain, and this was the dominant factor explaining the grip of traditional religion on mass publics.

2. The Religious Culture Hypothesis

The predominant religious cultural traditions in any society, such as the legacy of Protestantism and Catholicism in Western Europe, are expected to leave a distinct imprint upon the contemporary moral beliefs and social attitudes that are widespread among the public in these nations. Nevertheless, if secularization has occurred in postindustrial nations, as we suggest, then the influence of religious traditions can be expected to have faded most in these societies.

Predominant religious cultures are understood here as path-dependent, adapting and evolving in response to developments in the contemporary world, and yet also strongly reflecting the legacy of the past centuries.[37] The major faiths of the world express divergent teachings and doctrines on many moral values and normative beliefs, such as those surrounding the roles of women and men, the sanctity of life, and the importance of marriage and the family. To focus our analysis, we examine the impact of the predominant religious culture on contemporary societies in the context of Max Weber's theory of the Protestant ethic and the rise of capitalism,[38] and also the more recent claims about the importance of Western and Muslim religious cultures made by Samuel Huntington's theory of a "clash of civilizations."[39]

3. The Religious Participation Hypothesis

We anticipate that the declining importance of religious values in postindustrial nations has in turn eroded regular participation in religious practices, exemplified by attendance at services of worship and engagement in regular prayer or meditation.

Each major religion defines its own important and distinct practices in spiritual rituals, ceremonies, and observances, often associated with the life-changes of birth, marriage, and death, as well as celebration of certain holy days, and there are multiple variations within each religion's sects, denominations, and communities. Christian religious practices are exemplified by habitual church attendance on Sundays and special holidays, as well as by the role of prayer, charitable giving, the significance of communion, and the rituals of baptism, confirmation, and marriage. But within this common repertoire, Anglicans, Methodists, and Baptists each emphasize their own specific rituals. Elsewhere meditation rituals and ceremonies are central to Buddhism, along with the observation of festivals, blessings and initiations, and the role of monastic communities. For Muslims, the Qur-an specifies the five Pillars of Islam, including public profession of faith by recitation of the shahada, daily performance of the salat prayer ritual, annual giving of obligatory alms, fasting during Ramadan, and performance once in a lifetime in the rituals of the Great Pilgrimage to Mecca (the Hajj). Alternative New Age forms of spirituality involve an even wider range of activities, including psychic, pagan, metaphysical, personal growth, and holistic healthcare, with practices exemplified by yoga, meditation, aroma therapies, channeling, divination, and astrology.

In this limited study, we cannot hope to compare all the varied forms of religious behavior found in each of the world's major religions, but, as discussed in the next chapter, we can analyze the most common aspects of religious practices, symbolized by attendance at services of worship and regular engagement in prayer or meditation. We predict that the strongest decline in religious participation will occur in affluent and secure nations, where the importance of religion has faded most. By contrast, where religious values remain a vital part of people's everyday lives, in poor agrarian societies, we also expect that people will be most active in worship and prayer.

4. The Civic Engagement Hypothesis

In turn, there are good reasons to believe that regular religious participation, particularly collective acts at services of worship, will probably
encourage political and social engagement and also electoral support for
religious parties.

Theories of social capital claim that, in the United States, regular churchgoing encourages belonging to faith-based organizations and joining a
broader range of community groups in civic society. Mainline Protestant
churches in the United States have long been regarded as playing a central role in the lives of their local communities by providing places for
people to meet, fostering informal social networks of friends and neighbors, developing leadership skills, informing people about public affairs,
drawing together people from diverse social and ethnic backgrounds, and
encouraging active involvement in associational groups concerned with education, youth development, and human services. The role of churches in
the United States raises important questions: in particular, do religious
institutions function in similar ways in other countries, fostering social
networks, associational activism, and civic engagement? And, if so, has
secularization contributed to an erosion of social capital? Classic theories of voting behavior have also long claimed that in Western Europe
electoral cleavages between Protestants and Catholics, reinforced by the
organizational links between the Catholic Church and Christian Democratic parties, encourage the religious to vote for parties of the right.
Yet again if religious participation and values have eroded in postindustrial societies, as we argue, then we would also expect to see a process of
religious dealignment, with denominational identities playing a less important role in voting behavior. By contrast, in developing societies we
would predict that religion would continue to play an important role in
politics.

5. The Demographic Hypothesis

Yet while this series of hypotheses might lead to the assumption that secularization is spreading worldwide, in fact the situation is far more complex.
We find that human development and growing conditions of existential
security erode the importance of religious values, and thereby also reduce
rates of population growth in postindustrial societies. Thus we expect to
find that rich societies are becoming more secular in their values but at the
same time they are also shrinking in population size. By contrast we expect
that poor nations will remain deeply religious in their values, and also will

display far higher fertility rates and growing populations. One of the most central injunctions of virtually all traditional religions is to strengthen the family, to encourage people to have children, to encourage women to stay home and raise children, and to forbid abortion, divorce, or anything that interferes with high rates of reproduction. As a result of these two interlocking trends, rich nations are becoming more secular, but the world as a whole is becoming more religious.

Cultures have been defined as survival strategies for a society, and one can see this as a competition between two fundamentally different survival strategies. (1) Rich, secular societies produce fewer people, but with relatively high investment in each individual, producing knowledge societies with high levels of education, long life expectancies, and advanced economic and technological levels. This also provides greatly enhanced military potential and national security, but because families are placing an important investment in few offspring, these societies place a relatively high valuation on each individual and show a relatively low willingness to risk lives in war. On the other hand (2) poorer traditional societies produce large numbers of children, investing much less in each individual. Sons are valued more highly than daughters, but if one has several sons, the loss of one or two is tragic but not catastrophic. Infant mortality rates and death rates are sufficiently high that people implicitly do not expect all of their children to survive.

The modern strategy emphasizes high investment in relatively few individuals, with equal investment in both sons and daughters and a heavy investment of human capital in a smaller but more highly skilled workforce in which women are utilized as fully as men. The traditional strategy narrowly limits women's opportunities for education and the paid workforce, leaving few options except motherhood and family, with much less investment in each individual.[40] Within this strategy, talented women are not educated and are not allowed careers outside the home, which means that their potential contribution to society beyond the home is wasted. This strategy also has an indirect cost: it means that uneducated mothers raise children, so girls and boys receive less intellectual stimulation in their crucial early years. On the other hand, this strategy produces far greater numbers of children.

It is not clear which strategy is more effective. The modern strategy produces a much higher standard of living, higher life expectancy, and greater subjective well-being, and modern nations have greater technological and military power. But insofar as sheer numbers count, traditional societies are clearly winning: they are becoming an increasingly large proportion of the world's population. As a result we expect to find, and indeed demonstrate, enormous contrasts between the fertility rates of traditional and modern societies. Today, virtually all advanced industrial societies have fertility rates far below the population replacement level – and some of them are producing only about half as many children as would be needed to replace the adult population. Conversely, poorer societies have birth rates well above the population replacement level, and many are producing two or three times as many children as would be needed to replace the adult population. The net effect is that the religious population is growing fast, while the secular number is shrinking, despite the fact that the secularization process is progressing steadily in rich nations.

6. The Religious Market Hypothesis

Yet we do not rest our argument upon simply proving this series of propositions. To consider the core proposition of the alternative religious market school, we also test the empirical evidence for the assumptions at the heart of this rival theory. Religious market theory expects that religious participation will be influenced by the supply of religion, in particular: greater religious pluralism and also greater religious freedom will both increase religious participation.

To examine the evidence for these propositions, in subsequent chapters we compare the impact on religious participation (frequency of attending services of worship) of both religious pluralism (computing the standard Herfindahl Index) and a new 20-point Religious Freedom Index. We demonstrate that pluralism has no positive relationship with participation, either within postindustrial societies or in worldwide perspective. The theory fits the American case but the problem is that it fails to work elsewhere. State regulation provides a more plausible explanation of patterns of churchgoing in affluent societies, but even here the relationship is weak and the correlation may well be spurious. In post-Communist Europe, religious pluralism and religious freedom have a negative relationship with participation. Overall we conclude that the degree of religious pluralism in a society is far less important than people's experience with whether survival is seen as secure or insecure.

Conclusions

Three important conclusions flow from this study. First, we conclude that due to rising levels of human security, *the publics of virtually all advanced industrial societies have been moving toward more secular orientations.* We demonstrate that "modernization" (the process of industrialization, urbanization, and rising levels of education and wealth) greatly weakens the influence of religious institutions in affluent societies, bringing lower rates of attendance at religious services, and making religion subjectively less important in people's lives.

The overall trend is clear: within most advanced industrial societies, church attendance has fallen, not risen, over the past several decades; moreover, the clergy have largely lost their authority over the public and are no longer able to dictate to them on such matters as birth control, divorce, abortion, sexual orientation, and the necessity of marriage before childbirth. Secularization is not taking place only in Western Europe, as some critics have claimed (though it was first observed there). It is occurring in most advanced industrial societies, including Australia, New Zealand, Japan, and Canada. The United States remains an outlier among postindustrial societies, having a public that holds much more traditional worldviews than that of any other rich country except Ireland. But even in America, there has been a lesser but perceptible trend toward secularization; the trend has been partly masked by massive immigration of people with relatively traditional worldviews (and high fertility rates) from Hispanic countries as well as by relatively high levels of economic inequality; but when one controls for these factors, even within the United States there has been a significant movement toward secularization.

Nevertheless, it would be a major mistake to assume that secularization is triumphantly advancing and that religion will eventually disappear throughout the world. Our second conclusion is that *due to demographic trends in poorer societies, the world as a whole now has more people with traditional religious views than ever before* – and they constitute a growing proportion of the world's population. Rich societies are secularizing but they contain a dwindling share of the world's population; while poor societies are not secularizing and they contain a rising share of the world's population. Thus, modernization does indeed bring a de-emphasis on religion within virtually any country that experiences it, but the percentage of the world's population for whom religion is important, is rising.

The differential fertility rates of religious and secular societies is by no means a sheer coincidence; quite the contrary, it is directly linked with secularization. The shift from traditional religious values to secular-rational values brings a cultural shift from an emphasis on a traditional role for women, whose lives are largely limited to producing and raising many children, first under the authority of their fathers and then their husbands, with little autonomy and few options outside the home, to a world in which women have an increasingly broad range of life choices, and most women have careers and interests outside the home. This cultural shift is linked with a dramatic decline in fertility rates. Both religiosity and human development have a powerful impact on fertility rates, as we will demonstrate. The evidence suggests that human development leads to cultural changes that drastically reduce (1) religiosity and (2) fertility rates. Rising affluence does not automatically produce these changes, but it has a high probability of doing so, because it tends to bring about important changes in mass belief systems and social structure.

Lastly we predict, although we cannot yet demonstrate, that *the expanding gap between the sacred and the secular societies around the globe will have important consequences for world politics, raising the role of religion on the international agenda*. Despite popular commentary, this does not mean that this situation will necessarily generate more intense ethno-religious conflict, within or between nations. In the aftermath of 9/11, and U.S. military intervention in Afghanistan and Iraq, many commentators believe that these events reflect a deep-rooted clash of civilizations, but we should not assume a simple monocausal explanation. In recent years, many protracted civil wars have been settled through negotiated settlements, including in Angola, Somalia, and Sudan. The most reliable independent estimate of the number and severity of incidents of ethnic conflict and major wars around the globe suggests that a sizeable "peace dividend" has occurred during the post–Cold War era. The Minorities at Risk report estimates that the number of such incidents peaked in the mid-1980s, and subsequently declined, so that by late-2002 ethnic conflict had reached its lowest level since the early 1960s.[41] We do believe, however, that the accommodation of divergent attitudes toward moral issues found in traditional and modern societies, exemplified by approval or disapproval of sexual liberalization, women's equality, divorce, abortion, and gay rights, provides an important challenge to social tolerance. The contemporary debate over these issues is symbolized by the potential schism within the Anglican Church surrounding the consecration in the United States of Canon Gene Robinson, an openly gay bishop. Cultural contrasts between more religious and more secular values will probably fuel heated debate about many other complex ethical questions, such as the legalization of euthanasia in the Netherlands, the enforcement of strict Sharia laws for the punishment of adultery in Nigeria, or the availability of reproductive rights in the United States. Nevertheless we remain strictly agnostic about whether cultural differences over religious values will inevitably generate outbreaks of protracted violence, armed hostilities, or international conflict, an important issue well beyond the scope of this study.

Demonstrating the Theory

This book will examine systematic evidence concerning this series of propositions, probing into whether societal development levels are consistently related to patterns of religious values, beliefs, and behavior. If we are correct, we should find marked contrasts between agrarian, industrial, and postindustrial societies in indicators of religiosity, such as participation in daily prayer and regular churchgoing, beyond the purely symbolic rituals associated with birth, marriage, and death, and the celebration of religious holidays.

This study examines evidence for the alternative cognitive, functionalist, and supply-side accounts of secularization we have discussed, finding little evidence consistently supporting these theories. The central claim in the Weberian argument is that the spread of scientific knowledge and rising levels of education will bring a universal trend toward an increasingly rational worldview, in all industrial societies. If this is correct, then it suggests that secularization should have progressed furthest among the most educated and those who emphasize and respect science. Yet we do not find any such universal trend: as we shall demonstrate, secularization is most closely linked with whether the public of a given society has experienced relatively high levels of economic and physical security. Moreover, the Weberian interpretation emphasizes cognitive factors that tend to be irreversible and universal: the spread of scientific knowledge does not disappear in times of crisis or economic downturn. If this were the dominant cause of secularization, we would not expect to find the fluctuations in religiosity that are linked with varying levels of security.

If this revised theory of secularization based on existential security is correct, and if cultural patterns of religiosity are coherent and predictable, then certain specific propositions or hypotheses follow – each of which will be tested in this study using cross-national comparisons, time-series trends, and generational analysis.

(i) Cross-National Comparisons

Our first basic proposition is that levels of societal modernization, human development, and economic equality shape the strength of religiosity – meaning the *values*, *beliefs*, and *practices* of religion existing in any society.

We expect that poorer pre-industrial societies, which are most vulnerable to the threat of natural disasters and social risks, are most likely to emphasize the central importance of religion. By contrast, religion will be given lower priority by the publics of affluent postindustrial societies, who live under higher levels of physical and social security. We expect to find similar comparisons for many other indicators of religiosity, including the strength of religious identities, theological beliefs, adherence to traditional moral attitudes, and habits of religious observance and practices such as prayer and attendance at services of worship. The fact that we have survey data from almost eighty societies, covering the full range of variance from low-income economies to affluent postindustrial nations, and including all major religious traditions, makes it possible to test these hypotheses in a more conclusive fashion than has ever before been possible.

(ii) Comparing Predominant Religious Cultures

Yet we also expect that each society's historical legacy of predominant religious traditions will help shape adherence to particular religious values, beliefs, and practices. Consequently, we expect that the predominant religious culture will stamp its mark on each society, affecting how societal modernization influences patterns of religious beliefs and practices. As a result, important variations in religiosity can exist even among societies at similar levels of socioeconomic development. To examine this proposition, we will compare societies classified according to their predominant religious culture.

(iii) Generational Comparisons

In societies that have experienced sustained periods of rising economic growth and physical security (such as Germany, the United States, and Japan), or very rapid economic growth (such as South Korea and Taiwan), we expect to find substantial differences in the religious values held by older and younger generations. In such societies, the young should prove least religious in their values, attitudes, and practices while the older cohorts should display more traditional orientations, since basic values do not change overnight; instead, socialization theory suggests that we should find a substantial time lag between changing economic circumstances and their impact on prevailing religious values, because adults retain the norms, values, and beliefs that were instilled during their formative pre-adult years.[42] Cultural values change as younger birth cohorts, shaped by distinctive formative experiences, replace their elders. Since we hypothesize that these generational differences reflect economic growth and human development, we would not expect to find large generational differences concerning religion in societies such as Nigeria, Algeria, or Bangladesh, that have not experienced major progress toward human development over the past several decades. In such cases we would expect the young to be fully as religious as their elders. The decline of religiosity does not reflect the inevitable spread of scientific knowledge and education; it is contingent on whether a society's people have experienced rising existential security – or whether they have experienced economic stagnation, state failure, or the collapse of the welfare state, as has happened in the less successful post-Communist economies.

(iv) Sectoral Comparisons

The thesis of secularization based on existential security suggests that the primary cleavage predicting religiosity will be the contrast between rich and poor societies. We also expect that more vulnerable social sectors *within* any given society, such as the poor, the elderly, those with lower education and literacy, and women, will be more religious, even in postindustrial societies. Furthermore, the largest social differences are expected in countries where income is most unequally distributed.

(v) Patterns of Demography, Fertility Rates, and Population Change

Our thesis argues that fertility rates are systematically linked to the strength of religiosity and human development. Although life expectancy is far lower in poorer societies, we expect to find that countries with the strongest religiosity have much greater population growth than secular societies.

(vi) Social and Political Consequences

Where the process of secularization has occurred, we expect this to have important consequences for society and for politics, in particular by weakening the influence of religiosity on the acquisition of moral, social, economic, and political values, as well as by eroding active engagement in religious organizations and parties, and by reducing the salience of religious identities and ethno-religious conflict in societies.

Plan of the Book

To develop and test these propositions, Chapter 2 describes our research design, the comparative framework, and our main data source – the World Values Survey and European Values Survey. We outline the procedure used to classify 191 societies worldwide by their predominant religious culture, allowing us to compare Protestant, Catholic, Orthodox, Muslims, Hindus, and others. Chapter 3 goes on to examine global trends in religiosity and secularization. If cultural shifts were predictable, we would expect patterns of religiosity in each society to be consistently associated with levels of human development and economic equality. More specifically, we expect religious beliefs and practices to be strongest in poorer, pre-industrial societies; while by contrast the publics of the most affluent, secure, and egalitarian societies will prove most secular. Within any society in which substantial economic development has occurred, we expect secularization to have progressed furthest among the younger generations, who will be less religious than their parents and grandparents. With data from the Values Surveys we can test these core propositions more systematically than ever before, using cross-national comparisons, time-series trends, and generational analysis.

In Part II we go on to consider specific regional case studies in greater depth. Much of the previous literature has focused on the distinctive imprint of religion in specific countries or regions of the world, and the role of the state and organized religion. Most of the literature has examined patterns of churchgoing and religious beliefs in the United States and Western Europe, focusing on affluent postindustrial societies with similar levels of education and mass communications, and sharing a common Christian heritage. Chapter 4 considers the longstanding puzzle of why religiosity appears to have remained stable in the United States; while most studies find that churchgoing practices have eroded in other rich countries. We explore the evidence for trends and explanations for these differences offered by functionalist and by religious market theories. Chapter 5 analyzes whether religion has seen an erosion in Central and Eastern Europe, similar to the secularization process experienced in Western Europe, or whether, as supply-side theory suggests, the last decade has witnessed a resurgence of religiosity after the Soviet policy of state atheism was abolished. On the other hand, these patterns might be affected by other developments. For example, where the church became associated with nationalistic protest for the independence forces against control by the Soviet Union, in Catholic Poland or Lutheran Estonia, then once the Berlin Wall fell after a temporary "honeymoon" effect we might expect an erosion of religiosity. Chapter 5 examines the most extensive body of systematic cross-national survey evidence ever assembled concerning Muslim values and beliefs, from a wide range of countries around the world. In particular we focus on whether there is a cultural clash between the democratic values held in Western

Christianity and those held by the Muslim world, as Huntington argues.[43] We compare predominantly Islamic societies in the Middle East and elsewhere, such as Indonesia, Egypt, Iran, Nigeria, Indonesia, and Pakistan.

Theories of secularization are important in themselves, but they also have major social and political implications, as discussed in Part III. Although most people continue to express nominal adherence to traditional denominational identities, where religiosity has declined, it is unclear how far these identities matter. One of the strongest, most enduring, and yet contentious claims in the literature is Weber's theory that the Protestant Reformation generated a distinctive work ethos, which generated the underlying conditions leading to the rise of bourgeois capitalism. We cannot examine the historical patterns, but if religious cultural traditions have left an enduring legacy, we can examine the contemporary evidence. Chapter 7 compares the extent to which orientations toward work, and broader attitudes toward capitalism, differ by the type of religious faith. Chapter 8 considers the role of organized religion on social capital. The work of Robert Putnam has stimulated a recent revival of interest in whether social networks, social trust, and the norms and values generally associated with cooperative behavior, are shaped by participation in religious organizations.[44] While studies have examined this issue in depth within the United States, few have analyzed whether this relationship holds across different types of religious faith. Chapter 9 analyzes the strength of the linkages between religious identities and support for political parties, and in particular whether there is evidence of religious dealignment in postindustrial societies, but of strong relationships with religiosity continuing to predict electoral behavior and party support in agrarian societies. There is some evidence supporting these claims. In European countries where the Protestant and Catholic populations were once strongly "pillarized" into segmented party and social networks, exemplified by the Netherlands, the religious-based "pillars" have lost much of their relevance for electoral behavior.[45] Also in Western Europe, religious dealignment appears to have eroded denominational identities as a social cue guiding patterns of partisanship and voting choice. Adherence to the Catholic Church has become less closely related to electoral support for Christian Democratic parties in France, Italy, and Belgium.[46] But in the United States religiosity appears to have exerted a stronger impact on partisan divisions in the electorate in recent years.[47] It remains unclear how far religion, especially fundamentalist appeals, has shaped support for political parties and patterns of voting behavior in poorer developing societies and in newer electoral democracies. To draw together the analysis, the conclusion in Chapter 10 summarizes the key findings throughout the book and considers their broader implications for economic and political development and for demographic change. Chapter 2 provides technical details about our research design and methods; those who are mainly interested in the substantive results may prefer to skip directly to Chapter 3, which starts to examine the evidence.

Measuring Secularization

THE CONTEMPORARY DEBATE about secularization, once intellectually dormant, is currently alive and well, but unfortunately much of the evidence cited by both sides remains partial and selective. It is difficult to draw systematic generalizations about the vitality of religious life around the globe from studies focused on one or two nations, a limited time period, or a single indicator of secularization.[1] One scholar may examine the evidence of lapsed churchgoing habits in Britain and Ireland since the 1960s, for example, and conclude that secularization is proceeding apace, then another may challenge this by citing the vigorous resurgence of radical Islam in Iran and Algeria during the last decade, the rise of Pentecostal churches in Latin America, the Presbyterian expansion in South Korea, or the existence of ethno-religious conflict in Bosnia-Herzegovina. Many arguments simply point toward the continuing popularity of religion in the United States, as though this exception by itself refutes general patterns worldwide. The process of selecting case studies based on the dependent variable generates more heat than light. A more systematic overview is needed, comparing multiple indicators of religiosity across many cultures and regions of the world. In this chapter we outline the comparative framework used in the book and describe the sources of evidence, the societal classifications, and the measures adopted in this study. Building on this foundation, the next chapter compares the systematic evidence for religiosity and secularization occurring during the last fifty years.

Research Design

The basic research design adopted by this study uses a triangulation of approaches. Taken in isolation, no single indicator, set of data, or analytical technique can provide a comprehensive picture. As with other controversies in the social sciences, the core concepts, definitions, and measures concerning religiosity can be understood and operationalized in many alternative ways. Any one piece of the puzzle can be reasonably challenged. But where alternative approaches using multiple indicators, social surveys, and methods of analysis produce results that are consistent, then their cumulative effect increases confidence in the reliability and robustness of the findings, and the conclusions become more compelling. Patterns of religiosity are analyzed here by three basic analytical techniques.

Cross-National Surveys

First, our empirical evidence is based on large-N comparisons, drawing on macro-level data from 191 nations worldwide and on survey data from almost 80 societies around the globe. Cross-national surveys are compared among many contemporary societies that have sharply contrasting levels of societal development, including some of the richest and poorest nations in the world. One limitation of most previous studies is that they have usually been limited to affluent postindustrial studies (usually focusing on Christendom), which is an inappropriate framework to determine how far religiosity varies according to levels of societal modernization. The pooled World Values Surveys/European Values Surveys permit us to examine a broad range of variation in religious attitudes and behavior across widely different types of societies, regions, and faiths. The availability of evidence from a large number of societies also makes it possible to combine the mean scores for each nation with macro-level data on socioeconomic and political characteristics of each nation, creating an integrated dataset that permits us to analyze cross-level linkages, such as the impact of individual-level beliefs and values on a society's fertility rate; or the linkages between a society's level of economic development, and the religious beliefs of its people. This also makes it possible to identify outliers to general patterns, such as the anomalously high rate of religiosity in the United States and Ireland, relative to their levels of development. Such findings highlight the need for in-depth case studies, to understand the reasons behind deviations from the general pattern.

Correlations at any one point in time cannot, by themselves, demonstrate the underlying causality. Moreover, many aspects of societal modernization are closely interrelated, such as growing levels of affluence, education, and urbanization, so it is difficult to disentangle their effects. Furthermore, in cross-national research, differences in fieldwork and sampling practices, coding and translations, can generate substantial amounts of measurement error. If significant cross-national differences emerge, after applying appropriate controls, this random noise has probably caused such effects to be *under*estimated.

Longitudinal Trends

To complement the World Values surveys executed from 1981 to 2001, we also need to examine longitudinal evidence of historic trends in religious attitudes and behavior over even longer periods of time. We utilize such time-series survey data when it is available. The comparison of many decades of data gives more reliable indications of the processes at work and the patterns of causality behind changes in attitudes and behavior, such as the possibility that an erosion of religious beliefs undermined habitual churchgoing practices. Yet here we also encounter two important limitations. First, the geographic scope for such time-series analysis is sharply limited, because until quite recently, most surveys were conducted in advanced industrialized societies. No early benchmarks exist to monitor changes in religiosity in most developing countries – and no such benchmarks exist for most types of religion other than Christianity. Even with the data on religiosity from the early Gallup polls carried out in the 1950s, we are limited to examining trends that have occurred over the last fifty years, and more often we can only compare data from the last two or three decades, or even later. Thus, after comparing the results of the International Social Science Program surveys on religion in 1991 and 1998, Greeley concludes that any indicators of changes in religiosity are inconclusive, with some gains and some losses.[2] But given this limited seven-year time period, combined with the usual measurement errors that arise from comparing cross-sectional surveys, this approach could not be expected to shed much light on long-term processes of secularization: over a short period, random fluctuations combined with minor changes in fieldwork practices, sampling procedures, or even question order in the survey will probably swamp the effects of long-term trends. Since societal modernization in the shift from agrarian to industrial, and then from industrial to postindustrial, is a process that occurs at a glacial pace over many decades, our longitudinal evidence of trends from existing surveys in Western Europe and the Anglo-American democracies often covers too few years to capture the full effects taking place.

Generational Analysis

Generational analysis of cross-sectional surveys is an alternative technique that can throw light on long-term cultural change. If the socialization process imprints the effects of shared experiences during their formative years on successive generations, then analysis of the attitudes and behavior shared among distinct birth cohorts can be used as a proxy indicator of longitudinal trends.[3] We can explore how far those born in the prewar era differ from the postwar generation, or from the younger generation that came of age during the 1960s. The sheer size of the cross-national survey samples that are available through the World Values Survey increases the reliability of this approach. This is especially true when we analyze pooled groups of nationalities, for example, comparing the overall pattern of cohort differences in agrarian societies with those in industrial and postindustrial societies. This approach falls short of what we would ideally like to do – which would be to analyze successive waves of panel survey data collected among the same respondents at successive points in time, which would facilitate disentangling life-cycle effects, period effects, and birth cohort effects.[4] Life-cycle effects could theoretically account for differences detected among cohorts, such as lower churchgoing among the postwar than prewar generation, if one assumes that people have an inherent tendency to become more religious as they age. The availability of data from fundamentally different types of societies sheds light on the interpretation of these effects, because (as we will demonstrate later) there does not seem to be any inherent tendency for people to become more religious as they age: we *do* find lower levels of religiosity among the younger cohorts than among the older ones in postindustrial societies, but we do *not* find this phenomenon in agrarian societies.

We simply do not have the massive longitudinal database that would be required to demonstrate beyond any doubt whether secularization is or is not taking place. In its absence, no single approach can be absolutely conclusive, and the results will always remain open to challenge. But if a combination of methods, indicators, and datasets generates findings that all point in the same direction – and this direction is consistent with our basic theoretical argument – then the case becomes more compelling. This is the approach that we will take.

The Comparative Framework

To examine the theory and specific propositions discussed in Chapter 1, the comparative framework adopted in this book follows Prezeworski and Teune's *most different systems* research design, seeking to maximize contrasts among a diverse range of almost eighty societies to distinguish systematic clusters of characteristics associated with different dimensions and types of religiosity.[5] Some important trade-offs are involved in this approach, notably the loss of contextual depth that can come from focusing on historical developments over time in one or two nations. But the strategy of carrying out global comparisons has major advantages. Most importantly, it allows us to examine whether, as theories of societal modernization claim, basic religious values, beliefs, and practices weaken with the shift from traditional agrarian societies, having largely illiterate and impoverished populations, to industrial economies based on manufacturing, with a growing urban working class, to postindustrial economies with a large professional and managerial middle class based in the service sector.

Human development is a complex process of social transformation, including changes in the economy with the shift from agricultural production to industrial production and the rise of the service sector. It includes a massive expansion of education, increasing affluence and leisure, rising life expectancy and health, urbanization and suburbanization, the spread of the mass media, and changes in family structures and community social networks; and it tends to be linked with the process of democratization. Not all these developments necessarily go hand in hand with changes in religiosity. Our research design allows us to compare societies representing each of the major world faiths, including societies that were historically shaped by Protestant, Catholic, Orthodox, Muslim, Hindu, Jewish, and Buddhist/Confucian/Shinto belief systems. Any analysis of this topic faces the problem of "too many variables, not enough cases," where it becomes almost impossible to control for all the factors that could affect religiosity. For example, almost all Muslim countries are developing societies with autocratic political systems. To overcome this limitation, Part II considers regional patterns, where we can focus in more depth on comparisons that analyze variations in moral values and religious beliefs while holding constant certain societal features, notably the role of religious pluralism in the Anglo-American democracies and in Western Europe, the legacy of the suppression of religion in post-Communist states, and the impact of Muslim beliefs on government in the Islamic world.

The World Values Survey/European Values Survey

Evidence concerning religious values, beliefs, and behavior draws on the World Values Survey/European Values Survey, a global investigation of socio-cultural and political change. This project has carried out representative national surveys of the values and beliefs of the publics in seventy-six nation states (see Figure 2.1), containing almost five billion people or over 80% of the world's population and covering all six inhabited continents. It builds on the European Values Surveys, first carried out in twenty-two countries in 1981. A second wave of surveys, in forty-one nations, was completed in 1990–1991. The third wave was carried out in fifty-five nations in 1995–1996. The fourth wave, with fifty-nine nations, took place in 1999–2001 (see Table A1).[6] The pooled WVS survey used in this book includes data from all four waves, containing almost one quarter million respondents, facilitating analysis even for smaller religious groups. We make a further distinction within nation states that contain distinct societies, each with different historical religious traditions, including within Germany (East and West),[7] as well as in the United Kingdom (Northern Ireland and Britain) and the Federal Republic of Yugoslavia (Serbia and Montenegro). The pooled WVS therefore allows us to compare seventy-nine societies in total.

The WVS survey includes some of the most affluent market economies in the world, such as the United States, Japan, and Switzerland, with per capita annual incomes as high as $40,000; together with middle-level industrializing countries including Taiwan, Brazil, and Turkey, as well as poorer agrarian societies, exemplified by Uganda, Nigeria, and Viet Nam, with per capita annual incomes of $300 or less. Some smaller nations have populations below one million, such as Malta, Luxembourg, and Iceland, while at the other extreme almost one billion people live in India and over one billion live in China. The pooled survey with all waves contains older democracies such as Australia, India, and the Netherlands, newer democracies including El Salvador, Estonia, and Taiwan, semi-democracies such as Russia, Brazil, and Turkey, and non-democracies such as China, Zimbabwe, Pakistan, and

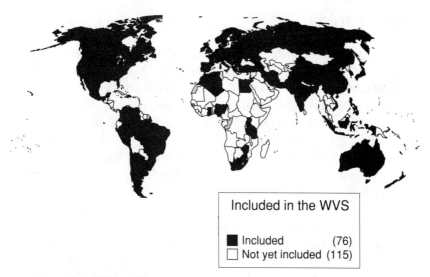

Figure 2.1. Nation States Included in the Pooled World Values Surveys, and European Values Surveys, 1981–2001.

Egypt. The transition process also varies markedly: some nations have experienced a rapid consolidation of democracy during the 1990s; the Czech Republic, Latvia, and Argentina currently rank as high on political rights and civil liberties as Belgium, the United States, and the Netherlands, which have a long tradition of democracy.[8] The survey includes some of the first systematic data on public opinion in many Muslim states, including Arab countries such as Jordan, Iran, Egypt, and Morocco, as well as in Indonesia, Iran, Turkey, Bangladesh, and Pakistan. The most comprehensive coverage of countries in the surveys is available in Western Europe, North America, and Scandinavia, where public opinion surveys have the longest tradition, but countries are included from all world regions, including some Sub Saharan African nations. Although the four waves of this survey took place from 1981 to 2001, the same countries were not always included in each wave, so time-series comparisons over the full period can be carried out in a subset of twenty societies. Data drawn from other sources facilitates long-term comparisons in a limited range of nations, including from the Eurobarometer surveys, conducted bi-annually since 1970, and from the postwar Gallup International polls on religion. The International Social Survey Programme surveys of religion conducted in 1991 (in 18 societies) and in 1998 (in 32 societies) provide comparable data.

Measures of Secularization

Both "religion" and "secularization" are multidimensional phenomena and we recognize an important distinction between religion as a societal institution and religion as an individual practice.[9] In this study we do not examine direct evidence for the power and status of religious institutions and authorities, such as the role of evangelical churches in the "bible-belt" American South, ideological divisions within the Anglican synod, the influence of radical Islamic parties in the Middle East, or the structure, resources, and leadership of the Roman Catholic Church in Italy. Nor do we focus primarily upon the relative organizational strength of different denominations and sects within specific countries, leaving area specialists to study important developments such as attempts to build churches and expand congregations by U.S. evangelicals in South Korea or rivalry for hearts and souls between Catholic clergy and Pentecostal missionaries in Guatemala and El Salvador.[10] These are all important issues, studied by scholars from many disciplines, but they are also well beyond the scope of this book. Instead we concentrate here upon examining systematic survey evidence among the mass public in multiple countries concerning three core dimensions of secularization – to see whether there has been a widespread erosion of religious participation, values, and beliefs at the individual level – using the specific indicators outlined in Table 2.1:

- *Religious participation:* Secularization concerns the role of religious behavior in people's lives. Most importantly for this study, the secularization process is understood to involve the decline of *collective* religious practices in everyday life, exemplified by the ritual of regular church attendance for Protestants and Catholics, and also the erosion of *individual* religious practices, such as participation in daily prayer or meditation for Muslims and Buddhists. Much of the recent literature disputing secularization has argued that rather than simple decline in religiosity, there has been an evolution, particularly in rich societies, with a shift from collective forms of engagement via traditional religious institutions toward individual or personal spirituality exercised in the private sphere.[11] The comparison of both aspects of religious behavior is therefore important to settle this issue.

- *Religious values:* A related feature of secularization concerns "values," meaning the goals that people prioritize for their society, community, families, and themselves. Secularization is reflected in the lessening importance of religion in people's lives, and growing indifference to

Table 2.1. Indicators of Religiosity

	Name	Coding	Waves	Item	Mean (%)
RELIGIOUS PARTICIPATION					
Apart from weddings, funerals, and christenings, how often do you attend religious services?	GoChurch	1–7	1–4	V185	2.0
How often do you pray to God outside of religious services?	OftPray	1–7	4	V199	2.3
RELIGIOUS VALUES					
How important is God in your life?	Imp_God	1–10	1–4	V196	6.3
How important is religion in your life?	Imp_Rel	1–4	2–4	V9r	2.8
RELIGIOUS BELIEFS					
Do you believe in heaven?	Heaven	0/1	1–4	V195	49.2
Do you believe in hell?	Hell	0/1	1–4	V194	36.8
Do you believe in life after death?	Life	0/1	1–4	V192	47.3
Do you believe people have a soul?	Soul	0/1	1–4	V193	52.9

Source: World Values Survey/European Values Survey, 1981–2001.

spiritual matters among the public. Secularization also erodes traditional religious identities, such as a sense of belonging to distinct Protestant and Catholic communities in Northern Ireland, until these become purely nominal labels rather than holding substantive meaning.

- *Religious beliefs:* In this regard, secularization refers to the erosion of faith in the core beliefs held by different world theologies. Skepticism about matters of faith is greatest among agnostics, while atheists express outright rejection of religious creeds and teachings. Secularization also involves the waning ability of religious authorities to shape mass views on such issues as abortion, divorce, and homosexuality, as well as by growing ethical relativism and individualism.

Some studies prefer to focus attention upon one or another of these dimensions. Karel Dobbelaere, for example, regards secularization as a broad process reducing the societal significance and meaning of religion, notably how far the public regards spiritual values as important to their lives and how far they listen to religious leaders as an important source of moral authority and spiritual guidance.[12] Others such as Rodney Stark emphasize the decline of religious participation, monitored through church and census historical records of congregations and through social surveys of reported churchgoing. It can be argued that behavior provides a concrete indicator of the importance of religion for social norms and habitual practices. Still other commentators, such as Andrew Greeley, give greater attention to the strength of common religious beliefs, such as faith in an afterlife or in metaphysical beings, since people can continue to adhere to these beliefs even if they no longer participate regularly in services of worship.[13] But instead of reducing the idea of secularization to a single meaning or indicator, this study recognizes that this phenomenon is multi-dimensional, thereby requiring a systematic overview operating at several distinct levels.

Where there is evidence that religious values, beliefs, and practices have eroded among the mass public, this clearly has significant implications for religion as a societal institution, but there is not necessarily a simple relationship at work; churches can maintain their traditional resources derived from centuries earlier even when their membership base has declined among the contemporary public. The role of the Anglican Church vividly illustrates this process; there is a wealth of evidence that the British public became increasingly indifferent to religion during the twentieth century. For example, Steve Bruce compares patterns of church attendance, church membership, Sunday school attendance, the number of full-time clergy, the popularity of religious rites including baptisms, confirmations, as well as in Easter and Christmas communicants, and support for religious beliefs. "All of them point the same way," Bruce concludes, "declining involvement with religious organizations and declining commitment to religious ideas. And the trends in the data have been regular and consistent for between 50 and 100 years, depending upon the index in question."[14] Yet the residual status and resources of the Church of England, accumulated for centuries, are largely preserved. The Anglican Church continues to enjoy the legacy of substantial holdings of land, commercial and residential property, stocks and shares, and financial assets, as well as the inheritance of dozens of magnificent cathedrals and 16,000 historic parish churches. Anglicans have also retained a voice in government through the inclusion since the fourteenth century of the "Lords Spiritual" in the House of Lords. Anglican, Methodist, and Presbyterian organizations continue to engage in charitable work for the poor, in fund-raising for missionaries or in running schools.[15] In short, this study focuses upon indicators of religiosity among the mass public, and any consistent erosion that has occurred will probably eventually have consequences for church institutions, but the impact may well be long delayed and indirect.

The Classification of Religious Cultures

Identifying the predominant religious culture in each country is important because we expect that the values and beliefs of Catholicism, Protestantism, Orthodoxy, Islam, and eastern religions will imprint themselves on each society, via the major channels of cultural transmission and socialization, irrespective of how far individuals actively participate in religion through churches, mosques, shrines, and temples. Hence, for example, we expect that through experience of schools, the mass media, and the workplace, the younger generation of Pakistanis and Bangladeshi Muslims growing up in Bradford, Birmingham, or Leicester will gradually absorb certain social and political values from their local communities, along with a fusion of Asian-British lifestyles, fashions, and music, contributing toward a more multicultural Britain, so that over time the religious, social, and political values of Asian-British will gradually come to differ from their compatriots remaining in South East Asia. We also need to identify the size of the major religious sectors in each country to facilitate calculation of religious pluralism or fractionalization in each country, discussed in Chapter 4, which is an essential component of religious market theory. Where one religious culture is clearly shared in any nation, so that 80% or more share a similar faith, then the identification of the predominant or majoritarian religion is relatively straightforward. This process is more complicated where a plural society is fragmented among multiple religions, so that we have to identify the plurality faith.

Estimates of the distribution of religious adherents around the world are usually drawn from a few common reference sources, each with certain important limitations. The classification of the predominant religion in 191 nations around the world used in this study is drawn from a standard reference work, the *Encyclopaedia Britannica Book of the Year 2001*, using a dataset on religious pluralism derived from this source collected by Alesina and colleagues.[16] As with any compilation of secondary data, the consistency and reliability of the *Encyclopaedia Britannica* figures can be questioned. The estimates of the precise number of religious adherents given in each faith depend on the level of aggregation that is employed, for example whether the total number of Protestants is counted in each country, or whether this is broken down into detailed Protestant denominations or sects, such as Baptists, Anglicans, and Methodists. The identification and classification of many traditional or folk religions that persist in parts of Africa, Asia, and the Caribbean remain problematic. Where information about self-reported religious identities is collected and published in an official national census this provides more reliable statistics, but also more detailed enumerations, than in countries where such information is not collected by the government. The classification of the estimated number of non-believers, agnostics, and atheists, as well as non-respondents, also varies from one reference source to another, and this is particularly important in countries where some or all religions are suppressed or restricted by the government.

Nevertheless, bearing in mind these important limitations, the *Encyclopaedia Britannica* dataset provides an overview of the distributions of the major religions around the world. The reliability and consistency of the data were crosschecked against two alternative reference sources that are widely cited in the literature. The *World Christian Encyclopedia* compares churches and religions around the globe, and estimates trends over time, based on an annual religious "megacensus" completed by ten million church leaders, clergy, and other Christian workers.[17] This source monitors the number and proportion of adherents to different world religions, as well as the distribution of religious personnel, resources, and missionaries. The *World Christian Encyclopedia* provides a comprehensive global overview yet it is difficult to evaluate the reliability of the data, as the surveys from which the estimates are derived are not based on representative samples of the general population in each country. For a further crosscheck, the classification of data used by the *Encyclopaedia Britannica* was also compared for consistency with the *CIA World Factbook 2002*, another standard reference source that is widely used in the literature.[18]

Figure 2.2, based on the *Encyclopaedia Britannica* data, illustrates the historically predominant religious culture identified in each country. The map shows the distribution of just under one billion people living in sixty-seven countries worldwide sharing a Roman Catholic culture, notably large parts of Southern and Central Europe, and the Spanish and Portuguese ex-colonies in Latin America. About half a billion people live in twenty-eight countries with a predominant Protestant culture, especially many people in Northern Europe as well as in their former colonies in sub-Saharan Africa, the Caribbean, and the Pacific, divided among multiple denominations and sects, including Anglicans, Lutherans, Methodists, Baptists, Pentecostals, and others. We estimate that another fifty states worldwide, containing over one billion people, share a predominately Muslim culture, the majority Sunni although the minority Shi'a, especially throughout large parts of Northern Africa, the Middle East, and some parts of South East Asia. Only three states are classified as Hindu, although due to the inclusion of India (as well as the smaller states of Mauritius and Nepal) this religious culture covers about one billion people. The culture of the Orthodox Church

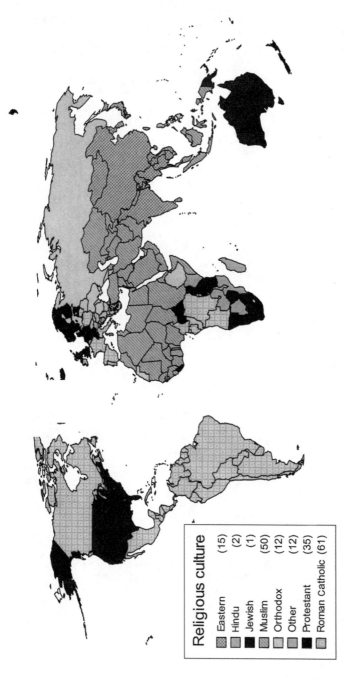

Figure 2.2. Historically Predominant Religions in 188 Nations Worldwide. Source: Classification from the Alesina et al. Dataset, derived from the *Encyclopaedia Britannica Book of the Year 2001*. Also Alesina et al., 2003. "Fractionalization." *Journal of Economic Growth.* 82: 219–258.

Religious culture

Eastern	(15)
Hindu	(2)
Jewish	(1)
Muslim	(50)
Orthodox	(12)
Other	(12)
Protestant	(35)
Roman Catholic	(61)

Table 2.2. Classification of Societies by Their Historically Predominant Major Religions

	Christian			Non-Christian	
	Catholic	Protestant	Orthodox	Muslim	Eastern
Postindustrial (23)	Austria Belgium Canada France Ireland Italy Luxembourg Spain	Australia Britain Denmark Finland Germany, West Germany, East Iceland Netherlands New Zealand Northern Ireland Norway Sweden Switzerland United States			Japan
Industrial (33)	Argentina Brazil Chile Colombia Croatia Czech Rep. Hungary Lithuania Malta Mexico Philippines Poland Portugal Slovakia Slovenia Uruguay Venezuela	Estonia Latvia	Belarus Bulgaria Georgia Greece Macedonia Montenegro Romania Russia Serbia Ukraine	Bosnia- Herzegovina Turkey	Korea, South Taiwan
Agrarian (23)	Dominican Rep. El Salvador Peru	South Africa Tanzania Uganda Zimbabwe	Armenia Moldova	Albania Algeria Azerbaijan Bangladesh Egypt Indonesia Iran	China India Viet Nam

	Christian			Non-Christian	
	Catholic	Protestant	Orthodox	Muslim	Eastern
				Jordan	
				Morocco	
				Nigeria	
				Pakistan	
Total *nation states*	67	28	12	50	13
Total *societies* in the WVS	28	20	12	13	6

NOTE: This study subdivides independent *nation states* with distinctive historical religious traditions into distinct *societies*, including the UK (Northern Ireland and Great Britain), Germany (East and West), and the Federal Republic of Yugoslavia (Serbia and Montenegro).

Sources: States classified by the historically predominant (plurality) religion, derived from the *Encyclopaedia Britannica Book of the Year 2001*. Alberto Alesina et al., 2003. "Fractionalization." *Journal of Economic Growth*. 82: 219–258. The dataset is available online at: www.stanford.edu/~wacziarg/papersum.html. For the classification of societies, see Appendix A.

predominates in Central Europe, Eastern Europe, and parts of the Balkans, in a dozen states containing about one quarter of a million inhabitants, although many people living in these countries identify themselves as atheists. Another ten states in South East Asia, covering thirty million people, have cultures emphasizing a range of Buddhist, Taoist, Confucians, Shinto, and related Eastern belief systems. Lastly, some nations are more difficult to classify into any major religious grouping: Israel is the only Jewish state. A variety of indigenous folk religions and beliefs continue to predominate in certain countries in Africa and Asia-Pacific, such as Cameroon, Angola, Benin, and Ghana.

Based on this distribution, Table 2.2 classifies societies contained in the World Values Survey into five major religious cultures based on the historically predominant religion identified in each society. In homogeneous countries the categorization proved straightforward, although this judgment was more problematic in fragmented societies where only the largest plurality of the population adhered to one particular religion. The pooled WVS survey from 1981 to 2000 covers a wide range of twenty-eight predominately Roman Catholic societies and twenty Protestant societies, including those at widely differing levels of socioeconomic development and levels of democratization. The surveys also cover twelve Orthodox religious cultures and thirteen Muslim societies, as well as six societies containing diverse Asian religions that are more difficult to categorize into a single coherent religious culture. At the individual level, people's denominational affiliations are monitored in the World Values Survey where people were asked, "Do you belong to a religious denomination?" If yes, people were asked to identify which one based on eight major categories: Roman Catholic, Protestant, Orthodox, Muslim, Buddhist, Jewish, Hindu, or "other" religions.

Type of Societies

In the global comparison, 191 nation states were also classified according to levels of societal modernization. The Human Development Index produced annually by the United Nations Development Program (UNDP) provides the standard 100-point scale of societal modernization, combining levels of knowledge (adult literacy and education), health (life expectancy at birth), and standard of living (real per capita gross domestic product). This measure is widely used in the development literature and it has the advantage of providing a broader and more reliable indicator of societal well-being than monetary estimates based on levels of affluence or financial wealth.[19] Using the 1998 Human Development Index, "*postindustrial* societies" were defined as the twenty most affluent states around the world, ranking with a HDI score over .900 and mean per capita GDP of $29,585. The classic definition of postindustrial societies emphasizes the shift in production from fields and factories toward the white-collar knowledge-based professions and management. Almost two-thirds of gross national product in the postindustrial societies derives from the service sector. "*Industrial* societies" are classified as the fifty-eight nations with a moderate HDI (ranging from .740 to .899) and a moderate per capita GDP of $6,314. These are characterized by an economy based on manufacturing industry, with moderate levels of income, education, and life expectancy. Lastly, "*agrarian* societies," based on agricultural production and the extraction of natural materials, includes ninety-seven nations worldwide with lower levels of development (HDI of .739 or below) and mean per capita GDP of $1,098 or less.[20]

Some contrasts in the most common indicators of social well-being can be compared to examine the relationship between patterns of human development and the predominant religious cultures worldwide. Table 2.3 summarizes the total distribution of populations and how patterns of population growth vary systematically across the different types of religious cultures,

Table 2.3. Social and Economic Indicators of the Major World Religions

Major Religion	Number of Nation States	Total Population 2000	Annual Pop. Growth (%)	Mean Life Expectancy (years) 2000	Mean GDP 2000	GINI Coefficient	Mean HDI 1998	Mean Rural Pop. 2000 (%)	Mean Religious Pluralism Index
Protestant	28	484,783,000	1.25	66	$14,701	40.2	.764	46	.573
Catholic	67	970,269,000	1.43	69	$11,170	40.8	.734	39	.414
Orthodox	12	320,104,000	−0.10	69	$7,508	34.5	.741	40	.485
Buddhist	10	147,078,000	1.71	66	$6,321	37.3	.635	63	.373
Other	20	1,534,932,000	1.38	56	$4,653	39.9	.620	54	.619
Hindu	3	1,040,152,000	1.67	65	$4,567	37.3	.599	73	.368
Muslim	50	1,042,558,000	2.10	61	$3,518	42.5	.594	49	.331
Mean			*1.50*	*65*	*$8,537*	*40.2*	*.681*	*46*	*.438*
Total	*190*	*5,546,112,000*							

NOTES: *Major religion*: Classified by the largest religion in each state identified from Alesina et al. 2003. *Total population 2000*: World Bank, *Developmental Indicators, 2002. Annual population growth*: World Bank, *Developmental Indicators, 2002. Mean per capita GDP 2000* (expressed in $US Purchasing Power Parity): World Bank, *Developmental Indicators, 2002. GINI coefficient of economic inequality* (latest year available): World Bank, *Development Indicators, 2002. HDI 1998*: Human Development Index, combining education and literacy, longevity and per capita GDP; UNDP 2000. *Mean percentage rural population, 2000*: World Bank, *Developmental Indicators, 2002. Mean life expectancy, 2000* (years): World Bank, *Developmental Indicators, 2002. Religious pluralism index*: 100-point scale estimating the degree of religious pluralism or fractionalization. Alesina et al. 2003.

along with levels of per capita income, human development, religious pluralism, rural populations, average life expectancy, and the GINI coefficient
of income equality. The Human Development Index provides the broadest
summary scale of modernization, showing the highest levels of development in predominantly Protestant, Catholic, and Orthodox religious cultures, while other religions all have lower levels of human development,
explored in detail in the next chapter. Even stronger contrasts are found
among levels of per capita income, which ranges from $14,701 on average
in affluent Protestant societies down to $3,518 in poorer Muslim societies.
Similar disparities reflecting these levels of income can be found among the
other societal indicators (discussed in Chapter 3), including in patterns of
population growth, urbanization, and income inequality. The fifty Muslim
societies are highly diverse, with over one billion people stretching around
the globe from Indonesia and Malaysia to Nigeria and Afghanistan. Beliefs
also range from the conservatism of the strict application of Sha'ria law to
the secular state of Turkey. Despite this diversity, nations with a predominant Muslim culture share certain important characteristics: compared with
other religious cultures, these societies are not only the poorest worldwide,
they also have the highest levels of economic disparities between rich and
poor, the second lowest life expectancy, the fastest population growth, and
the greatest religious homogeneity, as discussed further in Chapter 5.

Type of States

Recent years have seen increasingly sophisticated attempts to develop effective measures of a society's level of good governance in general, and
of democracy in particular. These indicators range from minimalist definitions, such as the dichotomous classification into democracies and au-
tocracies used by Przeworski and colleagues, through multidimensional
scales used by the World Bank to rank levels of corruption, stability, and
rule of law, to immensely rich and detailed qualitative "democratic audits"
conducted in just a few countries.[21] Alternative summary indices emphasize different components, and all measures suffer from certain conceptual
or methodological limitations in their reliability, consistency, and validity.
Nevertheless a comparison of nine major indices of democracy by Munck
and Verkuilen concluded that, despite these methodological differences, in
practice simple correlation tests showed that there was considerable similar-
ity in how nations ranked across different measures: "For all the differences

in conceptualization, measurement and aggregation, they seem to show that the reviewed indices are tapping into the same underlying realities."[22] Systematic biases may be generated from reliance by all the indices on similar sources of evidence or from common data limitations, but the correlation of outcomes suggests that the adoption of one or another measure is unlikely to generate widely varying classifications of countries.

The Gastil Index, used by Freedom House, has become widely accepted as one of the standard measures providing a multidimensional classification of political rights and civil liberties. This measure is adopted here from the range of alternatives, as in previous work by the authors, because it provides comprehensive coverage worldwide, including all nation states and independent territories around the globe.[23] The index also facilitates time-series analysis of trends in democratization, since an annual measurement for each country has been produced every year since the early 1970s. The 7-point Gastil Index is reversed in the presentations for ease of interpretation, so that a higher score on the index signifies that a country has greater political rights and civil liberties. We are also interested in historical patterns, and in particular how long democracy has endured in each society. To obtain a measure of length of democratic stability, the mean annual Freedom House ratings are calculated from 1972 to 2000.[24]

On this basis, *older democracies* are defined as the thirty-nine states around the world with at least twenty years' continuous experience of democracy from 1980 to 2000 and a Freedom House rating of 5.5 to 7.0 in the most recent estimate. *Newer democracies* are classified as the forty-three states with less than twenty years' experience with democracy and the most recent Freedom House rating of 5.5 to 7.0. Another forty-seven states were classified as *semi-democracies* (Freedom House describes them as "partly-free"; others use the terms "transitional" or "consolidating" democracies); these states have been democratic for less than twenty years and have current Freedom House ratings of 3.5 to 5.5. *Non-democracies* are the remaining sixty-two states, with a Freedom House score in 1999–2000 from 1.0 to 3.0; they include military-backed dictatorships, authoritarian states, elitist oligarchies, and absolute monarchies. Appendix A lists the classifications of nations used throughout the book, based on these measures. Clearly there is considerable overlap between human and democratic development at the top of the scale; many older democracies are also affluent postindustrial societies. But the pattern of states among industrial and agrarian societies shows a far more complex pattern, with newer democracies, semi-democracies, and non-democracies located at different levels of socioeconomic development.

Religious Freedom Index

To be able to compare the degree of religious freedom in each nation, we created a new scale based on information for each country contained in the U.S. State Department report on *International Religious Freedom, 2002*, a comprehensive comparison of state regulation and restrictions of all world faiths.[25] Our scale sought to replicate the methodology and expand upon the country coverage offered by the 1992 Chaves and Cann scale that has been used in previous studies to measure state regulation.[26] The new Religious Freedom Index that we developed focuses upon the relationship of the state and church, including issues such as whether the constitution limits freedom of religion, whether the government restricts some denominations, cults, or sects, and whether there is an established church. The new index was classified according to the twenty criteria listed in Appendix C, with each item coded 0/1. The 20-point scale was then reversed so that a higher score on the 20-point scale represents greater religious freedom.

To confirm the reliability and consistency of the new scale against alternative measures, the new Religious Freedom Index was tested and found to be moderately or very strongly correlated with the level of democracy in each nation, as measured by the Gastil Index of political rights and civil liberties produced by Freedom House, as well as with the Freedom House Index of religious freedom, the 1992 Chaves and Cann scale of state regulation of religion (discussed in Chapter 3), and the Alesina index of religious pluralism/ fractionalization.[27]

Given this comparative framework and typologies, the key questions to be explored in subsequent chapters concern how far the strength of religious beliefs, values, and practices vary in a predictable way by level of societal modernization and by the predominant religious culture, as theorized, and, in turn, how far patterns of secularization have important consequences for society and for politics. It is to these issues that we now turn.

Comparing Secularization Worldwide

THE THEORY DEVELOPED in this book argues that the erosion of religious values, beliefs, and practices is shaped by long-term changes in existential security, a process linked with human development and socioeconomic equality, and with each society's cultural legacy and religious traditions.[1] To clarify the core propositions, outlined earlier in Figure 1.1, we hypothesize that the process of societal modernization involves two key stages: (1) the transition from agrarian to industrial society, and (2) the development from industrial to postindustrial society. We argue that economic, cultural, and political changes go together in coherent ways, so that growing levels of existential security bring broadly similar trajectories. Nevertheless, situation-specific factors make it impossible to specify exactly what will happen in any given society: certain developments become increasingly likely to occur, but the changes are probabilistic, not deterministic. The modernization process reduces the threats to survival that are common in developing societies, especially among the poorest strata; and this enhanced sense of security lessens the need for the reassurance religion provides. The most crucial precondition for security, we believe, is *human* development even more than purely *economic* development: it involves how far all sectors of society have equal access to schooling and literacy, basic healthcare, adequate nutrition, a clean water supply, and a minimal safety net for the needy. Some developing countries have substantial national incomes derived from mineral and oil reserves, but many inhabitants remain illiterate, malnourished, or impoverished, due to social inequality, greedy elites, and governmental corruption. Private affluence can coexist with public squalor, and wealth alone is insufficient to guarantee widespread security.

Our theory is not deterministic or teleological. Even in affluent stable democracies, people can feel suddenly vulnerable from natural or manmade disasters, severe economic downturns, or personal tragedies. Within rich nations, certain sectors remain most at risk, typically the elderly, as well as poorer groups and ethnic minorities. Moreover, we agree with religious market theorists that contingent factors can also affect patterns of religiosity in particular contexts; the charismatic appeal of specific spiritual leaders can convert or mobilize their congregation, while conversely states can repress or persecute religious expression, as in China. In the long term and in global perspective, however, our theory predicts that the importance of religion in people's lives will gradually diminish with the process of human development. Moreover, it does so most dramatically during the *first* stage of human development, as nations emerge from low-income agrarian economies into moderate-income industrial societies with basic welfare safety nets safeguarding against the worst life-threatening risks; and, for reasons discussed in Chapter 1, this process does not reverse itself, but becomes less pronounced during the second stage, with the rise of postindustrial societies.

Secularization is also shaped by the spiritual and theological beliefs emphasized by each society's predominant religious culture. Denominations and sects adhere to specific ideas, teachings, and texts, for example distinguishing Unitarian and Mormon Christians, Shi'a and Sunni Muslims, and Theravada and Mahayana Buddhists. These creeds are expected to operate at both specific and diffuse levels. Members who belong to, and identify with, particular faiths and denominations will hold the core beliefs most strongly. But we also anticipate that, at diffuse levels, everyone living within a community will also be influenced by the predominant religious traditions within each society, through the shared public mechanisms of cultural socialization, including schools, universities, and the mass media, even if they never set foot in a church or participate in any particular religious service. We expect the central ideas embodied in the teachings in world religions will have their greatest impact upon those belonging to these faiths, although a fainter imprint from these ideas will be detectable among everyone living within each society. For this reason, for example, Muslim minority populations in Tanzania, Macedonia, and India are expected to hold different moral values, political ideas, and religious beliefs from Muslims living in Iran, Egypt, and Indonesia, all predominant Islamic states.

Evidence of Religious Behavior

Previous studies of long-term trends in religious participation have commonly monitored the historical records of Catholic and Protestant churches in Western Europe, such as diocesan reports, membership records, and church rolls of baptisms and marriages, as well as official statistics derived from government censuses and general household surveys. During the postwar era, these sources have been supplemented by data derived from opinion polls and representative social surveys. Here patterns of religious participation are examined through survey data by looking at (i) *cross-national comparisons* across many societies found today at different levels of development, as well as by considering (ii) *longitudinal trends* in participation and beliefs in a smaller subset of (mainly postindustrial) countries where time-series survey data is available, and lastly (iii) by using *generational comparisons* to detect evidence of intergenerational value change. Secularization is a long-term process extending over many decades, and we do not have the massive time-series database that would be needed to demonstrate it conclusively; but if the findings from these multiple approaches all point in the same direction, it increases our confidence in the conclusions to be drawn.

Standard survey measures used to monitor religious behavior include the frequency of attendance at services of worship, engagement in prayer or meditation, membership of churches, groups, and religious organizations, and religious self-identities. The primary indicator of religious participation analyzed in this chapter is measured by the standard question that is widely used in the literature: "*Apart from weddings, funerals and christenings, how often do you attend religious services?*" Responses in the World Values Survey ranged on a 7-point scale from "never" (scored 1) to "more than once a week" (scored 7). Based on this item, "regular" religious participation is understood to denote at least weekly attendance (i.e., combining either "once a week" or "more than once a week"). This item has been carried on all four waves of the WVS, allowing comparisons over time in the subset of countries included since 1981, as well as facilitating cross-national comparisons in the most recent 1995–2001 waves. This item has also been used in many other cross-national surveys, such as the Gallup International Millennium Survey in fall 1999, facilitating an independent check on the reliability of the WVS estimates.[2]

Yet one important limitation of this measure should be noted: Asian faiths such as Buddhism, Confucianism, and Shinto differ from Christianity in the notion of congregations, and how often people are expected to attend religious services at churches, mosques, temples, synagogues, and shrines, outside of special festivals and ceremonies.[3] Other forms of individual participation are often regarded as equally or even more important than collective service, such as private contemplation, meditation, and prayer, as well as other rituals, such as alms-giving, ancestor worship, or living a spiritual life. Asian religions are characterized by their private practices: membership has little or no meaning, people visit temples or monasteries as individuals or families rather than as collective congregations, and people may patronize more than one temple.[4] In Japan, for example, participation in religious rites at a shrine or temple is more a matter of custom, to commemorate the feast of the dead in August or to make annual visits at the New Year, rather than being indicative of religious commitment.[5] Indigenous and folk-religions in Africa are also characterized by varied rituals, informal practices, and diverse beliefs, often rooted in the subcultures of local communities, rather than embodied in formal church organizations. New Age spiritual movements that have developed in recent decades also employ highly diverse practices, such as channeling, meditation therapy, or crystals, which are often individualistic rather than collective. Comparing the frequency of attendance at congregations therefore, while common in the Western literature, may generate a systematic bias when gauging levels of engagement across different world religions.

To investigate whether serious bias arises from this measure, religious participation (monitored by the frequency of attending religious service) was compared against a second measure of religious behavior, using a 7-point scale monitoring how often people prayed or meditated outside of religious services. The correlation indicates that both items were significantly associated (at micro- and macro-levels) in every type of faith, although the association was strongest, as expected, among Roman Catholics and Protestants.[6] Some Muslim societies, such as Jordan and Egypt, proved more likely to follow the injunction to regular prayers than to engage often in regular services of worship. Religious participation was also significantly associated with religious values (the importance of religion) for different faiths, as well as with having a religious self-identity.[7] This suggests the important proviso that comparison of the frequency of attendance at services of worship may underestimate levels of engagement among world faiths that do not emphasize this practice, outside of ceremonies, rites of passage, and special occasions. The measure of regular attendance at services of

Table 3.1. Religiosity by Type of Society

	Agrarian	Industrial	Postindustrial	Eta	Sig.
RELIGIOUS PARTICIPATION					
Attend church at least weekly	44	25	20	.171	**
Pray "every day"	52	34	26	.255	***
RELIGIOUS VALUES					
Religion "very important"	64	34	20	.386	***
RELIGIOUS BELIEFS					
Believe in life after death	55	44	49	.229	*
Believe that people have a soul	68	43	32	.169	***
Believe in heaven	63	45	44	.094	*
Believe in hell	59	36	26	.228	***
Believe in God	78	72	69	.016	N/s

NOTES: Significance (Sig.): ***P = .001; **P = .01; *P = .05. N/s = not significant. The significance of the difference between group means is measured by ANOVA (Eta). Religious participation: "*Apart from weddings, funerals, and christenings, about how often do you attend religious services these days? More than once a week, once a week, once a month, only on special holy days, once a year, less often, never or practically never.*" The percentage attending religious services "*more than once a week*" or "*once a week.*" Frequency of prayer: Q199: "*How often do you pray to God outside of religious services? Would you say . . . Every day (7), more than once a week (6), once a week (5), at least once a month (4), several times a year (3), less often (2), never (1).*" The percentage "*every day.*" Religious values: Q10: "*How important is religion in your life? Very important, rather important, not very important, not at all important?*" The percentage "*very important.*" Religious beliefs: "*Which, if any, of the following do you believe in? Yes/No.*" The percentage "*yes.*"

Source: World Values Survey/European Values Survey, pooled 1981–2001.

worship is used here for comparability with many previous studies, but we also compare this indicator with the frequency of prayer, as an important alternative measure of religious behavior common in many world religions.

Cross-National Patterns of Religious Behavior

The comparison of religious behavior is summarized in Table 3.1 and Figure 3.1, based on the pooled WVS in 1981–2001 in the seventy-four societies where data was available. Important and striking contrasts are evident by the basic type of society, in a consistent and significant pattern, with affluent postindustrial nations proving by far the most secular in their behavior and values as well as, to a lesser extent, in their beliefs. Overall almost half (44%) of the public in the agrarian societies attended a religious service at least weekly, compared with one-quarter of those living

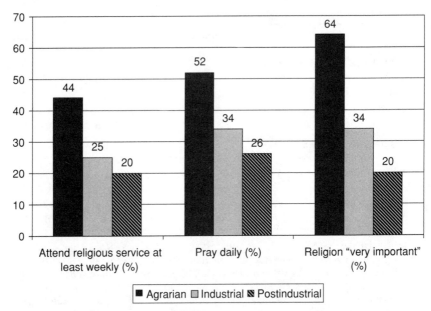

Figure 3.1. Religiosity by Type of Society. Notes: Religious participation: *"Apart from weddings, funerals, and christenings, about how often do you attend religious services these days? More than once a week, once a week, once a month, only on special holy days, once a year, less often, never, or practically never."* The percentage attending religious services *"more than once a week"* or *"once a week."* Frequency of prayer: Q199: *"How often do you pray to God outside of religious services? Would you say... Every day (7), more than once a week (6), once a week (5), at least once a month (4), several times a year (3), less often (2), never (1)."* Percentage "every day." Religious values: Q10: *"How important is religion in your life? Very important, rather important, not very important, not at all important?"* Percentage "Very important." Source: World Values Survey, pooled 1981–2001.

in industrial societies, and only one-fifth in postindustrial societies. Nor was this simply the product of the measure used since the propensity to engage in daily prayer showed similar disparities: over half of the population in agrarian societies prayed regularly, compared with only a third of those living in industrial nations, and only one-quarter of those in postindustrial states. Both measures, therefore, showed that *religious participation was twice as strong in poorer than in richer societies.* The contrasts were even more marked when it came to the importance of religious values in people's lives: two-thirds of those living in poorer societies regarded religion as "very important" compared with only one-third of those living in industrial nations, and only one-fifth of those in postindustrial societies. It is true that religious beliefs are less sharply demarcated by the basic type of society, but even here there are similarly consistent patterns: for example, about two-thirds of the public in postindustrial and in industrial societies expressed belief in God, but the majority in these societies proved skeptical about other metaphysical doctrines, including belief in reincarnation, heaven and hell, and the existence of a soul.[8] By contrast in agrarian societies, however, the majority believed in these ideas.

By any of these measures, therefore, religious participation, values, and beliefs remain widespread in poorer developing nations, but today they engage less than the majority of the publics in the most affluent postindustrial societies. Nor is this simply the product of questions, survey design, or fieldwork practices in the World Values Survey; a forty-four-nation survey conducted in 2002 for the Pew Global Attitudes Project confirms stark global contrasts in the personal importance of religion, with all wealthier nations except the United States placing less importance on religion than in poorer developing countries.[9] Similar differences in religiosity among rich and poor societies were also confirmed in the Gallup International Millennium Survey on religion conducted in sixty countries.[10]

Yet there are some important exceptions to these patterns, where specific countries are either more or less religious than would be expected from human development alone. To analyze these cross-national variations in more depth, Figure 3.2 presents the distribution of societies in the core indicators of religious behavior. The scatter gram shows that the religious societies (in the top-right quadrant) include some of the poorest societies in the world, notably Nigeria, Tanzania, Uganda, and Zimbabwe, where about three-quarters of the population or more attend religious services at least weekly, as well as Indonesia, the Philippines, and Bangladesh. But the most religious societies were not confined to Africa and Asia, as the top rankings also include El Salvador, Poland, and Mexico, all with moderate levels of socioeconomic development. Moreover, although many of the most religious nations are poor, this phenomenon is not simply a matter of economic development as there are some striking exceptions in this category, notably Ireland and the United States, as discussed further in the next chapter.[11] The most religious category includes predominately Catholic, Muslim, and Protestant societies, as well as some plural cultures divided among multiple faiths.

The moderately religious category in the middle of the scatter gram includes many West European nations, although there is no clearly observable pattern allowing us to explain the distribution in terms of a single factor,

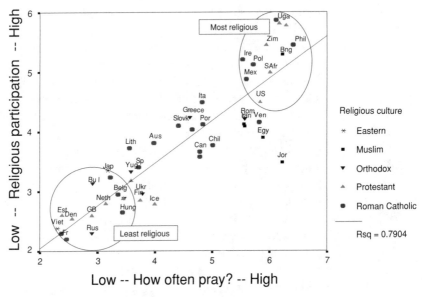

Figure 3.2. Religious Behavior in 76 Societies. Notes: Religious participation: Q185: *"Apart from weddings, funerals, and christenings, about how often do you attend religious services these days? More than once a week (7), once a week (6), once a month (5), only on special holy days (4), once a year (3), less often (2), never or practically never (1)."* Mean frequency of participation per society. How often pray? Q199: *"How often do you pray to God outside of religious services? Would you say . . . Every day (7), more than once a week (6), once a week (5), at least once a month (4), several times a year (3), less often (2), never (1)."* Mean frequency per society. Source: World Values Survey, pooled 1981–2001.

such as the particular type of society, religious culture, or even world region. Lastly, the most secular states in the bottom left-hand corner include many affluent postindustrial societies such as Denmark, Iceland, Finland, Norway, and Sweden, all sharing a cultural heritage as Protestant Nordic nations with established churches from the Lutheran side of the Reformation, characterized by persistently low, and eroding, levels of church attendance during the last sixty years.[12] Japan is also in this category, as well as many of the post-Communist nations, whatever their predominant faith, including (Orthodox) Russia, (Muslim) Azerbaijan, (Catholic) Czech Republic, and (Protestant) Estonia. The Communist state actively repressed religion, including closing Orthodox churches, limiting legal parish activities, persecuting the faithful, and using intensive atheist indoctrination, and this legacy continues to leave a contemporary imprint in Central and

Eastern Europe.[13] Chapter 6 goes on to explore whether a religious revival occurred in these regions during the 1990s, following the fall of the Soviet Union, as many suspect, in particular whether the younger generation that grew up under conditions of greater freedom are more religious than their parents and grandparents.

What is the role of societal modernization and human development in this process? To look at this issue more systematically, the two indicators of religious behavior were correlated with a range of standard indicators associated with the process of societal development and human security, without any prior controls. The measures selected for comparison include the UNDP Human Development Index, combining income, literacy and education, and longevity into a single 100-point scale. This measure has been widely used to compare rich and poor nations around the globe, providing a broader indicator of human security and the distribution of basic public goods than economic growth alone. We also compare the separate effect of alternative indicators of economic development (logged per capita GDP in $US standardized in purchasing power parity), the proportion of the population living in urban and rural areas, and the GINI coefficient (used to summarize the distribution of income inequality in any society). Education and communication are compared by measures of the level of adult literacy for women and men, gross educational enrollment, and also access to mass communications, including the distribution of television, radios, telephones, and newspapers. The provision of healthcare is measured using multiple social indicators standardized for population size, including the number of HIV/AIDS cases, infant and child mortality rates, access to an improved water source, immunization rates, and the distribution of physicians. Lastly, demographic data includes the annual percentage population growth, the average life expectancy at birth, and the distribution of the population among the young and elderly.

The simple correlations in Table 3.2, without any prior controls, confirm that all the indicators concerning human development, education, healthcare, and population demographics are powerfully and significantly related to both forms of religious behavior, with correlation coefficients (R) ranging from about .40 to .74, depending upon the particular measure used. The extent to which sacred or secular orientations are present in a society can be predicted by any of these basic indicators of human development with a remarkable degree of accuracy, even if we know nothing further about the country. To explain and predict the strength and popularity of religion in any country we do not need to understand specific factors such as the activities and role of Pentecostal evangelists in Guatemala and Presbyterian

Table 3.2. Human Security and Religious Behavior

Indicators	Religious Participation	Frequency of Prayer	Nations
SOCIOECONOMIC DEVELOPMENT	R Sig.	R Sig.	N.
Human Development Index 2001 (UNDP 2003)	−.530***	−.530***	73
GINI coefficient for income inequality, latest year (WDI 2002)	.426**	.530**	59
Logged per capita GDP (in $US PPP), 2000 (WDI 2002)	−.469***	−.512***	67
% Urban population, as % of total, 2000 (WDI 2002)	−.451**	−.490**	65
% Rural population, as % of total, 2000 (WDI 2002)	.452**	−.493**	65
EDUCATION AND COMMUNICATIONS			
Adult illiteracy rate, 1998 (UNDP 2000)	.406**	.522**	73
Education (Gross enrollment ratio) 1998	−.487***	−.435***	73
Access to mass communications (% TV, radio, telephones, mobile telephones, newspapers, and the Internet)	−.533***	−.468***	59
HEALTHCARE			
AIDS cases (per 100,000 people), 1997	.403***	.375***	67
Infant mortality rate, under 12 months per 1,000 live births 2000 (WDI 2002)	.600***	562***	62
Child mortality rate, under 5 years, per 1,000 live births 2000 (WDI 2002)	.604***	.608***	64
Access to an improved water source (% pop) (WDI 2002)	−.481**	−.507*	43
Immunization (against measles, % of children under 12 months) (WDI 2002)	−.583**	−.455**	64
Doctors (per 100,000 people), 1993 (UNDP 2001)	−.582***	−.708***	66
DEMOGRAPHICS			
Population growth (annual %) (WDI 2002)	.548***	.742***	65
Life expectancy at birth, total years, 2000 (WDI 2002)	−.535***	−.454***	64

Indicators	Religious Participation	Frequency of Prayer	Nations
Population ages 0–14 (% of total) (WDI 2002)	.607***	.722***	64
Population ages 65 and above (% of total) (WDI 2002)	−.557***	−.743***	64

NOTES: The figures show the simple correlation (without any controls) and significance (Sig.): ***P = .001; **P = .01; *P = .05. Religious participation: *"Apart from weddings, funerals, and christenings, about how often do you attend religious services these days? More than once a week (7), once a week (6), once a month (5), only on special holy days (4), once a year (3), less often (2), never or practically never (1)."* Scaled 1–7. Frequency of prayer: Q199: *"How often do you pray to God outside of religious services? Would you say... Every day (7), more than once a week (6), once a week (5), at least once a month (4), several times a year (3), less often (2), never (1)."* Scaled 1–7.

Sources: Indicators of human security: United National Development Program, 2003, *World Development Report,* New York: UNDP/Oxford University Press; WDI: World Bank, *World Development Indicators 2002.*

missionaries in South Korea, the specific belief-systems in Buddhism, the impact of madrassa teaching Wahhabism in Pakistan, the fund-raising capacity and organizational strength of the Christian Right in the U.S. South, the philanthropic efforts of Catholic missionaries in West Africa, tensions over the imposition of Sharia law in Nigeria, the crackdown on freedom of worship in China, or divisions over the endorsement of women and homosexual clergy within the Anglican church. What we do need to know, however, are the basic characteristics of a vulnerable society that generate the demand for religion, including factors far removed from the spiritual, exemplified by levels of medical immunization, cases of AIDS/HIV, and access to an improved water source.

Now, establishing correlations at the macro-level provides only limited insights into the factors causing these relationships and we should always bear in mind the possibility of reverse causation; it could always be argued that religious participation and the frequency of prayer (both indicators of spiritual values) somehow systematically *cause* countries to develop more slowly. But this hypothesis does not seem very plausible theoretically; there are classic Weberian theories suggesting that Protestant values should matter for the process of industrialization, as examined further in Chapter 7. Yet no generally accepted theory claims that *all* forms of religion deter economic development.[14] Nor could such an explanation account satisfactorily for why religiosity should lead to the diverse range of social indicators used, which are not purely economic, all generating similarly strong correlations, whether we compare rates of medical immunizations, child mortality, or literacy. It could also be argued by critics that a spurious relationship could be at work, with a mis-specified model, so that we may have exaggerated the role of human security in this process. For example, religious beliefs could be undermined primarily by the effect of rising education and growing cognitive awareness on human rationality, as Weberian theory suggests. Since countries with widespread access to schooling, universities, and literacy also usually have higher levels of affluence, healthcare, and lower population growth, it is admittedly difficult, if not impossible, to disentangle these effects to isolate the individual impact of existential security per se that we suspect underlies all these factors. But there is no direct correlation at the individual level between faith in science and religiosity. It is true that we do not have a *direct* specific measure of existential security, in part because the manifestation of this phenomenon differs in the specific risks and threats common in different societies; in South Africa, for example, vulnerability of the population to HIV/AIDS has created a national pandemic, while citizens in Colombia face substantial threats from drugs and drug-cartel-related crime. In Bangladesh, many peasant farmers face problems of disastrous floods wiping out their homes and farms, while in Eritrea, Rwanda, and Liberia, which were pulled apart by bloody civil wars, the public faced grave risks of becoming a victim of deep-seated ethnic conflict. At the same time, although the type of risks differ, what poorer developing countries share in common are precarious lives vulnerable to insecurity, lacking the basics of healthcare and food, literacy, and a clean water supply, and we believe that these typify the conditions of uncertainty and unpredictability which lead many people to emphasize religion.

Given the much shorter life spans generally found in poorer and less secure societies, one might expect that demographic trends would lead toward steadily rising levels of secularization around the world. But as we discuss further in the conclusion, the reality is more complex – and culminates in exactly the opposite result. Although poorer societies such as Nigeria, Bangladesh, and Uganda have infant mortality rates of eighty deaths per one thousand live births, compared with rates of four deaths per one thousand live births in Sweden, the former countries also have incomparably higher levels of population growth. These factors are linked, we argue, because social vulnerability and lack of human development drive both religiosity *and* population growth. This means that the total number of religious people continues to expand around the globe, even while secularization is *also* taking place in the more affluent nations.

Multivariate analysis at the macro-level provides some additional insight. The theory we have outlined holds that conditions of human security and experience of greater economic equality influence rates of religious participation indirectly, by reducing the importance of religious values in people's everyday lives. A society's predominant type of religious culture may also shape participation through religious beliefs. Table 3.3 tests empirical evidence of the main propositions in this theory using a series of OLS regression analysis models. *Model A* first enters two indicators of societal security, namely the UNDP Human Development index and also the GINI coefficient summarizing the economic inequality in each nation. The dependent variable here is the aggregate-level strength of participation in services of worship for the fifty-six societies for which complete data is available. Since many aspects of human security are closely interrelated (with greater affluence and the industrialization of the workforce often leading to improvements in healthcare and education), the other social indicators we have already examined are dropped from the regression models to avoid problems of multicollinearity and to produce a reasonably parsimonious model. *Model B* then adds measures of religious values (the importance of religion, using a 4-point scale). *Models C* and *D* repeat this process with frequency of prayer as the dependent variable, to see whether the main relationships remain robust and consistent.

The first results in Model A show that by itself, without any controls, the level of human development and economic inequality alone explained 46% of the variance in participation in services of worship. But our analytical model, outlined in Figure 1.1, hypothesizes that growing human security influences participation indirectly, by reducing the importance of religious values in each society. Model B therefore adds the measures of religious values, which proved strongly and significantly related to religious participation, and at this stage the index of human development and the GINI coefficient become insignificant in the model. Most importantly, this confirms that human security operates as expected by reducing the importance of religious values, and thereby *indirectly* influencing religious behavior. Moreover, the simple model proves highly successful: overall Model B explains over two-thirds (66%) of the variance in participation in services of worship in these societies, an impressive amount given the measurement error inherent in cross-national survey research and the data limitations in the analysis. Models C and D repeat this process with frequency of prayer as the key dependent variable and the results are very similar, confirming the findings are robust independent of the specific measure selected for comparison.

Yet we acknowledge that it is always difficult to establish causality conclusively, and in the present case, the massive time-series database that would be required to do so is not available. We will simply say that the regression analysis results are fully consistent with our argument that human security,

Table 3.3. Explaining Religious Behavior

| | Religious Participation | | | | | | | | Frequency of Prayer | | | | | | | |
| | Model A: Security | | | | Model B: Security + values | | | | Model C: Security | | | | Model D: Security + values | | | |
	b	s.e.	Beta	Sig.	B	s.e.	Beta	Sig.	b	s.e.	Beta	Sig.	B	s.e.	Beta	Sig.
SOCIETAL SECURITY																
Level of human development (HDI)	4.27	.85	.28	***	1.23	.86	.16	N/s	4.05	1.3	.44	***	.889	.55	.10	N/s
Levels of economic inequality (GINI coeff.)	.027	.01	.25	*	.000	.01	.01	N/s	.050	.02	.35	**	.005	.01	.03	N/s
RELIGIOUS ORIENTATION																
Religious values (4-point scale)					1.19	.211	.701	***					2.18	.14	1.05	***
Constant	6.23				1.29				5.94				2.34			
Adjusted R²	**.464**				**.667**				**.42**				**.925**			

NOTES: The models use ordinary least squares regression analysis. In Models A and B the dependent variable was the mean frequency of attendance at services of worship, measured on a 7-point scale from "never" to "at least weekly," analyzed at macro-level. In Models C and D the dependent variable was the frequency of prayer, measured on a 7-point scale at macro-level. The columns represent the unstandardized beta coefficients (b), the standard error (s.e.), the standardized betas (B), and the significance of the coefficients: ***P = .0001; **P = .01; P = .05. All items were checked to be free from problems of multicollinearity using tolerance statistics. *Human Development Index (HDI)*: UNDP index 2001 based on longevity, literacy, and education, and per capita GDP (in PPP). UNDP. *Human Development Report 2003*. New York: UNDP/Oxford University Press. *GINI coefficient*: This measures the extent to which the distribution of income among households within a society deviates from a perfectly equal distribution. It ranges from perfect equality (0) to perfect inequality (100). World Bank. *World Development Indicators 2002*. Religious values: "How important is religion in your life?" Very (4), rather (3), not very (2), or not at all (1). Religious participation: "Apart from weddings, funerals, and christenings, about how often do you attend religious services these days? More than once a week (7), once a week (6), once a month (5), only on special holy days (4), once a year (3), less often (2), never or practically never (1)." Scaled 1–7. Frequency of prayer: Q199: "How often do you pray to God outside of religious services? Would you say . . . Every day (7), more than once a week (6), once a week (5), at least once a month (4), several times a year (3), less often (2), never (1)." Scaled 1–7.

Source: World Values Survey, pooled 1981–2001.

measured here by the process of human development and the degree of socioeconomic equality, has an impact on the priority given to religious values and beliefs, as more affluent and egalitarian societies reduce vulnerability to daily life-threatening risks. These initial models do not take account of many other factors that could plausibly shape the strength and vitality of spiritual life in particular countries, including restriction of religious freedom experienced in China and Viet Nam, the role of Pentecostal missionaries in Latin America, the legacy of post-Communist states in Eastern and Central Europe, and the degree of religious pluralism in Protestant Scandinavia and Catholic Europe. Some of these factors are examined further in subsequent chapters. Nevertheless, the fairly simple and parsimonious models presented so far suggest that, among the factors that we have compared cross-nationally, religious values play the strongest role in mobilizing religious participation. And the importance of these values is, in turn, intimately related to patterns of societal modernization, human security, and socioeconomic equality.

The cross-national analysis that we have presented cannot by itself *prove* causation, and it could always be argued that some other unspecified cause is driving human security *and* religiosity. So far, however, no one has come up with a satisfactory explanation of what this other factor might be. What we can do is to rule out the Weberian argument, discussed in Chapter 1, that belief in science and technology has undermined faith in the magical and metaphysical. If the adoption of a rational worldview had played this role, then we might expect that those societies with the most positive attitudes toward science would also prove the most skeptical when it came to religious beliefs. Instead, as clearly shown in Figure 3.3, societies with greater faith in science also often have *stronger* religious beliefs. Far from a negative relationship, as we might expect from Weberian theory, in fact there is a positive one. The publics in many Muslim societies apparently see no apparent contradictions between believing that scientific advances hold great promise for human progress and that they have faith in common tenets of spiritual beliefs, such as the existence of heaven and hell. Indeed, the more secular postindustrial societies, exemplified by the Netherlands, Norway and Denmark, prove most skeptical toward the impact of science and technology, and this is in accordance with the countries where the strongest public disquiet has been expressed about certain contemporary scientific developments such as the use of genetically modified food, biotechnological cloning, and nuclear power. Interestingly, again the United States displays distinctive attitudes compared with similar European nations, showing greater faith in both God and scientific progress. Of course

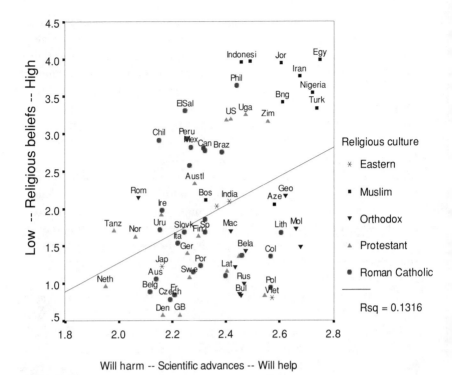

Figure 3.3. Faith in Science and Religion. Note: Attitudes toward science: Q 132: *"In the long run, do you think the scientific advances we are making will help or harm mankind?"* 1 *"Will harm"*; 2 *"Some of each"*; 3 *"Will help."* Religious beliefs: Summary 4-point scale composed of whether respondents expressed belief in heaven, in hell, in life after death, and in whether people have a soul. Source: World Values Survey, pooled 1981–2001.

the Weberian account could still be valid if the rise of the rational worldview was interpreted as a broader shift in social norms and values occurring during earlier centuries of European history, associated with the gradual spread of education and literacy, and the rise of industrialization and modern technology, rather than reflecting contemporary attitudes toward science. But, as discussed further in Chapter 7, this historical interpretation of the Weberian argument cannot be tested with any contemporary evidence. What the survey data does show is that, rather than a clear trade-off, many people can believe in the beneficial effects of science without apparently abandoning faith in God.

At this point, let us simply emphasize the consistency of the correlations between human security and secularization, which prove robust regardless of the particular developmental indicator selected from the wide range that are available. Although it does not prove causality, the results are consistent with our argument that religion becomes less central as people's lives become less vulnerable to the constant threat of death, disease, and misfortune. As the first stage of modernization progresses, and people escape the Hobbesian condition where life is nasty, brutish, and short, they often become more secular in their concerns. To enhance our confidence in our proposed interpretation, we will examine further relevant evidence concerning macro-level time-series trends, generational comparisons, and micro-level comparisons of religiosity by social sectors within nations.

Social Characteristics

So far we have explored some of the primary factors driving religious engagement at the macro- or societal-level. To explore the data further we can also examine the individual-level background characteristics of religious participants, to determine whether religiosity proves strongest, as expected, among the more vulnerable strata of society. Table 3.4 shows the patterns of regular religious participation in agrarian, industrial, and postindustrial societies broken down by the standard social characteristics. In the agrarian societies, religiosity was strong and broadly distributed across most social groups by gender, age, work status, income, and marital status, although, as expected, participation was indeed strongest among the least educated and the poorest groups. Since religious participation is so pervasive in all of these developing societies, there may well be a "ceiling" effect limiting variance in the data, with most social sectors participating fairly equally. In industrial societies, however, as secular orientations become more widespread, sharper social differences emerge among the residual religious population. Religiosity remains stronger in industrial societies among the more vulnerable populations who are most vulnerable to risks, including among women, the older population, poorer households, the less educated, and the unskilled working class.[15] In postindustrial societies, as well, religion is also more pervasive among women than men, and there is a sharp division by age, with the older population twice as likely to attend services regularly as the youngest group (under 30). Nevertheless, in these societies the patterns of religiosity by education and class remain mixed and inconsistent.[16] Further exploration, discussed in the next chapter, suggests that in postindustrial societies with the sharpest socioeconomic disparities, including in the United States, religion remains strongest among the poorest classes,

Table 3.4. Social Characteristics of Religious Participation

	Agrarian	Industrial	Postindustrial	All
All	49	25	22	28
Sex				
Women	49	26	26	30
Men	49	22	18	26
Age group				
Younger (Under 30 years old)	49	22	15	26
Middle (30–59 years old)	47	23	21	26
Older (60+ years old)	47	29	35	34
Education				
Low education	55	34	21	36
Medium education	47	23	16	28
High education	48	22	24	28
Employment status				
In paid work	49	29	26	27
Income				
Lowest income deciles	56	30	22	34
Highest income deciles	45	17	22	26
Social Class				
Manager/professional	52	22	23	28
Lower middle	46	22	17	22
Skilled working	42	21	17	23
Unskilled working	52	30	19	31
Marital and family status				
Married	49	24	23	28
With children	48	25	23	29

NOTE: Religious participation: *"Apart from weddings, funerals, and christenings, about how often do you attend religious services these days? More than once a week, once a week, once a month, only on special holy days, once a year, less often, never, or practically never."* The percentage attending religious services *"more than once a week"* or *"once a week."*

Source: World Values Survey, pooled 1981–2001.

but these differences diminish in more egalitarian postindustrial societies such as Norway and Sweden.

Two other general observations are important. First, overall the basic type of society has a far greater impact on religiosity than differences by so-cial sector; *all* groups in agrarian societies are more religious than *any* single group in postindustrial societies. In other words, the macro-level factors determining conditions of socio-tropic security in any country are more important than the micro-level predictors of ego-tropic security. We can interpret this pattern as indicating that even the affluent professional classes living in secure, gated communities in Johannesburg, San Paolo, or Lagos, located well away from the shanty-towns and favelas, with deep pockets for private healthcare, private education, and private insurance, cannot insulate themselves and their families entirely from the risks of crime, the threat of violence, and the problems of political instability endemic in society. On the other hand, even political refugees and unemployed first-generation immigrants from Afghanistan, Algeria, or Bangladesh now living in Stockholm, Paris, or Manchester, despite encountering serious poverty and discrimination, usually have access to basic public healthcare, state welfare benefits, and schooling for their children. Human security therefore has a diffuse effect upon the whole of society, both rich and poor, which generates the conditions leading to religiosity. In addition, the evidence shows that the sharpest reduction in religiosity occurs following the first stage of societal modernization, in the shift from agrarian to industrial societies. The second stage is also associated with a modest erosion of religiosity, but this step is far less dramatic. The process of development is not a linear process steadily and continuously generating a more secular and secure society. Nor is greater affluence alone sufficient where economic inequalities are severe. Instead, it appears that societies become less responsive to the appeals of the metaphysical world when people's lives are lifted out of dire poverty and its life-threatening risks, and life in this world becomes more secure with the complex process of human development.

Trends in Religious Participation and Beliefs

So far we have established that agrarian societies are far more religious than either industrial or postindustrial societies. But cross-sectional analysis cannot *prove* the causality underlying our interpretation. Is there any longitudinal evidence demonstrating the erosion of religious participation over relatively long periods of time, as suggested by our theory of secularization and existential security? The most extensive available time-series survey evidence is relatively limited in geographic coverage, because surveys about religion were not conducted in most developing nations until recently – but we can compare trends over recent decades from surveys in many postindustrial societies.

Table 3.5 shows the annual trends in regular (weekly) religious participation in thirteen European societies from 1970 to 1998, based on a comparable 5-point scale measuring attendance at religious services from the Eurobarometer surveys. To monitor the significance and direction of any change over time, models are used where the year of the survey is regressed

Table 3.5. Decline in Religious Participation, EU 1970–1998

	France	Belgium	Netherlands	Germany	Italy	Lux.	Denmark	Ireland	Britain	N. Ireland	Greece	Portugal	Spain
1970	23	52	41	29	56								
1971	27	58	49	39	58								
1973	19	38	33	22	48	48	5	91	16	59			
1975	22	45	44	26	39	44	6	93	8	60			
1976	23	45	45	30	37	40	6	93	17	56			
1977	18	50	48	26	37	42	5	91	17	64			
1978	14	45	45	23	36	39	5	90	10	69			
1980	13	38	31	21	37	41	5	91	9	59			
1981	12	36	29	20	35	36	7	91	7	59	27		47
1985	13	27	24	19	37	32	6	88	8	58	26		
1988	14	31	36	19	42	30	6	85	7	61	24	39	34
1989	13	29	34	18	44	28	4	83	10	60	21	40	31
1990	10	30	36	21	46	32	4	85	13	62	24	42	35
1991	9	24	35	19	46	28	4	82	13	61	24	39	33
1992	12	22	22	17	43	29	3	79	6	54	26	33	27
1993	11	27	33	15	45	27	4	81	7		25	31	33
1994		27	28	16	41	22	3	77	12		24	37	36
1998	5	10	14	15	39	17	4	65	4	46	21	30	20
Beta	–0.620	–1.290	–0.780	–0.589	–0.188	–1.041	–0.099	–0.855	–0.233	–0.371	–0.250	–1.095	–1.303
Sig.	0.000	0.000	0.001	0.000	0.316	0.000	0.005	0.000	0.075	0.081	0.067	0.023	0.004
Obs.	18	18	18	18	18	16	16	16	16	13	10	8	9

NOTE: Religious participation: Q: *"Do you attend religious services several times a week, once a week, a few times during the year, once a year or less, or never?"* The percentage attending religious services *"several times a week"* or *"once a week."* Sig. = significance; Obs. = number of observations in the series.

Source: The Mannheim Eurobarometer Trend File 1970–1999.

on the proportion of the population attending weekly religious services in each society. The result of the analysis clearly confirms that a substantial fall in regular attendance has occurred in every society, with negative regression coefficients, and the models demonstrate that this decline proved statistically significant (at the .10 level) in every European society except for Italy. We can monitor trends across the full series of surveys available since 1970 in the five core EU member states (France, Belgium, the Netherlands, Germany, and Italy). In these countries, on average about 40% of the public attended church regularly in 1970, with this proportion falling by half in recent years. The predominately Catholic nations saw the greatest shrinkage of their church population, notably the dramatic fall in Belgium, Luxembourg, and Spain, although these countries also started from the highest levels of religiosity.

To examine the trends in a broader range of nations (but over a shorter time span), religious participation can be compared in the twenty-two industrial and postindustrial societies contained in the 1981, 1990, and 2001 waves of the World Values Survey. As in the Eurobarometer surveys, the strongest declines of churchgoing (of over 10% over two decades) are registered in Catholic Europe (see in Table 3.6), notably in Ireland, Spain, Belgium, and the Netherlands. Six other Catholic societies, including Argentina, France, and Canada, experienced more modest erosions. Religious participation in most of the Northern European Protestant nations was extremely low at the start of the series but possibly for this reason, if there is a "floor" effect, it remains largely stable over these decades in most countries. By contrast, only three societies registered a modest increase during this period: the United States (+3%), Italy (+8%), and South Africa (+13%). The overall picture confirms one of secular decline in most, although not all, countries, with Catholic churches facing the greatest loss of congregations and emptying church pews.

Therefore, the cross-sectional analysis suggests that the strength of religious participation can be predicted with a fair degree of accuracy from contemporary levels of human development, as well as from the strength of religious values and beliefs in any society. Moreover, the time-series evidence lends further confirmation to our arguments; where we have survey evidence for many postindustrial and some industrial societies, this demonstrates that religious participation has usually (not everywhere) fallen. The next chapter demonstrates that in rich nations this erosion has been accompanied by a fall in subjective religiosity, measured by trends in belief in God and in life after death. Any one indicator can be questioned, as the patterns are not always clean-cut; different series start in different periods; and the

Table 3.6. Trends in Religious Participation, 1981–2001

Nation	1981	1990	2001	Change
Ireland	82	81	65	−17
Spain	40	29	26	−15
Belgium	31	27	19	−12
Netherlands	26	20	14	−12
Argentina	31	32	25	−6
Northern Ireland	52	50	46	−6
Canada	31	27	27	−4
France	11	10	8	−4
South Korea	19	21	15	−4
West Germany	19	18	16	−3
Britain	14	14	14	0
Denmark	3	3	3	0
Hungary	11	21	11	0
Norway	5	5	5	0
Finland	4	4	5	+1
Iceland	2	2	3	+1
Japan	3	3	4	+1
Mexico	54	43	55	+1
Sweden	6	4	7	+1
United States	43	44	46	+3
Italy	32	38	40	+8
South Africa	43	56	57	+13

NOTE: Religious participation: *"Apart from weddings, funerals, and christenings, about how often do you attend religious services these days? More than once a week, once a week, once a month, only on special holy days, once a year, less often, never or practically never."* The percentage attending religious services *"more than once a week"* or *"once a week."*
Source: World Values Survey, 1981–2001.

country coverage remains limited. Nevertheless, the time-series evidence examined so far adds great plausibility to the story told on the basis of the cross-sectional comparisons.

A significant exception to this general pattern of growing secularization in affluent postindustrial societies lies in evidence that although the publics of these nations are becoming increasingly indifferent to traditional religious values, they are not abandoning private or individualized spirituality. Table 3.7 examines the trends during the last twenty years in responses to an item monitoring how often people took time to think about the "meaning and purpose of life." While the existing hierarchical religious institutions seem to be losing their ability to dictate to the

Table 3.7. Rise in Thinking about the Meaning of Life, 1981–2001

	1981	1990	1995	2001	Change
Argentina	29	57	51	51	22
Sweden	20	24	28	37	17
Mexico	31	40	39	47	16
Canada	37	44		52	15
South Africa	39	58	51	54	15
Italy	37	48		50	13
South Korea	29	39		41	12
Australia	34		45		9
United States	49	49	46	58	9
Netherlands	23	31			8
Ireland	26	34			8
Denmark	29	29		37	8
Finland	32	38	40	40	8
Belgium	22	29			7
Norway	25	31	32		7
Japan	21	21	25	26	5
Northern Ireland	28	33			5
West Germany	27	30		31	4
France	36	39			3
Hungary	44	45	45		1
Iceland	37	36			-1
Spain	24	27	24	22	-2
Britain	33	36		25	-8

NOTE: Q: *"How often, if at all, do you think about the meaning and purpose of life? Often, sometimes, rarely, or never?"* The percentage *"often."*
Source: World Values Survey, 1981–2001.

masses, the publics of most countries showed increasing interest in the meaning and purpose of life, from the first available surveys in 1981 until the latest survey conducted in 1995 or around 2000. Growing proportions of the public thought about spiritual concerns, broadly defined. In a world where survival was uncertain, the main motivation for mass attachment to religion was the need for security. The need for meaning becomes more salient at high levels of existential security so that, even in rich countries, although church attendance is declining, spiritual concerns more broadly are not disappearing. At the same time, it is clear that these publics are not continuing to support the traditional religious authorities, institutionalized, hierarchical forms of religion, and established religious practices.

Generational Comparisons

The last approach we can use to examine the evidence is generational comparisons, where we break down the cross-sectional data into ten-year birth cohorts. The theory of value change argued here suggests that secular social trends have only a glacial effect on cultural norms, but that, through the socialization process, the experience of the prevailing conditions during the formative years of childhood and early adolescence leave a lasting imprint on people: the religious values held in later life are largely shaped by one's formative experiences. Certain decisive historical events and common experiences can stamp their imprint on a generation. Those growing up during the interwar era in Western nations experienced the dramatic collapse of stocks and savings, mass unemployment and soup kitchens in the 1930s triggered by the Great Depression, followed by the military conflict that engulfed the world at the end of the decade. Given these conditions, the interwar generation in postindustrial societies is likely to prioritize materialist social goals, like the importance of secure and full employment, low inflation, and the underlying conditions for economic growth, as well as traditional views toward religion and support for religious authorities. In contrast, the postwar generation in these nations, coming of age during periods of unprecedented affluence, domestic peace, and social stability, are more likely to adhere to secular values and beliefs.

Of course with only cross-sectional survey evidence, rather than numerous waves of cross-sections, or with panel surveys among the same respondents over successive waves, it is impossible to disentangle generational effects from life-cycle effects that may alter attitudes and values as people move from youth to middle age and then retirement.[17] As people age they enter different stages of life, and the experience of education, entry into the labor force, the formation of family through marriage and childrearing, and then retirement from the workforce, could each be expected to shape beliefs about religion. Cultural messages conveyed in the mass media, and contact with church organizations and religious social networks, could also color perceptions about the appropriate norms and practices of religious attitudes and behavior in any community. Significant events could also generate a period effect, exemplified by the impact of the events of 9/11 which the Pew survey estimated boosted churchgoing, at least temporarily, in the United States, or the influence on Catholicism of the Papal encyclical on contraception issued during the 1960s, or deep internal divisions splitting the Anglican church leadership over the ordination of women and homosexuals.[18] But there is strong evidence that religious values are learned

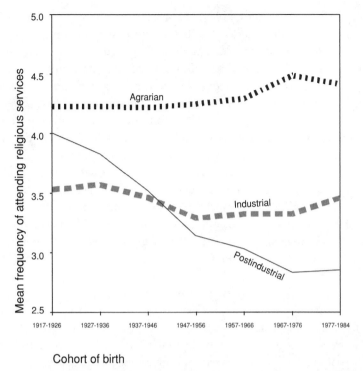

Cohort of birth

Figure 3.4. Religious Participation by Birth Cohort. Note: Religious participation: Q185: *"Apart from weddings, funerals, and christenings, about how often do you attend religious services these days? More than once a week, once a week, once a month, only on special holy days, once a year, less often, never or practically never."* The proportion who attended *"Once a week or more."* Sources: World Values Survey, pooled 1981–2001.

early in life, in the family, school, and community, as part of the primary socialization process, so that the enduring values of different birth cohorts can be attributed mainly to their formative experiences in childhood and adolescence.[19]

When religious participation is analyzed by birth cohort and by type of society, as illustrated in Figure 3.4, the results are clear and consistent. Postindustrial societies show a sharp and steady decline in religiosity from the oldest cohort born in the interwar years down to the postwar cohort, and then a more modest slide down to the sixties generation, before reaching a plateau among the youngest cohort. Among industrial societies there is only a modest slide among the interwar generation, and perhaps a very modest increase detectable among the youngest cohort. And among agrarian societies the pattern across birth cohorts is a completely flat plateau and actually shows a slight upward shift among the sixties cohort. Figure 3.4 makes a crucial point very clear: previous literature (based entirely on data from advanced industrial societies) has found that the young are less religious than the old, which could be interpreted as reflecting an historic decline of religiosity, or which could be interpreted as a life-cycle effect. Critics of secularization prefer the latter interpretation, dismissing any suggestion of historic change and interpreting this finding as reflecting a life cycle effect: "Everyone knows that people naturally get more religious as they grow older. It's inherent in the life cycle." Figure 3.4 demonstrates that there is *not* any inherent tendency for people to get more religious as they grow older: in agrarian societies, the young are fully as religious as the old. But in postindustrial societies, the young are much less religious than the old – which seems to reflect historic changes linked with the emergence of high levels of human development, rather than anything inherent in the human life cycle.

As a result of these patterns, a substantial religious gap has developed between societies. If we interpret Figure 3.4 as reflecting a process of intergenerational change, it implies that the most affluent nations have become far more secular over the years, overtaking the (largely ex-Communist) industrial societies in this process, and generating a large gap between them and developing societies. The pattern strongly suggests that the religious gap is not due to agrarian societies becoming *more* religious over time, as is often suggested. Their values have remained relatively constant. What has happened instead is that rapid cultural changes in the more affluent societies have shifted their basic values and beliefs in a more secular direction, opening up a growing gulf between them and the less affluent societies. This phenomenon may sometimes produce a backlash where religious groups and leaders in poorer societies seek to defend their values against the global encroachment of secular values. This phenomenon occurs, we believe, not because the agrarian societies have gradually become more religious over time, but rather because the prevailing values of richer societies have moved apart from traditional norms.

Conclusions

None of the evidence considered in this chapter is sufficient by itself, but if we put together the different pieces of the puzzle through triangulation, then the cross-sectional comparisons of many different countries, the available time-series data of trends over time, and the generational comparisons all point in a consistent direction. The evidence strongly suggests that the first stage of societal modernization, as countries move from traditional agrarian communities to the industrial phase, tends to be accompanied by a decline in feelings of personal piety, in expressions of spirituality, and in habitual observances at services of worship. Through human development, as lives become more secure and immune to daily risks, the importance of religion gradually fades away. The consistency of the correlation between religiosity and diverse indicators of human development, whether child mortality rates, educational enrollment, access to improved water, or urbanization, all point in a similar direction. Affluence such as per capita GDP is not sufficient by itself, as the distribution of resources and economic equality plays an important role as well. Vulnerable populations experiencing considerable uncertainty and risk in their lives, and in the lives of their family and community, regard religion as far more important, and therefore participate far more keenly in spiritual activities, than those living without such threats. As lives gradually become more comfortable and secure, people in more affluent societies usually grow increasingly indifferent to religious values, more skeptical of supernatural beliefs, and less willing to become actively engaged in religious institutions, beyond a nominal level of formal religious identities, participation in symbolic ceremonies of birth, marriage, and death to mark life's passages, and enjoyment of traditional holidays.

But despite this general picture, there could well be particular factors influencing particular regions or exceptional countries that fail to conform to this pattern. We still need to explain some important anomalies to secularization among postindustrial societies, notably the case of the United States. Many observers also suggest that a religious revival has occurred in Central and Eastern Europe with the overturn of the Communist state.[20] Following the events of 9/11, and the subsequent developments in Afghanistan and Iraq, numerous popular commentators have reported a resurgence of fundamentalist parties, extremist religious groups, and ethnoreligious conflict within the Muslim world. It is to these issues that we now turn.

PART II

Case Studies of Religion and Politics

The Puzzle of Secularization in the United States and Western Europe

DESPITE THE WEALTH of evidence for secularization that we have documented in postindustrial societies, critics could argue that we still have not accounted for important anomalies in these patterns. The strongest challenge to secularization theory arises from American observers who point out that claims of steadily diminishing congregations in Western Europe are sharply at odds with U.S. trends, at least until the early 1990s.[1]

To consider these issues, Part I describes systematic and consistent evidence establishing the variations in religiosity among postindustrial nations, in particular contrasts between America and Western Europe. This chapter focuses upon similar postindustrial nations, all affluent countries and established democracies, most (but not all) sharing a cultural heritage of Christendom, although obviously there remains the critical cleavage dividing Catholic and Protestant Europe. All these are service-sector knowledge economies with broadly similar levels of education and affluence, as well as established and stable democratic states.[2] This framework helps to control for many of the factors that might be expected to shape patterns of religiosity, allowing us to compare like with like. This process facilitates the "most-similar" comparative framework, thereby narrowing down, or even eliminating, some of the multiple factors that could be causing variations in religious behavior. This chapter examines whether the United States is indeed "exceptional" among rich nations in the vitality of its spiritual life, as the conventional wisdom has long suggested, or whether, as Berger proposes, Western Europe is "exceptional" in its secularization.[3] On this basis, Part II then considers evidence to test religious market, functionalist, and security theories of secularization. Religious market theory postulates that intense competition between rival denominations generates a ferment of activity explaining the vitality of churchgoing. Functionalist explanations focus on the shrinking social role of religious institutions, following the growth of the welfare state and the public sector. We compare evidence supporting these accounts with the theory of secure secularization, based on societal modernization, human development, and economic inequality, that lies at the heart of this book.

Comparing Religiosity in Postindustrial Nations

We can start by considering the cross-national evidence for how the indicators of religiosity that we have discussed earlier apply to postindustrial nations. Figure 4.1 shows the basic pattern of religious behavior, highlighting the substantial contrasts between the cluster of countries that prove by far the most religious in this comparison, including the United States, Ireland, and Italy. At the other extreme, the most secular nations include France, Denmark, and Britain. There is a fairly similar pattern across both indicators of religious behavior, suggesting that both collective and individual forms of participation are fairly consistent in each society. Therefore, although religion in the United States is distinctive among rich nations, it would still be misleading to refer to American "exceptionalism," as so many emphasize, as though it were a deviant case from *all* other postindustrial nations, as we can observe similarities with both Ireland and Italy.

The marked contrasts within Europe are illustrated further in Figure 4.2, mapping secular Northern Europe compared with the persistence of more regular churchgoing habits in Southern Europe, as well as differences within Central and Eastern Europe that will be explored in subsequent chapters. The "North-South" religious gap within the European Union is, admittedly, a puzzle that cannot be explained by the process of societal development alone, since these are all rich nations. More plausible explanations include the contemporary strength of religiosity in Protestant and Catholic cultures, as well as societal differences in economic equality. These contrasts are important and certainly deserve scrutiny.

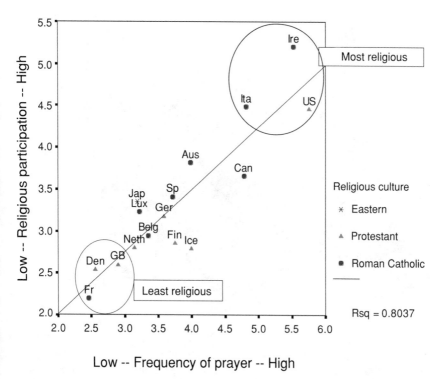

Figure 4.1. Religious Behavior in Postindustrial Societies. Notes: Religious participation: Q185: *"Apart from weddings, funerals, and christenings, about how often do you attend religious services these days? More than once a week, once a week, once a month, only on special holy days, once a year, less often, never or practically never."* Mean frequency of attendance at religious services. Frequency of prayer? Q199: *"How often do you pray to God outside of religious services? Would you say . . . Every day (7), more than once a week (6), once a week (5), at least once a month (4), several times a year (3), less often (2), never (1)."* Mean frequency per society. Source: World Values Survey, pooled 1981–2001.

Trends in Secularization in Western Europe

One reason for these cross-national variations could be that most postindustrial societies have experienced a significant erosion of religiosity during the postwar era, but that these trends have occurred from different starting points, in a path-dependent fashion, due to the historic legacy of the religious institutions and cultures within each country. Where the church ends up today could depend in large part upon where they start out.

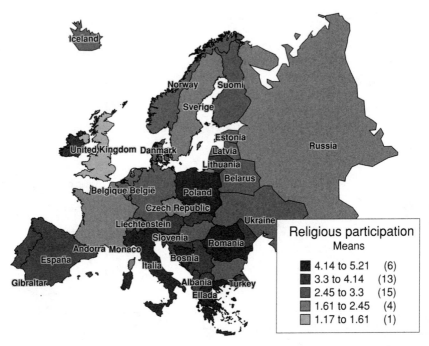

Figure 4.2. Religious Participation in Europe. Note: Religious participation: Q185: *"Apart from weddings, funerals, and christenings, about how often do you attend religious services these days? More than once a week, once a week, once a month, only on special holy days, once a year, less often, never or practically never."* Mean frequency of attendance at religious services. Source: World Values Survey, pooled 1981–2001.

We will demonstrate that the existing evidence in Western Europe consistently and unequivocally shows two things: traditional religious beliefs and involvement in institutionalized religion (i) vary considerably from one country to another; and (ii) have steadily declined throughout Western Europe, particularly since the 1960s. Studies have often reported that many Western Europeans have ceased to be regular churchgoers today outside of special occasions such as Christmas and Easter, weddings and funerals, a pattern especially evident among the young.[4] Jagodzinski and Dobbelaere, for example, compared the proportion of regular (weekly) churchgoers in seven European countries from 1970 to 1991, based on the Eurobarometer surveys, and documented a dramatic fall in congregations during this period in the Catholic states under comparison (Belgium, France, the Netherlands, and West Germany). Overall levels of church disengagement had advanced furthest in France, Britain, and the Netherlands: *"Although the timing and pace differ from one country to the next,*" the authors conclude, "*the general tendency is quite stable: in the long run, the percentage of unaffiliated is increasing.*"[5] Numerous studies provide a wealth of evidence confirming similar patterns of declining religiosity found in many other postindustrial nations.[6]

Trends in recent decades illustrate the consistency of the secularization process irrespective of the particular indicator or survey that is selected. Figure 4.3 illustrates the erosion of regular church attendance that has occurred throughout Western Europe since the early 1970s. The fall is

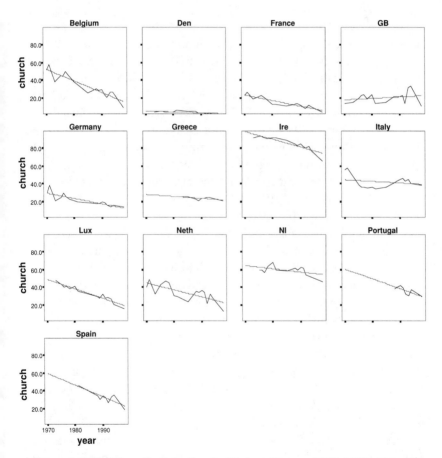

Figure 4.3. Religious Participation in Western Europe, 1970–1999. Note: The percentage of the population who said they attended a religious service "at least once a week" and the regression line of the trend. Source: The Mannheim Eurobarometer Trend File 1970–1999.

steepest and most significant in many Catholic societies, notably Belgium, France, Ireland, Luxembourg, the Netherlands, Portugal, and Spain.[7] To conclude, as Greeley does, that religion is "still relatively unchanged" in the traditional Catholic nations of Europe seems a triumph of hope over experience, and sharply at odds with the evidence.[8] Marked contrasts in the strength of churchgoing habits remain clear, say between contemporary rates of religious participation in Ireland and Denmark. Nevertheless, all the trends point consistently downward. Moreover, the erosion of religiosity is not exclusive to Western European nations; regular churchgoing also dropped during the last two decades in affluent Anglo-American nations such as Canada and Australia.[9]

Another interpretation of these patterns is offered by those who emphasize that trends in churchgoing are interesting but also out-of-date, if religiosity has evolved and reinvented itself today as diverse forms of personal "spirituality." Observers such as Wade Clark Roof suggest that collective engagement with religion in public life has eroded in America among the younger generation. Reasons for this are thought to include the declining status and authority of traditional church institutions and clergy, the individualization of the quest for spirituality, and the rise of multiple "New Age" movements concerned with "lived religion."[10] These developments are exemplified by a revival of alternative spiritual practices such as astrology, meditation, and alternative therapies, involving a diverse bricolage of personal beliefs. If similar developments are also evident in Europe, as a result public engagement with churches could have been replaced by a "private" or "personal" search for spirituality and meaning in life, making the practices, beliefs, and symbols of religiosity less visible.[11] Moreover, beyond patterns of churchgoing, the trends in European religiosity can be regarded as complex; Greeley, for example, proposes that indicators of subjective beliefs in Europe, exemplified by faith in God or in life after death, display a mixed picture during the last two decades, rather than a simple uniform decline: "*In some countries, religion has increased (most notably the former communist countries and especially Russia) in others it has declined (most notably Britain, the Netherlands, and France) and in still other countries it is relatively unchanged (the traditional Catholic countries), and in yet other countries (some of the social democratic countries) it has both declined and increased.*"[12] Given such divergence, Greeley suggests that simple attempts to discover secularization should be abandoned, and instead attention should focus on explaining persistent and well-established cross-national patterns, for example, why people in Ireland and Italy are consistently more religious than those living in France and Sweden.

Yet we find that, far from divergent patterns, one reason for the decline in religious participation during the late twentieth century lies in the fact that during these years many common spiritual beliefs have indeed suffered considerable erosion in postindustrial societies. There is, in fact, a consistent link between the "public" and "private" dimensions of religiosity. The Greeley results are based primarily upon analysis of the International Social Survey Program, which conducted opinion polls on religion in 1991 and 1998. Unfortunately this provides too limited a time period to detect longitudinal change. Instead, here we monitor trends in religious beliefs in God and in life after death during the last fifty years or so by matching survey data in the Gallup polls starting in 1947 to the more recent data where the same questions were replicated in the World Values Surveys.

Table 4.1 shows that in 1947, eight out of ten people believed in God, with the highest levels of belief expressed in Australia, Canada, the United States, and Brazil. The regression models show a fall in faith in God occurred across all but two nations (the United States and Brazil). The decline proved sharpest in the Scandinavian nations, the Netherlands, Australia, and Britain. The regression models show a negative slope across the series but given the limited series of time points (7 at most), not surprisingly the fall only proved statistically significant in six countries. Table 4.2 illustrates very similar patterns for belief in life after death, where again an erosion of subjective religiosity occurs in thirteen of the nineteen countries where evidence is available. The greatest declines during the fifty-year period studied are registered in Northern Europe, Canada, and Brazil, and the only exceptions to this pattern, where there is a revival of religious faith, is in the United States, along with Japan and Italy.

Trends in Religiosity in the United States

In the light of these European patterns, many have regarded the United States as an outlier, although in fact the evidence remains somewhat ambiguous. At least until the late 1980s, analysis of trends in church attendance derived from historical records and from representative surveys commonly reported that the size of congregations in the United States had remained stable over decades. For example, studies published during the 1980s indicated that Protestant church attendance had not declined significantly in America; and, while it fell rapidly among Catholics from 1968 to 1975, it did not erode further in subsequent years.[13] The first benchmark of the Gallup organization measuring religiosity found that in March 1939, 40%

Table 4.1. Belief in God, 1947–2001

Nation	1947	1968	1975	1981	1990	1995	2001	Change	b.	Sig. (P)
Sweden	80	60		52	38	48	46	−33.6	−.675	**
Netherlands	80	79		64	61		58	−22.0	−.463	*
Australia	95		80	79		75	75	−19.9	−.379	**
Norway	84	73		68	58	65		−18.9	−.473	**
Denmark	80			53	59		62	−17.9	−.387	*
Britain		77	76	73	72		61	−16.5	−.461	*
Greece		96					84	−12.3	−.364	–
West Germany		81	72	68	63	71	69	−12.0	−.305	N/s
Belgium			78	76	65		67	−11.2	−.487	N/s
Finland	83	83	72	59	61	73	72	−10.8	−.296	N/s
France	66	73	72		57		56	−10.1	−.263	N/s
Canada	95		89	91	85		88	−7.2	−.387	N/s
Switzerland		84			77	77		−7.2	−.277	N/s
India			98		93	94		−4.0	−.231	N/s
Japan			38	39	37	44	35	−3.0	−.016	N/s
Austria		85			78		83	−1.9	−.097	N/s
United States	94	98	94	96	93	94	94	0.4	−.027	N/s
Brazil	96	98			98	99		3.0	.056	N/s
ALL-10 1947–2001	85						72	−13.5	−.315	**

NOTES: The proportion of the public who express belief in God (% "Yes") in 19 societies. "Change" is the change in the proportion from the first to the last observation in the series. In the ordinary least squares regression models, year is regressed on the series. The unstandardized beta (b.) summarizes the slope of the line and the statistical significance (Sig.) of change in the time-series (P). ALL-10 are the average means for the 10 nations with observations in both 1947 and 2001.

Sources: 1947 Gallup Opinion Index "Do you, personally, believe in God?" Yes/No/Don't Know. 1968 Gallup Opinion Index "Do you believe in God?" Yes/No/Don't Know. 1975 Gallup Opinion Index "Do you believe in God or a universal spirit?" Yes/No/Don't Know. 1981–2001 World Values Survey/European Values Survey "Do you believe in God?" Yes/No/Don't Know. Source for Gallup polls: Lee Sigelman. 1977. "Review of the Polls: Multination Surveys of Religious Beliefs." Journal for the Scientific Study of Religion 16(3): 289–294.

Table 4.2. Belief in Life After Death, 1947–2001

	1947	1961	1968	1975	1981	1990	1995	2001	Change
Norway	71	71	54		41	36	43		−28
Finland	69		55			44	50	44	−25
Denmark	55				25	29		32	−23
Netherlands	68	63	50		41	39		47	−22
France	58		35	39	35	38		39	−20
Canada	78	68		54	61	61		67	−11
Brazil	78					70	67		−11
Sweden	49		38		28	31	40	39	−10
Greece			57					47	−10
Belgium				48	36	37		40	−8
Australia	63			48	49		56		−7
Britain	49	56	38	43	46	44		45	−4
Switzerland		55	50			52	52		−3
West Germany		38	41	33	36	38	50	38	0
United States	68	74	73	69	70	70	73	76	8
Japan					18	33	30	33	32	14
Italy				46	46	53		61	15
ALL-8 1947–2001	68							46	−22

NOTES: The proportion of the public who express belief in life after death (% "Yes") in 19 societies. "Change" is the change in the proportion from the first to the last observation in the series. The average means for the 8 nations with observations in both 1947 and 2001.

Sources: Data sources: 1947–1975 *Gallup Opinion Index* "Do you believe in life after death?" Yes/No/Don't Know. 1981–2001 *World Values Survey/European Values Survey* "Do you believe in life after death?" Yes/No/Don't Know. Source for Gallup polls: Lee Sigelman. 1977. "Review of the Polls: Multination Surveys of Religious Beliefs." *Journal for the Scientific Study of Religion* 16(3): 289–294.

of American adults reported attending church the previous week, exactly the same figure given by Gallup more than sixty years later (in March 2003).[14]

Yet serious difficulties are encountered in obtaining reliable estimates of churchgoing from survey data. Woodberry and others compared aggregate data on levels of church attendance in America derived from counting participants at services against the available estimates of self-reported church attendance derived from social surveys. They concluded that the self-reported figures are subject to systematic and consistent exaggeration, due to a social desirability bias concerning churchgoing in American culture.[15]

Studies suggest that the Gallup organization's procedures may systematically exaggerate attendance due to a lack of social desirability filters in the measurement of churchgoing (thereby unintentionally "cueing" respondents) and also unrepresentative sample completion rates based on a limited number of random digit dialing callbacks and respondent substitution.[16] Other data suggests that these estimates may be inflated; for example the American National Election Survey (NES), conducted every two years since the late 1950s, suggests that weekly church attendance never rises much above 25% in the United States. Moreover, when the NES modified the question sequence to assure the social desirability of not attending, the proportion reporting that they never attended church jumped from 12% to 33% and has stayed at that level in subsequent surveys.[17] The U.S. General Social Survey (GSS), conducted annually by NORC during the last three decades, also indicates that weekly church attendance in America hovers around the 25–30% region, with a significant fall in church attendance occurring during the last decade. According to the GSS, the proportion of Americans reporting that they attended church at least weekly fell to one-quarter in the most recent estimate, while at the same time the proportion saying that they never attended church doubled to one-fifth of all Americans (see Figure 4.4).[18]

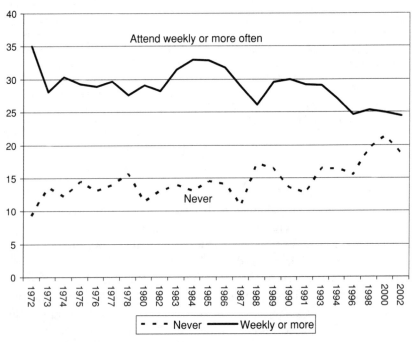

Figure 4.4. Religious Participation in the United States, 1972–2002. Note: Q: *"How often do you attend religious services?" Never/ At least once a week or more often.* Source: U.S. General Social Survey 1972–2002 N.43,204.

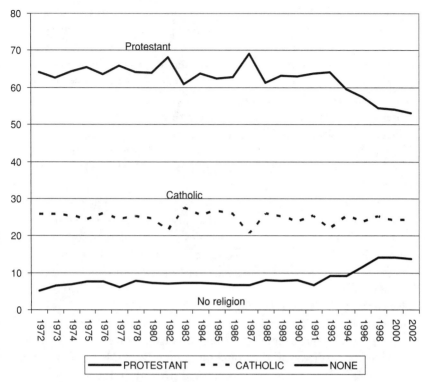

Figure 4.5. Religious Identities in the United States, 1972–2002. Note: Q: *"What is your religious preference? Is it Protestant, Catholic, Jewish, some other religion, or no religion?" The graph excludes religious identities adhered to by less than 3% of Americans.* Source: U.S. General Social Survey 1972–2002 N. 43,532.

Other indicators also suggest that traditional religious participation may have eroded in the United States, parallel to the long-term trends experienced throughout Europe. For example, Gallup polls registered a modest decline in the proportion of Americans who are *members* of a church or synagogue, down from about three-quarters (73%) of the population in 1937 to about two-thirds (65%) in 2001. The GSS has monitored religious identities in annual studies during the last three decades. They found that the proportion of Americans who are secularists, reporting that they have *no* religious preference or identity, climbed steadily during the 1990s (see Figure 4.5). During this decade, the main erosion occurred among American Protestants, while the proportion of Catholics in the population remained fairly steady, in part fueled by a substantial influx of Hispanic immigrants with large families. At the same time, changes have occurred among denominations within the religious population in the United States; for example many studies report that congregations for newer evangelical churches have expanded their membership at the expense of "mainline" Protestant denominations such as the United Methodist Church, Presbyterians, and Episcopalians, in part due to changes in the American population and also patterns of immigration from Latin America and Asia.[19] Moreover, even where we have reliable estimates of churchgoing, Brian Wilson emphasizes that little relationship may exist between these practices and spirituality, for example if churchgoing in America fulfills a need for social networking within local communities, and if U.S. churches have become more secular in orientation.[20]

Despite the overall popularity of religion in the United States, it would also be a gross exaggeration to claim that all Americans feel the same way, as important social and regional disparities exist. Secularists, for example, are far more likely to live in urban cities on the Pacific Coast or in the Northeast, as well as to have a college degree, and to be single and male. By contrast, committed evangelicals are far more likely to live in small towns or rural areas, especially in the South and Midwest, as well as being female and married. These regional divisions proved important for politics: in the 2000 U.S. presidential election, for example, religion was by far the strongest predictor of who voted for George W. Bush and who voted for Al Gore.[21] The election result reflected strongly entrenched divisions in public opinion and values between social conservatives and liberals on issues such as approval of the use of the death penalty, reproductive rights, and homosexuality. The regional patterns of religiosity are important and may even have led to two distinctive cultures within the United States; for example Himmelfarb argues that one culture in America is religious, puritanical, family-centered, patriotic, and conformist. The other is secular, tolerant, hedonistic, and multicultural. These cultures, she argues, coexist and tolerate each other, in part because they inhabit different worlds.[22]

We can conclude that the United States remains one of the most religious in the club of rich countries, alongside Ireland and Italy, and indeed as observed earlier this makes America one of the most religious countries in the world. The pervasive importance of these values is apparent in many American practices, especially in public life (even prior to the Bush administration and 9/11), despite the strict division of church and state. In the same way, American cultural values are more individualistic, more patriotic, more moralistic, and more culturally conservative than those in Europe. Nevertheless, there are some indicators that secular tendencies may have strengthened in America, at least during the last decade, which may bring the United States slightly closer to public opinion in Western Europe.

Explaining Variations in Religiosity: The Religious Market Model

Given the existence of important and consistent cross-national variations in religiosity, what best explains these patterns? Religious market theory provides the most critical and sustained challenge to the traditional secularization thesis. This account suggests that supply-side factors, notably denominational competition and state regulation of religious institutions, shape levels of religious participation in the United States and Europe. As discussed earlier in the introduction, during the last decade many American commentators have enthusiastically advanced this account, and the principal proponents include Roger Finke, Rodney Stark, Lawrence R. Iannaccone, William Sims Bainbridge, and R. Stephen Warner, although it has also encountered sustained criticism.[23] Market-based theories in the sociology of religion assume that the demand for religious products is relatively constant, based on the otherworldly rewards of life after death promised by most (although not all) faiths.[24] Dissimilar levels of spiritual behavior evident in various countries are believed to result less from "bottom up" demand than from variance in "top down" religious supply. Religious groups compete for congregations with different degrees of vigor. Established churches are thought to be complacent monopolies taking their congregations for granted, with a fixed market share due to state regulation and subsidy for one particular faith that enjoys special status and privileges. By contrast, where a free religious marketplace exists, energetic competition between churches expands the supply of religious "products," thereby mobilizing religious activism among the public.

The theory claims to be a universal generalization applicable to all faiths, although the evidence to support this argument is drawn mainly from the United States and Western Europe. The proliferation of diverse churches in the United States, such as Methodists, Lutherans, Presbyterians, and Episcopalian mainline churches, as well as Southern Baptist Convention, the Assemblies of God, the Pentecostal and Holiness churches among conservative denominations, is believed to have maximized choice and competition among faiths, thereby mobilizing the American public. American churches are subject to market forces, depending upon their ability to attract clergy and volunteers, as well as the financial resources that flow from their membership. Competition is thought to generate certain benefits, producing diversity, stimulating innovation, and compelling churches to actively recruit congregations by responding to public demands. For example, the National Congregations Study found that American churches commonly seek to attract new adherents by offering multiple social activities (or "products") beyond services of worship, including religious education, cultural and arts groups, engagement in community politics, and welfare services such as soup kitchens and baby-sitting cooperatives.[25] By contrast, Starke and Finke emphasize that most European nations sustain what they term "a *socialized* religious economy," with state subsidies for established churches. Religious monopolies are believed to be less innovative, responsive, and efficient. Where clergy enjoy secure incomes and tenure regardless of their performance, such as in Germany and Sweden, then it is thought that priests will grow complacent, slothful, and lax: "when people have little need or motive to work, they tend not to work, and . . . Subsidized churches will therefore be lazy."[26] Finke and Stark believe that if the "supply" of churches was expanded in Europe through disestablishment (deregulated), and if churches just made more effort, this would probably lead to a resurgence of religious behavior among the public ("Faced with American-style churches, Europeans would respond as Americans do").[27] In short, they conclude, "To the extent that organizations work harder, they are more successful. What could be more obvious?"[28]

What indeed? Yet, after considerable debate during the last decade, the evidence that religious competition provides a plausible explanation of religious participation remains controversial.[29] Criticisms have been both theoretical and empirical. Conceptually Bryant has questioned the appropriateness of the cost-benefit model, and the use of metaphors such as "markets," "products," "commodities," and "capital," in the analysis of religion.[30] In terms of the evidence, commentators have noted serious flaws with the measures commonly used to gauge the degree of religious competition. Most studies have employed the Herfindahl Index. This is derived from economics where the Herfindahl Index is a measure of the size of firms in relationship to the industry and an indicator of the amount of competition among them. It is defined as the sum of the squares of the market shares of each individual firm. As such, it can range from 0 to 1, moving from numerous very small firms to a single monopolistic producer. In economics, decreases in the Herfindahl Index generally indicate a loss of the ability of firms to control prices and an increase in competition, whereas increases imply the opposite. To gauge religious fractionalization or pluralism, the Herfindahl Index is computed along similar lines as one minus the sum of the squares of the percentage share of the churchgoing population held by each denomination within a particular universe (whether the unit of analysis is a local community, city, region, or country).[31] The religious pluralism index represents the probability that two randomly selected individuals from a population belong to different denominations.[32] It is analogous to the Pedersen Index of party competition.[33] Stark and Finke emphasize two points about the characteristics of this index: (i) "ceiling" effects are commonly evident, and (ii) the impact of pluralism on participation is essentially curvilinear, so that the first shift from single church religious monopolies to greater competition with two or more churches has a substantial impact upon church attendance, whereas the effects become saturated at later levels of pluralism. Multiple studies using different datasets and specifications have compared the correlation between the religious pluralism index and religious participation within specific geographic areas (usually communities in the United States), and a positive regression coefficient has been interpreted as providing support for the religious market theory.

Yet although commonly used in the literature, there are many difficulties concerning the operationalization of the concept of religious competition, and these problems are exacerbated in cross-national research. Chaves and Gorski conducted a thorough meta-review of the literature by examining the results of 193 tests of the evidence, drawn from different geographical and historical settings, from a series of 26 articles published on this subject. They concluded that the theory lacked consistent support, as some studies found a significant correlation between religious pluralism and religious participation while others failed to confirm any linkage.[34] The most critical study by Voas, Olson, and Crockett concluded that any observed relationships are spurious and a purely mathematical association between the pluralism index and religious participation rates can explain any positive or negative correlations. The study concludes that there is no compelling evidence from *any* of the existing studies that religious pluralism, measured by the Herfindahl Index, influences church participation rates.[35]

The appropriate geographic unit of analysis is also problematic. The original supply-side theory conceived of religious competition as rivalry between different churches within a particular local community, typified by the role of Baptists, Episcopalians, and Catholic churches in the United States. Once we extend the comparison more broadly cross-nationally, however, it becomes unclear how competition should be gauged, for example whether the key comparison should be competition among different denominations and sects, or whether we should focus on rivalry between and among multiple churches, temples, mosques, synagogues, and shrines representing all the major world religions.

What evidence supports the argument that greater religious competition leads to more churchgoing in the United States than in Western Europe? Finke and Starke provide numerous examples of specific limitations experienced by particular denominations and faiths in Western European countries. This includes quoting incidents of limited religious freedoms, such as harassment experienced by Jehovah's Witnesses in Portugal, Germany, and France, and legal regulations such as tax-free status that provide positive fiscal benefits for established churches.[36] Yet this approach is unsystematic, and a systematic bias may arise from the particular selection of cases. It is true that the United States displays a diverse range of churches and temples in many communities, and relatively high rates of churchgoing and subjective religiosity, fitting the theory. But clear anomalies to this relationship also exist, notably high levels of churchgoing evident in Ireland, Italy, Poland, Colombia, and Venezuela, despite the fact that the Catholic Church predominates as a virtual monopoly in these nations.[37]

More systematic cross-national evidence is provided in a study by Iannaccone comparing church attendance in eight West European nations (excluding six predominant Catholic cultures) plus four Anglo-American democracies. Regression analysis found a significant and very strong relationship between the degree of denominational pluralism in these countries (measured by the Herfindahl Index) and levels of religious participation (rates of weekly church attendance).[38] It remains unclear, however, why the six predominant Catholic cultures in Southern and Western Europe are excluded from this comparison, as they challenge the model. Smith, Sawkins, and Seaman compared eighteen societies based on the 1991 ISSP religion survey and reported that religious pluralism was significantly related to regular religious participation.[39] Yet the literature remains divided about this issue as other cross-national studies have reported results inconsistent with the supply-side thesis. For example, Verweij, Ester, and Nauta conducted a cross-national comparison using the 1990 European Values Survey in sixteen countries. They found that irrespective of the model specification, religious pluralism in any particular country, measured by the Herfindahl Index, was an insignificant predictor of levels of religious participation, whether measured against rates of church attendance or church membership. By contrast, the degree of state regulation was important, along with the predominant religious culture and the overall level of societal modernization.[40] Research by Bruce, comparing religiosity in the Nordic and Baltic states, also concluded that trends in religious observance contradicted a number of core supply-side propositions.[41] The empirical evidence supporting the supply-side thesis has come under serious attack, as the conclusions of most of the studies by Stark and Finke were contaminated by a coding error; there was a negative 1 in the formula rather than a positive 1. The use of the Herfindahl Index in this particular situation generated a methodological artifact that leads to all of the supply-side conclusions in the United States data.[42] Nevertheless, despite these critical flaws in the empirical evidence, the supply-side theory provides an alternative perspective that is open to testing with indicators that avoid these problems.

Leaving aside the strong normative thrust of the supply-side argument and concepts, derived from free market economics, what specific propositions flow from this account that are open to systematic cross-national testing with empirical evidence? We can compare four separate indicators to test the religious markets model, with the results summarized in Table 4.3. Again any one indicator may be flawed, due to the limitations of data or measurement error, but if all results from the independent measures

Table 4.3. Human Security, Religious Markets, and Religiosity in Postindustrial Societies

Indicators	Religious Participation		How Often Pray?		Number of Nations
	R	Sig.	R	Sig.	
RELIGIOUS MARKETS					
Religious pluralism	.018	N/s	.119	N/s	21
Religious Freedom Index	.367	N/s	.477	N/s	21
State regulation of religion	.427	N/s	.423	N/s	18
Freedom House religious freedom scale	−.314	N/s	−.550	N/s	13
HUMAN SECURITY					
Human Development Index	−.249	N/s	.077	N/s	21
Economic inequality (GINI coefficient)	**.496**	*	**.614**	*	18

NOTE: Pearson's simple correlations (R) without prior controls and their significance (Sig.): *P = 0.05 level; **P = 0.01 level (2-tailed). *Religious pluralism*: the Herfindahl Index (see text for the construction and data) (Alesina 2002). *The state regulation of religion*: Scale measured by Mark Chaves and David E. Cann (1992). *Religious Freedom Index*: See Appendix C for details of the construction of this scale. *Freedom House religious freedom scale, 2001*; available online at: www.freedomhouse.org. *Human Development Index, 2001*: United National Development Program, 2003, *World Development Report*, New York: UNDP/Oxford University Press; available online at: www.undp.org. *Economic inequality GINI coefficient*: WDI: World Bank, *World Development Indicators, 2002*, Washington, DC; available online at: www.worldbank.org.

point in a generally consistent direction, then this lends greater confidence
to the results.

Religious Pluralism

If the supply-side theory is correct, then religious pluralism and state regulation of religion should both be important in predicting rates of churchgoing in postindustrial societies: in particular, countries with great competition among multiple pluralist religious churches, denominations, and
faiths should have the highest religious participation.[43] Religious pluralism is gauged here by the Herfindahl Index using the data on the major
religious populations derived from the *Encyclopaedia Britannica Book of the
Year 2001*, discussed earlier, compiled by Alesina and colleagues.[44] The religious pluralism index is calculated as the standard Herfindahl indicator for
each country, monitoring fractionalization in each society, ranging from
zero to one. This is the standard measure used by supply-side theorists,
and so appropriate for testing their claims. One important qualification,
however, concerns the unit of comparison, since this study measures religious pluralism among the major world faiths at the societal level, which is
necessary for cross-national research. Nevertheless this means that we cannot gauge competition among religious organizations representing diverse
denominations and sects at local or regional levels, and in the U.S. context,
competition is understood to reflect the propensity of rival churches within
a community – whether Baptist, Episcopalian, Lutheran, or Methodist – to
attract congregations.

   Contrary to the predictions of supply-side theory, the correlations between religious pluralism and religious behavior all prove insignificant in
postindustrial societies, with the distribution illustrated in Figure 4.6. The
results *lend no support to the claim of a significant link between religious pluralism
and participation*, and this is true irrespective of whether the comparison focuses on frequency of attendance at services of worship or the frequency of
prayer.[45] Among postindustrial societies, the United States is the exception
in its combination of high rates of religious pluralism *and* participation: the
theory does indeed fit the American case, but the problem is that it fails to
work elsewhere. The scatter gram shows that other English-speaking nations share similar levels of religious pluralism, however in these countries
far fewer people regularly attend church. Moreover, in Catholic postindustrial societies the relationship is actually *reversed*, with the highest participation evident in Ireland and Italy, where the Church enjoys a virtual religious
monopoly, compared with more pluralist Netherlands and France, where

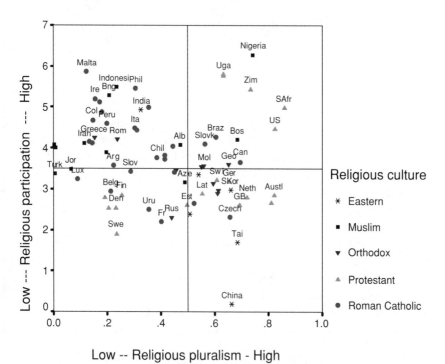

Figure 4.6. Religiosity and Pluralism. Notes: *Religious Pluralism Index* (Alesina 2002). Religious participation: Q185: *"Apart from weddings, funerals, and christenings, about how often do you attend religious services these days? More than once a week, once a week, once a month, only on special holy days, once a year, less often, never or practically never."* Mean frequency of attendance at religious services. Source: World Values Survey, pooled 1981–2001.

churchgoing habits are far weaker. Nor is this merely due to the comparison of postindustrial societies: the global comparison in all nations confirms that there is no significant relationship between participation and pluralism across the broader distribution of societies worldwide.

Of course the account could always be retrieved by arguing that what matters is less competition among the major faiths, since people rarely convert directly, but rather competition among or within specific denominations, since people are more likely to switch particular churches within closely related families. This proposition would require testing at the community level with other forms of data, at a finer level of denominational detail than is available in most social surveys, and indeed even in most census data. Nevertheless, if the claims of the original theory were modified, this would greatly limit its applicability for cross-national research.

Despite the extensive literature advocating the supply-side theory, based on the measure of pluralism of faiths and religious participation used in this study, no empirical support is found here for this account.

State Regulation and Freedom of Religion

An alternative version of religious market theory predicts that participation will also be maximized where there is a strong constitutional division between church and state, protecting religious freedom of worship and toleration of different denominations, without hindrance to particular sects and faiths. This is one of the explanations for American exceptionalism advanced by Lipset, who argues that the long-standing separation of church and state in the United States has given the churches greater autonomy and allowed varied opportunities for people to participate in religion.[46] Three indicators are available to analyze this relationship:

(i) *The state regulation of religion* was measured by Mark Chaves and David E. Cann in eighteen postindustrial nations. The 6-point scale was classified using data provided by the *World Christian Encyclopedia* (1982) based on whether or not each country had the following characteristics:

- There is a single, officially designated state church;
- There is official state recognition of some denominations but not others;
- The state appoints or approves the appointment of church leaders;
- The state directly pays church personnel salaries;
- There is a system of ecclesiastical tax collection;
- The state directly subsidizes, beyond mere tax breaks, the operation, maintenance, or capital expenses for churches.[47]

(ii) These results can be cross-checked against the *Freedom of Religion Index*, discussed in Chapter 2. This index was constructed by coding the twenty items contained in Appendix C including indicators such as the role of the state in subsidizing churches, state ownership of church property, registration requirements for religious organizations, constitutional recognition of freedom of religion, and restrictions of certain denominations, cults, or sects. The 20-item scale was standardized to 100 points, for ease of interpretation, and then coded so that a higher score represented greater religious freedom.

(iii) Lastly, we can also compare the results of the summary analysis of religious freedom generated every year by Freedom House.[48] The survey criteria used by this organization develop a 7-point scale based on the International Covenant on Civil and Political Rights, the United Nations

Declaration on the Elimination of All Forms of Intolerance and of Discrimination Based on Religion or Belief, the European Convention on Human Rights. The annual survey defines religious freedom in terms of three major components. First, it refers to the freedoms of particular bodies, houses of worship, humanitarian organizations, educational institutions, and so forth. Second, it refers to freedom for particular individual religious practices, such as prayer, worship, dress, proclamation, and diet. Lastly, it refers to human rights in general, insofar as they involve particular religious bodies, individuals, and activities.

Yet, contrary to the supply-side theory, the results of the simple correlations in Table 4.3 suggest that no significant relationship exists between any of these indicators of religious freedom and levels of religious behavior. Moreover, this pattern was found both within the comparison of post-industrial nations and also in the global comparison of all countries where data was available. We will return to consider this issue in greater detail in the next chapter, when comparing religiosity in Central and Eastern Europe, because the historical legacy of the role of the Communist state in promoting state atheism and repressing the church provides a stronger test case than Western democracies. There are many reasons why one might imagine that the spread of greater tolerance and freedom of worship, facilitating competition among religious institutions, might prove conducive to greater religious activity among the public. But so far the range of evidence using multiple indicators fails to support the supply-side claims.

Functional Theories and the Social Role of Religious Institutions

As discussed earlier, the alternative classic functionalist account derives originally from Émile Durkheim's seminal sociology of religion. For functionalists, the public gradually deserted churches as societies industrialized due to the process of functional differentiation and specialization, where the church's comprehensive role for education, health, and welfare was gradually displaced by other institutions offering an extensive series of public services. During the medieval era, for example, the seminaries trained priests, hospices and apothecaries cared for the sick, and alms-houses provided refuge for the poor. Through disestablishment and the growth of state-funded schools, churches lost their educational monopoly and thereby their ability to mold, inculcate, and socialize young minds into religious habits and beliefs. Churches continue to run schools and orphanages, but their staff became trained, certified, and accountable to professional bodies and state regulators located outside the church's control. Universities became the home of scientific knowledge, technical skills, and professional training. In healthcare, medieval beliefs in magical cures, homeopathic remedies, and spiritual healers were gradually displaced by reliance upon modern hospitals, surgical intervention, drug-based medicine subject to testing by random experiments and certified by professional regulators, and trained medical staff. Even the important residual functions of the church to provide social and communication networks within local communities, to reinforce social sanctions, and to maintain the institutions of marriage and the family, were eroded by the proliferation of channels of mass communication, as well as by changes in the mores governing traditional relationships in the family, marriage, and childcare. The growing separation of church and state across Europe meant that the legitimacy and power of spiritual authorities in the medieval era was challenged by the rise of legal-bureaucratic states in industrialized societies, and eventually by democratically elected governments.[49] As a result of institutional differentiation, where alternative organizations have developed an extensive range of functions for schooling, healthcare, and care of dependents, then although a residual spiritual or moral role for the church may persist, the social role of religious institutions is believed to have diminished in people's lives.

If this argument were correct, then religious participation should have weakened most in postindustrial societies where the social welfare role of religious institutions has been displaced most fully by public services for health, education, and social security provided by the state sector, and indeed there is some evidence supporting this argument.[50] To examine evidence here we can compare public perceptions of the different functions and competencies of religious authorities. The Values Surveys asked people to agree or disagree with the following statements: "*Generally speaking, do you think that the religious authorities in your country are giving adequate answers to . . .*

- *The moral problems and needs of the individual.*
- *The problems of family life.*
- *People's spiritual needs.*
- *The social problems facing our country today.*"

This is an imperfect measure of the perceived role of the church, since responses may relate more strongly to the performance and competency of the clergy, rather than reflecting attitudes toward the legitimate role of religious institutions per se. Competency and legitimacy can remain distinct; for example there are well-established patterns in how far the American

Table 4.4. The Perceived Functions of Religious Authorities

Type of Society	Moral Role (% Agree)	Spiritual Role (% Agree)	Family Role (% Agree)	Social Role (% Agree)	Total Function Scale
Postindustrial	39	34	39	58	1.6
Industrial	59	53	59	76	2.4
Agrarian	75	72	75	80	3.0
All nations	57	51	57	72	2.3

NOTE: *"Generally speaking, do you think that the religious authorities in your country are giving adequate answers to . . .*

- *The moral problems and needs of the individual.*
- *The problems of family life.*
- *People's spiritual needs.*
- *The social problems facing our country today."*

(Yes/No) Percentage who agree.
Source: WVS data, pooled 1981–2001.

public dislikes Congress as an institution, and yet how far they often approve of the particular elected representative from their own district. Nevertheless if, as functionalists suggest, the institutional role of the church has been displaced in advanced industrialized societies by the process of institutional differentiation and the rise of the welfare state, then we would expect that perceptions of the *social* role of religious authorities would have been eroded most by this process, while leaving their spiritual and moral role intact. We can analyze the evidence by comparing how far agrarian, industrial, and postindustrial societies differed in perceptions of the moral, spiritual, family, and social roles of religious authorities.

Table 4.4 confirms that the perceived role of religious authorities was indeed strongest, as expected, in agrarian societies, where about three-quarters or more of the public felt that religious authorities played an important moral, spiritual, family, and social role. In postindustrial societies, by contrast, between one-third and one-half of the public agreed with the important moral, spiritual, and family roles of the church. Yet at the same time stronger support was expressed in postindustrial societies for the role of religious authorities in dealing with "*the social problems facing our country today*" (supported by 58%) rather than in their capacity to deal with "*people's spiritual needs*" (supported by only 34%). This is the reverse of what would have been expected if the church's role in philanthropy, education, and healthcare had been eroded most sharply by societal modernization, as the functionalist argument claims. More direct measures would be needed, evaluating the perceived legitimacy of the role of religious authorities compared with many other types of leaders, to explore this issue in greater depth. But the available data used here does not appear to give any direct support to the functionalist argument.

The Role of Security and Economic Inequality

The explanations that we have considered, including both supply-side religious markets and the traditional functional arguments, have therefore provided only limited insights into the diversity of religious participation found in rich nations. To summarize, in postindustrial nations no empirical support that we examined could explain why some rich nations are far more religious than others, and the study failed to establish a significant link between patterns of religious behavior and the indicators of religious pluralism, religious freedom, and the perceived functions of the church. But, of course, this still leaves us with the question that we considered at the start of the chapter: why are some societies such as the United States and Ireland persistently more religious in their habits and beliefs than comparable Western nations sharing a Christian cultural heritage?

Our answer rests on the same arguments that we have already developed at length to explain cross-national variations worldwide, namely patterns of human security and, in particular, conditions of socioeconomic inequality. What matters for societal vulnerability, insecurity, and risk, that we believe drives religiosity, are not simply levels of national economic resources, but their distribution as well. The growth of the welfare state in industrialized nations ensures large sectors of the public against the worst risks of ill health and old age, penury and destitution, while private insurance schemes, the work of nonprofit charitable foundations, and access to financial resources have transformed security in postindustrial nations, and also reduced the vital role of religion in people's lives. Even relatively affluent nations have multiple pockets of long-term poverty, whether afflicting unemployed African Americans living in the inner cities of Los Angeles and Detroit, farm laborers in Sicily, or Bangladesh, Pakistani, and Indian émigrés in Leicester and Birmingham. Populations typically most at risk in industrialized nations, capable of falling through the welfare safety net, include the elderly and children, single-parent female-headed households, the long-term disabled, homeless, and unemployed, and ethnic minorities. If we are correct that feelings of vulnerability are driving religiosity, even in rich nations, then this should be evident by comparing levels of economic inequality across societies, as well as by looking at how far religiosity is strongest among the poorer sectors of society.

We can analyze the distribution of economic resources in postindustrial societies by comparing the GINI coefficient, estimated in the latest available year by the World Bank, which measures the extent to which the distribution of income among households within a society deviates from a perfectly equal distribution. The GINI coefficient ranges from perfect equality (0) to perfect inequality (100). Table 4.3 indicates that the Human Development Index fails to predict variations in levels of religious behavior within postindustrial nations, not surprisingly since all these countries are highly developed. Yet the level of economic inequality measured by the GINI coefficient proves strongly and significantly related to both forms of religious behavior, but especially to the propensity to engage in individual religiosity through prayer. Figure 4.7 illustrates this relationship; the United States is

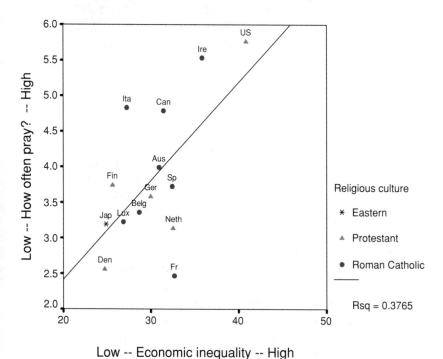

Low -- Economic inequality -- High

Figure 4.7. Religiosity and Economic Inequality. Notes: How often pray? Q199: *"How often do you pray to God outside of religious services? Would you say . . . Every day (7), more than once a week (6), once a week (5), at least once a month (4), several times a year (3), less often (2), never (1)."* Mean frequency per society. Economic inequality is gauged by the GINI coefficient, latest year, World Bank 2002. Source: World Values Survey, pooled 1981–2001.

exceptionally high in religiosity in large part, we believe, because it is also one of the most unequal postindustrial societies under comparison. Relatively high levels of economic insecurity are experienced by many sectors of U.S. society, despite American affluence, due to the cultural emphasis on the values of personal responsibility, individual achievement, and mistrust of big government, limiting the role of public services and the welfare state for basic matters such as healthcare covering all the working population. Many American families, even in the professional middle classes, face risks of unemployment, the dangers of sudden ill heath without adequate private medical insurance, vulnerability to becoming a victim of crime, and the problems of paying for long-term care of the elderly. Americans face greater anxieties than citizens in other advanced industrialized countries about whether they will be covered by medical insurance, whether they will be fired arbitrarily, or whether they will be forced to choose between losing their job and devoting themselves to their newborn child.[51] The entrepreneurial culture and the emphasis on personal responsibility has delivered overall prosperity but one trade-off is that the United States has greater income inequality than any other advanced industrial democracy.[52] By comparison, despite recent restructuring, the secular Scandinavian and West European states remain some of the most egalitarian societies, with an expansive array of welfare services, including comprehensive healthcare, social services, and pensions.[53] As Gill and Lundgaarde (forthcoming) demonstrate, high levels of welfare expenditure show a strong negative relationship with church attendance – even controlling for urbanization, literacy, religious pluralism, and other indicators of modernization.

If this argument rested only on the cross-national comparisons then, of course, it would be too limited, as multiple other characteristics distinguish Western Europe and the United States. But evidence can also be examined at individual-level by looking at how far the distribution of income relates to religious behavior. The patterns in Figure 4.8 show that religiosity is systematically related at individual-level to the distribution of income groups in postindustrial societies: *the poor are almost twice as religious as the rich*. Similar patterns can be found in the United States (see Figure 4.9); for example two-thirds (66%) of the least well-off income group pray daily, compared with 47% of the highest income group.

No single indicator is ever sufficient by itself to confirm or refute the secularization thesis, since the specific choice of measures and concepts always remain open to question, studies use alternative time-periods and cross-national comparative frameworks, and often we lack the long-term evidence that would be more persuasive. Yet the range of evidence presented

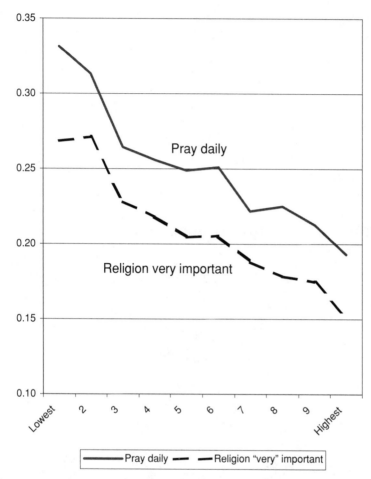

Figure 4.8. Religiosity by Income in Postindustrial Societies. Note: The percentage of the public who pray daily and who regard religion as very important by decile household income group (counting all wages, salaries, pensions and other incomes, before taxes and other deductions) in postindustrial societies. Source: World Values Study, pooled 1981–2001.

here in postindustrial societies serves to confirm the broader pattern established in earlier chapters. Secularization is not a deterministic process but it is still one that is largely predictable, based on knowing just a few facts about levels of human development and socioeconomic equality in each country. Despite all the numerous possible explanatory factors that could be brought into the picture, from institutional structures, state restrictions on freedom of worship, the historical role of church-state relations, and

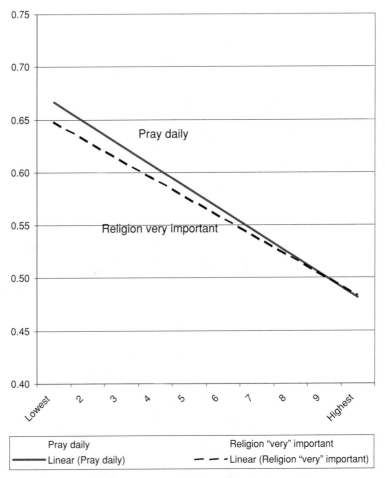

Figure 4.9. Religiosity by Income in the United States. Note: Linear trends in the percentage of the American public who pray daily and who regard religion as very important by decile household income group (counting all wages, salaries, pensions and other incomes, before taxes and other deductions). Source: World Values Study, pooled 1981–2001.

patterns of denominational and church competition, the levels of societal and individual security in any society seem to provide the most persuasive and parsimonious explanation. But does this explanation continue to hold elsewhere, even in the Muslim world? We go on to test this thesis.

a long time-series, we think that the best alternative way to probe into long-term trends is to examine surveys carried out during the 1990s using generational comparisons, based on the assumption that the attitudes toward religion that were instilled during a given generation's formative years will leave lasting traces in subsequent years. If we find substantial intergenerational differences within given countries, they suggest (although they do not prove) the direction in which prevailing trends are moving. Where important cross-national differences are evident, such as contrasts between a relatively religious Romania and a relatively secular Estonia, then we need to explore their causes at the societal level, examining the role of such factors as state regulation of religious institutions, and the impact of human development indicators.

The Secularization versus Supply-Side Debate

Theories of demand-side secularization and of supply-side religious markets have both been used to explain developments in the region, but previous studies have been unable to resolve which is most clearly supported. On one hand, the traditional secularization thesis implies that religiosity has gradually decayed in Central and Eastern Europe over successive decades, for the same reasons that operate in other industrialized societies. In particular, the salience of religious values and habitual churchgoing would be expected to erode as a society experiences the long-term transition from poorer agrarian to more affluent industrial states. Social policies in the Soviet Union emphasized the expansion of the welfare state, employment security, and widespread access to public services in healthcare, housing, unemployment benefits, childcare, and pensions. The state invested heavily in broadening access to schools and universities, so that by the early 1980s levels of participation in higher education in Soviet bloc nations were only slightly behind those in the West.[2] Official repression of religion would be expected to have reinforced these factors, although its impact varied widely from one country to another: in Poland, for example, Soviet-led attempts at repression of religion were counter-productive, leading the Polish people to emphasize their attachment to religion as a way to preserve their Polish identity. After the collapse of communism, the tendency toward secularization linked with development should have accelerated in countries that experienced a successful transition to democracy, such as Poland, Hungary, and the Czech Republic, and more secure external relationships where states are becoming integrated into the European Union and NATO. In those post-Communist societies where people's lives gradually became more secure during the late twentieth century, a simple version of the modernization thesis would lead us to expect a linear relationship between age and religious values (such as the importance attached to religion), as well as between age and religious participation (such as attendance at religious services and daily prayer): in both cases, we would expect to find that the young were less religious than the old. Conversely, religion would be expected to remain strong among both young and old in post-Communist agrarian societies that remain poor and underdeveloped (such as Albania, Moldova, and Azerbaijan), for the same reasons that apply to other low-income societies around the world. Countries such as Turkmenistan, Kazakhstan, and Uzbekistan in Central Asia lost ground markedly during the 1990s, with economies characterized by large numbers of peasant farmers, faltering heavy manufacturing industry, structural underemployment, negative growth, poor basic healthcare, shrinking average life spans, social inequality, and widespread poverty (with per capita Gross National Incomes in 2000 below $5,000).

Support for the traditional secularization thesis can be found in the literature. For example, Need and Evans compared patterns of religiosity in 1993–1994 in ten post-Communist societies that they classified as predominately Catholic (the Czech Republic, Hungary, Poland, Lithuania, Slovakia) and Orthodox (Belarus, Bulgaria, Romania, Russia, and Ukraine). Tested with both linear and logged age regression models, the study reports that rates of church participation usually showed a pattern of linear decline as one moved from older to younger generations, precisely as secularization theory implies.[3] Qualitative case studies also support these findings; Borowik argues that the break-up of the Soviet Union brought a radical shift in Central and Eastern Europe when the legal position of the churches changed dramatically, with the new regimes recognizing freedom of religion as a basic human right.[4] In Russia, Belarus, and Ukraine, the number of those who declared their belief in God and their adherence to the Orthodox tradition rose in the short-term, immediately after the fall of communism, but the study found that commitment to the Church, and the level of religious practice, are as low today as in the most secularized Western European societies. Borowik concludes that the contemporary picture of religiosity in these countries, where atheism was imposed for many years, remains quite similar to that in Western Europe, where secularization developed spontaneously. Kaariainen also concludes that a brief religious resurgence occurred in Russia at the beginning of the 1990s, but after that the situation stabilized. By the late 1990s, he found, only one-third of the Russian population considered themselves believers, the majority remaining indifferent toward religion. Furthermore, because of their atheist heritage, most people have only a cursory knowledge of common Orthodox beliefs and many also believe in astrology, magic, reincarnation, and so on. The Russian Orthodox Church is respected but only a minority of the people describe themselves as Orthodox. Despite the growing number of churches and parishes across the country, Kaariainen found that Russians go to church less often than other Europeans.[5] Some have also emphasized that new forms of "individualized" spirituality outside the church are emerging in Central and Eastern Europe.[6]

If the process of secularization is related to human development and existential security, as the evidence presented earlier in this book suggests, then we might expect the long-term erosion of religiosity across a broad range of post-Communist societies to be more complex than simpler versions of modernization theory suggest. Where living standards have gradually risen in the region, this should tend to erode religiosity gradually over succeeding birth cohorts, as traditional secularization theory suggests. On the other hand, the collapse of living standards and the disappearance of the welfare state that occurred during the past decade would lead us to expect a short-term *revival* of religiosity in low- to moderate-income societies, especially for the more vulnerable segments of the population such as the elderly living on dwindling state pensions while facing hyperinflation in food and fuel costs. Widespread feelings of existential insecurity were also engendered by the sudden introduction of neo-liberal free markets, which produced severe recessions, throwing millions of public sector employees out of work; and where household savings are threatened by hyperinflation (as in Azerbaijan and Belarus); where political stability and government leadership is undermined by scandals over corruption or a banking crisis; and where ethnic conflict sharply worsens or where domestic security is threatened by secessionist movements, as in the Chechnya conflict.[7] In the most dramatic case, the disintegration of the former Yugoslavian republic led to the outbreak of bloody civil war in Bosnia-Herzegovina, heightening ethno-religious identities and the salience of religiosity among the Catholic, Orthodox, and Muslim communities co-existing in the Balkans. The theory of secularization based on existential security therefore predicts that the process of societal modernization in post-Communist Europe would tend to generate a long-term linear decline of religiosity over successive birth cohorts, but that this gradual transformation would tend to be offset by short-term factors linked with the collapse of communism. Thus (1) it will only occur in those Central and East European countries that have experienced a long-term process of human development and economic equality, (2) it will be clearest among the most secure and affluent social sectors, and also (3) specific countries in the region are likely experience a *short-term* revival of religiosity if conditions since the fall of communism generate widespread feelings of sharply diminished existential security.

In contrast to this interpretation, a very different set of expectations is generated by theories of supply-side religious markets. The evidence considered earlier threw serious doubt on the capacity of this theory to explain variations within Western Europe, but it might be that this account provides a more convincing case under the conditions operating in post-Communist states. Supply-side theory emphasizes that patterns of religiosity in post-Communist states are determined by the role of religious organizations competing actively for "hearts and minds," and in particular the degree of state regulation of the church. During the Soviet era, religious organizations were strongly constrained or persecuted throughout most of Central and Eastern Europe, with the "Godless" Communist party actively promoting atheist beliefs and practice.[8] Religion was not destroyed, but it was strongly discouraged in most of these societies.[9] The dissolution of the Soviet Union and the collapse of communism brought a radical change in the relationship between church and state, with freedom of religion becoming officially recognized as a basic human right and a multitude of denominations becoming free to compete for followers. If the policy of atheism under the Soviet state discouraged religiosity, then we might expect a curvilinear pattern of age differences in religiosity. We might expect to find a U-shaped curve, with religiosity being relatively strong among the older generation that grew up in pre-Communist societies, and also the youngest cohort that came of age under more liberal conditions, while by contrast the middle-aged generation should prove the least religious. This can be tested by seeing whether age is most closely related to indicators of religiosity in either a linear (monotonic) or a logged (curvilinear) fashion.

Some studies have detected support for this thesis; for example, Greeley compared public opinion toward religion in nine former Communist countries, mostly located in the Baltics and Central Europe (Russia, Hungary, Slovenia, Slovakia, East Germany, Poland, Latvia, Bulgaria, and the Czech Republic), derived from analysis of the 1991 and 1998 International Social Survey Program.[10] Greeley found that common Christian beliefs, such as faith in God and in reincarnation, are quite widespread in this region. He argues that generational comparisons of these beliefs suggest a curvilinear U-shaped curve, with the oldest and the post-1960s generation being more likely to express faith than the middle-aged. Greeley concludes that a revival in religious convictions has occurred among the younger generation in the region, especially in Russia, although he acknowledges that this has not, as yet, been accompanied by a rise in church attendance. Other dimensions of religious behavior, including affiliation to the Orthodox Church and engagement in prayer, remain relatively low and show clear erosion over successive birth cohorts.[11] Another study by Froese also concludes that the supply-side theory fits the cases of Hungary, Poland, and East Germany, where a religious resurgence occurred after independence, driven, he believes, by a revival of church organizations.[12]

Additional Relevant Factors

The debate between secularization demand-siders and religious market supply-siders has been difficult to resolve, in part because of the limited time-series survey data that is available, but also because previous studies have focused on different periods and comparative frameworks. One classic danger in the case study approach, focusing on historical studies of the role of the church in given countries such as Poland or the United States, is that specific countries can be selected to fit almost any given theory. The ten-nation comparative study by Need and Evans was more wide-ranging, but it was based on surveys conducted during the early 1990s, just a few years after independence, when many societies remained in the midst of democratic and neo-liberal market economic transitions. Generational changes emerge too slowly to be captured so quickly. Any generational shifts in religious values and beliefs that did occur after independence would take many years to become apparent. Most comparative survey work has also analyzed religiosity among Catholic Central European countries, with less attention given to developments in Eastern Orthodox and in Muslim societies.

This limits the generalizations that can be drawn about post-Communist Europe, as dramatic contrasts are evident within this vast region, stretching longitudinally from the Baltic to the Bering Strait and latitudinally from the Arctic to the Caucuses. Societies in Central and Eastern Europe differ significantly in numerous factors that could plausibly act as intervening variables conditioning the relationship between age and religion. These factors include a society's experiences during the transition and consolidation of democracy, as well as in its historical religious culture, the duration of Soviet rule, the relationship between church and state under Communism, the success of its economic adjustment to the free market during the last decade, its integration into international organizations such as NATO and the European Union, as well as in its degree of ethno-religious homogeneity and fractionalization. Any systematic study therefore will need to utilize multivariate analysis controlling for the intervening factors that could affect the relationship between age and religiosity.

The most successful post-Communist societies, such as Poland, Hungary, Slovakia, Slovenia, and the Czech Republic, have developed stable representative democracies with multiparty competition, free elections, and thriving civic societies. With economies that adjusted relatively successfully to the free market, and positive rates of economic growth, by the end of 2000 these nations achieved per capita incomes ranging from $8,000 to $16,000. Just over a decade after achieving independence, these countries entered the European Union and NATO. The Baltic states, Latvia, Lithuania, and Estonia also engineered a fairly rapid transition from a Soviet-style command economy to the free market and integration with Western Europe. By contrast, economic growth and progress on human rights and political liberties proved sluggish, or even failed outright, in many other former Communist nations. Russian per capita GDP fell by 6% per year during the 1990s, while economic inequality (measured by the GINI coefficient) rose to the highest level in the region, and the average life expectancy declined sharply. Belarus under President Lukashenko experienced economic stagnation and decline, experiencing a 3% fall in per capita GDP from 1990–1999, together with hyperinflation of consumer prices, and rigged elections. The countries of the South Caucuses and Central Asia are characterized by failing economies, repressive regimes with no transition to even competitive elections, and endemic poverty and hardship. Azerbaijan has considerable reservoirs of oil and gas, but GDP fell by a massive 9.6% annually during the 1990s, and the ruling regime has often been criticized for extensive corruption and vote rigging. Kyrgyzstan has experienced flawed parliamentary and presidential elections, the harassment and imprisonment of opposition leaders, and the closure of dissident newspapers, as well as negative annual economic growth during the last decade. In this country, with average per capita income around $2,420, the economy has failed: factories remain closed, unemployment has soared, and malnutrition is rife. After the breakdown of Soviet control, Balkan societies within the former Yugoslavia descended into chaos and the bloody Bosnian war, fueled by deep-rooted ethnic conflict.

In short, post-Communist societies have shown very diverse rates of progress toward democratization and economic development, and the historical relationships between church and state also differed radically. Johnston suggests that public religiosity continues to be relatively high in nations where the church was actively involved in resistance against the Soviet regime and the struggle for independence.[13] In Poland and the Czech Republic, for example, the role of the Catholic Church in opposing the Communist state, and the Western orientation and organizational links of Roman Catholicism, meant that the Church maintained or even strengthened its role after independence. Strassberg argues that the Catholic Church has been involved in politics throughout the history of Poland, and after 1945 it functioned as the main opposition to the Communist party.[14] In this regard, Polish Catholicism became associated with nationalism, freedom, human rights, and democracy.[15] By contrast, in Hungary the state established a policy of a "church within socialism," where the credibility of the Catholic Church was eroded by collaboration with the Communist government. Religious freedoms expanded after Hungarian independence, but nevertheless people did not flock back to the Church.[16] In Croatia, by contrast, during the Bosnian war religion played a key symbolic role in reinforcing a sense of distinct national identity, distinguishing between the Catholic Croats, the Orthodox Serbs, and the Islamic groups in Bosnia and elsewhere.[17]

    Comparisons also need to take account of the historically predominant religious culture in each nation, since the Soviet Union included Catholic, Protestant, Orthodox, and Muslim societies. In previous chapters we found that beliefs and values differed in Western Europe by the type of predominant faith, and Need and Evans also found that Catholics in Central and Eastern Europe are generally more regular churchgoers than Orthodox Christians.[18] The post-Communist countries in the World Values Survey include seven Catholic societies – Croatia, the Czech Republic, Hungary, Lithuania, Poland, Slovakia, and Slovenia. From 70% to 95% of the population is Catholic in these countries, with a substantial Protestant minority in Hungary. The survey also covers eleven Eastern Orthodox societies, including Armenia, Belarus, Bulgaria, Georgia, Macedonia, Moldova, Montenegro, Romania, Russia, Ukraine, and Serbia. Some of these countries contain more homogeneous populations than others, with substantial religious minorities (of 10% or more) coexisting in Belarus (Catholics), Bulgarian (Muslims), Macedonia (Muslims), and Montenegro (Muslims and Catholics), as well as smaller populations of Muslims and Catholics living elsewhere. The Protestant ex-Communist societies in the survey include Estonia, East Germany, and Latvia, and there are three Muslim ex-Communist nations, Albania, Azerbaijan, and Bosnia-Herzegovina, although both Albania and Bosnia-Herzegovina contain substantial Catholic and Orthodox minorities.

Generational Change in Religiosity

Because time-series data covering a reasonably long period of time (such as the five decades that were used to test secularization in Western countries) are not available from the ex-Communist countries, we will use generational comparisons of the twenty-two post-Communist societies covered in the World Values Survey (WVS) as a proxy indicator of long-term change. We will compare linear and logged regression models to see which provides a better fit to the data. Our revised version of secularization theory implies that we should find a linear relationship between age and religious participation, with religiosity falling through successive birth cohorts, in the economically more developed societies. If, however, we find no significant age-related differences; or that the young are more religious than the old; or a curvilinear relationship between age and religiosity, it will tend to refute our theory (and we will we need to explore further the causes of any apparent religious revival among the younger generation). We will also compare patterns of religiosity in given societies, to see whether post-Communist countries vary systematically according to their level of human development and economic equality, as predicted by the theory of secularization and existential security – or whether state regulation of religious institutions and religious pluralism proves a more convincing explanation, as the supply-side thesis contends. As in previous chapters, our core dependent variables will be religious *values*, measured by the importance of religion, and religious *participation*, as indicated by frequency of attendance at services of worship, and by frequency of prayer. For comparison with the work of Greeley, we will also determine whether any generational differences exist in a range of common religious *beliefs*. In general we anticipate that generational differences will be strongest with religious *values*, although if they exist, these will also tend to be linked with one's patterns of religious *behavior*.

Table 5.1 presents the results of the fitted regression models for age in years, using all the pooled surveys in post-Communist Europe from 1995 to 2001. The results of the models show that for all the dependent variables except one (belief in life after death) the linear models provide a slightly better fit than the logged ones. Among all post-Communist societies, across nearly all indicators, we find that (1) religiosity was stronger among the older generation than among the young; and (2) the age-related differences tend to be linear, rather than curvilinear.[19] This is precisely the pattern that is predicted by the theory of secularization and existential security.

To illustrate these patterns graphically, and to help examine variations across these countries, the trends by birth cohort are shown for religious

Table 5.1. Age and Religiosity in Post-Communist Europe, Without Controls

	Linear Age Effects		Logged Age Effects	
	R^2	Sig.	R^2	Sig.
RELIGIOUS PARTICIPATION				
Religious participation	.006	.000	.005	.000
Frequency of prayer	.039	.000	.032	.000
RELIGIOUS VALUES				
Importance of religion	.026	.000	.022	.000
Importance of God	.016	.000	.013	.000
RELIGIOUS BELIEFS				
Believe in God	.008	.000	.006	.000
Believe in life after death	.001	.000	.002	.000
Believe in hell	.001	.000	.000	N/s
Believe in heaven	.001	.000	.000	.000
Believe in soul	.000	N/s	.000	N/s

NOTES: The models represent the results of individual-level regression analysis models where age (in years) was regressed as a linear or logged variable on indicators of religiosity, without any prior controls, using curvefit. The coefficients represent the amount of variance (R^2) in religiosity, and the significance of the relationship, explained by age. N = 18,595; N/s = Not significant; Sig. = Significance. Religious values: *"How important is religion in your life?"* Very (4), rather (3), not very (2) or not at all (1). Religious participation: *"Do you attend religious services several times a week, once a week, a few times during the year, once a year or less, or never?"* The percentage that reported attending religious services *"several times a week"* or *"once a week."* Frequency of prayer: Q199: *"How often do you pray to God outside of religious services? Would you say...Every day (7), more than once a week (6), once a week (5), at least once a month (4), several times a year (3), less often (2), never (1)."* Mean frequency per type of society. Importance of God scale: *"How important is God in your life? Please use this scale to indicate – 10 means very important and 1 means not at all important."* Mean per nation. Religious beliefs: Whether respondents expressed belief in God, in heaven, in hell, in life after death, and in whether people have a soul.
Source: World Values Survey, pooled 1995–2001.

values (in Figure 5.1) and for religious participation (Figure 5.2). Linear and logged regression models for the effects of age on religious values and participation were also run for each nation. Regardless of whether we focus on religious values or religious participation, the results show two clear patterns. First, there is a clear overall decline in all indicators of religiosity across successive birth cohorts; the older generations are almost always significantly more religious than the young. Second, there are important differences in levels of religiosity in post-Communist societies today, similar to those we have already observed in Western Europe. Poland, Romania, and Bosnia-Herzegovina, for example, tend to be consistently more religious

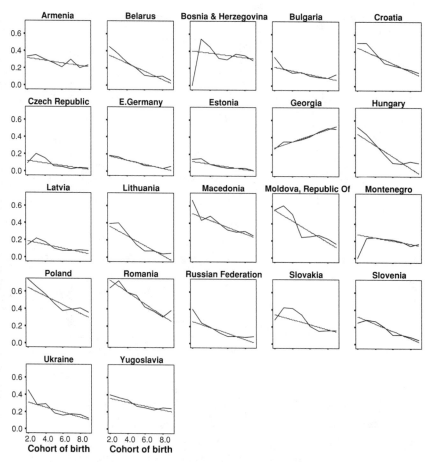

Figure 5.1. Religious Values by Cohort of Birth. Note: The proportion saying that religion was "very important" to their lives, with the regression line of the trend. Source: World Values Survey, pooled 1990–2001.

than East Germany, Estonia, and Montenegro. For the moment, we will leave aside the causes of these cross-national contrasts (which could be due to such factors as the historical relationship between church and state, or differences in levels of human development). These cross-national contrasts are interesting in themselves: the countries where the older generation is most secular generally display relatively flat patterns across successive birth cohorts – while in those countries in which the older generation is relatively religious, we find a more dramatic decline in religiosity among the younger cohorts. In other words, we find much stronger indications of

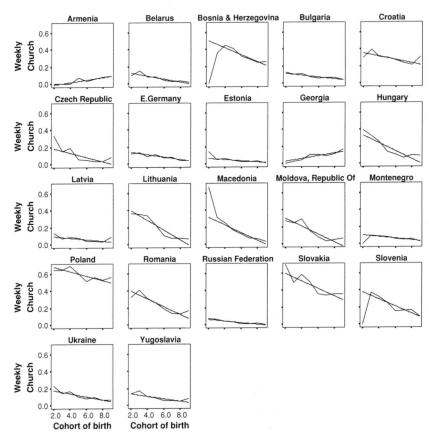

Figure 5.2. Religious Participation by Cohort of Birth. Note: Religious participation (the proportion that attended church at least weekly) by cohort of birth,
with the regression line of the trend. Source: World Values Survey, pooled
1990–2001.

historical change in some countries than in others. The generational contrasts are most marked in Hungary, Moldova, and Romania, and less evident
in some other nations with a more secular older generation, such as in East
Germany, Estonia, and Latvia. These trends are strikingly similar whether
the comparisons are based on the importance of religious values, attendance at services of worship, or the frequency of prayer, which enhances
our confidence that we are dealing with a robust and reliable phenomenon.

To control for the many other factors that could affect the relationship
between age and religiosity, we will use multivariate analysis to confirm

Table 5.2. Explaining Individual Religious Participation in Post-Communist Europe

	B	s.e.	Beta	Sig.
Societal level of human development (HDI 1998)	.992	.314	.016	.002
SOCIAL BACKGROUND				
Age (linear in years)	.001	.001	.008	.050
Male gender (0 women/1 men)	−.164	.017	−.041	.000
Education (4-point scale low to high)	.207	.012	.074	.000
Income (10-point scale low to high)	−.018	.003	−.023	.000
RELIGIOUS VALUES AND BELIEFS				
Importance of religion (4-point scale low to high)	.594	.010	.308	.000
Religious beliefs (5-point scale)	.312	.006	.232	.000
TYPE OF RELIGIOUS FAITH				
Protestant	1.10	.046	.105	.000
Catholic	1.67	.025	.377	.000
Orthodox	.565	.023	.130	.000
Muslim	−.080	.080	−.004	N/s
Constant	−1.097			
R^2	.453			

NOTE: Models use ordinary least squares regression analysis with religious participation (7-point scale measuring frequency of attendance at services of worship) as the dependent variable measured at individual level in 22 post-Communist societies. The table lists the unstandardized regression coefficient (B), the standard error (s.e.), the standardized regression coefficient (Beta), and the significance (Sig.) of the coefficients. N = 32,348. Religious participation: *"Do you attend religious services several times a week, once a week, a few times during the year, once a year or less, or never?"* The percentage that reported attending religious services "several times a week" or "once a week." Importance of religion scale: *"How important is religion in your life?"* 4-point scale. Religious beliefs: Whether respondents expressed belief in God, in heaven, in hell, in life after death, and in whether people have a soul. Type of religious faith: Dummy variables (0/1) for whether the respondent belonged to each type of major world religion.

Source: World Values Survey, pooled 1990–2001.

whether these patterns hold up – or seem to reflect the influence of specific variables. The regression models in Table 5.2 control for the society's level of human development as well as for the standard social and attitudinal variables that Chapter 3 demonstrated tend to influence patterns of churchgoing, such as gender, education, and income, in addition to the impact of religious values and beliefs, and belonging to different world religions. The pooled World Values Survey 1990–2001 is used to analyze patterns across the twenty-two post-Communist societies. The results show that the linear effects of age continue to be significant even with these multiple controls, with religiosity continuing to be stronger among the older generations. A similar regression model was replicated using logged age and the beta coefficients for age proved slightly weaker and statistically insignificant (at the conventional .05 level). The other social and attitudinal factors performed as expected, with religious attendance in post-Communist societies being relatively strong among women, the less educated, and the less affluent, as well as (unsurprisingly) among those who held religious values and beliefs. Catholics were the most regular churchgoers, with Protestants and Orthodox being moderate in attendance, and Muslims in this region the least likely to attend services of worship. The analysis of individual religiosity in post-Communist Europe therefore largely confirms the patterns found earlier in Western Europe, meaning that we do not need to resort to particularistic explanations based on factors distinctive to the history of the church under the Soviet state, whether the traditional beliefs and practices of the Eastern Orthodox church, the repression or persecution of Catholic leaders, or the cultural legacy of the Communist Party. Nevertheless there remain important national contrasts within the region, such as between religious Poland and secular Russia, which require further exploration.

The Impact of Religious Markets versus the Impact of Human Development

To examine the societal-level factors that could be causing the cross-national differences, we can compare how far religiosity is systematically related to religious markets and societal development. Four indicators are compared to see how strongly these correlated with the indicators of religious values, beliefs, and participation that we have used throughout this book.

Religious Pluralism

The supply-side theory of Stark and Finke suggests that the degree of competition among religious institutions plays a crucial role in creating religious vigor; and above all, that religious pluralism increases religious participation.[20] Religious pluralism is gauged here by the Herfindahl Index used in earlier chapters, as calculated by Alesina and colleagues using the data on the major religious populations derived from the *Encyclopaedia Britannica Book of the Year 2001*.[21] The religious pluralism index is calculated as the standard Herfindahl indicator for each country, ranging from zero to one.

State Regulation of Religion

A related hypothesis developed by Greeley argues that state regulation of religion in the Soviet Union restricted the churches, but that a religious revival occurred after the fall of communism in countries where there is a strong constitutional division between church and state, protecting religious freedom of worship and toleration of different denominations, without hindrance to particular sects and faiths (which, of course, would tend to enhance the degree of religious pluralism). In Communist China, for example, observers suggest that the state continues to actively repress, ban, or deter religious practices, exemplified by the prosecutions, killings, torture, and arrests practiced since 1999 against members of the Falun Gong cult.[22]

To examine this argument, we need to make a systematic comparison of state-church relations, and the degree of religious tolerance that now exists. To generate such a comparison, the degree of religious freedom in the twenty-seven nation states in post-Communist Europe was classified based on information for each country contained in the U.S. State Department report on *International Religious Freedom, 2002*, a comprehensive comparison of state regulation and restrictions of all world faiths.[23] As discussed in Chapter 2, the Religious Freedom Index that we developed focuses upon the relationship of the state and church, including issues such as whether the constitution limits freedom of religion, whether the government restricts some denominations, cults, or sects, and whether there is an established church. The index was classified according to the twenty criteria listed in Appendix C, with each item coded 0/1. The 20-point scale was then reversed so that a higher score represents greater religious freedom.

Societal Development

For comparison, we also examined how far the indicators of religiosity correlated with the Human Development Index and also with change in per capita GDP from 1990 to 2000 (measured in Purchasing Power Parity estimates in U.S. dollars), both of which are regarded as core indicators of societal modernization and human security.

The simple correlations in Table 5.3, without any prior controls, show that, despite the legacy of seven decades of Soviet repression of the church, the Religious Freedom Index was not significantly related (at the .05 level) to *any* of the indicators of religiosity used in this study, whether of

Table 5.3. Explaining Societal-Level Religiosity in Post-Communist Europe

| | Religious Market Indicators | | Societal Development Indicators | | |
| | Religious Freedom Scale | Religious Pluralism | Human Development Index, 1998 | Change in per capita GDP 1990–2000 | N. Nations |
	R Sig.	R Sig.	R Sig.	R Sig.	
RELIGIOUS PARTICIPATION					
Religious participation	.011	−.466*	−.069	−.118	22
How often pray?	−.305	−.747**	−.060	−.123	14
RELIGIOUS VALUES					
Importance of religion	−.335	−.285	−.467*	−.468*	20
Importance of God	−.333	.032	−.621**	−.590**	21
RELIGIOUS BELIEFS					
Believe in god	−.313	.035	−.684***	−.693**	21
Believe in life after death	−.275	−.091	.070	−.102	20
Believe in hell	−.396	−.098	−.399	−.489*	21
Believe in heaven	−.356	−.129	−.246	−.332	20
Believe in soul	−.228	.399	−.595**	−.673**	20

NOTE: Macro-level regression models of the impact of the religious market and societal development indicators on the dependent variables in 22 post-Communist societies, without any prior controls. *Correlation is significant (Sig.) at the 0.05 level (2-tailed). **Correlation is significant at the 0.01 level (2-tailed). *Religious Freedom Index, 2002*: see the Technical Appendix at the end of Chapter 6, Table A6.1, and text for details. This is an expanded and updated version of the Chaves and Cann (1992) scale. *Religious pluralism: The Herfindahl Index of religious pluralism or fractionalization*, from Alesina et al. 2003. See Chapter 4 note 32 for details of its construction. *Human Development Index, 1998*: Index based on longevity, literacy, and education, and per capita GDP (in PPP), UNDP *Human Development Report 2002*, New York: UNDP/Oxford University Press. *Change in Per Capita Gross Domestic Product, 1990–2000*: World Bank, *World Development Indicators*, 2002.

Source: World Values Survey, pooled 1990–2001.

participation, values, or beliefs. Of course this could be due in part to the limited number of cases, but even if this conventional test is relaxed, the correlation coefficients that did emerge were usually *negative*, which is in the opposite direction to that suggested by religious market theory. The results suggest that greater religious freedom in post-Communist nations is associated with *lower*, not higher, levels of religiosity. Religious pluralism was strongly and significantly related to religious participation and frequency of prayer, but again, contrary to religious market theory, in a *negative* direction. Post-Communist countries with more heterogeneous religious cultures and institutions proved to be more secular, not more religious, than those where religion is more homogeneous. The other indicators of religiosity showed insignificant correlations, but all but one was *negatively* related to pluralism. Our findings not only fail to support supply-side religious markets theory – they have the opposite sign from that which religious market theory would predict: in post-Communist Europe, religious pluralism is linked with relatively *low* levels of religiosity.

By contrast, the indicators of societal security show that religious values are negatively related to both human development and levels of affluence, as implied by the theory of secularization and existential security. People living in post-Communist countries that had achieved the most successful transition, with higher standards of living, longevity, and education, also regarded religion as less important to their lives than the publics living in poorer and less secure states in the region. Similar patterns were evident for belief in God. The other coefficients proved statistically insignificant, given the limited number of cases, although again their direction usually pointed in the expected direction.

To explore this further the results were examined in multivariate models (in Table 5.4) monitoring the combined effects of human development and religious markets on the mean level of religious values (the importance of God scale) measured at societal-level, and some scatter grams illustrating the relationships under comparison. Figure 5.3 tests the extent to which religious values (the 10-point importance of God scale) can be predicted in post-Communist Europe using standard indicators of human security, including the Human Development Index and the rate of economic growth during the last decade. These factors predict the vitality of religion in people's lives in this region so successfully that we do not need to resort to institutional explanations based on the history of the relationship between the church and state, the persecution of religious authorities, levels of rivalry and competition among religious organizations, or whether a particular culture is mainly Catholic or Protestant, Orthodox or Muslim. The sharp contrast in the scatter grams between the secular values evident in Czech Republic and Estonia, and the spiritual values manifested in Romania and Albania, can largely be attributed simply to different levels of human development and thus the social conditions of greater security.

Table 5.4. Explaining Societal Religious Values in Post-Communist Europe

	B	s.e.	Beta	Sig.
HUMAN DEVELOPMENT				
Level of human development (HDI 1998)	−17.99	5.97	−.602	.008
RELIGIOUS MARKETS				
Religious Freedom Index (20 points from low to high)	−.022	.024	−.176	.381
Religious pluralism scale	−1.416	1.86	−.146	.459
Constant	22.2			
R²	.332			

NOTE: Models use ordinary least squares regression analysis with mean religious values (the 10-point scale measuring importance of God) as the dependent variable measured at societal level in 19 post-Communist societies. The table lists the unstandardized regression coefficient (B), the standard error (s.e.), the standardized regression coefficient (Beta), and the significance of the coefficients (Sig.). The small number of cases (19) created problems of multi-collinearity and instability when the type of religious culture was introduced (because of the close association between Catholicism and the societies which were highest in human development *and* in religiosity), so this variable was excluded from the final model. See Figure 5.3. The growth in per capita GDP was also closely correlated with the Human Development Index, so this was also dropped to avoid problems of multi-collinearity. *Importance of religion scale: "How important is God in your life?"* 10-point scale. *Human Development Index, 1998*: Index based on longevity, literacy, and education, and per capita GDP (in PPP); *UNDP Human Development Report 2002*. New York: UNDP/Oxford University Press. *Religious Freedom Index*: 20-point measure explained in the text and in the Technical Appendix, Table A6.1, at the end of Chapter 6. *Religious pluralism: The Herfindahl index of religious pluralism or fractionalization*, from Alesina et al. 2003. See Chapter 4 note 32 for details of its construction.

Source: World Values Survey, pooled 1990–2001.

To confirm the finding of negative correlations between religiosity and religious markets we can also examine the scatter gram to see what is underlying this relationship. Contrary to religious market theory, Figure 5.4 shows how the salience of religious values is related to both the Herfindahl measure of religious pluralism and the Religious Freedom Index. The most secular countries (such as the Czech Republic and Estonia) have the greatest religious pluralism and freedom of the church from state regulation. This is no accident; the reason, we believe, is that human development generates more secular values among the general population – and also greater religious freedoms, social tolerance, and democracy. Religion not only becomes less important to people's lives in secure societies, but freedom of

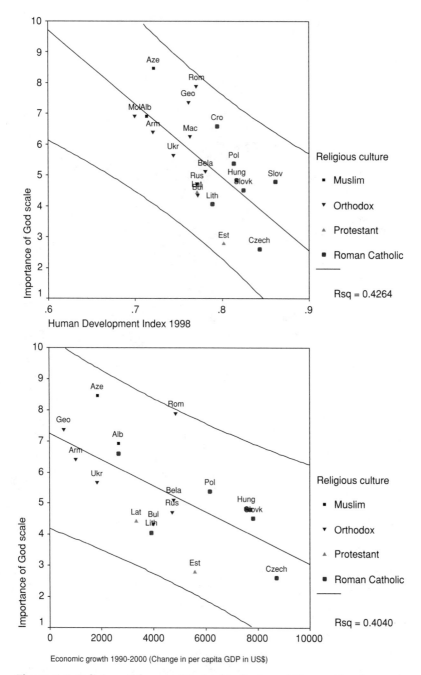

Figure 5.3. Religious Values and Societal Indicators of Human Development.

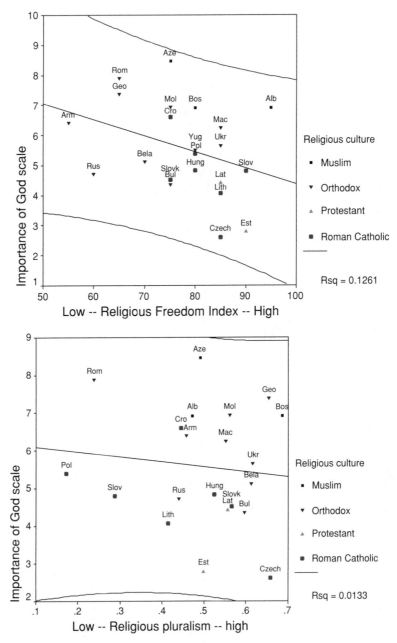

Figure 5.4. Religious Values, Religious Pluralism, and the Religious Freedom Index. Note: See the text for details of the 20-point Religious Freedom Index. Source: World Values Survey, pooled 1981–2001.

worship is also expanded as part of human rights and democratic liberalization. In poorer and less developed post-Communist societies, by contrast, religion remains a vital force in people's lives, and authoritarian states in the region limit religious liberties, just as they consistently restrict human rights in other spheres.

Conclusions

There are many reasons why patterns of secularization in post-Communist Europe might plausibly be expected to differ from those we have already found in the West. The role of the state in restricting religion under Communism is well established and we do not need to document its history here.[24] But the key question for us is whether this repression actually generated the erosion of mass spirituality in the Soviet bloc, or whether it may have exacerbated, but not necessarily caused, a long-term growth of secularization in this region which parallels similar developments in other countries. The fact that Western European democracies have a long history of religious tolerance, human rights, and civic liberties during the twentieth century means that the comparison of these regions provides an exceptionally well-designed "natural experiment" to test the "bottom-up" and "top-down" claims in the sociology of religion.

The generational comparisons suggest that there has been a long-term decline of religiosity across succeeding generations in post-Communist Europe, and we found no convincing evidence of a curvilinear pattern from the generational comparisons, suggesting that the younger generation has not experienced a significant revival of religious values, beliefs, or behavior. Moreover, the cross-national comparisons indicate that the cross-national differences that do remain important today can be satisfactorily explained by levels of human development among post-Communist nations, just as these factors explain patterns elsewhere. The supply-side thesis that religious markets are critical, so that participation is determined by religious pluralism and the lack of state regulation of church institutions, is given no positive support from the evidence; instead, the opposite position seems to be the case. It is the more homogenous religious cultures, exemplified by the role of Catholicism in Poland, which have best-preserved faith in God and habitual church attendance, not the most plural. And today the post-Communist states with the greatest regulation of the church turn out to be the *most* religious, not the least. We argue that this is no accident;

it reflects the fact that human security encourages secularization, together with the political rights and civil liberties associated with religious freedom in transitional and consolidating democracies. But what about values elsewhere in the world in other types of religious culture, particularly Muslim states? It is to examine these issues that we now turn.

Religion and Politics in the Muslim World

IN SEEKING TO understand the role of religion in the Muslim world, many popular commentators have turned to Samuel P. Huntington's provocative and controversial thesis of a "clash of civilizations." This account emphasized that the end of the Cold War brought new dangers. Huntington argued:

> *In the new world,...* the most pervasive, important and dangerous conflicts will not be between social classes, rich and poor, or other economically defined groups, but between people belonging to different cultural entities. Tribal wars and ethnic conflicts will occur within civilizations... And the most dangerous cultural conflicts are those along the fault lines between civilizations... For forty-five years the Iron Curtain was the central dividing line in Europe. That line has moved several hundred miles east. It is now the line separating peoples of Western Christianity, on the one hand, from Muslim and Orthodox peoples on the other.[1]

For Huntington, Marxist class warfare, and even the disparities between rich and poor nations, have been overshadowed in the twenty-first century by Weberian culture.

This influential account appeared to offer insights into the causes of violent ethno-religious conflicts exemplified by Bosnia, the Caucuses, the Middle East, and Kashmir. It seemed to explain the failure of political reform to take root in many Islamic states, despite the worldwide resurgence of electoral democracies around the globe. The framework seemed to provide a powerful lens that the American media used to interpret the underlying reasons for the terrorist attack on the World Trade Center and subsequent developments in Afghanistan and Iraq. Commentators often saw 9/11 as a full-scale assault on the global hegemony of America, in particular, and a reaction by Islamic fundamentalists against Western culture, in general. Nevertheless, the Huntington thesis has been highly controversial. The claim of rising ethnic conflict in the post–Cold War era has come under repeated and sustained attack.[2] Many scholars have challenged the existence of a single Islamic culture stretching all the way from Jakarta to Lagos, let alone one that held values deeply incompatible with democracy.[3] What has been less widely examined, however, is systematic empirical evidence of whether the publics in Western and Islamic societies share similar or deeply divergent values, and, in particular, whether any important differences between these cultures rest on democratic values (as Huntington claims) or on social values (as modernization theories suggest).

This chapter seeks to shed light on this issue by examining cultural values from the World Values Survey in almost eighty societies around the globe, including nine predominately Islamic societies. First we briefly outline the Huntington thesis and the response by critics. We then lay out and analyze the evidence. The data supports the first claim in Huntington's thesis: culture *does* matter, and matters a lot: religious legacies leave a distinct and lasting imprint on contemporary values. But Huntington is mistaken in assuming that the core "clash" between the West and Islamic societies concerns *political* values: instead, the evidence indicates that surprisingly similar attitudes toward democracy are found in the West and the Islamic world. We do find significant cross-cultural differences concerning the role of religious leaders in politics and society, but these attitudes divide the West from many other countries around the globe, not just Islamic ones. The original thesis erroneously assumed that the primary cultural fault line between the West and Islam concerns democratic government, overlooking a stronger cultural divide based on issues of gender equality and sexual liberalization. Cohort analysis suggests that as younger generations in the West have gradually become more liberal toward sexuality, this has generated a growing cultural gap, with Islamic nations remaining the most traditional societies in the world. The central values separating Islam and the West revolve far more centrally around Eros than Demos.

The "Clash of Civilizations" Debate

The clash of civilizations thesis advances three central claims. First, Huntington suggests that "culture matters"; in particular that contemporary values in different societies are path-dependent, reflecting long-standing legacies associated with core "civilizations." The concept of civilization is understood by Huntington as a "culture writ large": *"It is defined both by common objective elements, such as language, history, religion, customs, institutions, and by the subjective self-identification of people."*[4] Of these factors, Huntington sees religion as the central defining element (p. 47), although he also distinguishes regional subdivisions within the major world religions, such as the distinct role of Catholicism in Western Europe and Latin America, due to their different historical traditions and political legacies.

Second, the "clash" thesis claims that there are sharp cultural differences between the core political values common in societies sharing a Western Christian heritage – particularly those concerning representative democracy – and the beliefs common in the rest of the world, especially Islamic societies. For Huntington, the defining features of Western civilization include the separation of religious and secular authority, the rule of law and social pluralism, the parliamentary institutions of representative government, and the protection of individual rights and civil liberties as the buffer between citizens and the power of the state: *"Individually almost none of these factors was unique to the West. The combination of them was, however, and this is what gave the West its distinctive quality."*[5] Other accounts have commonly stressed that the complex phenomenon of "modernization" encompasses many additional social values that challenge traditional beliefs, notably faith in scientific and technological progress, belief in the role of economic competition in the marketplace, and the diffusion of modern social mores, exemplified by sexual liberalization and equality for women.[6] But Huntington's claim is that the strongest distinguishing characteristic of Western culture, the aspect which demarcates Western Christianity most clearly from the Muslim and Orthodox worlds, concerns the values associated with representative democracy. This claim is given plausibility by the failure of electoral democracy to take root in most states in the Middle East and North Africa.[7] According to the annual assessment made by the Freedom House (2002), of the 192 countries around the world, two-thirds (121) are electoral democracies. Of the 47 countries with an Islamic majority, one-quarter (11) are electoral democracies. Furthermore, none of the core Arabic-speaking societies in the Middle East and North Africa falls into this category. Given this pattern, in the absence of survey evidence concerning the actual beliefs of Islamic publics, it is commonly assumed that they have little faith in the principles or performance of democracy, preferring strong leadership and rule by traditional religious authorities to the democratic values of pluralistic competition, political participation, and political rights and civil liberties.

Lastly, Huntington argues that important and long-standing differences in political values based on predominant religious cultures will lead to conflict between and within nation states, with the most central problems of global politics arising from an ethno-religious "clash."[8] It remains unclear whether Huntington is claiming that the core cleavage concerns Western democratic values versus the developing world, or whether the main contrast lies as a fault line between the West and Islam, but the latter has been the primary popular interpretation of the thesis, and the one that has aroused the most heated debate.

Middle Eastern area studies specialists, scholars of the Koran, and students of Islamic law have contested a series of issues about the "clash" thesis. Critics have challenged the notion of a single Islamic culture, pointing to substantial contrasts found among one billion people living in diverse Islamic nations, such as Pakistan, Jordan, Azerbaijan, Indonesia, Bangladesh, and Turkey, and the differences between Muslims who are radical or moderate, traditional or modern, conservative or liberal, hard-line or revisionist.[9] Observers stress the manifold differences within the Islamic world due to historical traditions and colonial legacies, ethnic cleavages, levels of economic development, and the role and power of religious fundamentalists in different states, claiming that it makes little sense to lump together people living in Jakarta, Riyadh, and Istanbul. Along similar lines, the idea that we can recognize a single culture of "Western Christianity" is to oversimplify major cross-national differences, even among affluent postindustrial societies as superficially similar as the United States, Italy, and Sweden, for example the contrasts between Catholic Mediterranean Europe and Protestant Scandinavia, as well as among social sectors and religious denominations within each country.

Moreover, setting this issue aside for the moment, even if we accept the existence of a shared "Islamic" culture, scholars have also argued that the core values and teaching of the Koran are not incompatible with those of democracy.[10] Edward Said decried Huntington's thesis as an attempt to revive the "black-white," "us-them," or "good-evil" world dichotomy that had been so prevalent during the height of the Cold War, substituting threats from "Islamic terrorists" for those from "Communist spies."[11] Western leaders, seeking to build a global coalition against the followers of Osama bin Laden, took pains to distance themselves from the clash of civilizations thesis, stressing deep divisions within the Islamic world between the extreme fundamentalists and moderate Muslims. Leaders emphasized that the events of September 11 arose from the extreme ideological beliefs held by particular splinter groups of Al-Qaeda and Taliban fundamentalists, not from mainstream Muslim public opinion. Just as it would be a mistake to understand the 1995 bombing in Oklahoma City as a collective attack on the federal government by all Christian fundamentalists, rather than the work of a few individuals, it would be inappropriate to view the attack by Al-Qaeda terrorists on symbols of American capitalism and financial power as a new "clash of civilizations" between Islamic and Western cultures.

As well as challenging the basic premises of the clash of civilizations thesis, alternative explanations of radical Islamic fundamentalism suggest that the underlying root causes lie in deep disparities between rich and poor within societies, buttressed by the pervasive inequalities in political power in Middle Eastern regimes.[12] Structural or neo-Marxist theories suggest that the best predictors of radical disaffection lie in uneven patterns of modernization around the world and the existence of pervasive inequalities *within* many Muslim societies. The most important cleavage may be between middle class, more affluent, educated, and professional social sectors on the one hand – the teachers, doctors, and lawyers in Cairo, Beirut, and Islamabad – and the substrata of poorer, uneducated, and unemployed younger men living in Saudi Arabia, Libya, and Syria who, if disaffected, may become willing recruits to Islamic fundamentalist causes. Huntington distinguishes certain demographic characteristics of Islamic societies, notably the phenomena of the "youth bulge," but does not pursue the consequences of this generational pattern, in particular whether younger men from poorer sectors of society are particularly prone to political disaffection.

Yet there are plausible alternative theories about the major cultural contrasts we could expect to find between Islam and the West. In work presented elsewhere we document how the modernization process has transformed values by generating a rising tide of support for equality between women and men in postindustrial societies, and greater approval in these societies of a more permissive and liberal sexuality, including tolerance of divorce, abortion, and homosexuality.[13] The version of modernization theory developed by Inglehart hypothesizes that human development generates changed cultural attitudes in virtually any society, although values also reflect the imprint of each society's religious legacies and historical experiences. Modernization brings systematic, *predictable* changes in gender roles. The impact of modernization operates in two key phases:

i. Industrialization brings women into the paid workforce and dramatically reduces fertility rates. Women attain literacy and educational opportunities. Women are enfranchised and begin to participate in representative government, but still have far less power than men.

ii. The postindustrial phase brings a shift toward greater gender equality as women move into higher status economic roles in management and the professions, and gain political influence within elected and appointed bodies. Over half of the world has not yet entered this phase; only the more advanced industrial societies are currently moving on this trajectory.

These two phases correspond to two major dimensions of cross-cultural variation: (i) A transition from traditional to secular-rational values; and (ii) a transition from survival to self-expression values. The decline of the traditional family is linked with the first dimension. The rise of gender equality is linked with the second. Cultural shifts in modern societies are not sufficient by themselves to guarantee women equality across all major dimensions of life; nevertheless, through underpinning structural reforms and women's rights they greatly facilitate this process.[14] If this theory is applied to cultural contrasts between modern and traditional societies, it suggests that we would expect one of the key differences between the Western and Islamic worlds to focus around the issues of gender equality and sexual liberalization, rather than the democratic values that are central to Huntington's theory.

Classification and Measures

To summarize, many issues arising from the "clash" thesis could be considered, but here we focus upon testing two alternative propositions arising from the theoretical debate. Huntington emphasizes that the political values of democracy originated in the West with the separation of church and state, the growth of representative parliamentary institutions, and the expansion of the franchise. As such, he predicts that, despite the more recent emergence and consolidation of "Third Wave" democracies in many parts of the world, democratic values will be most deeply and widely entrenched in Western societies. If true, we would expect to find *the strongest cultural clash in political values would be between the Western and Islamic worlds.* In contrast, Inglehart's modernization theory suggests that a rising tide of support for women's equality and sexual liberalization has left a particularly marked imprint upon richer postindustrial nations, although traditional attitudes continue to prevail in poorer developing societies. Accordingly, given this interpretation, we also test the alternative proposition that *any deep-seated cultural divisions between Islam and the West will revolve far more strongly around social rather than political values, especially concerning the issues of sexual liberalization and gender equality.*

The issues of cultural conflict and value change have generated considerable controversy but, as yet, little systematic survey data has been available to compare public opinion toward politics and society in many Middle Eastern and Western societies. Interpretations by area scholars and anthropologists have relied upon more qualitative sources, including personal interviews, observations, and direct experience, and traditional textual exegesis of the literature, religious scriptures, and historical documents.[15] Recently commercial companies have started to conduct opinion polls that are representative of the public in a limited range of Muslim nations;[16] Gallup's survey examined attitudes toward other countries in nine Middle Eastern societies and the United States,[17] while Roper Reports Worldwide compared social values in the United States and Saudi Arabia.[18] Moreover, a study by Mark Tessler examined orientations toward democracy in four Arab states (Egypt, Jordan, Morocco, and Algeria), reporting that support for political Islam does not lead to unfavorable attitudes toward democracy.[19] Richard Rose compared attitudes among Muslims in Kazakhstan and Kyrgyzstan, and also concluded that being a Muslim does not make a person more likely either to reject democracy or to endorse dictatorship.[20] To build on previous studies, this chapter focuses on analyzing attitudes and values in the last two waves of the World Values Survey, from 1995 to 2001. To test the evidence for the clash of civilizations thesis, this study compares values at *societal*-level, based on the assumption that predominant cultures exert a broad and diffuse influence upon all people living under them.

Classifying Cultural Regions

In Huntington's account, nine major contemporary civilizations can be identified, based largely on the predominant religious culture in each society:

- Western Christianity (a European culture that subsequently spread to North America, Australia, and New Zealand),
- Muslim (including the Middle East, Northern Africa, and parts of South East Asia),

- Orthodox (Russian and Greek),
- Latin American (predominately Catholic yet with a distinct corporatist, authoritarian culture),
- Sinic/Confucian (China, South Korean, Viet Nam, and Korea),
- Japanese,
- Hindu,
- Buddhist (Sri Lanka, Burma, Thailand, Laos, and Cambodia), and (possibly)
- Sub-Saharan Africa.[21]

Huntington treats states or societies as the core actors exemplifying these civilizations, although recognizing that populations with particular cultural and religious identities spread well beyond the border of the nation state. Moreover, some plural societies are deeply divided, so there is rarely a clean one-to-one mapping, apart from exceptional cases such as Japan and India.

To analyze the survey evidence for these propositions, societies were classified into these categories (see Table 6.1) based on the predominant religious culture within each nation. The comparison includes eleven societies with a Muslim majority (ranging from 71% to 96%), including Algeria, Jordan, Pakistan, Turkey, Azerbaijan, Indonesia, Bangladesh, Albania, Morocco, Iran, and Egypt. This compares diverse states within the Islamic world, including semi-democracies with elections and some freedoms, exemplified by Albania, Turkey, and Bangladesh, as well as constitutional monarchies (Jordan), and suspended semi-democracies under military rule (Pakistan). Geographically these nations are located in Eastern Europe, the Middle East, and South Asia. In addition, the comparative framework includes twenty-two nations based on a culture of "Western Christianity" (using Huntington's definition to include both predominately Catholic and Protestant postindustrial societies, and countries like Australia and New Zealand, which are not located regionally in the "West" yet which inherited a democratic tradition from Protestant Britain). Other nations are classified into distinct religious cultural traditions, including Latin America (10), Russian or Greek Orthodox (12), Central Europe (10 nations sharing a common Western Christian heritage with the West yet with the distinct experience of living under Communist rule), sub-Saharan Africa (5), South East Asia (4 societies reflecting Sinic/Confucian values), plus Japan and India. In addition, ten societies contain a significant *minority* Islamic population (ranging from 4% to 27%), including Bosnia, Macedonia, Nigeria, and India, although these nations have Orthodox, Protestant, or Hindu

Table 6.1. Classification of Societies by Religious Cultures

Protestant	Catholic	Islamic	Orthodox	Central Europe	Latin America	Sinic/Confucian	Sub-Saharan Africa
Australia	Austria	Albania	Belarus	Croatia	Argentina	South Korea	Nigeria
Britain	Belgium	Algeria	Bosnia	Czech Republic	Brazil	Taiwan	South Africa
Canada	France	Azerbaijan	Bulgaria	East Germany	Chile	Viet Nam	Tanzania
Denmark	Ireland	Bangladesh	Georgia	Estonia	Colombia	China	Uganda
Finland	Italy	Egypt	Greece	Hungary	Dominican Rep		Zimbabwe
Iceland	Malta	Indonesia	Macedonia	Latvia	El Salvador		
New Zealand	Portugal	Iran	Moldova	Lithuania	Mexico		
Netherlands	Spain	Jordan	Montenegro	Poland	Peru		
Northern Ireland	Switzerland	Morocco	Romania	Slovakia	Uruguay		
Norway		Pakistan	Russia	Slovenia	Venezuela		
Sweden		Turkey	Serbia				
United States			Ukraine				
West Germany							

NOTE: This study dividing states with distinctive historical traditions, religious, legacies, and political institutions, including the UK (Northern Ireland and Great Britain), Germany (East and West), and the Federal Republic of Yugoslavia (Serbia and Montenegro). The Catholic and Protestant societies are analyzed together as "Western Christianity." In addition, India and Japan are each treated as separate religious cultures.

Source: World Values Survey/European Values Survey, 1995–2001.

majority populations. In the multivariate regression models, each type of society was coded as a dummy variable and the "Western" societies category was used as the (omitted) reference category. The models therefore measure the impact of living in each of these types of society, with controls, compared with living in the West.

To rule out intervening variables, multivariate regression models compare the influence of predominant religious cultures in each type of society controlling for levels of human and political development. Modernization theories suggest that this process brings certain predictable shifts in cultural values, including declining belief in traditional sources of religious authority and rising demands for more participatory forms of civic engagement.[22] Structural differences among societies are measured by the United Nations Development Program (UNDP) Human Development Index (HDI) 2000 (combining levels of per capita income, literacy and schooling, and longevity), and levels of democratization, which are classified based on the 1999–2000 Freedom House analysis of political rights and civil liberties.[23] The structural differences among groups within societies are measured by the standard social indicators, including income (as the most reliable cross-cultural measure of socioeconomic status in different societies), education, gender, age, and religious values. The latter was included to see whether the *strength* of religious values was more significant than the predominant *type* of religious culture in any society. Religious values were measured by whether people said that religion was "very important" in their lives.

Measuring Political and Social Values

Attitudes were compared toward three dimensions of political and social values: (i) support for democratic ideals and performance, (ii) attitudes toward political leadership, and (iii) approval of gender equality and sexual liberalization. As argued elsewhere, an important distinction needs to be drawn between support for the *ideals* of democracy and evaluations of the actual *performance* of democracy.[24] Evidence from previous waves of the World Value Survey suggests that citizens in many countries adhere strongly to the general principles of democracy, such as believing that it is the best form of government and disapproving of authoritarian alternatives, and yet at the same time many remain deeply dissatisfied with the way that democratic governments work in practice.[25] The phenomenon of more "critical citizens" or "disenchanted democrats" has been widely observed.[26] To examine these dimensions, attitudes toward the principles and performance of democracy are measured in this study using the items listed in Table 6.2,

Table 6.2. Factor Analysis of Political Values

	Democratic Performance	Democratic Ideals	Religious Leadership	Strong Leadership
V170 *Democracies are indecisive and have too much squabbling*	.862			
V171 *Democracies aren't good at maintaining order*	.854			
V172 *Democracy may have its problems but it's better than any other form of government*		.853		
V167 *Approve of having a democratic political system*		.780		
V200 *Politicians who do not believe in God are unfit for public office*			.881	
V202 *It would be better for [this country] if more people with strong religious beliefs held public office*			.879	
V165 *Approve having experts, not government, make decisions*				.838
V164 *Approve having a strong leader who does not have to bother with parliament and elections*				.721
% of total variance	19.6	17.7	19.6	15.7

NOTE: Principal component factor analysis was used with varimax rotation and Kaiser normalization. The total model predicts 72.6% of cumulative variance. The democratic performance scale was reversed so that a positive response expressed greater satisfaction with democracy.

Source: World Values Survey/European Values Survey, Waves III and IV (1995–2001).

where respondents are invited to express agreement or disagreement with the statements. It should be noted that the performance items do not ask people about their experience of democracy in their own country, such as how well their government works, but rather tap their expectations of how well democratic governments generally function in taking decisions and maintaining order.

In addition, it is commonly assumed that one of the primary contrasts between Muslim and Western cultures relates to attitudes toward the role

of religious leaders, who exercise power by virtue of their spiritual authority, or secular leaders who hold authority through elective office, reflecting
deeper beliefs about the separation of church and state. We therefore also
monitored support for the role of religious leaders in public life, with the
items listed in Table 6.2. Neither leadership item cued respondents with
any explicit reference to "democracy" and indeed, in principle, there is no
inconsistency in believing both in the important role of spiritual authorities and in the principles of democracy, if the religious leaders exercise
power through elected office, exemplified by Christian Democrat parties
in Germany or politicians from the Christian far right in the United States.
We also sought to compare attitudes toward preferences for strong leadership, measured by questions tapping support for non-democratic forms
of government by experts or by leaders unaccountable to parliament or
elections. Factor analysis confirmed that these political items did indeed
fall into four distinct dimensions. Accordingly summary scales were constructed, each standardized to 100 points for ease of interpretation and
consistent comparison across measures.

Yet the alternative proposition is that the transformation of social values
toward sexuality and women's equality, which has profoundly affected the
younger generation in postindustrial societies, may lie at the heart of any
cultural clash between modern and traditional societies in general, and between the West and Islam in particular. In this regard, Huntington may have
correctly identified the importance of civilizational values, but may have
misdiagnosed the root causes of any cultural differences. To explore this
proposition we can compare support for gender equality, using a standardized scale developed elsewhere, also based on factor analysis, monitoring
attitudes toward the roles of women and men in the workforce, education,
politics, and the family.[27] The Gender Equality items are similar to those
commonly contained in the more comprehensive psychological scales of sex
roles. The gender equality scale was summed across the component items
and standardized to 100 points for ease of interpretation. We also compared
attitudes using 10-point scales monitoring approval or disapproval of three
related dimensions of changing sexual mores, concerning homosexuality,
abortion, and divorce.

Attitudes toward Democracy

The multivariate ordinary least squares regression models presented in
Table 6.3 compared the impact of living within each type of religious
culture after including controls for the societal-level of human and political

Table 6.3. Political Values by Type of Religious Culture, with Controls

Scale	Approve of Democratic Performance 0–100				Approve of Democratic Ideals 0–100				Favor Religious Leadership 0–100				Favor Strong Leadership 0–100			
	B	s.e.	Beta	Sig.	B	s.e.	Beta	Sig.	B	s.e.	Beta	Sig.	B	s.e.	Beta	Sig.
Type of religious culture																
Muslim	0.2	.36	.02	N/s	0.2	.31	.01	N/s	8.3	.51	.14	***	0.3	.38	.01	N/s
Orthodox	−10.2	.28	−.20	***	−9.1	.24	−.20	***	9.1	.39	.12	***	8.2	30	.15	***
Central European	−7.6	.23	−.15	***	6.0	.20	−.14	***	2.4	.31	.04	***	8.4	.25	.15	***
Latin American	−6.5	.26	−.12	***	−3.7	.22	−.08	***	1.6	.39	.02	***	5.3	.28	.09	***
Sinic/Confucian	0.2	.44	.01	N/s	−4.3	.37	−.05	***	−0.3	.89	−.01	N/s	13.3	.467	.12	***
Sub-Saharan African	−6.3	.47	−.10	***	−7.2	.39	−.13	***	11.2	.59	.15	***	2.8	50	.04	***
Hindu	−8.0	.67	−.05	***	−4.6	.55	−.03	***	N/a				14.0	.72	.08	***
Japanese	2.3	.66	.02	***	−4.1	.55	−.03	***	4.8	.61	.03	***	3.1	.65	.02	***
(Constant)	70.7				84.3				71.3				56.6			
Adjusted R² Block 1 (Control variables only)	.02				.02				.38				.04			
Adjusted R² Block 2 (Controls + type of society)	.07				.06				.39				.08			
N.	82865				82536				47703				80986			

NOTE: Ordinary least squares regression models with blockwise entry with the political value scales as the dependent variables. The full model is illustrated in the Technical Appendix at the end of this Chapter, Table A6.1. *Block 1* in all models controls for the *level of human development* (Human Development Index 1998), *level of political development* (Freedom House 7-point index [reversed] of political rights and civil liberties 1999–2000), age (years), gender (male=1), education (3 categories from low to high), income (10 categories), and religious values (importance of religion). *Block 2* then enters the type of culture, based on the predominant religion, coded as dummy variables. Western culture represents the (omitted) reference category. The coefficients can be understood to represent the effect of living in each type of culture compared with living in Western culture, net of all prior controls. *Political value* scales: For details see Table 6.2. *Type of culture*: see Table 6.1. B = unstandardized regression coefficient; s.e. = standard error; Beta = standardized regression coefficient. Significance (Sig.): ***P = .001; **P = .01; *P = .05. N/s = Not Significant.

Source: All World Values Survey/European Values Survey (WVS), pooled sample 1995–2001.

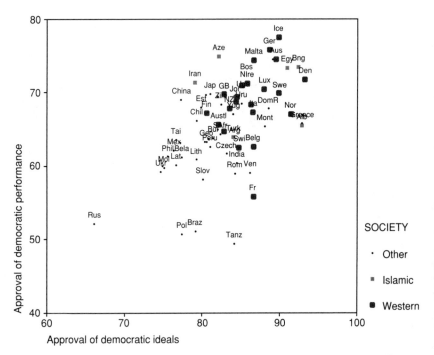

Figure 6.1. Democratic Values. Source: World Values Survey/European Values Survey (WVS), pooled sample 1995–2001.

development, and individual-level measures for age, gender, education, income, and strength of religiosity. In these models, each type of society was coded as a dummy (0/1) variable. The Western category was excluded from the analysis, so that the dummy coefficients can be interpreted as the effect of living in these societies, after applying prior controls, compared with the effect of living in the West. The data was entered in blocks, including development and social controls in the first block, then the additional effects of the full model in the second block, including the type of society as well.

The results show that after controlling for all these factors, contrary to Huntington's thesis, compared with Western societies, *there were no significant differences between the publics living in the West and in Muslim religious cultures in approval of how democracy works in practice, in support for democratic ideals, and in approval of strong leadership.* By marked contrast, less support for democratic values was evident in many other types of non-Western society, especially countries in Eastern and Central Europe, and Latin America, while the Sinic/Confucian states showed the greatest approval of strong government. At the same time, after introducing all the controls, *Muslim publics did display greater support for a strong societal role by religious authorities than do Western publics.* This pattern persists despite controlling for the strength of religiosity and other social factors, which suggests that it is not simply reducible to the characteristics of people living in Muslim societies. Yet this preference for religious authorities is less a cultural division between the West and Islam than it is a gap between the West and many other types of less secular societies around the globe, especially in sub-Saharan Africa and, to a lesser extent, in Latin America.

To examine these results in more detail, Figures 6.1 and 6.2 compare the location of each nation on these scales. Of all countries under comparison, Russia proved a striking outlier, displaying widespread disillusionment with the way that democratic processes worked, as well as little enthusiasm for democratic ideas. Other Orthodox societies also showed minimal faith in democracy, including the Ukraine, Moldova, Belarus, Georgia, and Macedonia. A few other developing countries from different cultures proved extremely critical of the way that democracy worked in practice, although showing greater support for democratic ideals, including

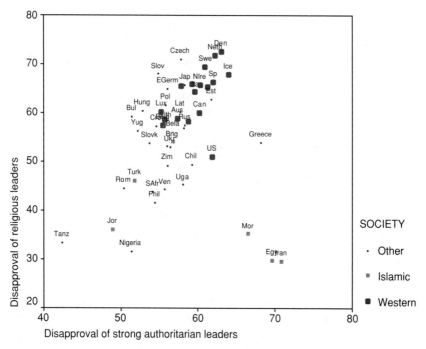

Figure 6.2. Leadership Attitudes. Source: World Values Survey/European Values Survey (WVS), pooled sample 1995–2001.

Tanzania, Brazil, and Poland. Many diverse cultures were located in the middle of the distribution, including Turkey and Jordan as Islamic societies, as well as the United States, Italy, and the Netherlands. Nations that gave the strongest endorsement for democratic ideals and practices included the Scandinavian societies of Denmark, Iceland, and Sweden, along with Germany and Austria, but high support was also registered in Muslim Bangladesh, Egypt, and Azerbaijan. Therefore, in general, slightly lower levels of support for democracy were evident in some Eastern European states, notably in Russia, lending some confirmation for claims of a division between the Orthodox and Western worlds. But attitudes toward democratic principles and performance generally showed a broad distribution across many diverse cultural groups, providing minimal support for the stronger claim that the West is particularly distinctive to Islam in its faith in democracy. Indeed, the difference between public opinion in Eastern and Western Europe could be explained equally satisfactorily as reflecting a residual hangover from the Cold War era, and the poor performance of electoral democracies and states in these nations, rather than being interpreted as the result of cultural legacies or the emergence of any "new" ethno-religious cleavage.

Figure 6.2 compares leadership attitudes by nation. Support for religious leaders was lowest in many secular societies in Scandinavia and Western Europe, as well as in certain nations in Eastern Europe like the Czech Republic. The United States proved distinctive, showing higher than average support for religious leaders, compared with other Western nations, while Greece was another outlier. At the other extreme, support for religious leaders was relatively strong in African societies including Nigeria, Tanzania, and South Africa, as well as the Philippines, all countries with strong religiosity. Compared with Western nations, many of the Islamic nations expressed greater support for the principle of religious authorities, but they were far from alone in this regard. There is also a fascinating split over the issue of strong leadership evident within the Islamic world; more democratic countries with greater political rights and civil liberties and parliamentary traditions, exemplified by Bangladesh and Turkey, expressed greater reservations about authoritarian leadership. To a lesser extent, Jordan also fell into this category. In contrast, the public living in Islamic countries characterized by more limited political freedoms, less democratic states, and by strong executives, expressed greater support for authoritarian leadership, notably in Egypt, Iran, and Morocco.

Yet so far we have not compared the alternative modernization thesis that the social values of gender equality and sexual liberalization could plausibly lie at the heart of any "clash" between Islam and the West. The analysis of these social attitudes in Table 6.4 reveals the extent of the gulf between Islam and the West, with a far stronger and more significant gap on these issues than across most of the political values. Many structural factors are also important; more egalitarian and liberal values are evident among the young, women, the well educated, and the more secular, as discussed in Chapter 7, as well as in societies with greater human and democratic development. After these controls are introduced, the results show that there remains a strong and significant difference across all the social values (including approval of gender equality, homosexuality, abortion, and divorce) among those publics living in Western versus Muslim societies. Figure 6.3 shows the distribution of nations on the scales for gender equality and homosexuality in more detail. The results confirm the consistency of the sharp differences between Islam and the West on these issues. All the Western nations, led by Sweden, Germany, and Norway, strongly favor equality for women and also prove tolerant of homosexuality. Many other societies show a mixed pattern, falling into the middle of the distribution. In contrast the Muslim cultures, including Egypt, Bangladesh, Jordan, Iran, and Azerbaijan, all display the most traditional social attitudes, with only Albania proving slightly more liberal.

We lack time-series survey data that would allow us to trace trends in the postwar era, to see whether these cultural differences between societies have widened, as we suspect, due to the modernization process in postindustrial economies. Nevertheless, if we assume that people acquire their basic moral and social values as the result of the long-term socialization process in the family, school, and community, leading to generational rather than life-cycle effects, we can analyze these attitudes for different ten-year cohorts of birth. The results in Figure 6.4 confirm two striking and important patterns: first, there is a persistent gap in support for gender equality and sexual liberalization between the West (which proves most liberal), Islamic societies (which prove most traditional), and all other societies (which are in the middle). Moreover, even more importantly, the figures reveal that the gap between the West and Islam is usually narrowest among the oldest generation, but that this gap has steadily widened across all the indicators as the younger generations in Western societies have become progressively more liberal and egalitarian, while the younger generations in Islamic societies remain as traditional as their parents and grandparents. The trends suggest that Islamic societies have not experienced a backlash against liberal Western sexual mores among the younger generations, but rather that young Muslims remain unchanged, in contrast to the transformation of lifestyles and beliefs experienced among their peers living in postindustrial societies.

Table 6.4. Social Values by Type of Religious Culture, with Controls

Scale	Approve of Gender Equality (0–100)				Approve of Homosexuality (1–10)				Approve of Abortion (1–10)				Approve of Divorce (1–10)			
	B	s.e.	Beta	Sig.	B	s.e.	Beta	Sig.	B	s.e.	Beta	Sig.	B	s.e.	Beta	Sig.
Type of religious culture																
Muslim	**−8.2**	**.35**	**−.18**	***	**−1.9**	**.05**	**−.18**	***	**−0.67**	**.05**	**−.07**	***	**−0.25**	**.05**	**−.03**	***
Orthodox	−8.9	.30	−.17	***	−2.1	.04	−.26	***	0.24	.04	.03	***	−0.20	.04	−.03	***
Central European	−6.6	.30	−.09	***	−1.6	.03	−.18	***	0.24	.03	.03	***	0.01	.03	.01	N/s
Latin American	2.6	.25	.05	***	−1.0	.03	−.11	***	−1.20	.03	−.14	***	0.15	.04	.02	***
Sinic/Confucian	−0.3	.69	−.01	N/s	−2.9	.07	−.13	***	−2.10	.06	−.10	***	−2.30	.07	−.11	***
Sub-Saharan African	7.3	.42	13	***	−0.6	.06	−.05	***	−0.08	.06	−.01	N/s	0.29	.06	.03	***
Hindu	3.4	.53	.03	***	−1.2	.08	−.05	***	−0.05	.08	−.01	N/s	−0.10	.08	−.01	N/s
Japanese	−14.4	.52	−.09	***	−1.5	.06	−.06	***	−0.45	.06	−.02	***	−0.05	.07	−.01	N/s
(Constant)	32.7				1.6				3.1				2.16			
Adjusted R² Block 1 (Control variables only)	**.26**				**.20**				**.23**				**.26**			

Adjusted R² Block 2 (Controls + type of society)	.33	.26	.21	.31
N.	63476	103290	99980	105432

NOTE: OLS regression models with blockwise entry with the social value scales as the dependent variables. The full model is illustrated in the Technical Appendix at the end of this chapter, Table A6.1. Block 1 in all models controls for the *level of human development* (Human Development Index 1998), *level of political development* (Freedom House 7-point index [reversed] of political rights and civil liberties 1999–2000), age (years), gender (male = 1), education (3 categories from low to high), income (10 categories), and religious values (importance of religion). Block 2 then enters the type of culture, based on the predominant religion, coded as dummy variables. Western culture represents the (omitted) reference category. The coefficients can be understood to represent the effect of living in each type of culture compared with living in Western culture, net of all prior controls. *Type of culture:* see Table 6.1. *Gender equality scale:* For details see note 7 and Appendix B. *Sexual liberalization scales:* "Please tell me for each of the following statements whether you think it [Homosexuality/ abortion/ divorce] can always be justified, never be justified, or something in-between, using this card from 1 (never justifiable) to 10 (always justifiable)." B = unstandardized regression coefficient; s.e. = standard error; Beta = standardized regression coefficient. Significance (Sig.): ***P = .001 ** P = .01 *P = .05. N/s = Not significant.

Source: All World Values Survey/European Values Survey (WVS), pooled sample 1995–2001.

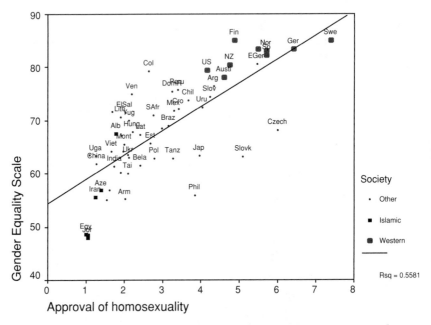

Figure 6.3. Social Values. Source: World Values Survey/European Values Survey (WVS), pooled sample 1995–2001.

Conclusion and Discussion

The thesis of a "clash of civilizations" has triggered something of a "clash of scholarship" among those seeking to understand the causes and consequences of ethnic-religious conflict. This task has long been of interest to academe but it has received fresh impetus from the dramatic events and aftermath of 9/11. Alternative interpretations of these issues are important for themselves, but also because they carry important policy implications, not least for how far differences between the United States and Middle Eastern states primarily reflect the views of political elites and governing regimes, or whether they tap into deeper currents of public opinion. To summarize the core components of the Huntington thesis, the claims are threefold: societal values in contemporary societies are rooted in religious cultures; the most important cultural division between the Western and Islamic world relates to differences over democratic values; and, in the post–Cold War era, this "culture clash" is at the source of much international and domestic ethnic conflict.

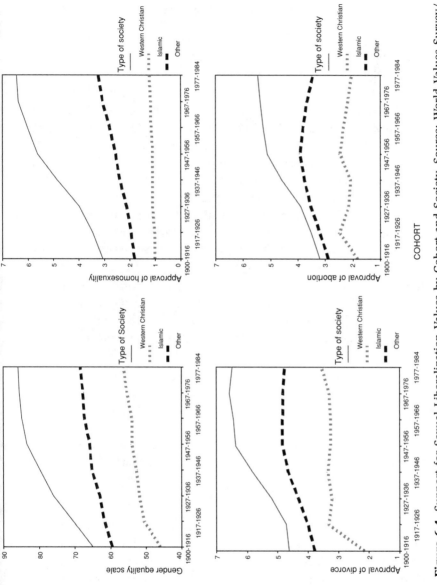

Figure 6.4. Support for Sexual Liberalization Values by Cohort and Society. Source: World Values Survey/European Values Survey (WVS), pooled sample 1995–2001.

153

The comparative evidence from this chapter suggests four main findings:

(i)   First, when political attitudes are compared (including evaluations of how well democracy works in practice, support for democratic ideals, and disapproval of strong leaders), far from a clash of values, there is minimal difference between the Muslim world and the West.

(ii) Instead, the democratic clash (if it can be called a clash) divides post-Communist states in Eastern Europe (exemplified by Russia, Ukraine, and Moldova), which display minimal support for democracy, from many other countries that display far more positive attitudes, including both Western *and* Islamic nations. This pattern could be explained equally well as reflecting the residual legacy of the Cold War and a realistic evaluation of the actual performance of democracy in these states, rather than by the reemergence of ethnic conflict based on the values of the Orthodox church, which are, after all, part of Christendom.

(iii) Support for religious authorities is stronger in Muslim societies than in the West, but here it is not a simple dichotomy, as many other types of society also support an active role for religious leaders in public life, including the sub-Saharan African countries under comparison as well as many Catholic nations in Latin America.

(iv) Yet there *is* a substantial cultural cleavage, although one underestimated by Huntington, in social values toward gender equality and sexual liberalization. In this regard, the West is far more egalitarian and liberal than all other societies, particularly Muslim nations. Moreover, cohort analysis suggests that this gap has steadily widened as the younger generation in the West has gradually become more liberal in their sexual mores, while the younger generation in Muslim societies remains deeply traditional.

The results indicate that modern Western societies are indeed different, in particular concerning the transformation of attitudes and behavior associated with the "sexual revolution" that has occurred since the 1960s, fundamental changes in the nature of modern families, and more expressive lifestyles. Equality for women has progressed much further, and transformed traditional cultural beliefs and values about the appropriate division of sex roles far more deeply, in affluent Western societies. But at the same time, any claim of a clash of civilizations, especially of fundamentally different *political* values held by Western and Islamic societies, represents an oversimplification of the evidence. Across many political dimensions examined here, both Muslim and Western societies are similar in their positive orientation toward democratic ideals. Where Islam societies do differ significantly from the West, in supporting religious authorities, they are far from exceptional around the world. Any black-and-white "Islam versus the West" interpretation of a "culture clash" as conveyed by the popular media is far too simplistic. It would be desirable to be able to compare public opinion across more dimensions, and across a wider range of nations in the Middle East, Africa, and Asia. Moreover, it remains unclear how far different understandings of democracy are culturally determined, giving rise to the familiar problems of equivalence in cross-national research. Nevertheless, the results urge strong caution in generalizing from the type of regime to the state of public opinion in any particular country. Support for democracy is surprisingly widespread among Islamic publics, even among those who live in authoritarian societies. The most basic cultural fault line between the West and Islam does not concern democracy – it involves issues of gender equality and sexual liberalization, as discussed further in Chapter 7.

Technical Appendix

Table A6.1. Illustration of the Full Regression Model used in Tables 6.3 and 6.4

	Approve of Democratic Performance			
	B	s.e.	Beta	Sig.
Developmental controls				
Level of human development (100-point scale)	−9.2	1.0	−.07	***
Level of political development	.13	.06	.01	***
Social controls				
Age (Years)	−.03	.01	−.02	***
Gender (Male = 1)	0.15	.12	.01	N/s
Education (3 categories low to high)	1.86	.09	.07	***
Income (10 categories low to high)	0.67	.03	.10	***
Religious values (importance of religion)	−0.42	.07	−.03	***
Type of religious culture				
Muslim	**.12**	**.36**	**.01**	**N/s**
Orthodox	−10.1	.28	−.20	***
Central European	−7.6	.23	−.15	***
Latin American	−6.5	.26	−.12	***
Sinic	.19	.43	.01	N/s
Sub-Saharan African	−6.3	.47	10	***
Hindu	−8.0	.67	−.05	***
Japanese	2.3	.66	.01	***
(Constant)	70.7			
Adjusted R^2 Block 1 (Control variables only)	.02			
Adjusted R^2 Block 2 (Controls + type of culture)	.07			

NOTE: This illustrates the full ordinary least squares regression model, with blockwise entry, in this case with the approval of democratic performance 100-point scale as the dependent variable. *Block 1* of the model controls for the level of development of the society and the social background of respondents. *Block 2* then enters the type of culture, based on the predominant religion, coded as dummy variables. Western societies represent the (omitted) reference category. The coefficients represent the effects of living in each type of society compared with living in Western societies, net of all prior controls. *Democratic performance* scale: For details see Table 6.2. *Level of human development:* Human Development Index (HDI) 2000, including longevity, literacy, and education, and per capita GDP in $US PPP (UNDP Development Report 2000). *Level of political development:* Freedom House 7-point index (reversed) of political rights and civil liberties 1999–2000 (www.freedomhouse.org). *Type of culture:* see Table 6.1. Sig. = significance of the coefficients: ***P = .001; **P = .01; *P = .05. N/s = Not significant. B = unstandardized regression coefficient. s.e. = standard error. Beta = standardized regression coefficient.
Source: World Values Survey/European Values Survey (WVS), pooled sample 1995–2001.

PART III

The Consequences of Secularization

Religion, the Protestant Ethic, and Moral Values

so far, this book has explained that the authority of established religion has been weakening among the publics of postindustrial societies (and especially among the more secure strata of these societies). The concluding section of the book shifts its focus from explaining secularization to examining the influence of religion on important social and political phenomena. What are the consequences of secularization? In particular, to what extent has this process eroded the social values, moral beliefs, and ethical teachings of the church; diminished the role of churches, faith-based organizations, and social capital in civic society; weakened the traditional base of electoral support for religious parties; and diluted the symbolic meaning of religious identities in situations of deep-seated ethnic conflict? If the process of secularization has occurred along the lines that we suggest, then we expect that religiosity will continue to exert a strong imprint on society and politics in developing nations, but that its power will have faded in many industrial and postindustrial societies.

Sociologists, political scientists, and economists have long sought to understand how given belief systems produce enduring cross-national differences in cultural values. In Chapter 6 we demonstrated how religion helps shape attitudes toward gender roles, and attitudes toward abortion, divorce, and homosexuality.[1] This chapter examines the impact of religion on orientations toward work and broader economic attitudes, starting with a seminal

159

theory in the sociology of religion: Max Weber's claim that the Protestant ethic generated the spirit of capitalism. We also analyze how religion shapes moral values, including ethical standards such as honesty and bribery, as well as beliefs about issues of life and death, including euthanasia, suicide, and abortion. The conclusion considers the implications of our findings and how they contribute toward understanding processes of value change.

The Protestant Ethic and the Spirit of Capitalism Thesis

Weber's argument about the origins of modern capitalism has been among the most influential in the history of the social sciences, attracting confirmation and refutation by sociologists, historians, psychologists, economists, and anthropologists throughout the twentieth century.[2] The central puzzle he addressed concerned why the Industrial Revolution, economic modernization, and bourgeois capitalism arose first in the West, and specifically in Protestant rather than Catholic Western societies, rather than elsewhere. Weber argued that legal and commercial changes, institutional developments, and technological innovations in Europe were insufficient by themselves to provide an adequate explanation; other societies had developed banking, credit institutions, and legal systems, as well as the foundations of science, mathematics, and technology. He notes that the material conditions for capitalism existed in many earlier civilizations, including the rise of the merchant class engaged in trade and commerce in China, Egypt, India, and the classical world, well before the Protestant Reformation.[3] What they lacked, however, he believed, was a particular and distinctive cultural ethos. For Weber, it was the particular values associated with the Protestant Reformation and Calvinist doctrine that gave birth to the spirit of Western capitalism.[4] Ascetic Protestantism preached that people have a duty to work diligently, to pursue financial rewards, and to invest prudently. The aim of working and accumulating resources was not just to meet minimal material needs, still less to dissipate profits on material display and hedonistic and worldly pleasures in the enjoyment of life, but rather work was regarded as a moral duty pursued for its own sake: *"Labour must, on the contrary, be performed as if it were an absolute end in itself, a calling."*[5] The Protestant ethic interpreted ethical activities, not as monastic asceticism renouncing this life, but rather as the fulfillment of worldly obligations. In turn, the virtues of hard work, enterprise, and diligence, Weber argued, were the underlying cultural foundation for capitalist markets and investment: *"Honesty is useful, because it assures credit; so are punctuality, industry, frugality, and that is the reason they are virtues."*[6] The Protestant ethic was therefore understood by Weber as a unique set of moral beliefs about the virtues of hard work and economic acquisition, the need for individual entrepreneurial initiative, and the rewards of a just God. Its specific values emphasized self-discipline, hard work, the prudent reinvestment of savings, personal honesty, individualism, and independence, all of which were thought to generate the cultural conditions most conducive to market economies, private enterprise, and bourgeois capitalism in the West.

It should be stressed that Weber did not claim that the restless go-getting entrepreneurial class of merchants and bankers, shopkeepers and industrial barons were also the most devout ascetic Protestants; on the contrary, he argued that *"those most filled with the spirit of capitalism tend to be indifferent, if not hostile, to the Church."*[7] He therefore did not expect an individual-level relationship to exist between personal piety, churchgoing habits, and adherence to the Protestant work ethic. Instead, this cultural ethos was thought to be pervasive, influencing devout and atheists alike, within Protestant societies. Any attempt to analyze the Weberian theory should therefore be tested at the macro-level, not the individual-level.

This Weberian thesis, like any classic in the literature, has attracted widespread debate and criticism during the last century.[8] Much of the work has focused on understanding the historical relationship between Protestantism and the subsequent rise of capitalism; for example Tawney, and later Samuelson, questioned the direction of causality in this relationship, arguing that the early growth of capitalism in late-Medieval Europe preceded and encouraged subsequent cultural shifts, such as greater individualism and more acquisitive attitudes that were conducive to the adoption and spread of Protestantism.[9] Historians have disputed whether economic activities actually flourished most, as Weber claimed, where Calvinism was predominant in the seventeenth-century Dutch Republic.[10] Economists have examined whether contemporary religion generates cultural attitudes that are conducive to economic development and growth; for example Guiso, Sapienza, and Zingales provide some limited evidence in support of this argument, finding that religiosity was linked to attitudes such as social trust, that were conducive to the working of free markets and institutions; but when comparing specific economic attitudes within Christian denominations, in both Protestant and Catholic cultures, they found mixed results.[11] Political sociology has also studied these issues; previous work by Granato and Inglehart showed a strong linkage between macro-level economic growth rates and some of the core values of the Weberian Protestant ethic (which are not unique to Protestant societies today) – including an emphasis on the values of individual autonomy and economic achievement.[12]

We lack historical evidence that could examine cultural conditions at the time when capitalism was burgeoning in the West. But if Weber's thesis is correct, we might expect that the culture of Protestantism would have left an enduring legacy in values that still remain visible today. To develop these arguments further, we will focus here on the core Weberian hypothesis, namely that, compared with those living in all other religious cultures (especially Catholic societies), Protestant societies should display the strongest work ethic conducive to modern capitalism, exemplified by valuing the virtues of work as a duty, as well as favoring markets over the state. Moreover, Weber stresses that an important aspect of Protestantism concerns the teaching of broader ethical standards, including those of honesty, willingness to obey the law, and trustworthiness, which serve as the foundation of business confidence, good faith dealings, and voluntary contract compliance. Since Weber's claim concerned societal-level cultural effects, we focus on analyzing macro-level values when classifying societies by their predominant religious culture, using the categories developed in Table 2.2.[13] We describe the mean distribution of attitudes by religious culture, then use multivariate models to control for the factors that we have already demonstrated are closely related to the strength of religious values and practices. This includes the level of human development; we suspect that societies sharing a common Protestant heritage still display an affinity in basic values, but that the forces of development have subsequently transformed the cultural legacy of religious traditions. Thus, Inglehart argued:

> In Western history, the rise of the Protestant Ethic – a materialistic value system that not only tolerated economic accumulation but encouraged it as something laudable and heroic – was a key cultural change that opened the way for capitalism and industrialization. But precisely because they attained high levels of economic security, the Western societies that were the first to industrialize, have gradually come to emphasize Postmaterialist values, giving higher priority to the quality of life than to economic growth. In this respect, the rise of Postmaterialist values reverses the rise of the Protestant Ethic. Today, the functional equivalent of the Protestant Ethic is most vigorous in East Asia and is fading away in Protestant Europe, as technological development and cultural change become global.[14]

If true, we would interpret the Protestant ethic as a set of values that are most common in societies of scarcity; they may be conducive to an emphasis on economic growth, but insofar as they reflect an environment of scarcity, they would tend to fade away under conditions of affluence.

Evidence for the Protestant Ethic

Work Ethic

What values are intrinsic to capitalism and how can the Protestant work ethos best be measured? Social psychological studies have used detailed multi-item scales to gauge orientations toward work, although a systematic meta-review of the literature found that they have generally been tested on small groups, rather than on nationally representative random samples of the general population.[15] These studies suggest that the most suitable scales measuring attitudes toward work need to be multidimensional, since the Weberian thesis predicted that the Protestant ethic involved a range of personal values conducive to early capitalism.[16] Table 7.1 shows the items from the World Value Survey selected to examine work values in this chapter. Factor analysis using principle component analysis revealed that these fell into three main dimensions. (1) The *intrinsic benefits of work* included items such as the priority that people gave to the opportunities in their work to use initiative, to achieve something, to gain respect, and to have interesting employment. (2) The second dimension concerned the *material rewards of work*, indicating that people who valued good hours and generous holidays also gave high priority to good pay, little work pressure, and job security. (3) The third dimension concerned broader attitudes toward *work as a duty*, which lie at the heart of ascetic forms of Protestantism, where people were asked to express agreement or disagreement with statements such as *"people who don't work turn lazy," "work is a duty to society,"* and *"it is humiliating to receive money without work."* The scales were recoded where necessary, so that a high score was consistent with more positive attitudes toward work values and the capitalist economy, summed across the items. The scores were then standardized to 0–100 point scales, for consistent comparison across the different dimensions.

Table 7.2 examines whether Protestant societies differ from other religious cultures in the priority given to the intrinsic and material rewards of work, as well as attitudes toward work as a duty. The results are striking and consistent across all three measures: contrary to the Weberian thesis, compared with all other religious cultures, *those living in Protestant societies today display the weakest work ethic*. The contrasts between Protestant and the other religious cultures are consistent across scales, although they are usually very modest in size, with the important exception of Muslim cultures, which display by far the strongest work ethic. An important reason for this pattern comes from the comparison of the same scales by the type

Table 7.1. Factor Analysis of Work Ethic

Var	Code		Intrinsic Rewards	Material Rewards	Work as a Duty
V91R	0/1	Value: An opportunity to use initiative	.740		
V93R	0/1	Value: A job in which you feel you can achieve something	.683		
V94R	0/1	Value: A responsible job	.649		
V96R	0/1	Value: A job meeting one's abilities	.603		
V89R	0/1	Value: A job respected by people in general	.544		
V95R	0/1	Value: A job that is interesting	.515		
V90R	0/1	Value: Good hours		.701	
V92R	0/1	Value: Generous holidays		.667	
V86R	0/1	Value: Good pay		.620	
V87R	0/1	Value: Not too much pressure		.528	
V88R	0/1	Value: Good job security		.510	
V99R	1-5	Agree/disagree: People who don't work turn lazy			.724
V100R	1-5	Agree/disagree: Work is a duty to society			.708
V98R	1-5	Agree/disagree: It is humiliating to receive money without work			.702
V102R	1-5	Agree/disagree: Work should always comes first			.651

NOTE: Factor analysis using Principal Component Analysis with varimax rotation and Kaiser normalization. Work values: Q: *"Here are some more aspects of a job that people say are important. Please look at them and tell me which ones you personally think are important in a job."*
Source: World Values Survey/European Values Survey, Waves III and IV (1995–2001).

of society; postindustrial economies today have the weakest work ethic, because rich nations place the greatest importance on the values of leisure, relaxation, and self-fulfillment outside of employment. Industrial societies are moderate in the value they place on the rewards of employment. But in the poorer developing nations, where work is essential for life, often with long hours and minimal leisure time, and an inadequate welfare safety net,

Table 7.2. Mean Scores on the Work Ethic Scales

	Intrinsic Rewards	Material Rewards	Work as a Duty
All	54	55	72
Type of religious culture			
Protestant	50	49	68
Catholic	52	52	72
Orthodox	51	55	73
Muslim	70	70	90
Eastern	53	52	75
Type of society			
Postindustrial	50	46	65
Industrial	53	55	74
Agrarian	61	63	81
Difference by religious culture	.537***	.542***	.628***
Difference by type of society	.330**	.496***	.794***
Number of societies	73	73	46

NOTE: For the classification of societies see Table 2.2. For items in the scales see Table 7.1. All scales have been standardized to 100 points. The significance of the difference between group means is measured by ANOVA (Eta) without any controls. Significance: ***P = .000. Work values: Q: "*Here are some more aspects of a job that people say are important. Please look at them and tell me which ones you personally think are important in a job.*" (Code all mentioned.) Intrinsic rewards: "*An opportunity to use initiative; A job in which you feel you can achieve something; A responsible job; A job meeting one's abilities; A job respected by people in general; A job that is interesting.*" Material rewards: "*Good hours; generous holidays; Good pay; not too much pressure; Good job security.*" Work as a duty: Agrees or agrees strongly: "*People who don't work turn lazy; Work is a duty to society; It is humiliating to receive money without work; Work should always comes first.*"
Source: World Values Survey/European Values Survey, Waves III and IV (1995–2001).

people place by far the highest emphasis on the value of work. The contrasts between rich and poor societies in attitudes toward work as a duty were greater than those generated by religious culture.

If we limit the comparison to Catholic and Protestant societies – the main focus of attention in Weber's work – some modest differences do emerge on individual items within the composite scales; Catholic societies, for example, place slightly greater weight on the value of pay and holidays. Protestant cultures give greater priority to jobs requiring initiative, as well as those generating interest and a sense of achievement. But overall, Protestant societies score slightly *lower* on the summary work scales than Catholic cultures, not higher, as the Weberian thesis originally predicted.

Table 7.3. Work Ethic by Type of Predominant Religious Culture, with Controls

Scale	Intrinsic Rewards 1–100				Material Rewards 1–100				Work Ethos 1–100			
	B	s.e.	Beta	Sig.	B	s.e.	Beta	Sig.	B	s.e.	Beta	Sig.
Type of religious culture												
Catholic	4.30	.261	.06	***	6.88	.245	.11	***	7.01	.192	.22	***
Orthodox	2.43	.358	.03	***	6.32	.336	.08	***	6.25	.137	.14	***
Muslim	29.08	.393	.38	***	21.3	.369	.30	***	9.52	.131	.13	***
Eastern	7.17	.416	.06	***	5.40	.391	.05	***	7.93	.129	.13	***
(Constant)	34.4				61.1				99.3			
Adjusted R² Block 1	**.034**				**.041**				**.098**			
Adjusted R² Block 2	**.046**				**.046**				**.163**			
Adjusted R² Block 3	**.114**				**.082**				**.199**			
Number of respondents	107681				107681				39377			

NOTE: Ordinary least squares regression models with block-wise entry with the value scales as the dependent variables. See Table 7.2 for the items contained in the value scales. The full model is illustrated in the Technical Appendix, Table A7.1. *Block 1* in all models macro-level controls for the *level of human development* (Human Development Index 1998) and the *level of political development* (Freedom House 7-point index [reversed] of political rights and civil liberties 1999–2000). *Block 2* adds micro-level controls for age (years), gender (male = 1), education (3 categories from low to high), income (10 categories), and religiosity. *Block 3* then enters the type of predominant religious culture, based on Table 2.2, coded as dummy variables. Protestant societies represent the (omitted) reference category. The coefficients can be understood to represent the effect of living in each type of religious culture compared with living in Protestant societies, net of all prior controls. *Value scales:* Significance (Sig.): ***P = .001; **P = .01; *P = .05. N/s = Not significant. s.e. = standard error. B = unstandardized beta coefficients. Beta = standardized beta.

Source: World Values Survey/European Values Survey (WVS), pooled sample 1981–2001.

Yet these results could always prove spurious if there is some other characteristic about Protestant societies that could influence these patterns, such as greater levels of higher education or the older age profile of the populations in these nations. To test for this, regression analysis was used at individual-level in Table 7.3, where the predominant religious culture in each society was coded as a dummy variable, with the Protestant culture representing the reference category. The coefficients can be understood to represent the result of living in each type of religious culture compared with the effects of living in Protestant societies, controlling for the other factors in the model. The results confirm the significance of the observed cultural patterns, even after controlling for levels of human and political development and the social background of respondents. Overall the work ethic weakened by levels of human development, as well as by the education and income of individuals, as expected. Growing affluence, and the development of the welfare state in richer countries, mean that work is no longer such an essential necessity of life, and people turn increasingly toward other opportunities for individual self-fulfillment. But even after entering these factors, all other religious cultures proved significantly more work-oriented than Protestant societies, and the strongest coefficients were in Muslim nations.

To examine the consistency of this pattern among particular countries, as well as systematic variations among richer and poorer Protestant societies, the scatter plot in Figure 7.1 illustrates the distribution in more detail. Societies that emphasize the intrinsic value of work most strongly *also* place the greatest importance on the material rewards as well (there is a strong and significant correlation between the two scales R = .618). The Protestant societies are scattered across the graph but are mostly located in the bottom-left quadrant, indicating nations that are consistently low on both the intrinsic and the material work scales. This includes the more affluent Protestant societies such as Finland and Denmark, but also Latvia and Zimbabwe. The United States is relatively high among Protestant societies in its work ethic, although moderate in comparison with all countries of the world. The Orthodox and Catholic societies are also scattered around the middle of the distribution, whereas by contrast most (not all) of the Muslim societies are high in both dimensions of the work ethic, including Jordan, Morocco, Indonesia, Turkey, and Nigeria, as well as Egypt and Bangladesh.

Our conclusion is reinforced by Figure 7.2, which compares how far people believe that work is a duty to society and how far they feel that work should be given priority over leisure. Fewer societies can be compared using these items, which were not carried in all waves of the WVS. Nevertheless,

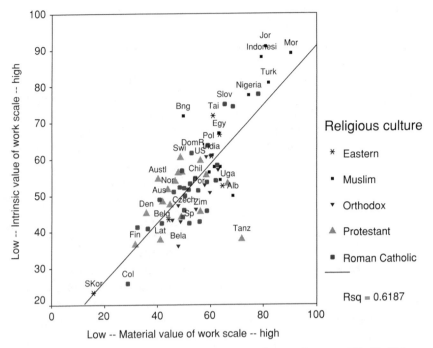

Figure 7.1. Work values by Religious Culture. Source: World Values Survey/European Values Survey (WVS), pooled sample 1981–2000.

the results confirm that many of the affluent Protestant nations express the least agreement with these sentiments, including Britain, the Netherlands, and the United States. Other cultures prove more mixed, but once more Morocco and Bangladesh, some of the poorest Muslim nations, place the heaviest emphasis on the value of work as a duty or calling. The consistency of this general pattern using alternative attitudinal indicators lends greater confidence to our interpretation of the results, suggesting that the findings are robust and do not depend upon the particular indicator that is chosen for comparison.

Of course the results are limited; contemporary survey data cannot tell us how these cultural attitudes compared in many previous centuries, and we lack historical evidence at the time of the Reformation. It is entirely possible that a strong orientation toward work as a duty characterized the Protestant societies of Northern Europe during the rise of bourgeois capitalism – and that this ethos gradually dissipated precisely because these societies were the first to become rich – and to shift toward emphasizing a more leisured lifestyle in subsequent centuries. Although some historians doubt the thesis, Weber's analysis could be correct for the historical era when he claimed that

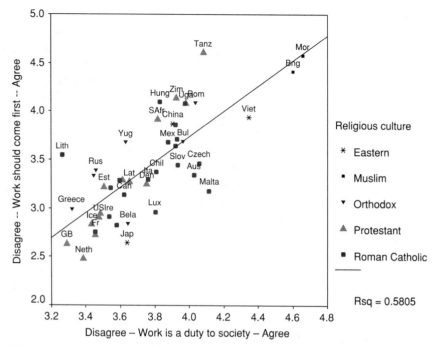

Figure 7.2. Work Orientations by Religious Culture. Note: Q: *"Do you agree or disagree with the following statements?"* (1) Strongly agree, (2) agree, (3) neither, (4) disagree, (5) strongly disagree. Q102: *"Work should always come first, even if it means less spare time."* (Agree coded high). Q100: *"Work is a duty toward society."* (Agree coded high). Source: World Values Survey/European Values Survey (WVS), pooled sample 1981–2001.

the Protestant ethos fueled the capitalist spirit.[17] But it seems clear that *today*, contemporary Protestant societies place relatively little value on the virtues of labor, in terms of both material and intrinsic rewards, especially compared with contemporary Muslim societies. Systematic survey evidence from a broad range of societies indicates that by the late twentieth century the work ethic was no longer a distinctive aspect of Protestant societies – quite the contrary, they are the societies that emphasize these characteristics least of any cultural region in the world. Any historical legacy, if it did exist in earlier eras, appears to have been dissipated by processes of development.

Attitudes toward Capitalism

What of broader attitudes toward some of the key principles of capitalism, such as attitudes toward the role of the market versus the state? We have already noted that Guiso, Sapienza, and Zingales, drawing on the first three waves of the WVS, concluded that religiosity was associated with personal trust, which social capital theory claims is broadly conducive to effective free-markets and better governing institutions.[18] The logic suggests that a cultural trait affects certain values or beliefs, and those beliefs in turn influence economic decision-making and thus economic outcomes. Yet the linkages in this chain of reasoning between social trust and economic growth remain controversial.[19] Guiso, Sapienza, and Zingales' more direct comparison of economic attitudes among Christian denominations, however, found mixed results: *"Protestants are more trusting and favor incentives more, Catholics are more thrifty and favor private property and competition more."*[20] In this chapter economic values related to support for capitalism can be compared by focusing upon four 10-point scale items concerning: (1) the priority of maintaining individual economic incentives rather than achieving greater income equality; (2) whether people should take responsibility for themselves rather than the government providing for everyone; (3) whether competition is regarded as good or harmful; and lastly (4) preferences for the role of the state or the private market in ownership of business and industry. Table 7.4 summarizes the mean distribution of responses by the type of religious culture and the type of society.

If we just compare Protestant and Catholic societies, Protestants are slightly more pro-capitalist in orientation on three out of four indicators. This does provide some limited support for the Weberian thesis. Yet comparisons across all religious cultures show a more mixed pattern, according to the particular dimension under comparison. Overall compared with all religious cultures, those living in Protestant societies gave the least support to the position that individuals should be responsible for providing for themselves, rather than the government being responsible to ensure that everyone is provided for. This response is consistent with the extensive welfare states and cradle-to-grave protection that exist in Protestant Scandinavia and Northern Europe, along with relatively high trust in government commonly found in the Nordic nations.[21] Compared with all other cultures, Protestant societies ranked toward the middle on attitudes favoring economic incentives over economic equality. They also were more positive than average toward the value of competition, and they were highest of all cultures on support for private ownership of business and industry, rather than state ownership. While the latter finding could be interpreted as approval of a key dimension of capitalist economies and private property, the overall pattern remains mixed. The evidence does not provide consistent support for the thesis that those living in Protestant societies today have a stronger commitment to free market economic values and a minimal

Table 7.4. Economic Attitudes by Religious Culture and Society (Coding of V143 still to check)

	Favor Economic Incentives over Economic Equality	Favor Individual Responsibility over State Responsibility	Favor Competition	Favor Private Ownership
	V141	V143	V144R	V142R
All	**5.9**	**5.6**	**7.5**	**6.1**
Type of religious culture				
Protestant	5.8	5.1	7.6	6.8
Roman Catholic	5.6	5.6	7.2	6.2
Orthodox	6.4	6.4	7.5	5.4
Muslim	6.4	5.4	8.0	5.6
Eastern	5.7	5.9	7.6	5.6
Type of society				
Postindustrial	5.7	5.3	7.2	6.8
Industrial	5.8	5.8	7.4	5.8
Agrarian	6.4	5.4	8.0	5.6
Difference by religious cultures	.120***	.131***	.097***	.182***
Difference by type of society	.088****	.080***	.110***	.177***
Number of respondents	188,401	204,949	187,400	172,549

NOTE: The mean scores on the following 10-point scales recoded so that low = leftwing, high = rightwing: Q141–144: *"Now I'd like you to tell me your views on various issues. How would you place your views on this scale? 1 means you agree completely with the statement on the left; 10 means you agree completely with the statement on the right; and if your views fall somewhere in-between, choose any number in-between ... "*

- Q141: (1) *"We need larger income differences as incentives for individual effort."* Or (10) *"Incomes should be made more equal."*
- Q143: (1) *"The government should take more responsibility to ensure that everyone is provided for."* Or (10) *"People should take more responsibility to provide for themselves."*
- Q142R: (1) *"Private ownership of business and industry should be increased."* Or (10) *"Government ownership of business and industry should be increased."*
- Q144R: (1) *"Competition is harmful. It brings out the worst in people."* Or (10) *"Competition is good. It stimulates people to work hard and develop new ideas."*

The significance of the difference between group means is measured by ANOVA (Eta). *** Significance: P = .001; ****P = .0001.

Source: World Values Survey/European Values Survey, Waves II to IV (1990–2001).

role for the state. Many factors may be influencing capitalist attitudes in any given society, such as the public's experience of government services, the benefits offered by the welfare state, and the performance of public sector industries.

Ethical Standards

Yet the Weberian thesis might still apply to contemporary Protestant societies, if we found that certain ethical standards, which grease the wheels of capitalism, were more pronounced in them. Willingness to obey the law, voluntary compliance with the payment of taxes, honesty in public transactions, and lack of corruption are all standards of public life that are widely believed to play an important role in the economy. Indeed, during the last decade the issue of corruption has witnessed a marked revival of interest among many international developmental agencies, including the World Bank and Transparency International. Widespread bribery and corruption in the public sector is now commonly regarded as one of the most important problems for economic development, as otherwise international aid only benefits the governing elites. Is it true that religious cultures play a critical role in setting certain ethical standards that encourage business confidence, investment, and contract compliance? The WVS contains four 10-point scale items that are designed to test the public's ethical attitudes, including how far people believe that certain actions are either always justified, never justified, or somewhere in-between. For the comparison, we take the strictest standard, which is the proportion that regarded certain actions as never justified. The items we compared included claiming government benefits to which you are not entitled, avoiding a fare on public transport, cheating on taxes, and someone accepting a bribe during the course of their duties.

There was a broad consensus about these ethical standards; Table 7.5 shows that overall almost two-thirds of the public thought that claiming false benefits, avoiding fares, and cheating taxes were never justified, with this proportion rising to three-quarters concerning bribery. Comparison across religious cultures shows that Protestant societies proved only moderately ethical on all four scales; usually slightly more ethical than the Catholic societies but not displaying the highest ethical standards across all groups; indeed, by contrast the Eastern religious cultures showed the highest disapproval of moral infringements. Any argument that today Protestant societies display higher ethical standards that may be conducive to business confidence and good governance is not supported by this analysis.

Table 7.5. Ethical Scales by Religion (% "Never justified")

Type of Religious Culture	Claiming Government Benefits to Which You Are Not Entitled	Avoiding a Fare on Public Transport	Cheating on Taxes If You Have a Chance	Someone Accepting a Bribe in the Course of Their Duties
All	61	59	60	74
Religious culture				
Protestant	67	61	56	76
Catholic	57	54	57	71
Orthodox	54	47	50	72
Muslim	66	71	75	81
Eastern	68	75	79	80
Type of society				
Postindustrial	66	63	56	75
Industrial	55	50	57	71
Agrarian	65	69	71	79
Difference by religious culture	.114***	.171***	.176***	.081***
Difference by type of society	.108***	.155***	.120***	.065***
Number of societies	75	75	75	75

NOTE: Q: *"Please tell me for each of the following statements whether you think it can always be justified (10), can never be justified (1), or something in-between."* Percentage *"Can never be justified."* The significance of the differences between groups without any controls is measured by ANOVA (Eta). *** Significant at the .001 levels.

Source: World Values Survey/European Values Survey, Waves III and IV (1995–2001).

Moral "Life Issue" Values

Lastly, to put these cultural differences into a broader context, we can also compare attitudes toward "life and death" matters where religious institutions have traditionally played a strong role and spoken with most moral authority in seeking to set standards concerning the issues of euthanasia, suicide, and abortion. Studies have commonly found that the type of religious faith plays a major role in explaining attitudes toward abortion in the United States, with growing polarization between fundamentalist protestants and liberals over recent decades.[22] Comparative research has also established that the strength of religiosity, and contrasts between Protestants and Catholics, influence abortion attitudes in Western Europe, as well as

Table 7.6. Moral "Life Issue" Values by Religious Culture (% "Never justified")

	Abortion	Suicide	Euthanasia
All	41	67	44
Religious culture			
Protestant	31	58	32
Catholic	45	65	43
Orthodox	25	69	41
Muslim	60	86	72
Eastern	40	65	34
Type of society			
Postindustrial	25	50	26
Industrial	38	68	42
Agrarian	60	88	65
Difference by religious culture	.480***	.526***	.596***
Difference by type of society	.575***	.715***	.705***
Number of societies	75	75	75

NOTE: Q: *"Please tell me for each of the following statements whether you think it can always be justified (10), can never be justified (1), or something in-between."* Percentage *"Can never be justified"* (1). The significance of the differences between groups without any controls is measured by ANOVA (Eta). *** Significant at the .001 levels.

Source: World Values Survey/European Values Survey (WVS), pooled sample 1981–2001.

broader moral values.[23] How do the differences among religious cultures that we have observed so far on economic attitudes compare with these issues? The WVS contains three 10-point scales measuring how far people felt that euthanasia, suicide, and abortion were or were not justified, similar to those already used to compare economic attitudes. Again we can compare those who believe that these issues were "never" justified as the strictest test.

The results of the comparison in Table 7.6 show that on these issues there were far larger contrasts in moral attitudes, both between Protestant and Catholic societies, as well as among all the world's faiths and by type of society. On abortion, for example, in Orthodox societies only one-quarter thought that abortion was never justified (where, under Communism, these facilities had long been easily available to women as part of Soviet reproductive policy). Similar sentiments were expressed by just under one-third of those living in Protestant nations. By contrast, in Catholic societies almost-one-half (45%) thought that abortion was never justified, rising to almost two-thirds (60%) of those living in Muslim nations. Equally strong contrasts were found among societies by levels of development; by far the most liberal attitudes toward abortion were evident in postindustrial societies (where only one-quarter thought it was never justified) compared with almost two-thirds (60%) disapproving in agrarian societies. Nor was this contrast confined to the issue of reproductive rights; instead very similar, or even stronger, patterns were found concerning attitudes toward suicide and euthanasia. This suggests that the differences by levels of development, and to a lesser extent by type of religious culture, were not confined to specific theological teachings, but instead reflected a broader and more general ethos toward these life and death issues. Overall, as expected, postindustrial societies were significantly more liberal in their moral attitudes while poorer developing nations proved by far the most traditional.

Again the results could be spurious, since liberal attitudes are commonly found to be closely associated with education and income. The multivariate models presented in Table 7.7 confirm that the impact of religious culture on moral attitudes remains significant, even after controlling for levels of development and for individual social background factors. Catholic and Muslim societies were significantly more traditional toward abortion, suicide, and euthanasia than Protestant nations. Those living elsewhere displayed a more mixed pattern. The impact of age has a significant and consistent effect in these models by generating more traditional attitudes across these three moral issues, while education and income, as expected, were persistently associated with more liberal attitudes. The effects of gender proved mixed, with women slightly more liberal toward abortion, while men were more liberal toward the issues of suicide and euthanasia. But after controlling for these differences, people living in Catholic and in Muslim societies proved consistently more traditional than those in Protestant nations across all three moral issues.

The scatter gram in Figure 7.3, comparing attitudes toward abortion and euthanasia, illustrates these contrasts most clearly among different societies. The most liberal countries on these life-and-death issues included some of the Nordic Protestant states, including Denmark and Sweden, as well as the Netherlands and New Zealand, and also some of the Catholic societies such as France, the Czech Republic, and Canada. By contrast, many of the Muslim states proved highly traditional, including Bangladesh, Algeria, Egypt, and Nigeria, as well as Latin American Catholic societies such as Chile, El Salvador, and Brazil.

Table 7.7. Moral Values by Type of Predominant Religious Culture, with Controls

Scale	Abortion 1–10			Suicide 1–10			Euthanasia 1–10		
	B	s.e.	Beta Sig.	B	St. Err.	Beta Sig.	B	s.e.	Beta Sig.
Type of religious culture									
Catholic	−.745	.024	−.12***	−.245	.019	−.05***	−.750	.027	−.11***
Orthodox	.684	.034	.08***	−.146	.027	−.02***	.069	.038	.01
Muslim	−.644	.038	−.08***	−.313	.030	−.05***	−1.43	.044	−.17***
Eastern	.072	.038	.01	.080	.030	.01***	.180	.044	.02***
(Constant)	−1.45			−.607			−.717		
Adjusted R² Block 1	**.097**			**.064**			**.096**		
Adjusted R² Block 2	**.121**			**.080**			**.119**		
Adjusted R² Block 3	**.151**			**.083**			**.145**		
Number of respondents	95625			95625			95625		

NOTE: Ordinary least squares regression models with block-wise entry with the value scales as the dependent variables. See Table 7.6 for the items contained in the value scales. The full model is illustrated in the Technical Appendix at the end of this chapter, Table A7.1. *Block 1* in all models macro-level controls for the *level of human development* (Human Development Index 1998) and the *level of political development* (Freedom House 7-point index [reversed] of political rights and civil liberties 1999–2000). *Block 2* adds micro-level controls for age (years), gender (male = 1), education (3 categories from low to high), income (10 categories), and religiosity. *Block 3* then enters the type of predominant religious culture, based on Table 2.2, coded as dummy variables. Protestant societies represent the (omitted) reference category. The coefficients can be understood to represent the effect of living in each type of religious culture compared with living in Protestant societies, net of all prior controls. *Value scales*: Significance (Sig.): ***P = .001; **P = .01; *P = .05. N/s = Not significant.

Source: World Values Survey/European Values Survey (WVS), pooled sample 1981–2001.

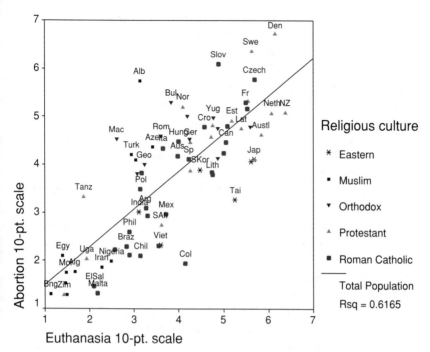

Figure 7.3. Moral "Life Issue" Values by Type of Religion. Note: Q: "Please tell me for each of the following statements whether you think it can always be justified (10), never be justified (1), or something in-between..." V210: "Abortion." V212: "Euthanasia – ending the life of the incurably sick." Source: World Values Survey/European Values Survey (WVS), pooled sample 1981–2001.

Conclusions

There are many reasons why we might expect that the moral and ethical values taught by the world's major faiths would exert an enduring impact on the publics living in these societies. Those who are brought up attending religious services as active adherents to these religions will be most exposed to the teachings of religious leaders, and their interpretation of moral standards in holy texts, but through a broader process of diffusion everyone in these societies might be affected by these cultural values. The claims of Weberian theory suggest that the church's values are important, not just for themselves, but also because cultural factors may have a decisive impact on patterns of economic growth and development. In particular, Weber argued, after the Reformation the ethos of Protestantism in Europe fueled the spirit of capitalism. But do denomination cultures continue to exert a decisive influence on economic attitudes and moral standards today? If secularization has weakened the strength and vitality of religion in affluent nations, then instead of the church imposing clear and distinct ethical standards and rules for society, we might expect contemporary modern societies to display a bricolage, or a diverse patchwork of moral values, beliefs, and practices derived from many sources.[24]

We cannot examine the sort of historical evidence that would unravel the relationship that Weber discussed between Calvinistic values found in Western Europe at the time of the Reformation and the subsequent rise of the merchant class of bourgeois shopkeepers, industrialists, and business entrepreneurs dueling early capitalism. What we can do, however, is see whether any legacy from Protestantism continues to stamp an enduring cultural imprint on economic attitudes in Protestant societies in the late twentieth century that distinguish these from other world religions. What the comparison reveals is that those living in contemporary Protestant societies display the weakest work ethic today, not the strongest, in comparison with all the other major religious cultures. Given the choice, those living in Protestant nations give roughly equal weight to the importance of work and leisure. On broader economic attitudes, there is a modest difference, with Protestant societies slightly more pro-free market on most measures under comparison than Catholic cultures. Nevertheless, Protestant societies are not *the* most pro-market across all religions. On ethical issues, it is not the case that Protestant cultures display higher moral standards of probity and honesty. By contrast, stronger differences by types of religious culture emerged on life-and-death issues, including attitudes toward abortion and suicide, rather than on economic attitudes. It appears that the teaching of spiritual authorities has greatest impact today regarding more basic moral questions. But as we have also observed throughout, long-term processes of societal development are also transforming these basic cultural values, moving publics toward greater moral liberalism on issues of sexuality and toward pursuit of opportunities for self-fulfillment outside of the workplace and economic sphere. We go on in the next chapter to see how far this process has also influenced the role of the church and religious institutions in encouraging engagement in voluntary associations and therefore social capital in local communities.

Technical Appendix

Table A7.1. Illustration of the Full Regression Model Used in Tables 7.3 and 7.7

	Duty to work scale			
	B	s.e.	Beta	Sig.
Developmental controls				
Level of human development (100-point scale)	−52.7	1.04	−.41	***
Level of political development	.857	.079	.09	***
Social controls				
Age (Years)	.206	.005	.21	***
Gender (Male = 1)	1.05	.146	.03	***
Education (3 categories low to high)	−1.58	.103	−.08	***
Income (10 categories low to high)	−.200	.029	−.03	***
Type of religious culture				
Catholic	7.01	.192	.22	***
Orthodox	6.25	.281	.14	***
Muslim	9.52	.409	.13	***
Eastern	7.93	.374	.13	***
(Constant)	99.3			
Adjusted R² Block 1 (Macro control variables only)	.098			
Adjusted R² Block 2 (Macro + micro controls)	.163			
Adjusted R² Block 3 (All controls + type of culture)	.199			

NOTE: This illustrates the full ordinary least squares regression model, with block-wise entry, in this case with the duty of work measured using a 100-point scale as the dependent variable. *Block 1* of the model controls for the level of development of the society. *Block 2* then enters the social background of respondents. *Block 3* then enters the type of religious culture, based on the predominant religion, coded as dummy variables. Protestant societies represent the (omitted) reference category. The coefficients represent the effects of living in each type of society compared with living in Protestant societies, net of all prior controls. *Level of human development:* Human Development Index (HDI) 2000, including longevity, literacy, and education, and per capita GDP in $US PPP (UNDP Development Report 2000). *Level of political development:* Freedom House 7-point index (reversed) of political rights and civil liberties 1999–2000 (www.freedomhouse.org). *Type of society:* see Table A1. Significance (Sig.): ***P = .001; **P = .01; *P = .05. B = unstandardized regression coefficient. Beta = standardized regression coefficient. s.e. = standard error. N/s = Not significant.

Source: World Values Survey/European Values Survey (WVS), pooled sample 1981–2001.

Religious Organizations and Social Capital

EARLIER CHAPTERS HAVE demonstrated that where religious values are undermined by the first stage of the modernization process, this influences
participation in services of worship. What are the broader consequences
of secularization for engagement in faith-based organizations, civic networks, and social capital in postindustrial societies? Mainline Protestant
churches in the United States – Methodists, Presbyterians, Episcopalians,
and Lutherans – have long been regarded as playing a central role in the
lives of their local communities. They are believed to do so by providing
places for people to meet, fostering informal social networks of friends
and neighbors, developing leadership skills in religious organizations and
church committees, informing people about public affairs, delivering welfare services, providing a community meeting place, drawing together people from diverse social and ethnic backgrounds, and encouraging active
involvement in associational groups concerned with education, youth development, and human services, exemplified by the Rotary clubs, YMCA,
and school boards.[1]

The role of churches in the United States raises important questions:
in particular, do religious institutions function in similar ways in other
countries, fostering social networks, associational activism, and civic
engagement? And, if so, has secularization contributed to an erosion of
social capital in postindustrial societies? To focus on these issues, the first

section of this chapter outlines Robert Putnam's influential theory about the role of religion in social capital. We then analyze the extent to which religious participation seems to affect belonging to voluntary organizations and community associations, both faith-based and non-religious, in different faiths and types of society. The last section considers the effects of religious participation on a broader range of civic attitudes and behaviors.

Putnam's Theory of Social Capital

Theories of social capital originated in the ideas of Pierre Bourdieu and James Coleman, emphasizing the importance of social ties and shared norms for societal well-being and economic efficiency.[2] Robert Putnam generated widespread debate when he expanded this notion in *Making Democracy Work* (1993) and in *Bowling Alone* (2000).[3] For Putnam, social capital means *"connections among individuals – social networks and the norms of reciprocity and trustworthiness that arise from them."*[4] This is understood as both a *structural* phenomenon (social networks of friends, neighbors, and colleagues) and a *cultural* phenomenon (social norms that facilitate collaborative cooperation).

The heart of Putnam's theory rests on three key claims. The first is that ① horizontal networks embodied in civic society, and the norms and values related to these ties, have important *social consequences*, both for the people in them and for society at large, by producing private goods and public goods. In particular, networks of friends, colleagues, and neighbors are associated with norms of generalized reciprocity in a skein of mutual obligations and responsibilities. Bridging networks are thought to foster the conditions for collaboration, coordination, and cooperation to create collective goods. Voluntary organizations such as parent-teacher associations, women's groups, and youth clubs are regarded as particularly important for this process because active engagement brings local people into face-to-face contact, achieves specific community goals, and encourages broader traits, including interpersonal trust. In turn, social capital is believed to function as an important resource leading toward a diverse array of benefits from individual health and happiness to child welfare and education, social tolerance, economic prosperity, reduced ethnic violence, and good institutional performance: *"social capital makes us smarter, healthier, safer, richer."*[5]

Moreover, in *Bowling Alone* Putnam argues that, as churches have traditionally played a vital role in American civic life, the process of secularization ② has significantly contributed to the erosion of community activism. Putnam regards religious organizations, particularly Protestant churches, as uniquely important for American civic society: *"Faith communities in which people worship together are arguably the single most important repository of social capital in America."* [6] Religious involvement is seen as central for American communities, with faith-based organizations serving civic life directly by providing social support for members and services to the local area, as well as indirectly, by nurturing organizational skills, inculcating moral values, and encouraging altruism. The decline in religious involvement during the twentieth century, he suggests, is most evident among the younger generations. *"Americans are going to church less often than we did three or four decades ago, and the churches we go to are less engaged with the wider community. Trends in religious life reinforce rather than counterbalance the ominous plunge in social connectedness in the secular community."* [7] Putnam suggests that the United States is far from unique in this regard, as a fall in church attendance is also evident in similar societies elsewhere: "The universal decline of engagement in these institutions is a striking fact about the dynamics of social capital in advanced democracies." [8]

Putnam also argues that social capital has significant *political consequences*, both for democratic citizenship and ultimately for government performance. The theory can be understood as a two-step model that claims that civic society directly promotes social capital (the social networks and cultural norms that arise from civic society), which in turn facilitates political participation and good governance. "Civic engagement" refers to a variety of activities, ranging from the act of voting to more demanding forms of participation exemplified by campaign work, party membership, contacting officials, and protesting. Others have confirmed the central role of churches in fostering civic engagement in America; for example Verba, Schlozman, and Brady found that being recruited to vote or to take some other form of political action through church, work, or other non-political organization was a powerful predictor of political participation, being approximately as powerful as education or political interest. [9] Rosenstone and Hansen argue that people are "pulled" into political activism by party organizations, group networks like churches, and by informal social networks. [10] Drawing on the American survey evidence available since the late 1960s and early 1970s, Putnam documents an erosion of traditional forms of conventional political engagement, exemplified by attending public meetings, working for a political party, and signing petitions, which he links with the decline in voluntary associations during the postwar era. [11] Putnam demonstrates that membership in many forms of civic associations, including labor unions, social clubs like the Elks and the Moose, and community organizations such as the Parent Teacher Association (PTA), expanded in the early twentieth century but then faded in postwar America.

But it remains unclear whether a steady erosion of membership in voluntary organizations has occurred during the postwar era, either in the United States or in other postindustrial nations.[12] Several investigators dispute the American evidence; Rotolo, for example, examined annual trends in American associational membership from 1974 to 1994 as measured by the General Social Survey, replicating Putnam's approach.[13] The study confirmed that some organizations, such as church-related groups, trade unions, fraternal organizations, sports-related groups, and college fraternities, experienced falling membership. But others had stable membership, and some groups, such as hobby clubs, literary groups, professional associations, school-related organizations, and veterans' groups, saw a substantial expansion in membership during these years. Wuthnow reaches similar conclusions concerning varied trends across diverse social sectors.[14]

The available research has generally failed to demonstrate a consistent and universal slump in grassroots affiliation across a broad range of associations in most postindustrial nations in recent decades. Instead, studies generally report diverse trends in membership and activism among different types of associational groups, for example a shrinkage in the mass base of trade unions in many (but not all) nations, but rising activism in new social movements, including those concerned with human rights, globalization, women's issues, and the environment.[15] Comparisons also reveal persistent differences in the strength and vitality of civic society among different cultural regions and nations around the globe, which may relate to the historic relationship between civic society and the state, such as sharp contrasts evident between Nordic societies and ex-Soviet states. Kees Aarts, for instance, reported trendless fluctuations in levels of membership in traditional organizations in Western Europe in the 1950s–1990s.[16] Historical case studies in particular nations have generally found a complicated pattern, for example Peter Hall examined trends in a wide array of indicators of social capital in Britain.[17] Membership in voluntary associations, he concluded, has been roughly stable since the 1950s, rising in the 1960s, and subsiding only modestly since then. While churches have faded in popularity in recent decades, environmental organizations and charities have expanded, so that overall the voluntary sector in Britain remains rich and vibrant. Case studies in Sweden, Japan, and Australia confirm similar complex trends.[18] An emerging array of studies of social

capital in post-Communist and developing societies also belie the existence
of any simple linkages among social networks and trust, human development, and good governance.[19] Therefore, although it seems clear that secularization has occurred in most affluent countries, it remains unclear from
the literature whether this process has contributed to an erosion of faith-
based organizations, such as church-related charities, social networks, and
youth clubs, as might well be expected; and it remains unclear whether
the decline in churchgoing has brought declining membership in community associations and engagement in civic affairs more broadly, as many
observers fear.

Comparing Associational Membership

To examine these issues, we will analyze systematic evidence concerning a
set of testable hypotheses. According to social capital theory, religious participation (defined as regular attendance at services of worship) is predicted
to affect:

i. *Membership in related religious organizations*, exemplified by faith-based
    welfare groups, where we expect the effects of religious participation
    to be strongest and most direct;

ii. *Belonging to a broader range of non-religious voluntary organizations and
    community associations*, for example, those concerned with the educa-
    tional and cultural groups, sports clubs, and trade unions; and lastly

iii. *Civic engagement more generally*, including social attitudes and polit-
    ical behavior, where we hypothesize that religious participation will
    probably have only a weaker and more indirect impact.

We will also examine the impact of intervening variables that could influence this relationship. In particular we will determine whether the linkage
between religious participation and these factors varies among different
faiths, for example between more "horizontal" and egalitarian organization
typical of Protestant churches and the more "hierarchical" organization
evident in the Catholic Church, as well as among different types of rich
and poor society. We will examine both the structural and cultural dimensions of social capital – that is, the strength of social networks (measured
by belonging to a wide range of associational groups), and the strength of
cultural norms (gauged by feelings of social trust). And since social capital is a relational phenomenon, found in the bonds between neighbors,
work colleagues, and friends, any linkages between religious participation,

voluntary associations, and civic engagement will be explored at both individual and societal-levels.

The empirical analysis focuses on two waves of the WVS (in the early 1990s and in 1999–2001) that carried identical measures of associational membership, as follows:[20] *"Please look carefully at the following list of voluntary organizations and activities and say . . . (a) Which, if any, do you belong to? (b) Which, if any, are you currently doing unpaid voluntary work for?"* The survey lists fifteen types of social groups, including church or religious organizations, sports or recreational organizations, political parties, art, music or educational organizations, labor unions, professional associations, health-related, charitable organizations, environmental organizations, and any other voluntary organization. The diverse range therefore includes traditional interest groups and mainstream civic associations, as well as some new social movements.

Levels of human and political development, as well as patterns of age, gender, education, and income, are often systematically associated with participation in religious services, as well as with membership in community associations and levels of civic engagement. The analysis therefore uses multivariate regression models analyzing the impact of religious participation with prior controls for levels of human and political development, as well as for the standard factors commonly linked to civic participation at the individual-level, such as education, income, gender, and age. Denominational differences may also matter; Robert Wuthnow has noted that in the United States, membership in mainline Protestant congregations generates the kinds of social networks, norms, and relationships that help individuals and communities attain important goals, encouraging volunteering, civic engagement, and political participation – but that membership in evangelical churches does *not* have these effects. He suggests that social capital in America may have fallen due to the demographic shrinkage of mainline Protestant congregations since the 1960s, in contrast with the rapid growth of Baptist churches and evangelicals such as Pentecostals, fueled by trends in population and immigration.[21] Levels of societal development are also relevant; we have already observed that religiosity is far stronger in poorer developing nations than in affluent societies. Nevertheless, associational membership is expected to be relatively widespread in postindustrial democracies, where parties, trade unions, professional associations, and other related organizations are well established among the professional middle classes in civil society. For these reasons, we also examine whether religious participation causes significant differences associated with the type of religious faith and the type of society.

(i) Explaining Membership in Religious Organizations

We will examine the impact of religious participation on belonging to church or religious-based voluntary associations, with the latter measured as a dummy variable. We hypothesize that attending religious services will be closely related to membership in other church groups, typified by congregations volunteering to help with Protestant Sunday schools, Jewish charities, or Catholic youth programs. The results of the multivariate logistic regression model in Table 8.1 confirm that membership in religious organizations rose with levels of human and political development; the growth of affluence, education, and leisure time, as well as the spread of civic society with democratization, boost membership in church-related associations, as well as belonging to many other interest groups and new social movements. Individual membership also rises with age and income levels, characteristics that have been found to be associated with civic engagement in many studies. But gender proves to be insignificant; the stronger religiosity of women appears to counterbalance the greater propensity of men to join most kinds of organizations.[22] Education also proves to have a negative impact, contrary to the usual pattern of participation; this suggests that faith-based organizations provide an important channel of community engagement for those who are religious but have lower educational levels. *Even after this battery of controls has been applied, regular attendance at churches, mosques, temples, and synagogues shows a significant impact on membership in religious organizations*, such as volunteering to help run faith-based charities, soup kitchens, and social clubs. Among those who attended a service of worship at least weekly, one-third belonged to a religious or church-related association, compared with only 4% of those who did not attend regularly. This pattern was found with every type of faith except Orthodox (which was negatively associated with belonging to religious organizations) and Islamic (with a positive but insignificant relationship, which reflects the limited number of cases from Muslim states). The relationship was strongest for Protestants and Hindus, where about one in four people belonged to a religious organization, followed by those of Jewish faith. Atheists, as expected, had lower than average involvement in religious organizations.

(ii) Explaining Membership in Non-Religious Organizations

Confirmation that church attendance is linked with belonging to faith-based associations is far from surprising. If this were all that it claimed, Putnam's theory would be trivial. Putnam's social capital theory, however,

Table 8.1. Explaining Membership in Religious Organizations

	Membership in Religious Organizations		
	B	s.e.	Sig.
Developmental controls			
Level of human development (100-point scale)	1.057	.1.42	***
Level of political development	.309	.015	***
Social controls			
Age (years)	.002	.001	**
Gender (Male = 1)	.028	.028	N/s
Education (3 categories low to high)	−.058	.019	***
Income (10 categories low to high)	.076	.005	***
Religious participation and type of faith			
Religious participation	.342	.008	***
Protestant	1.945	.128	***
Catholic	.331	.129	***
Orthodox	−1.22	.172	***
Muslim	.065	.135	N/s
Jewish	1.409	.250	***
Hindu	1.790	.191	***
Buddhist	.605	.166	***
None/Atheist	−1.013	.140	***
(Constant)	−6.519		
% correctly predicted	85		
Nagelkerke R²	**.356**		

NOTE: The table presents the results of a logistic regression model where membership in a religious organization is the dependent variable. The figures represent the unstandardized beta (B), the standard error (s.e.), and the significance of the coefficient (Sig.): ***P = .001; **P = .01; *P = .05. N/s = Not significant. Religious participation: Q185: *"Apart from weddings, funerals, and christenings, about how often do you attend religious services these days? More than once a week, once a week, once a month, only on special holy days, once a year, less often, never or practically never."* Membership in religious organization: *"Please look carefully at the following list of voluntary organizations and activities and say...(a) Which, if any, do you belong to? A religious or church-related organization (Coded 0/1).* Religious faith: *"Do you belong to a religious denomination"* If yes, *"Which one?"* If "No" coded None/atheist (0). Measured at individual level. Source: World Values Survey Wave IV 1999–2001.

makes a less obvious and more interesting claim: that civic society is denser and stronger if people belong to multiple overlapping categories, such as professional *and* philanthropic groups, or unions *and* environmental organizations, so that church attendance strengthens other overlapping linkages within the community. "Bridging" forms of social capital, which span different social sectors and ideological viewpoints, are strengthened by multiple memberships. Do religious institutions have the power to influence broader engagement in community life? To test this claim, we will compare the average number of *non-religious* community associations that people joined, using a 14-point scale summarizing membership in all the organizations listed in Table 8.3 except the religious or church-related category. Overall about half (50%) the public reported belonging to no voluntary associations, one-quarter (24%) belonged to just one type of organization, while the remaining quarter of the public were members of more than one type of group.[23]

Table 8.2 analyzes factors predicting membership in voluntary organizations and community associations. Once again, levels of political development are positively linked with associational membership; as many have observed, the growth of political rights and civic liberties, associated with the process of democratization, expands opportunities for participation in grassroots civil society. Human development is also positively related, although in this case the relationship proved insignificant. At the individual-level, higher education, higher income, and (male) gender were also associated with belonging to more groups, a finding already well established in the literature on political participation.[24] After applying these macro- and micro-level controls, the results demonstrate that *religious participation is positively associated with higher levels of membership in non-religious community associations*. Members of congregations were more likely than average to belong to a diverse range of voluntary organizations, as social capital theory claims. But this pattern varied by types of faith; Protestants had significantly higher than average membership in these associations, as did those of Jewish, Hindu, and Buddhist faith, whereas Catholics, Orthodox, Muslims, and atheists belonged to *fewer* than average groups. As Wuthnow found in the United States, Protestant churches may encourage a greater sense of engagement with the wider community than Catholic churches, although they are not unique in this regard.

To analyze how activism varies by type of association, Table 8.3 uses logistic regression models, with societal and individual social controls, presenting just the regression coefficients for the effects of religious participation on belonging to each type of organization, as well as describing the average membership for those who do and do not attend services of worship at least weekly. The results show that regular church attendance was most strongly associated with membership in associations concerned with the traditional philanthropic functions of religious institutions, including those for social welfare such as for the elderly or handicapped,

Table 8.2. Explaining Membership in Non-Religious Voluntary Organizations

	Belong to How Many Non-Religious Organizations (Vol-org)			
	B	s.e.	Beta	Sig.
Developmental controls				
Level of human development (100-point scale)	.070	.067	.007	N/s
Level of political development	.093	.005	.115	***
Social controls				
Age (years)	.000	.000	−.001	N/s
Gender (Male = 1)	.107	.012	.037	***
Education (3 categories low to high)	.178	.009	.093	***
Income (10 categories low to high)	.067	.002	.119	***
Religious participation and type of faith				
Religious participation	**.041**	**.003**	**.063**	***
Protestant	**.111**	**.030**	**.029**	***
Catholic	−.365	.044	−.112	***
Orthodox	−.815	.031	−.107	***
Muslim	−.446	.142	−.125	***
Jewish	.783	.096	.024	***
Hindu	.536	.062	.025	***
Buddhist	.256	.013	.019	***
None/Atheist	−.102	.028	−.029	***
(Constant)	−.396			
Adjusted R²	**.082**			

NOTE: The table uses ordinary least squares regression analysis where the number of memberships of all non-religious organizations is the dependent variable in the most recent wave of the WVS. The figures represent the unstandardized beta (B), the standard error (s.e.), the standardized beta (Beta), and the significance of the coefficient (Sig.). ***P = .001; **P = .01; *P = .05. N/s = Not significant. Vol-Any: Percentage belonging to at least one non-religious association. Religious participation: Q185: *"Apart from weddings, funerals, and christenings, about how often do you attend religious services these days? More than once a week, once a week, once a month, only on special holy days, once a year, less often, never or practically never."* Associational membership: *"Please look carefully at the following list of voluntary organizations and activities and say . . . (a) Which, if any, do you belong to? (Each coded 0/1 and summed into as 0–14 scale excluding belonging to a religious association.)* For the list of organizations see Table 8.3.
Source: World Values Survey Wave IV 1999–2001.

educational and cultural groups, local community action groups on issues such as poverty, housing, and racial equality, women's groups, and youth work. For example, 15% of those who attended services weekly also volunteered for social welfare organizations, compared with 9% of those

Table 8.3. Religious Participation and Associational Membership

	Attend Service Weekly (%)	Don't Attend Service Weekly (%)	B	s.e.	Sig.
Religious or church related	33	4	.342	.008	***
Peace movement	5	2	.280	.011	***
Women's groups	9	3	.200	.012	***
Youth work (e.g., scouts, guides, youth clubs)	9	5	.200	.011	***
Local community action on issues like poverty, employment, housing, racial equality	9	4	.141	.011	***
Social welfare services for the elderly, handicapped, or deprived people	15	9	.134	.005	***
Third world development or human rights	5	3	.113	.013	***
Education, arts, music, or cultural activities	18	13	.077	.004	***
Professional associations	12	10	.067	.005	***
Political parties or groups	12	10	.046	.005	***
Conservation, environment, or animal rights groups	10	8	.044	.005	***
Health-related	8	4	.028	.009	**
Sports or recreation	20	20	.026	.004	***
Labor unions	13	20	−.112	.004	***

NOTES: For details of the logistic regression models see Notes to Table 8.1. The models control for levels of human and political development in each society, as well as for the effects of age, gender, education, and income at individual-level. B = unstandardized beta; s.e. = standard error; Sig. = significance. Religious participation: Q185: *"Apart from weddings, funerals, and christenings, about how often do you attend religious services these days? More than once a week, once a week, once a month, only on special holy days, once a year, less often, never or practically never."* Associational membership: *"Please look carefully at the following list of voluntary organizations and activities and say . . . (a) Which, if any, do you belong to?"*
Source: World Values Survey 1999–2001.

who did not attend church so regularly. About 9% of regular churchgoers also volunteered for youth work, almost twice as many as those who didn't attend church so often. By contrast, churchgoing was only weakly related to other types of civic associations that are less closely related to the core philanthropic functions of religious institutions, such as membership in parties, professional associations, and sports clubs. The only organization that showed a negative relationship with churchgoing was membership in trade unions. The pattern confirms social capital theory's claim that the social networks and personal communications derived from regular churchgoing play an important role, not just in promoting activism within religious-related organizations, but also in strengthening community associations more generally. By providing community meeting-places, linking neighbors together, and fostering altruism, in many (but not all) faiths, religious institutions seem to bolster the ties of belonging to civic life.

(iii) Explaining Broader Patterns of Civic Engagement

Social capital theory argues that associational membership is only one aspect of this phenomenon, and we also need to examine whether church-going and membership in church-related organizations influence broader social attitudes including social trust, social tolerance, and confidence, in government, as well as civic activism and willingness to engage in political protest. In this regard we also need to examine both individual-level and societal-level relationships; social capital is essentially a relational phenomenon that exists as a collective good within each community, rather than simply an individual resource. As such, even though there may be no relationship at the individual-level between religious participation and civic engagement, there could be an important one evident at aggregate-level.[25]

Interpersonal trust is one of the most important components of social capital, for it is believed to foster cooperation and coordination, allowing communities to work together spontaneously without the formal sanction of laws or the heavy hand of the state.[26] Social trust was measured in the 2001 WVS by the standard question: *"Generally speaking, would you say that most people can be trusted or that you can't be too careful in dealing with people?"* This measure has several limitations. It offers a simple dichotomy, whereas most modern survey items today present more subtle continuous scales. The double negative in the latter half of the question may be confusing to respondents. No social context is presented to respondents, nor can they distinguish between different categories, such as relative levels of trust in friends, colleagues, family, strangers, or compatriots. Nevertheless this item has become accepted as the standard indicator of social or interpersonal trust, having been used in the Civic Culture surveys and the American General Social Survey since the early 1970s, so it will be used here to facilitate replication with previous studies. The other measures of civic attitudes and behavior include the propensity to engage in political discussion and the expression of political interest, confidence in the major political institutions (government, parties, parliament, and the civil service), voting participation, and actually having engaged in political protest, using the measures developed in the Political Action surveys, concerning signing a petition, supporting a consumer boycott, attending a lawful demonstration, and joining an unofficial strike.

Table 8.4 summarizes the relationship between religious participation, membership in a religious organization, and this range of indicators, after controlling for the macro- and micro-level factors used in earlier models. The pattern is inconsistent. We find that *church attendance* is associated with significantly *lower* than average levels of political discussion and interest, with *lower* levels of social trust (the opposite direction to that predicted by social capital theory), and with *less* participation in some of the more radical forms of political protest. On the other hand, all these indicators show significant and positive linkages with *membership* in religious organizations, with only one exception (political discussion). That is, people who belong to religious organizations display relatively *high* levels of civic attitudes and behavior, whether it is confidence in major political institutions, voting participation, support for democracy, social tolerance and trust, political interest and propensity to sign petitions, or participation in consumer boycotts.

Thus, different ways of measuring religious participation generate contrasting results. High rates of church attendance are *negatively* linked with civic activity, but high levels of membership in religiously affiliated organizations are *positively* linked with civic activity. Furthermore, the direction of causality is unclear; social capital theory suggests that *because* people interact face-to-face in church-related organizations, they learn to become more engaged in the social concerns and public affairs of their community. But the reverse causal process could equally well be at work – with people who are socially trusting "joiners" being most likely to engage in civic activity *and* to belong to religious associations. At this point, we can only conclude that *belonging to religious organizations does indeed go together with community engagement and democratic participation*, as social capital theory suggests – but the direction of the causal linkage is not clear. Simply attending religious services definitely does not seem to be conducive to civic activity; the more demanding activity of joining religious-linked organizations, does; we suspect that the latter involves a reciprocal causal process.

Table 8.4. The Effects of Religious Participation on Civic Engagement

	Religious Participation			Belong to a Religious Association		
	B	s.e.	Sig.	B	s.e.	Sig.
Civic Attitudes						
Political interest	−.032	.003	***	.119	.015	***
Political discussion	−.054	.004	***	−.056	.020	**
Social trust	−.003	.003	N/s	.083	.016	***
Social tolerance	.002	.000	***	.032	.002	***
Institutional confidence	.080	.004	***	.072	.017	**
Approve of democracy as an ideal	.272	.027	***	.848	.127	***
Approve of the performance of democracy	.138	.031	***	.485	.145	***
Political Activism						
Voted	.114	.003	***	.072	.017	**
Have signed a petition	.018	.003	***	.399	.016	***
Have joined a boycott	−.010	.005	*	.291	.024	***
Have attended a lawful demonstration	−.044	.004	***	.029	.019	*
Have joined an unofficial strike	−.065	.007	***	.066	.033	*

NOTES: All the models with dichotomous dependent variables use binary logistic regression, except for (i) with continuous scales, which use ordinary least squares regression. For details of the models see notes to Table 8.1. The models all control for levels of human and political development in each society, as well as for the effects of age, gender, education, and income at individual-level. B = unstandardized beta; s.e. = standard error; significance (Sig.): ***P = .001; **P = .01; *P = .05. Religious Participation: Q185: *"Apart from weddings, funerals, and christenings, about how often do you attend religious services these days? More than once a week, once a week, only on special holy days, once a year, less often, never or practically never."* Belong to religious organization: *"Please look carefully at the following list of voluntary organizations and activities and say... (a) Which, if any, do you belong to? A religious or church-related organization (Coded 0/1)."* Social trust: V25: *"Generally speaking, would you say that most people can be trusted (1) or that you can't be too careful in dealing with people? (0)"* Political discussion: V32: *"When you get together with your friends, would you say you discuss political matters frequently, occasionally or never?"* [% "Frequently" (1), else (0)]. Political interest: V133: *"How interested would you say you are in politics?"* (% "Very"/"somewhat interested" (1), "Not very"/"Not at all"/"Don't know" (0). Institutional confidence scale: Confidence in parliament, the national government, parties and the civil service, using a 16-point scale. For the questions and coding of the other indicators of civic engagement, see Appendix A.

Source: World Values Survey/European Values Survey, pooled 1981–2001.

Conclusions

Social capital theory has generated considerable controversy in recent years, as economists, sociologists, and political scientists have debated the claim that, just as the investment of economic capital is productive for manufacturing goods and services, so social capital encourages the production of private and public goods. The American literature has emphasized the function of religious institutions in the generation of social capital, in particular that mainline Protestant churches play a vital role in drawing together diverse groups of Americans within local communities, encouraging face-to-face contact, social ties, and organizational networks that, in turn, generate interpersonal trust and collaboration over public affairs. The theory suggests that people who pray together often also stay together to work on local matters, thereby strengthening communities.

The evidence we have examined tends to confirm the first part of this theory's core propositions – that religious participation (as measured by the frequency of attending worship services) is positively linked with membership in related religious organizations. Attendance at religious services is also positively linked with belonging to certain types of non-religious voluntary organizations and community associations. Finally, we also found that *membership* in religious organizations (but *not* attendance at religious services) was significantly associated with various indicators of civic engagement, including social attitudes and political behavior. The available database is inadequate to determine the causality in these associations, which requires panel surveys. But a process of mutually reinforcing reciprocal causation is probably underlying these relationships, whereby "joiners" who are active in local sports clubs, arts associations, and youth work, and who have a positive sense of political and social trust, also belong to religious organizations.

Consequently, whatever the other significant consequences, given the limits of cross-sectional surveys we cannot either prove or disprove that the process of secularization has weakened social capital and civic engagement. But systematic evidence, presented elsewhere, suggests that the decline of traditional hierarchical associations in postindustrial societies, including churches as well as labor unions and political party organizations, has been at least partially offset by complex societal developments that have transformed the nature of political activism. These developments have encouraged alternative forms of political mobilization and expression, best exemplified by the rise of new social movements, the surge in political communications through the Internet, and the expansion of participation in protest politics, through activities such as demonstrations, consumer boycotts, and petitions.[27] Given these important trends, the decline in church-going that we have observed in rich nations has been significant in itself, but we remain agnostic whether this phenomenon has thereby contributed to a decline in civic engagement. But has secularization influenced other important aspects of political participation, notably the process of elections, voting behavior, and support for religious political parties? The next chapter considers these issues.

Religious Parties and Electoral Behavior

THROUGHOUT THE CHRISTIAN world, popes, cardinals, and clergy once exercised immense political influence, sometimes bending kings and emperors to their will. They have lost this preeminent political role in modern Western democracies. Church leaders continue to take positions on controversial moral and social issues, ranging from gay marriages, the availability of divorce and abortion rights to questions of war and peace – but today, they are only one voice among many. Similarly, the once dominant function of the Church in education, healthcare, and alleviating poverty has been transformed by the emergence of the welfare state, so that even where faith-based organizations continue to offer these services, they are state-regulated and authorized by professional bodies. The role of religious symbols, rituals, and rhetoric has been reduced or abandoned both in public life and in the arts, philosophy, and literature. There is no question that the relationship between church and state has changed dramatically. Nevertheless, religion continues to have a major impact on politics. The rise of radical Islamic parties, and the consequence of this development for political stability in the Middle East, North Africa, and Asia, has revived popular interest in this phenomenon.

This chapter examines the impact of secularization on partisan support and voting behavior in the mass electorate. Religious dealignment, the evidence suggests, has diluted traditional loyalties linking Catholic voters and

Christian Democratic parties in postindustrial nations.[1] But has the process of secularization in postindustrial societies actually eroded the extent to which people vote along religious lines? Here, religion still seems to play a powerful role. In the 2000 U.S. presidential election, for example, religion was by far the strongest predictor of who voted for Bush and who voted for Gore – dwarfing the explanatory power of social class, occupation, or region. There was a stark difference in the 2000 election between "traditionalists" – middle-aged married voters with children living in the rural South and Midwest who came from a religious background, supporting Republican George W. Bush, and the "modernists" – including single college-educated professionals living in urban cities on both coasts, who rarely attended church, and who voted for Democrat Al Gore.[2] What are the common linkages between religion and support for given political parties elsewhere? And how does this relationship vary between industrial and agrarian societies?

Structural Theories of Partisan Alignment

The seminal cross-national studies of voting behavior during the 1960s by Seymour Martin Lipset and Stein Rokkan emphasized that social identities formed the basic building blocks of party support in Western Europe.[3] For Lipset and Rokkan, European nation-states were stamped by social divisions established decades earlier, including the regional cleavages of center versus periphery, the class struggle between workers and owners, and the religious cleavages that split Christendom between Catholics and Protestants, and between practicing Christians and non-practicing individuals who were only nominally Christians. These traditional social identities were thought to be politically salient for several reasons. First, they reflected major ideological fissions in party politics. Divisions over social class mirrored the basic schism between the left, favoring a strong role for the state with redistributive welfare policies, and interventionist Keynesian economic management; and the right, advocating a more limited role for government and laissez-faire market economics. Moreover, the religious division in party politics reflected heated moral debates concerning the role of women, marriage, and the family that have been discussed in previous chapters. Differences between core and periphery concerned how far governance in the nation state should be centralized with parliaments in London, Madrid, and Paris, or how far decision-making powers should be devolved to the regions and localities.

Lipset and Rokkan argued that organizational linkages gradually strengthened over the years, as the party systems that were in place in the 1920s gradually "froze," with stable patterns of party competition continuing to be based on the most salient primary cleavages dividing each society, such as social class in Britain, religion in France, and language in Belgium.[4] The electoral systems used in Western Europe when the mass franchise was expanded played a vital role in stabilizing party competition, reinforcing the legitimacy of those parties and social groups that had achieved parliamentary representation. Challenger parties, threatening to disturb the partisan status quo, faced formidable hurdles in the electoral thresholds needed to convert votes into seats and – an even more difficult hurdle – competing against the established party loyalties and party machines that had been built up by the existing major parties. Thus, patterned and predictable interactions in the competition for government became settled features of the electoral landscape throughout most established democracies. Lipset and Rokkan's structural theory became the established orthodoxy for understanding voting behavior and party competition in Western Europe, and in other established democracies such as Australia and Canada. In the United States, Campbell et al.'s *The American Voter* presented a social psychological model that gave central importance to the concept of partisan identification but which also emphasized that this orientation was deeply rooted in structural divisions within American society, above all those of socioeconomic status, race, religion, and region.[5]

Why did religious cleavages remain important in industrial societies? A large part of the explanation was the fact that the dominant churches in Western Europe had succeeded in creating organizational networks, including Christian Democratic and other religious parties, in the same way as trade unions had mobilized workers into supporting socialist, social democratic, and communist parties. The Church was linked with parties on the right that represented conservative economic policies and traditional moral values – initially concerning marriage and the family, and later including gender equality, sexual liberalization, and gay rights. In the United States, "born again" fundamentalist churches became closely linked to the Republican Party, especially in the South. During the early 1980s the Christian Right in America mobilized vigorously around conservative policies, such as the Right to Life movement advocating limiting or banning abortion, policies favoring the use of prayer in school, and later against legal recognition of homosexual marriage.[6] The role of religion in party politics elsewhere has developed within varying contexts. In Ireland, Poland, and Italy, for example, the Catholic Church has taken conservative positions on issues

such as divorce and reproductive rights, but in Poland the Church also became associated with nationalist opposition to the Soviet Union.[7] In Latin
American societies, the Church has often sided with liberal movements
and actively defended human rights in opposition to repressive states and
authoritarian regimes.[8]

The structural theory needs to be qualified. The mass basis of electoral
politics and party competition can be affected by such factors as the impact
of the Second World War or the end of the Cold War; the influence of major
electoral reforms on party fortunes; or significant expansions of the electorate.[9] Important shifts in the mass base of American parties, for example,
were triggered by the diverse coalition assembled by FDR during the Great
Depression, the postwar loss of "yellow-dog" democratic hegemony in the
South, and the emergence of the modern gender gap in the early 1980s.[10]
Nevertheless, until at least the mid-1960s, party systems in many established democracies seemed to exhibit a rock-like stability, characterized by
glacial evolution rather than radical discontinuities.

For most religious parties in Western Europe the two decades after
World War II were a period of unparalleled electoral success; in both
Italy and West Germany, the Christian Democrats became the dominant
parties during this era. Throughout Catholic Europe, including Belgium
and Austria, Christian Democratic counterparts became the largest or next
largest parties.[11] In postwar Britain, however, class was the dominant cleavage, reinforced by older religious divisions between high-Church Tories in
England and low-Church Liberals in the periphery.[12] Cleavages between
Protestant and Catholic communities deeply divided the electoral politics
of Northern Ireland[13] and in Latin America, Christian Democrat parties
have played a major role. Religion has also been viewed as a fundamental
political cleavage in party politics throughout the Middle East, South Asia,
and South East Asia, but until recently little systematic cross-national survey
data has been available to analyze electoral support in these countries.[14]

Theories of Partisan Dealignment

From the mid-1970s onward, a broad consensus developed in the literature
on electoral behavior, suggesting that the traditional linkages between social groups and party support have weakened, although structural factors
such as class, age, gender, and religion remain important predictors of voting choice, and there is little agreement among observers about the precise
reasons for this phenomenon.[15] Various observers have attributed trends

in partisan dealignment in established democracies to a variety of complex developments in postindustrial societies, including: the process of secularization, which tended to erode religious identities; intergenerational value change, leading to the rise of new issues that cut across established party cleavages; the impact of social and geographic mobility weakening community social networks; the rise of television broadcasting replacing older channels of political communications through partisan newspapers, personal discussion, and party campaign organizations; growing multiculturalism resulting from migration, which was generating cross-cutting social cleavages based on racial and ethnic identities; and the increased complexity of newer issues on the policy agenda, such as globalization, environmentalism, sexuality, and international terrorism, that do not comfortably fit into older patterns of party competition.[16] As a result of these processes, identities based on social class and religious denomination no longer seem as capable of generating unwavering and habitual party loyalties in many postindustrial societies as they were in the postwar era, opening the way for new types of parties challenging the status quo.

Electoral developments seemed to confirm these observations in many countries. New parties that were not based on the traditional social anchors of class and religion started to gain electoral momentum and parliamentary representation. These new parties ranged from ethno-nationalist parties in Canada, Spain, and the United Kingdom, to Green parties in Germany, France, Sweden and elsewhere, to the anti-immigrant radical right such as the National Front in Britain and France, and a range of diverse "protest" parties advocating cross-cutting moral and economic issues in Denmark, Italy, and the Netherlands.[17] In recent years, the decline of the Christian democratic parties and the center-right in Europe seems to have opened the way for electoral breakthrough by diverse new parties peddling a populist anti-immigrant, anti-multicultural campaign message. The most shocking recent example was the fact that Jean-Marie Le Pen, leader of the National Front, was able to supplant the Socialist candidate as the second strongest vote-winner in France's 2002 presidential elections; but other prominent successes won by such parties included the fact that Joerg Haider's far right Freedom Party won more than one-quarter of the vote in the 1999 Austrian general election; the dramatic rise of the neo-populist Pym Fortuyn List in the May 2002 elections in the Netherlands (linked with the assassination of its leader); and a surge in support for Vlaams Blok, winning one-fifth of the vote in Flanders in the May 2003 Belgian general election.

If the rock-like ballast of traditional social identities no longer ties voters to established parties, this is likely to have significant consequences by generating growing volatility in electoral behavior and in party competition; opening the door for more split-ticket voting across different electoral levels; facilitating the sudden rise of "protest" politics; and creating more vote-switching within and across the left-right blocks of party families. Moreover, this process should boost the political impact of short-term events during election campaigns, heightening the importance of short-term party strategies, the appeal of candidates and party leaders, and the impact of political communications, opinion polls, and the news media.[18]

Evidence of Partisan Dealignment

But has secularization actually eroded support for religious parties throughout postindustrial societies as a whole? Some light can be shed on these questions from the analysis of data drawn from the Comparative Study of Electoral Systems (CSES), presented elsewhere. The results demonstrate that religion remains more strongly and more consistently related to voting choice today than any of the various indicators of socioeconomic status.[19] In the pooled model used in the CSES study, comparing thirty-seven presidential and parliamentary elections from the mid- to late-1990s in thirty-two nations, almost three-quarters (70%) of the most devout (defined as those who reported attending religious services at least once per week) voted for parties of the right. By contrast, among the least religious, who never attended religious services, less than half (45%) voted for the right. The substantial 25-point mean voting gap based on religiosity is far stronger than that produced by any of the alternative indicators of socioeconomic status, such as education, social class, or income. Across all elections in the CSES, Catholic voters were significantly more likely to vote for parties of the right than were Protestants; and atheists were more likely to vote for the parties of the Left than were any other of the social groups examined. Religiosity was particularly strongly related to voting choice in Israel, the Netherlands, and Belgium – all countries where religious divisions have long been regarded as some of the most critical components of cleavage politics; but this was also true in such ex-Communist countries as Hungary and the Czech Republic.

Left-Right Orientations and Religion

The CSES provides evidence from thirty-two nations, including established and newer democracies, and both industrial and postindustrial societies.

The WVS covers a considerably wider range of nations, covering low-income societies, non-industrial societies, and Muslim and other cultural regions as well as industrial and postindustrial societies. Does the evidence from this broader range of variation show similar patterns? In particular, does it confirm the finding that the relative influence of religious participation, values, and identities is greater than that of social class? And what is the linkage between religiosity and voter choice in relatively traditional agrarian societies?

Classifying parties as belonging to the "Left" or the "Right" party is relatively straightforward among established democracies, but it becomes much more difficult when we undertake to compare the many parties in newer transitional and consolidating democracies, especially those based on personalized politics that lack a clear ideological or programmatic identity. We can, however, compare ideological orientations rather than voting intention, based on where respondents place themselves on a left-right ideological scale. Respondents were asked the following question: *"In political matters, people talk of 'the left' and 'the right.' How would you place your views on this scale generally speaking?"* The scale proved to be well balanced with minimal skew, and showed a normal distribution in all three types of society. We also found low non-response rates in most societies; even less educated respondents in poorer societies could place themselves on this scale. For descriptive comparisons the 10-point ideological orientation scale was dichotomized into "Left" and "Right" categories for ease of presentation. This 10-point ideological scale consistently proved to be a strong predictor of voting choice in those countries where the political parties could be unambiguously classified and placed on a right-left scale. Table 9.1 presents the proportion placing themselves on the Right half of the scale (those placing themselves at points 6 through 10), analyzed by type of society and by individual religious faith.

The descriptive results, without applying any social controls, indicate that religious participation was associated with Right ideological self-placement: across all nations, among those who attended services of worship at least weekly, 53% placed themselves on the Right; only 41% of those who did *not* attend this frequently placed themselves on the Right, generating a 12-point religious gap. This difference was relatively strong in postindustrial and industrial societies, but relatively weak in agrarian societies. The individual's self-described level of religiosity shows a similar pattern (not surprisingly, given the strong link that we have found between religious values and participation): 50% of those who believed that religion was "very important" placed themselves on the Right, compared with

Table 9.1. Support for the Right by Society and Religiosity

	Agrarian	Industrial	Postindustrial	All	Coef.	Sig.
Religious participation						
Attend church at least weekly	48	54	55	53		
Do not attend weekly	46	40	40	41	.112	***
Religious values						
Religion "very important"	48	51	52	50		
Religion not "very important"	45	40	40	40	.115	***
Religious faith						
None	52	37	32	36	.094	***
Catholic	46	49	45	47	.047	***
Protestant	47	50	48	48	.028	***
Orthodox	35	39	39	38	.033	***
Jewish	42	43	39	41	.007	**
Muslim	48	42	38	46	.033	***
Hindu	48	50	45	48	.015	***
Buddhist	76	63	63	64	.043	***
ALL	47	44	44	45	.049	***

NOTES: Left-right self-placement: Q: *"In political matters, people talk of 'the left' and 'the right.' How would you place your views on this scale generally speaking?"* Left (1) Right (10). The scale is dichotomized for this table into Left (1–5) and Right (6–10). The figures represent the proportion that is Right in each category, with the remainder categorized as Left. Religious participation: Q: *"Do you attend religious services several times a week, once a week, a few times during the year, once a year or less, or never?"* The percentage that reported attending religious services *"several times a week"* or *"once a week."* Religious values: Q10: *"How important is religion in your life? Very important, rather important, not very important, not at all important?"* The significance of the mean difference on the left-right scale is measured by the Eta coefficient using ANOVA. Significance (Sig.): ***P = .001; **P = .01; *P = .05

Source: World Values Survey/European Values Survey, pooled 1981–2001.

40% of those who viewed religion as less important. This religious gap was again in a consistent direction across all types of societies, although again, it was largest in postindustrial societies. Figure 9.1 confirms that the relationship between religious values (measured by the 10-point "importance of God" scale) and left-right self-placement also shows a similar relationship. In all three types of societies, rising levels of religiosity go with rising levels of political support for the right (with minor fluctuations in the trend line).

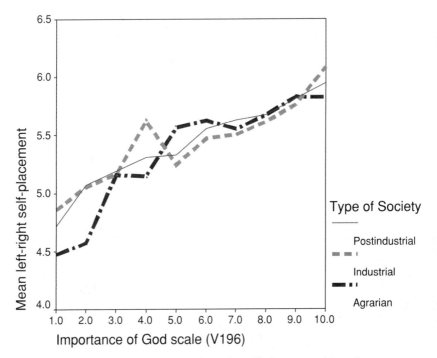

Figure 9.1. Religious Values and Left-Right Self-Placement. Note: See note to Table 9.3 for indicators. Source: World Values Survey, 1981–2001.

The contrasts by type of individual religious faith were also striking: only one-third of those who said they did not belong to any faith placed themselves on the Right half of the ideological spectrum, with fully two-thirds placing themselves on the Left. This pattern was clearest in postindustrial societies, and was not evident in agrarian states. Those of the Jewish faith were also more likely to place themselves on the Left than average, while Protestants, Hindus, and Buddhists were relatively likely to place themselves on the Right. People of the Orthodox faith tended to place themselves on the Left, but this is linked with the fact that the Orthodox tend to be concentrated in ex-Communist societies, where Left ideological affiliations are relatively widespread.

It seems likely that certain social characteristics that help to predict religiosity, such as age, could also be associated with more Right orientations. Multivariate analysis can help us sort out the impact of such variables. Table 9.2 presents a model with the full battery of developmental and social controls used throughout this book. In industrial and postindustrial societies the results show that religious participation remains a significant positive

	Agrarian				Industrial				Postindustrial			
	B	S. e.	Beta	Sig.	B	S. e.	Beta	Sig.	B	S. e.	Beta	Sig.
Developmental controls												
Level of human development (100-point scale)	−1.08	.235	−.05	***	−2.45	.548	−.04	***	2.43	1.74	.01	N/s
Level of political development	−.074	.021	−.04	***	.025	.014	.01	N/s	.977	.091	.10	***
Social controls												
Gender (Male = 1)	.179	.051	.03	***	.120	.029	.03	***	.199	.028	.05	***
Age (years)	.003	.002	.01	N/s	−.003	.001	−.02	***	.006	.001	.05	***
Education (3 categories low to high)	−.103	.040	−.03	**	−.212	.022	−.07	***	−.085	.022	−.07	***
Income (10 categories low to high)	.007	.010	.01	N/s	.005	.006	.01	N/s	.055	.006	.08	***
Class (4-point scale)	**−.053**	**.023**	**−.02**	*	**−.098**	**.014**	**−.05**	***	**−.147**	**.015**	**−.08**	***
Religious participation and type of faith												
Religious participation	**−.051**	**.015**	**−.04**	***	**.171**	**.008**	**.15**	***	**.151**	**.008**	**.15**	***
Protestant	.476	.098	.08	***	.393	.075	.04	***	.281	.077	.07	***
Catholic	.537	.107	.06	***	.321	.057	.07	***	.120	.081	.03	N/s
Orthodox	−.531	.172	−.03	***	.302	.081	.03	***	−3.71	.891	−.03	***
Muslim	.697	.096	.12	N/s	.035	.075	.01	N/s	−.242	.258	−.01	N/s
Jewish	.295	.285	.01	***	−.202	.332	−.01	N/s	−.670	.199	−.03	***
Hindu	.513	.114	.06	***	.331	.926	.01	N/s	.528	.464	.01	N/s
Buddhist	2.46	.302	.08	***	.631	.127	.03	***	.731	.133	.05	***
None/Atheist	1.04	.122	.09	***	.196	.052	.04	***	−.089	.082	−.02	N/s
(Constant)	6.54				7.23				−4.06			
Adjusted R²	**.025**				**.034**				**.067**			

NOTE: The table presents the results of an ordinary least squares regression model where ideological orientation on the 10-point left-right scale is the dependent variable, with left = 1, and right = 10. The figures represent the unstandardized beta (B), the standardized Beta, and the significance of the coefficient (Sig.): ***P = .001; **P = .01; *P = .05. N/s = Not significant. Religious participation: Q185: "Apart from weddings, funerals, and christenings, about how often do you attend religious services these days? More than once a week, once a month, only on special holy days, once a year, less often, never or practically never." Religious faith: "Do you belong to a religious denomination?" If yes, "Which one?" If "No" coded None/atheist (0). Measured at individual level.

Source: World Values Survey/European Values Survey, pooled 1981–2001.

Table 9.3. Correlations between Religious Values and Right Orientations

	Early 1980s		Early 1990s		Mid-1990s		2000		
	R.	Sig.	R.	Sig.	R.	Sig.	R.	Sig.	Chg.
Postindustrial									
Australia	.179	***			.113	***			−
Austria			.098	***			.163	***	+
Belgium	.391	***	.266	***			.173	**	−
Britain	.205	***	.111	***			.152	***	−
Canada	.148	***	.102	***			.065	**	−
Denmark	.263	***	.154	***			.095	**	−
Finland	.203	***	.139	***	.149	***	.208	***	+
France	.322	***	.281	***			.200	***	−
Germany, East			.306	***	.187	***	.219	***	−
Germany, West	.267	***	.224	***	.185	***	.220	***	−
Iceland	.137	***	.091	***			.087	**	−
Ireland	.244	***	.298	***			.267	***	+
Italy	.325	***	.288	***			.227	***	−
Japan	.097	***	.111	***	.136	***	.128	***	+
Netherlands	.346	***	.384	***			.164	***	−
Norway	.158	***	.126	***	.064	*			−
Spain	.434	***	.342	***			.360	***	−
Sweden	.151	***	.112	***	.048	N/s	.034	N/s	−
Switzerland			.188	***	.132	**			−
United States	.157	***	.220	***	.176	***	.172	***	+
Industrial									
Argentina	.270	***	.221	***	.233	***	.165	**	−
Brazil			.094	***	.081	**			−
Bulgaria			.258	***	.154	***	.154	***	−
Chile			.182	***	.077	*	.065	*	−
Croatia					.277	***	.194	***	−
Czech Rep					.188	***	.144	***	−
Hungary			.204	***	.158	***	.167	***	−
Latvia					.096	**	.129	***	+
Mexico	.160	***	.245	***	.090	***	.068	*	−
Poland			.140	**		***	.221	***	+
Portugal			.210	***			.136	***	−
Russia			.068	*	.065	*	.036	N/s	−
Serbia					.082	**	.066	N/s	−
Slovakia					.162	***	.221	***	+
Slovenia			.178	***	.252	***	.313	***	+
Turkey			.313	***			.314	***	+
Ukraine					.132	***	.192	***	+

(*Table 9.3 cont.*)

	Early 1980s		Early 1990s		Mid-1990s		2000		
	R.	Sig.	R.	Sig.	R.	Sig.	R.	Sig.	Chg.
Agrarian									
South Africa	.234	***	.109	***	.013	N/s	.003	N/s	−
Nigeria			.032	N/s	.014	N/s	−.013	N/s	
India			.157	***	.368	***			+
Bangladesh					.062	*	.183	***	+

NOTE: The coefficients represent simple correlations between *religious values* (measured by the 10-point "importance of God" scale) and *Right orientations* (measured by the 10-point left-right ideology scale when 1 = left and 10 = right), without any prior controls. Chg. represents change in the strength of the correlation coefficient from the earliest data point to the latest data point, where "−" = weaker, "+" = stronger. Significance: ***P = .001; **P = .01; *P = .05.

Source: World Values Survey, pooled 1981–2001.

predictor of Right orientations, even after entering controls for levels of human and democratic development, and the traditional social factors associated with ideological orientations including gender, age, education, income, and social class. Indeed in these societies, religious participation emerges as the single strongest predictor of Right ideology in the model, showing far more impact than any of the indicators of social class. Among the different types of faith, there is a mixed pattern, suggesting that this could relate to the political role of the church, temple, or mosque, but Protestants consistently emerge as more likely to place themselves on the Right than the average respondent in all societies. In agrarian societies, by contrast, religious participation is *negatively* associated with Right self-placement: the pattern that has been found consistently in industrial and postindustrial societies does *not* apply to agrarian societies.

To examine this pattern further, we need to examine the results within each nation, and also within each wave of the survey, to see whether secularization has generated religious dealignment and a weakening of the religious-ideological relationship during the last twenty years. Table 9.3 displays the simple correlations, without any controls, between religious values and Right orientations in each country and period. The results show two main patterns. First, the significance of the correlations demonstrates the consistency of the underlying relationships: those who regard religion as important to their lives are more Right in orientation in almost all nations, and at different time periods. The only exception is Nigeria, where the impact of religious values consistently proves to be insignificant. In large part, this reflects a lack of variation in religious values: almost all Nigerians consider religion to be very important.

Religion continues to be a relatively strong predictor of an individual's ideological positions. But we find indications that this relationship has weakened over time, as dealignment theory suggests. The summary "change" symbol in the right-hand column represents the shift in the correlation coefficient across each available wave of the survey: a negative polarity (-) indicates that the strength of the relationship between religious values and Right ideological self-placement has weakened over time, from the first to the last available observation. Table 9.3 shows that among the twenty postindustrial societies, this relationship has *weakened* in fifteen nations and grown stronger in only five (but these five include the United States). In industrial societies, we find a broadly similar pattern in which the correlations have weakened in eleven nations and grown stronger in only six. Lastly, in the few agrarian societies where comparison is possible over time, South Africa shows a complicated picture, in large part because of the ceiling effect already noted for Nigeria (almost everyone is religious); while India and Bangladesh both show increasingly strong links between religious values and Right orientations over time. The results suggest that religion has by no means disappeared as one of the factors predicting one's ideological positions. This is especially true in countries such as Spain, Ireland, Italy, France, and Belgium, as well as in Slovenia, Turkey, and Croatia, where the correlations between religion and ideological self-placement are still moderately strong in the latest wave. But there are indicators that during the last twenty years, this relationship has been gradual weakening as an ideological cue in most industrial and postindustrial countries, as predicted by secularization theory. This does *not* seem to be happening in the few agrarian societies for which we have time-series data.

Voting Support for Religious Parties

We have examined the relationship between religion and ideological placement on the left-right scale, but what about absolute level of support for religious parties? Let us compare the electoral strength of religious parties during the postwar era, as measured by their share of the vote cast in national elections in sixteen postindustrial societies from 1945 to 1994. Lane, McKay, and Newton classified parties as "religious," and monitored their share of the vote, in the second edition of the *Political Data Handbook OECD Countries*. The results in Table 9.4 and Figure 9.2 illustrate the trends,

Table 9.4. The Electoral Strength of Religious Parties in National Elections in Postindustrial Societies, 1945–1994

Nation	1945–49	1950–54	1955–59	1960–64	1965–69	1970–74	1975–79	1980–84	1985–89	1990–94	1995–2000
Catholic cultures											
Austria	46.9	41.3	45.1	45.4	48.3	43.9	42.4	43.0	41.3	29.9	42.3
Belgium	44.2	44.9	46.5	44.4	33.3	31.3	36.1	26.4	28.4	24.5	
France	26.4	12.5	11.2	8.9	11.5	16.2	5.3	5.2			
Ireland	19.8	28.9	26.6	32.0	34.1	35.1	30.5	37.7	28.2	24.5	
Italy	41.9	40.1	42.4	38.2	39.0	38.7	38.5	32.9	34.3	22.7	
Luxembourg	39.2	42.4	36.9	33.3	35.3	27.9	34.5	34.9	32.4	30.3	
Portugal							14.3	22.3	8.0	4.4	
Protestant cultures											
Finland	8.2		0.2	0.8	0.4	1.8	4.1	3.0	2.6	3.0	
Norway		10.5	10.2	9.6	8.8	12.3	12.4	9.4	8.4	7.9	
Germany, West	34.1	46.0	50.2	45.3	46.9	44.9	48.6	46.7	44.3	42.7	
Netherlands	55.4	54.7	52.5	52.2	47.4	41.9	37.8	36.7	40.5	27.0	
Switzerland	22.1	23.5	24.5	25.0	23.7	22.8	23.4	22.5	20.0	20.5	
Sweden						1.8	1.4	1.9	2.7	5.6	
Denmark				0.9	1.5	3.0	3.8	2.5	2.2	2.1	
Other religious cultures											
Japan					8.2	8.5	10.4	9.6	9.4	8.1	
Turkey						11.9	8.6	20.8	18.0	7.2	16.9
Mean	32.4	33.7	30.1	26.4	24.2	21.3	19.4	20.8	18.0	15.1	

NOTES: No religious parties with more than 1% of the vote were identified in Spain, Greece, Iceland, UK, Canada, New Zealand, the United States, or Australia. The table lists the percentage share of valid votes cast for religious parties in national elections. The percentage includes the CDU/CSU, ÖVP, and DC.

Source: Data 1945–1994: Jan-Erik Lane, David McKay, and Kenneth Newton. 1997. *Political Data Handbook OECD Countries. 2d edition.* Oxford: Oxford University Press. Table 7.5a. Data for 1995–2000 *Elections around the world.* Available online at: http://www.electionworld.org/election/.

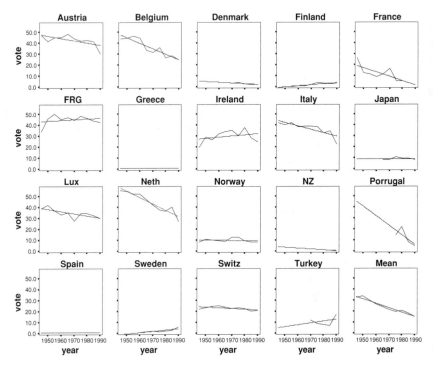

Figure 9.2. The Electoral Strength of Religious Parties in National Elections in Postindustrial Societies, 1945–1994. Source: Jan-Erik Lane, David McKay, and Kenneth Newton. 1997. *Political Data Handbook OECD Countries. 2d edition.* Oxford: Oxford University Press. Table 7.5a.

showing that a decline in support for religious parties has occurred during the last half century, especially in Catholic Europe. The decline of voting support for religious parties is sharpest in Belgium, France, and Italy (as well as a shorter-term trend in Portugal), with more modest erosion occurring in Luxembourg and Austria. By contrast, Ireland shows a slight strengthening of this relationship. Most countries in Protestant Europe, as well as in Shinto Japan and Orthodox Greece, show a pattern of weak but stable support for religious parties. The only traditionally Protestant country showing a sharp decline in support for religious parties is the Netherlands.

Conclusions

In earlier stages of history, one's religious identity provided a cue that oriented electors toward political parties, as well as toward their ideological positions on the political spectrum. In this regard, differences between Protestants and Catholics in Western Europe functioned as a cognitive shortcut, like the role of social class, which linked voters to parties; these linkages often persisted throughout an individual's lifetime. In recent decades, however, as secularization has progressively weakened religious identities in advanced industrial societies, we would expect to find that the political impact of denominational differences would also play less of a role in party and electoral politics. As a result parties that once had strong organizational links to the Catholic Church, notably the Christian Democrats in West Germany, Italy, and Austria, have become more secular in their electoral appeals, moving toward "bridging strategies" that enable them to win electoral support from many diverse social groups.

The pattern documented in this chapter at both individual and at macro-level is broadly consistent with these expectations; in postindustrial nations, religious values continue to predict a sense of affiliation with the political right, with a 15% gap among those who place themselves on the right among those who do and do not attend church regularly. This religious gap remains significant even after employing our standard battery of so-cietal and individual controls. This gap is also consistently found in many diverse societies, suggesting that there is a fairly universal pattern at work in people's ideological orientations. Nevertheless, we have also found that the relationship between religiosity and Right political orientations appears to have weakened during the last twenty years in most industrial and postindustrial societies, with some exceptions such as the United States and Austria. In an important sense, the bottom-line test lies in the votes actually cast in national elections – and we find that during the past fifty years, support for religious parties has fallen in most postindustrial nations, especially in Catholic Europe. This pattern almost perfectly reflects that which applies to patterns of regular churchgoing in Europe: as was demonstrated earlier, in both cases religion starts from a far higher base, and then falls more sharply, in Catholic than in Protestant European countries. Sec-ularization appears to be a process that started in Protestant Europe well before survey evidence began to become available, so that at the start of the postwar era, these countries already had lower levels of religious behavior and support for religious parties than those existing in Catholic countries. Consequently, during the past half-century the process of secularization has affected Catholic Europe most strongly, so that these countries are now approaching, but not yet attaining, the low levels of religiosity found in Northern Europe. And, precisely as we found earlier with regard to reli-gious practices, values, and beliefs, the United States remains an outlier in

CONCLUSIONS

Conclusions

Secularization and Its Consequences

SINCE THE SEPTEMBER 2001 terrorist attacks, and their aftermath in Afghanistan and Iraq, public interest in cultural and religious differences around the world has grown tremendously, and the debate about secularization theory and its recent critiques has seemed to become increasingly relevant to contemporary concerns. The idea of secularization has a long and distinguished history in the social sciences, with many seminal thinkers arguing that religiosity was declining throughout Western societies. Yet the precise reasons for this erosion of spirituality were not entirely clear. By the mid-1960s the popular claim that religion was in a state of terminal decline rested upon flimsy evidence. Its proponents cited empirical evidence of declining churchgoing in Western Europe, and a handful of case studies that fit the thesis, rather than a systematic examination of empirical evidence from many countries.[1]

It was not surprising, therefore, that during the last decade American sociologists mounted a sustained counterattack on the basic premises of secularization theory.[2] This critique put many former proponents on the defensive; Peter Berger recanted former claims, noting that many exceptions had accumulated that appeared to challenge the basic prophesies of Weber and Durkheim – pointing to the continuing vitality of the Christian Right in the United States, the evangelical revival in Latin America, the new freedom of religion in post-Communist Europe, the reported resurgence of Islam in the Middle East, or evidence that religious practices and beliefs continued to thrive throughout most of Africa and Asia.[3] Some of these reported phenomena may have been overstated, but the simplistic assumption that religion was everywhere in decline, common in earlier decades, had become implausible to even the casual observer. Too many counterexamples existed around the world. The religious market argument sought to reconstruct our thinking about the primary drivers in religious faith, turning attention away from long-term sociological trends in the mass public's demand for spiritual faith, and emphasizing instead institutional factors affecting the supply of religion, including the role of church leaders and organizations, and the role of the state in maintaining established religions or restrictions on freedom of worship for certain faiths.[4]

The attempt to reconstruct the early twentieth-century sociology of religion was long overdue but the religious market theory was, we believe, fundamentally mistaken in trying to generalize from the distinctive American experience to the world as a whole. It is clear that the U.S. public remains far more religious than the publics of almost any other postindustrial society, with unusually high levels of belief in God, prayer, and church attendance, but we believe that this largely reflects other causes than those cited by religious market theory. Moreover, the classic sociological thinkers never claimed that religion would erode universally; Weber's core argument was that the rise of rationality, following the Enlightenment, would undermine religious beliefs in the West. Durkheim claimed that the process of industrialization would lead to institutional differentiation, stripping the Christian church of key social functions. It is therefore knocking down a straw man to criticize these theories by pointing out that religion remains strong in countries that have not yet experienced the industrialization process.

This concluding chapter recapitulates and clarifies our core secularization theory, summarizes the findings from the evidence examined in this book, and discusses some potential criticisms. We also demonstrate how conditions of existential security interact with religiosity *and* with patterns of population growth.

Societies where people's daily lives are shaped by the threat of poverty, disease, and premature death remain as religious today as centuries earlier. These same societies are also experiencing rapid population growth. In rich nations, by contrast, the evidence demonstrates that secularization has been proceeding since at least the mid-twentieth century (and probably earlier) – but at the same time fertility rates have fallen sharply, so that in recent years population growth has stagnated and their total population is starting to shrink. The result of these combined trends is that *rich societies are becoming more secular but the world as a whole is becoming more religious.* Moreover, a growing gap has opened up between the value systems of rich and poor countries, making religious differences *increasingly* salient. There is no reason why this growing cultural divergence must inevitably lead to violent conflict, but it is a cleavage that fanatics and demagogues can seize, to use for their own ends.

Global differences over religion have been growing during the twentieth century, and this has important consequences for social change; for social capital, civic engagement, and partisan politics; and for the potential risk of cultural conflict in world politics.

The Theory of Existential Security and Secularization

Since there is so much room for confusion in debates about secularization, let us restate our theory concisely, making explicit the core assumptions and hypotheses on which we base our main analysis and conclusions. Our theory is not based on Weberian claims about the rationality of belief systems, nor on Durkheimian arguments of functional differentiation. These processes probably have some impact, but we will set these contentious claims aside in this chapter to construct a clear set of logical propositions concerning another process that, we believe, plays an even more important role. The theory of existential security and secularization developed throughout this book is based upon two simple axioms, illustrated in Figure 1.1, that prove to be extremely powerful in accounting for much of the variation in religious belief and practice that exists around the world.

The Security Axiom

The first premise, the security axiom, rests on the idea that societies around the world differ greatly in their levels of economic and human development and socioeconomic equality – and consequently, in the extent to which they provide their people with a sense of existential security. The more vulnerable populations, especially in poorer countries, chronically face life-threatening risks linked with malnutrition and lack of access to clean water; they are relatively defenseless against HIV/AIDS, malaria, and other diseases, and against natural disasters; they lack effective public healthcare and education; and their life expectancies are low and their child mortality rates are high.

Despite the spread of electoral democracy during the last decade, these problems tend to be compounded by lack of good governance, disregard for human rights, gender inequality and ethnic conflict, political instability, and ultimately state failure.

The World Bank and the United Nations Development Program (UNDP) have highlighted these conditions and the U.N. Millennium Development Goals urged rich countries to do more to cope with these problems. The U.N. development program is designed to help poor countries by reducing debt, and by strengthening aid, investment, trade, and technology transfers. The past thirty years saw dramatic improvements in some parts of the developing world: for example, the UNDP estimates that during this period average life expectancy increased by eight years and illiteracy was nearly cut in half. Some developing societies made tremendous strides, notably Taiwan, South Korea, Hong Kong, and Singapore, and parts of China and India have recently experienced impressive economic growth. There are also notable success stories in such countries as Botswana, Sri Lanka, and Mexico. Nevertheless the UNDP reports that worldwide progress has been erratic during the last decade, with some reversals: fully fifty-four countries (twenty of them in Africa) are poorer now than in 1990; in thirty-four countries, life expectancy has fallen; in twenty-one nations the Human Development Index declined. In Africa, trends in HIV/AIDS and hunger are worsening.[5] The gap between living conditions in rich and poor societies is growing.

The Cultural Traditions Axiom

Our theory also builds upon the premise that the predominant religious beliefs, values, and practices in any society are rooted in long-standing cultural traditions and histories. The religious traditions of Protestants and Catholics, Hindu and Muslim, shape the values, practices, and beliefs of people living in these societies, even if they never set foot in a church, temple, or mosque, or if they personally adhere to a minority faith. These religious and cultural differences mean that we need to be cautious in generalizing across countries; attendance at services of worship, for example, and the role of prayer or meditation, are less important rituals in some faiths than in others. The symbolic meaning of similar religious acts differs worldwide: in Tokyo spiritual expression might mean stopping at a Shinto shrine to celebrate the New Year or welcoming visiting ancestral spirits in the midsummer feast of lights; in Algeria religious behavior might mean visiting Mecca for the Great Pilgrimage at least once in their lifetime, as well as alms-giving, the daily prayer ritual, and Friday worship in the Mosque; in Italy, pious observation might mean attending Mass every day and observing confirmation and confession.

As the result of this diversity of beliefs and rituals, it is sometimes assumed that it is impossible to compare religions, because each is *sui generis*. We agree that one needs to be sensitive to variations in the core ideas, symbolic ceremonies, and specific rituals found among the world's faiths, denominations, and sects. But cross-national surveys can compare certain core common elements shared by major world faiths, namely religious *values* and the self-identified importance of religion for each person, whatever its particular form and beliefs. We can also examine core religious *practices* (measured by attendance at services of worship and by regular prayer or meditation), regardless of the specific ceremonies and rituals that are practiced. We do not seek to compare the specific forms of theology, such as the meaning of faith for Catholics, interpretations of the divine in Christian scriptures, the doctrine of Buddhism, Hinduism, or Baha'ism, the ceremonial rites of passage in Taoism, or the alternative forms of New Age spirituality that are becoming popular in the West. We do analyze the extent to which people in different societies and regions believe religion to be important in their lives, and how often they engage in worship and prayer, as core common religious practices. Our analysis indicates that these components of religion are cross-culturally comparable, and that they have a powerful impact on people's worldviews and behavior.

Hypotheses

A series of key propositions flow from these premises, tested throughout this book. None of these hypotheses are particularly startling, but they are building blocks that, when put together, cause us to rethink traditional accounts of the secularization process, and cast doubt on the most influential recent alternative, the supply-side theory.

1. The Religious Values Hypothesis

Our first hypothesis holds that the conditions that people experience in their formative years have a profound impact upon their cultural values. Growing up in societies in which survival is uncertain is conducive to a strong emphasis on religion; conversely, experiencing high levels of existential security throughout one's formative years reduces the subjective importance of religion in people's lives. This hypothesis diverges sharply from the religious market assumption that demand for religion is constant. On the contrary, our interpretation implies that the demand for religion should be far stronger among low-income nations than among rich ones; and among the less secure strata of society than among the affluent. We hypothesized that as a society moves past the early stages of industrialization, and life becomes less nasty, less brutish, and longer, people tend to become more secular in their orientations.

Analysis of data from societies around the world revealed that the extent to which people emphasize religion and engage in religious behavior could, indeed, be predicted with considerable accuracy from a society's level of economic development and other indicators of human development. Multivariate analysis demonstrated that a few basic developmental indicators such as per capita GNP, rates of AIDS/HIV, access to an improved water source, or the number of doctors per 100,000 people, predicted with remarkable precision how frequently the people of a given society worshiped or prayed. These factors explain most of the variance even without taking into account the specific belief-systems of given countries, or the institutional structures of religion, such as the organizational characteristics and financial resources of evangelical churches in Latin America, the philanthropic efforts of Catholic missionaries, the legal-institutional state regulation of freedom of worship in post-Communist Europe, or the role of the clergy in Africa. The most crucial explanatory variables are those that differentiate between vulnerable societies, and societies in which survival is so secure that people take it for granted during their formative years.

2. The Religious Cultures Hypothesis

Our theory hypothesizes that, although rising levels of existential security are conducive to secularization, cultural change is path-dependent: the historically predominant religious tradition of a given society tends to leave a lasting impact on religious beliefs and other social norms, ranging from approval of divorce, to gender roles, tolerance of homosexuality, and work orientations. Where a society started continues to influence where it is at later points in time, so that the citizens of historically Protestant societies continue to show values that are distinct from those prevailing in historically Catholic or Hindu or Orthodox or Confucian societies. These cross-national differences do not reflect the influence of the religious authorities today – they persist even in societies where the vast majority no longer attends church. They reflect historical influences that shaped given national cultures, and today affect the entire population; thus, within the

Netherlands, Catholics, Protestants, and those who have left the church all tend to share a common national value system that is very distinctive in global perspective.

A society's historical heritage leaves a lasting imprint, but the process of secularization tends to bring systematic cultural changes that move in a predictable direction, diminishing the importance of religion in people's lives and weakening allegiance to traditional cultural norms, making people more tolerant of divorce, abortion, homosexuality, and cultural change in general. It may seem paradoxical to claim that economic development brings systematic changes *and* that a society's cultural heritage continues to influence it, but it is not: if every society in the world were moving in the same direction, at the same rate of speed, they would remain as far apart as ever, and would never converge.

The reality is not that simple, of course: secularization started earliest and has moved farthest in the most economically developed countries; and little or no secularization has taken place in the low-income countries. But this means that the cultural differences linked with economic development not only are not shrinking, they are growing *larger*. Secularization and the persistence of cultural differences are perfectly compatible.

Weber claimed that Protestantism reshaped attitudes toward work, which had a decisive impact on economic growth and development, fueling the spirit of capitalism. But the very fact that the historically Protestant countries were the first to industrialize and attain high levels of mass existential security means that they should tend to have relatively secularized cultures today. Similarly, survey evidence reveals that those living in contemporary Protestant societies have the weakest, not the strongest, adherence to the work ethic today, in comparison with all the other major religious cultures. Those living in Protestant nations today give roughly equal weight to the values of work and leisure, whereas the publics of most other societies give overwhelming priority to work. A society's religious heritage has a lasting imprint on moral issues, such as attitudes toward abortion and suicide. But as we have observed, long-term processes of development are transforming basic cultural values, moving publics toward moral liberalism on issues of sexuality and toward pursuit of opportunities for self-fulfillment outside of the workplace and economic sphere.

Another influential thesis that we examined was Samuel Huntington's "clash of civilizations" thesis, which claims that one of the most important cultural divisions between the Western and Muslim worlds concerns differences over democratic political values. In the post–Cold War era,

Huntington argues that this "culture clash" is a major potential source of international and domestic conflict. The comparative evidence in Chapter 6 points to four main findings. First, when we compared political attitudes (including evaluations of how well democracy works in practice, support for democratic ideals, and disapproval of authoritarian leadership), far from a "clash of values," we found only modest differences between the Islamic world and the West. Instead, the largest cleavage over democratic values was between ex-Soviet states in Eastern European countries (such as Russia, Ukraine, and Moldova), which display minimal support for democracy, and most other countries that display far more positive attitudes, including both Western *and* Islamic nations. This pattern could as plausibly be explained as reflecting the residual legacy of the Cold War and a realistic evaluation of the actual performance of democracy in these states, as by the reemergence of ethnic conflict based on the values of the Orthodox Church. We did find that support for a strong role by religious authorities is stronger in Muslim societies than in the West, but again it is not a simple dichotomy; many other types of society also support an active role for religious leaders in public life, including the Sub-Saharan African countries and Latin American countries.

It is clear that religious cultures have an important impact (which was underestimated by Huntington) in predicting beliefs about gender equality and sexual liberalization. In this regard, the West is far more egalitarian and liberal than all other societies, particularly Muslim nations. Generational comparisons suggest that this gap has steadily widened as the younger birth cohorts in the West have gradually become more liberal in their sexual mores while the younger cohorts in Islamic societies remain deeply traditional. The results suggest that modern Western societies are indeed different, especially concerning the transformation of orientations associated with the sexual revolution that occurred in recent decades, fundamental changes in the nature of modern families, and more expressive lifestyles. Equality for women has progressed much further, and transformed traditional cultural beliefs and values about the appropriate division of sex roles far more deeply, in affluent Western societies than in the rest of the world, but these changes are beginning to reshape prosperous East Asian societies as well. Support for gender equality and tolerance of divorce, homosexuality, and so forth are not part of the Western Christian tradition – they are recent developments even there – and are not uniquely Western. They are cultural changes linked with high levels of economic development and the emergence of the knowledge society.

3. The Religious Participation Hypothesis

We expected that religious values and beliefs would heavily influence religious practices, such as attendance at services of worship and the frequency of prayer or meditation. The evidence strongly supports this expectation; Figure 10.1 compares the mean frequency of attendance in religious services against the strength of religious values in each society (using a four-point scale to monitor the importance of religion). The graph shows a remarkably strong correlation ($R^2 = .73$); religious values seem to have a strong impact on religious participation in most countries. Countries located in the bottom left-hand corner, such as the Czech Republic, Denmark, and France, consistently displayed relatively secular orientations on both indicators. By contrast, other societies located in the top right quadrant, such as South Africa, the United States, and El Salvador, are consistently highly religious by both measures. Yet a number of outliers were also evident, where religious participation was higher than expected, falling above the regression line near the top right corner, notably Nigeria, Uganda, and Zimbabwe, as well as Ireland, Poland, and India. In these societies, other factors seem to be important in encouraging religious engagement, such as social norms, communal networks, and informal group pressures to attend services for those living in highly religious communities. In the bottom right quadrant, located below the regression line, Muslims living in Iran, Turkey, and Egypt regarded religion as very important to their lives, yet fewer than expected actually participated regularly in worship services.

We followed a similar procedure to examine the relationship between core religious beliefs and patterns of religious participation. Some writers suggest that an important distinction can be drawn between "belonging" and "believing." Thus, Grace Davie argues that in Britain the shrinking number of people attending church services has not been accompanied by a widespread decline in religious beliefs.[6] In Western Europe as a whole, Davie argues that similar patterns can be observed: *"Western Europeans are unchurched populations, rather than simply secular. For a marked falling-off in religious attendance (especially in the Protestant North) has not resulted, yet, in the abdication of religious belief."*[7] Opinion polls also suggest the persistence of widespread adherence to many of the core ideas and beliefs in Christianity in the United States. As Wilcox and Jelen summarized the evidence, linking beliefs and participation:

> The United States has a remarkably high level of religious belief and observance, a fact that makes the country an outlier in the well-established

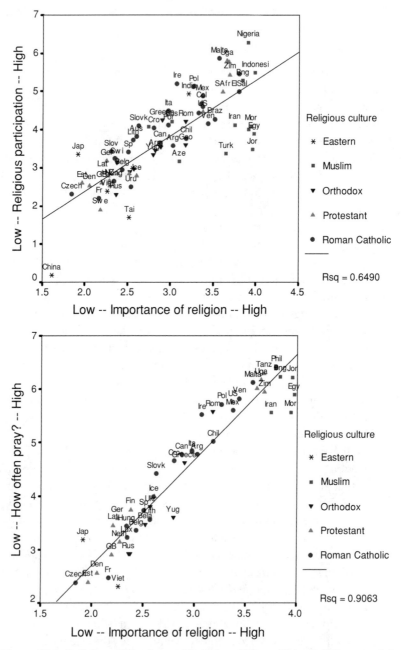

Figure 10.1. Religious Behavior and Religious Values. Note: Religious participation: Q185: *"Apart from weddings, funerals, and christenings, about how often do you attend religious services these days? More than once a week, once a week, once a month, only on special holy days, once a year, less often, never or practically never."* Source: World Values Survey, pooled 1981–2001.

relationship between socioeconomic development and religious observance. Citizens in the United States are more likely to believe in a personal God, in an afterlife, in heaven, and especially in Satan and hell than are citizens in Europe. They are more likely to attend church weekly or more often and to pray regularly.[8]

Andrew Greeley has suggested that many Central and Eastern European societies have also experienced a recent resurgence of spiritual beliefs, with the demise of the Soviet Union opening the door to freedom of worship in post-Communist states.[9] Systematic cross-national evidence comparing religious beliefs in much of the rest of the world is scarce, although observers have cited various signs of faith-based revivals and counter-secular movements including the strength of Orthodox Judaism in Israeli politics, the spread of evangelical Protestantism in Latin America, and the strength of conservative Islamic movements in some Middle Eastern and North African nations.[10]

The strength of common religious beliefs can be compared using a simple 4-point scale, summarizing faith in the existence of heaven, hell, life after death, and whether people have a soul. These items have varying shades of meaning and emphasis in diverse faiths, creeds, and sects,[11] but they go together to form a Religious Belief scale that has a high degree of statistical reliability and internal consistency across each of the major types of religion, suggesting that they tap a common dimension of core beliefs.[12] As Figure 10.2 illustrates, the strength of religious beliefs also predicts a country's level of religious participation with a fair degree of accuracy ($R^2 = .476$), although there was a broader scattering of societies around the regression line than was found with the measure of religious values. Nigeria, Uganda, Ireland, India, and the Philippines all showed higher levels of participation than would be expected from the strength of religious beliefs alone, while Egypt, Turkey, and Iran again proved lower than expected, suggesting that contingent factors in these countries help shape religious practice.

The distinctively high levels of churchgoing in the United States can be accounted for by the strength of religious values and beliefs in America, with this country falling where expected on the regression line – which still leaves open the question *why* all these indicators of religiosity are stronger in America than in most other rich postindustrial societies. One possibility is the fact that the United States was founded by religious refugees, who attached so much importance to religion that they were willing to risk their lives in a dangerous new environment in order to be able to

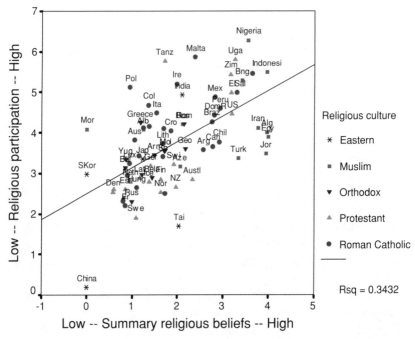

Figure 10.2. Religious Participation and Beliefs. Note: Religious Participation: Q185: *Apart from weddings, funerals, and christenings, about how often do you attend religious services these days? More than once a week, once a week, once a month, only on special holy days, once a year, less often, never or practically never."* The proportion that attended *"Once a week or more."* Source: World Values Survey, pooled 1981–2001.

practice their religion – and were able to transmit this outlook, to some extent, to succeeding waves of immigrants. We do not have data that enables us to test this hypothesis, but in Chapter 4 we examined another possibility, finding evidence that existential security interacts with conditions of socioeconomic equality. The United States has a less comprehensive social welfare safety net than most other countries with comparable levels of economic development, so that many still experience existential insecurity – a situation also found in many oil-rich states. One manifestation of this is the fact that life expectancy is slightly lower in America than in most other rich nations. The particular pattern of immigration and multiculturalism that characterizes the United States may also contribute toward this phenomenon; America contains many first- and second-generation migrants drawn originally from poorer nations in Central and South America, as well as from poorer countries in Asia, bringing relatively strong religiosity with them.[13]

4. The Civic Engagement Hypothesis

We also predicted (our fifth hypothesis) that greater engagement in religious practices would encourage political and social activism, and hence social capital and civic engagement, whether expressed through belonging to faith-based organizations, membership in civic society groups, or support for political parties. Social capital theory has attracted extensive interest in recent years, as many social scientists have sought to explore the role of voluntary associations and civic organizations. The claim of this theory is that social capital fosters the production of private goods (benefiting the individual) and also public goods (benefiting society). Social capital is regarded as generating capacity building for communities, just as the investment of economic capital is productive for manufacturing goods and services. Studies have emphasized that in the United States, mainline Protestant churches play a vital role in "bridging" diverse groups within local communities, encouraging the face-to-face contact, social linkages, and organizational networks that, in turn, are thought to generate interpersonal trust and collaboration in local communities on issues of common concern.

The evidence examined in Chapter 8 supports the claim that in many countries, not just the United States, religious participation (as measured by the frequency of attending worship services) is positively associated with belonging to related religious organizations, such as faith-based charities, youth groups, and social clubs, as well as to some non-religious voluntary organizations and community associations. Moreover, *membership* in religious organizations (but *not* attendance at religious services) was significantly linked with selected indicators of civic engagement, including social attitudes and political participation.

But it remains difficult to sort out the direction of causality in these associations. Belonging to churches may bring people into contact with a wider range of friends, neighbors, and colleagues, beyond their immediate family, thereby encouraging people to join other social networks and community associations. But it could also be true that the people who are most likely to join voluntary groups in their community are also most likely to join churches, or other religious organizations. It seems likely that a process of mutually reinforcing reciprocal causation underlies these relationships, so that sociable "joiners" not only attend churches, but also belong to various other civic organizations. In any case, the effect of declining churchgoing on civic engagement seems to have been largely offset by the emergence of new social movements, protest politics, and newer forms of virtual communications that encourage alternative forms of political mobilization and expression.[14]

In earlier eras, one's religious identity provided a cue that oriented voters toward political parties, and helped define one's ideological position on the political spectrum. In this regard, differences between Protestants and Catholics in Western Europe functioned as a cognitive shortcut, similar to the role of social class, which linked voters to parties; these linkages often persisted throughout an individual's lifetime. In recent decades, however, as secularization has progressively weakened religious identities in advanced industrial societies, we would expect to find that the political impact of denominational differences would play a declining role in party and electoral politics. In consequence, parties that once had strong organizational links to the Catholic Church, such as the Christian Democrats in West Germany, Italy, and Austria, have become more secular in their electoral appeals, moving toward "bridging strategies" that enable them to win electoral support from many diverse social groups.

The evidence examined in Chapter 9 serves to confirm these expectations; in postindustrial nations, religious values continue to predict a sense of affiliation with the political Right. This religious gap remains significant even after employing our standard battery of societal and individual controls. This gap is found in many diverse societies, suggesting a fairly universal pattern at work in people's ideological orientations. Nevertheless, we have also found that the relationship between religiosity and Right political orientations seems to have weakened during the last twenty years in most industrial and postindustrial societies, apart from the United States and Austria. In an important sense, the bottom-line test lies in the votes actually cast in national elections – and we find that during the past fifty years, support for religious parties has fallen in most postindustrial nations, especially in Catholic Europe.

This finding reflects the pattern that was found with churchgoing in Europe: in both cases religion starts from a far higher base, and then falls more sharply, in Catholic countries than in Protestant ones. Secularization appears to be a process that started in Protestant Europe well before survey evidence began to become available, so that at the start of the postwar era, these countries already had considerably lower levels of support for religious parties than those found in Catholic countries. Consequently, during the past half-century the process of secularization has affected Catholic Europe most strongly, and these countries are now approaching, but not yet attaining, the low levels of religiosity found in

Northern Europe. Precisely as we found with religious practices, values, and beliefs, the United States remains an outlier in its emphasis on the importance of politics in religion. Secularization has generally been sweeping through affluent nations, in politics as well as in society, although the pace of change and its effects differ from one country to another. We do not have any substantial body of time-series data with which to analyze trends in pre-industrial countries, as we do with the advanced industrial societies of Europe and North America, but the limited evidence that is available indicates that there is no worldwide decline of religiosity, or of the role of religion in politics: this is a phenomenon of industrial and postindustrial society.

5. The Religious Markets Hypothesis

Using multiple methods, we have analyzed evidence from almost eighty societies, carrying out cross-cultural comparisons at both the societal and individual levels and examining time-series survey data and generational comparisons to test a series of hypotheses concerning the relationship between secularization and existential security. We also tested empirically the core propositions of the most influential contemporary alternative interpretation; the supply-side based religious market theory.

Religious market theory holds that religious participation is mainly influenced by the institutional "supply" of religion and the role of the state. It predicts *that religious participation will increase with (1) greater religious pluralism and (2) less state regulation of religious institutions.* These institutional explanations appear plausible in the light of several historical examples of the relationship between the church and state.

The leading example cited as evidence that religious *pluralism* produces high levels of religious belief and participation is the United States. But although religious pluralism does indeed go together with relatively high levels of religiosity in the United States, such countries as Pakistan, Indonesia, Algeria, El Salvador, Puerto Rico, Bangladesh, Egypt, Nigeria, Uganda, Brazil, and Colombia all show much *higher* levels of both religious belief and religious practice – in societies where as much as 99% of the population belong to one politically and socially dominant religion. A few of these countries, such as Nigeria, show high degrees of religious pluralism, but most of them are extremely homogeneous: what they have in common is poverty. The American public is strongly religious only in comparison with the publics of other advanced industrial societies: it ranks far below most poor societies. Multivariate analysis of data from a wide range of societies does not support the hypothesis that religious pluralism produces high levels of religiosity. We suggested other reasons why the United States is a deviant case among rich countries.

Does less state *regulation* of religion produce high levels of religiosity? Again, a number of examples (including the United States) seem to support this hypothesis. Yet state persecution of religion can be counterproductive. Efforts to stamp out religion in Poland, for example, had the effect of turning the Roman Catholic Church into a bastion of Polish independence against Russian oppression both under the Czars and under the Soviet Union. And in Russia, where for seventy years official Soviet policy enforced state atheism, support for the Russian Orthodox Church persists to the present. To test Religious Markets theory, we used the Herfindahl Index of religious pluralism, and the Chaves and Cann Index of state regulation. We also developed a more comprehensive new 20-point Religious Freedom Index focusing upon the relationship of the state and church, monitoring such issues as whether the constitution constrains freedom of religion, whether the government restricts certain denominations or sects, and whether there is an established church. Using these separate and independent measures, no systematic empirical support was found for the propositions that religious pluralism or state regulation mattered; indeed, on the contrary, we found precisely the reverse. In the world as a whole, the most *homogeneous* religious cultures, and the societies with the *greatest* state regulation of religion, have the greatest religious participation and the strongest faith in God.

This is not accidental. In many poor societies, where religion is central to society, authoritarian rulers have a direct interest in promoting or controlling religious institutions in order to maintain their power and legitimacy. In such societies, religious and political power are closely linked. The process of modernization usually brings a decline in the salience of religion, for reasons already described, as well as encouraging the spread of human rights and political liberties, and the state no longer exerts so much control over religious authorities. Even where there are established churches, their societal significance gradually fades away: nominally, such countries as England and Sweden have established churches; their real power has become very modest. Human development tends to generate both greater tolerance for religious freedom and the erosion of religious values. There is no doubt that institutions can play a role maintaining religious vitality, but if the mass public is deserting the churches in advanced industrialized societies, supply-side efforts have modest effect: there is little that religious leaders can do to revive public demand.

6. The Demographic Hypothesis

Given the findings considered so far, one might assume that the process of secularization would gradually sweep through the world, as development gradually improved living conditions in poorer countries. This was the conventional wisdom a few decades ago. But the reality is more complex – and culminates in exactly the opposite result.

We hypothesized that one of the major factors driving religiosity is the need for a sense of certainty in a world where existence is full of danger and uncertainty. This is not the only motivating factor. Philosophers and theologians have sought to probe into the meaning and purpose of life since the dawn of history; but for the great majority of the population, who lived at the margin of subsistence, the need for reassurance and a sense of certainty was the main function of religion. In societies where existential insecurity has faded into the background, this factor has become less compelling.

But secularization and human development has a paradoxical secondary consequence. It is linked with a precipitate decline of fertility rates, driving demographic changes that prevent secularization from sweeping the world. Although poorer countries such as Pakistan, El Salvador, Uganda, and Nigeria have high infant mortality rates, their publics place much more emphasis on religious values than do the publics of rich countries – which is conducive to their also having much higher fertility rates than those found in richer countries, for the reasons discussed in Chapter 1. The net result is that poor nations also have incomparably greater population growth than rich, secularized countries, where the population is stagnant and starting to shrink. Thus, despite the fact that a large part of the world has begun to industrialize during the past century, and secularization occurs in virtually every industrialized country, there are more people with traditional values today than ever before in history.

The basic demographic indicators demonstrating these propositions are shown in Table 10.1, including macro-level rates of fertility, longevity, infant mortality, and survival, derived from the World Bank *World Development Indicators*. For comparison, seventy-three societies in the pooled World Values Survey, 1981–2001, are classified into three categories: the most secular, the moderate, and the most religious, based on their overall mean levels of religious values (using the 10-point "importance of God" scale).

Table 10.1. Demographic Indicators by Type of Society

Type of Society	Fertility (rate)		Life Expectancy (years)		Infant Mortality (rate)		Survival to Old Age (%)		Nations
	1970–75	2000–05	1970–75	2000–05	1970–75	2000–05	Females 2000–05	Males 2000–05	
Most secular	2.8	1.8	68.7	74.4	35.4	12.4	85.3	72.3	25
Moderate	3.3	1.7	68.3	74.7	43.5	15.7	85.9	75.0	24
Most religious	5.4	2.8	57.7	68.2	94.5	39.1	74.6	65.1	24
All nations	**3.8**	**2.1**	**65.0**	**72.5**	**56.8**	**22.4**	**82.0**	**70.8**	**73**

NOTES: Type of society: Based on macro-level mean religious values measured on the 10-point "importance of God" scale. Fertility: Total fertility rate per woman. Life expectancy: Life expectancy at birth (in years). Infant mortality: Infant mortality rate (per 1,000 live births). Survival: Probability at birth of surviving to age 65 (% cohort). Nations: Number of societies.

Source: World Bank 2003 *World Development Indicators*. Washington, DC: World Bank, available online at: www.worldbank.org.

A country's fertility rate reflects the average number of children born to women of childbearing years (16–44); these rates are shown for the period 1970–1975 and again for 2000–2005. The results show that women are having far fewer children during the last thirty years across all types of society: on average, the fertility rate dropped from 3.8 to 2.1. But there remain sharp contrasts between the most secular and religious societies; today women of childbearing age living in secular societies have an average of 1.8 children, while in societies where traditional religious beliefs prevail, women have an average of 2.8 children. The indicators for life expectancy, infant mortality, and rates of survival to old age all highlight the extent to which secular and religious societies differ in their life-chances; in secular nations, people live longer, fewer children die, and more people survive to old age. As argued in the introduction, culture can be viewed as a survival strategy for a given society, and we find two contrasting survival strategies. In subsistence-level traditional societies life is insecure and relatively short; their cultural systems vary in many respects, but in virtually every case they encourage people to produce large numbers of children, and discourage anything that threatens the family, such as divorce, homosexuality, or abortion. Rich, secular societies produce fewer people, but with relatively high investment in each individual, producing knowledge societies with high levels of education, long life expectancies, and advanced economic and technological levels. Virtually all affluent postindustrial countries have life expectancies of more than seventy years, and women in these societies have fertility rates of between one and two children – tending to hover near the population replacement level or even falling below it. The United States is an exception to the prevailing pattern among rich nations here, as in many other ways, with slightly higher fertility and lower life expectancy. At the other extreme, people have a life expectancy of forty years or less in the poorest agrarian nations in the world, such as Niger, Burkina Faso, and Guinea-Bissau, and the total fertility rate for women in these societies is seven to eight children.

The net effect of these survival strategies upon annual rates of population growth is illustrated in Table 10.2. From 1975 to 1997, the population in the two dozen most religious societies under comparison grew at a rate of 2.2% per annum, compared with 0.7% in secular, rich nations. For the second period, from 1997 to 2015, it is estimated that population growth in religious societies will have slowed to 1.5%, which still brings substantial growth. By contrast, in the more secular states, average population growth has plummeted to 0.2%, and in some countries has already become negative. In affluent societies, women today have greater control over

Table 10.2. Population Growth Rate by Type of Society

Type of Society	Nations	Annual Population Growth Rate, 1975–1997 (%)	Annual Population Growth Rate, 1997–2015 (%)
Most secular	25	0.7	0.2
Moderate	24	0.7	0.3
Most religious	24	2.2	1.5
All nations	**73**	**1.2**	**0.7**

NOTES: Type of society: Based on mean macro-level religious values measured on the 10-point "importance of God" scale, WVS 1981–2001. Nations: Number of societies.

Source: World Bank 2003, *World Development Indicators.* Washington, DC: World Bank, available online at: www.worldbank.org.

reproduction through widespread availability of contraception and abortion; they also have wider opportunities in education, the paid work-force, and the broader public sphere, and more egalitarian perceptions of sex roles.[15] The typical family structure has also been transformed during the last half century in postindustrial societies, for both men and women, by the rising age at which people first get married, patterns of cohabitation, growing numbers of single-parent households, rising rates of divorce, and the aging population.[16] Figure 10.3 illustrates the fact that societies where religion is considered most important are also the ones that have shown the highest population growth rates during the last thirty years, while secular societies have low rates of population growth.

What does this process mean for the world's population? The estimates in Table 10.3 give a broad indication of how this translates into demographic trends during the twentieth century, and also during the last three decades, according to our classification of these types of society. In the seventy-three societies under comparison, just over two billion live in relatively secular societies, and these countries have seen an 41% increase in the total size of their populations during the last thirty years. Almost as many people (1.7 billion) today live in relatively religious countries, but they have seen an 82% rise in their population during the same period, with greater female fertility producing twice as much growth, despite high infant mortality and low life expectancies. Another way to understand the effects of this process is to compare the proportion of the publics under comparison living in secular and religious societies; in 1970, 45% lived in secular societies and 29% lived in religious societies. By 2002, the figures had become 40% and 33%, respectively.

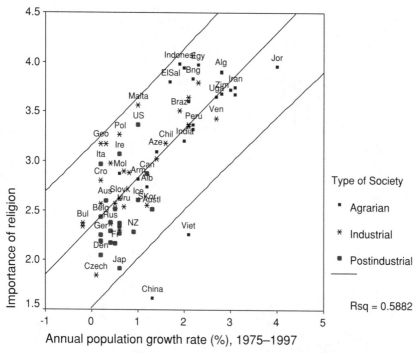

Figure 10.3. Religious Values and Population Growth Rates, 1975–1998. Notes: Importance of religion: Q10: "How important is religion in your life? Very important, rather important, not very important, not at all important." Annual population growth rate 1975–1997: World Bank 2003 *World Development Indicators*. Washington, DC: World Bank, available online at: www.worldbank.org. Source: World Values Survey, pooled 1981–2001.

Thus, as was pointed out in Chapter 1, we find two apparently contradictory trends:

1. The publics of virtually all advanced industrial societies have been moving toward more secular orientations during the past fifty years. Nevertheless,

2. The world as a whole now has more people with traditional religious views than ever before – and they constitute a growing proportion of the world's population.

These two propositions are not contradictory – because secularization has a powerful negative impact on human fertility rates. The rich countries, in which secularization is most advanced, now have human fertility rates far below the replacement level – while poor societies with traditional religious

Table 10.3. Estimated Population Growth by Type of Society, 1900–2002

	Total Estimated Population (in millions)			Population Growth (in millions)		Population Growth (percentage)	
	1900	1970	2002	1900–2002	1970–2002	1900–2002	1970–2002
Most secular	814	1,468	2,071	1,257	602	154	41
Moderate	379	839	1,350	971	511	256	61
Most religious	294	935	1,700	1,407	766	479	82
All nations	**1,486**	**3,242**	**5,122**	**3,635**	**1,879**	**245**	**58**

NOTES: Estimates based on the 73 societies classified in the pooled WVS 1981–2001. Type of society: Based on mean macro-level religious values measured on the 10-point "importance of God" scale, pooled WVS 1981–2001. It should be noted that we are therefore comparing contemporary macro-levels of religiosity, not those existing in 1900. Estimated population In 1900, 1970, and 2002 (in millions).

Source: *World Christian Encyclopedia.*

worldviews have fertility rates that are far above the replacement level, and contain a growing share of the world's population.

Both culture and human development influence this process. In previous research, we developed a powerful multi-item indicator of Traditional versus Secular-rational values that taps a major dimension of cross-cultural variation.[17] This dimension reflects how strongly given societies emphasize religion and a number of other related orientations. Traditionally oriented societies emphasize the importance of parent-child ties and family values; they strongly reject divorce, abortion, prostitution, and homosexuality. Societies with secular-rational values have the opposite preferences on all of these topics. To a large extent, traditional values focus on protecting the family, encouraging reproduction within marriage, and discouraging any other kind of sexual behavior. The move from traditional values to secular-rational values brings a cultural shift from an emphasis on a role for women, whose lives are largely limited to producing and raising as many children as possible, to a world where women have an increasingly broad range of life choices, and most have careers and interests outside the home. This development is linked with a dramatic decline in fertility rates, as illustrated in Figure 10.4. Thus, although it was not designed to do so, our multi-item indicator of Traditional/Secular-rational values is a remarkably powerful indicator of fertility rates, as Model 1 in Table 10.4 demonstrates. The single item measuring religious values (the importance of religion), used throughout this book, also proved highly significant as an alternative item predicting fertility rates, as show in Table 10.4 Model 2.[18]

Yet cultural values are not the whole story, because patterns of human development also contribute to human fertility rates, as Table 10.4 also demonstrates. The improvements in healthcare that accompany human development usually give women easier access to family planning, through the availability of contraception and abortion, while women's growing literacy, education, and paid employment in the labor force expand their awareness of family planning and opportunities outside of the private sphere. The improvements in infant mortality that come from better nutrition, immunization, and access to clean water mean that there are fewer risks from planning smaller families. The younger age profile of developing societies also means that these contain more women of childbearing age. Moreover, in peasant societies, children and adolescents play a vital role in sustaining small agricultural holdings, also providing parents with protection against disability in old age, whereas the economic role of the family shrinks in industrialized economies and the welfare state provides an alternative source

Table 10.4. Explaining Fertility Rates

	Model 1 Human Development and Traditional/Secular-Rational Values				Model 2 Human Development and Religious Values			
	B	s.e.	Beta	Sig.	B	s.e.	Beta	Sig.
Level of human development (100-point scale)	−4.23	.707	−.510	***	−4.51	.730	−.569	***
Religious values (4-point scale)					.521	.153	.313	***
Traditional/secular-rational value scale	−.695	.139	−.424	***				
Constant	5.46				4.19			
Adjusted R²	.688				.644			

NOTE: The table presents the results of ordinary least squares regression models where the fertility rate is the dependent variable in 73 societies. The figures represent unstandardized beta (B), the standard error (s.e.), standardized beta (Beta), and their significance of the coefficients: ***P = .0001. The models were checked with tolerance statistics for multicollinearity. *Level of human development*: Human Development Index 2001 (UNDP). *Fertility rate*: The average number of children a woman would bear if age-specific fertility rates remained unchanged during her lifetime, 2000. World Bank *Development Indicators 2002*. *Traditional/secular-rational values*: Measured by support of the following items: "God is very important in respondent's life; It is more important for a child to learn obedience and religious faith than independence and determination; Autonomy index; Abortion is never justifiable; Respondent has strong sense of national pride; Respondent favors respect for authority." In contrast, support for secular-rational values is measured by the opposite position on all of above. The scale uses the factor analysis scores. Religious values: Q10: "*How important is religion in your life? Very important, rather important, not very important, not at all important*." WVS. *Source*: World Values Surveys, pooled 1981–2001.

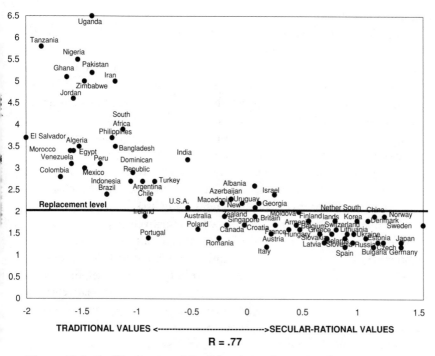

Figure 10.4. Fertility Rates and Traditional/Secular-Rational Values, mid-1990s.

of care for the elderly. For all these reasons, the combined impact of culture plus development explains, in total, two-thirds of the variations in fertility rates in the societies under comparison.

Implications and Challenges

Further research could deepen our understanding of these phenomena. Future surveys could look more directly at perceptions of risk and security, to provide direct attitudinal evidence linking the living conditions of rich and poor societies to individual levels of religiosity, and from there to fertility rates. This seems to be the most plausible interpretation of the evidence examined throughout this book, but it is possible that some other factor present in developing nations, not addressed by our theoretical framework or analyzed in our models, might provide an alternative explanation of the strong linkages we have found between economic development and fertility rates. In this regard, we need to develop new measures tapping perceptions of the ego-tropic and socio-tropic risks most common in different contexts and cultures. It will also be useful to go further in analyzing survey data monitoring the long-term evolution of religious beliefs, values, and practices in case studies of particular nations beyond the postindustrial societies usually studied in Western Europe, Scandinavia, and North America. We now have a half-century of survey data from a number of developed countries, along with complementary data drawn from church records and census records; but we have very little time-series data from low-income societies, and thus no direct measure of whether secularization or a resurgence of religiosity is occurring in them.

Moreover, the national outliers and anomalies to the general cultural patterns we have established are worth examining in detail. It is clear that the United States *is* exceptionally religious for its level of development, but it remains unclear *why*. Conversely, some relatively poor societies have relatively secular cultures: the Confucian-influenced societies, in particular, emphasize Secular-rational values significantly more than their economic level would predict – and this may be a contributing factor in helping explain why China has attained much lower fertility rates than other relatively poor societies. Strong, coercive governmental policies are the proximate cause of China's low fertility rates, but other governments have attempted to reduce birth rates without attaining comparable success.

A closer examination of differential patterns of development among Christian denominations within given countries and regions, such as the rise of evangelicalism and the erosion of Catholicism reported in Latin America, and complex patterns of religiosity found in Africa, would also provide important insights that go far beyond the materials considered in this book. We have also only started to compare systematic and representative cross-national survey data in a diverse range of Islamic societies, but the limited evidence we have examined suggests that this approach is likely to challenge some of the conventional wisdom about public opinion in these societies.

This book has demonstrated that, with rising levels of existential security, the publics of virtually all advanced industrial societies have been moving toward more secular orientations during at least the past fifty years. Earlier perceptions of this process gave rise to the mistaken assumption that religion was disappearing. "God is dead," proclaimed Nietzsche more than a century ago. A massive body of empirical evidence points to a very different conclusion. As a result of contrasting demographic trends in rich and poor countries, the world as a whole now has more people with traditional religious views than ever before – and they constitute a growing proportion of the world's population.

The expanding gap between the sacred and the secular societies around the globe will have important consequences for world politics, making the role of religion increasingly salient on the global agenda. It is by no means inevitable that the religious gap will lead to greater ethno-religious conflict and violence. Indeed, the best available evidence of long-term trends in ethno-religious conflict, the latest *Minorities at Risk* report, goes against this scenario, demonstrating falling levels of such conflict during the 1990s.[19] The main factors driving this development can be found in the dramatic spread of democratization that occurred worldwide since the late 1980s, which facilitated greater autonomy or self-determination for many ethno-religious minorities, and the end of some of the most repressive state regimes.

Nevertheless, the persistence of traditional religious beliefs in poorer agrarian societies may be stimulated by the contrast between their situation and the growing secularization pervasive elsewhere. The spread of sexual liberalization, emancipated women, and secular policies can generate powerful reactions among those who cherish traditional values. We have already seen symptoms such as the resurgence of fundamentalist movements, and support for leaders and parties who mobilize popular support based on appeals to religious values, among people with traditional beliefs. Even within moderately rich societies, fundamentalist Evangelical churches and sects have become visible politically.[20] This does not mean that the publics of these societies are becoming more religious and more traditional. The empirical evidence indicates that precisely the opposite is happening in advanced industrial societies. Evangelists with relatively traditional values are expanding at the expense of the more modernized mainline religious groups partly because of the differential fertility rates that are linked with traditional versus modern worldviews in the world as a whole. Waves of migrants entering the United States from developing countries in Latin America, the Caribbean, and Asia, bringing conservative cultural values with them, have reinvigorated religious life. Moreover, fundamentalist groups in advanced industrial societies have been galvanized into unprecedented levels of organized action because they perceive that many of their most basic values (concerning abortion, divorce, homosexuality, and family values) are being threatened by rapid cultural changes in their societies. In the post–Cold War world, the widening gap between the core values held by the more religious and more secular societies will probably increase the salience and importance of cultural issues in international affairs. How well we manage to accommodate and tolerate these cultural differences, or how far we fail, remains one of the core challenges for the twenty-first century.

Appendix A

Table A1. Classifications of Types of Society

Nation state (76 total)	In 1980 Wave	In 1990 Wave	In 1995 Wave	In 2000 Wave	HDI 1998	Type of State
Postindustrial						
1 Australia	Yes		Yes		.929	Older democracy
2 Austria		Yes		Yes	.908	Older democracy
3 Belgium	Yes	Yes		Yes	.925	Older democracy
4 Canada	Yes	Yes		Yes	.935	Older democracy
5 Denmark	Yes	Yes		Yes	.911	Older democracy
6 Finland	Yes	Yes	Yes	Yes	.917	Older democracy
7 France	Yes	Yes		Yes	.917	Older democracy
8 Germany[a]	Yes	Yes	Yes	Yes	.911	Older democracy
9 Iceland	Yes	Yes		Yes	.927	Older democracy
10 Ireland	Yes	Yes		Yes	.907	Older democracy
11 Italy	Yes	Yes		Yes	.903	Older democracy
12 Japan	Yes	Yes	Yes	Yes	.924	Older democracy
13 Luxembourg				Yes	.908	Older democracy
14 Netherlands	Yes	Yes		Yes	.925	Older democracy
15 New Zealand			Yes		.903	Older democracy

(continued)

Table A1 (*continued*)

Nation state (76 total)	In 1980 Wave	In 1990 Wave	In 1995 Wave	In 2000 Wave	HDI 1998	Type of State
			Included in World Values Study			
16 Norway	Yes	Yes	Yes		.934	Older democracy
17 Spain	Yes	Yes	Yes	Yes	.899	Older democracy
18 Sweden	Yes	Yes	Yes	Yes	.926	Older democracy
19 Switzerland		Yes	Yes		.915	Older democracy
20 United Kingdom[a]	Yes	Yes	Yes	Yes	.918	Older democracy
21 United States	Yes	Yes	Yes	Yes	.929	Older democracy
Industrial						
1 Argentina	Yes	Yes	Yes	Yes	.837	Newer democracy
2 Belarus		Yes	Yes	Yes	.781	Non-democratic
3 Bosnia & Herzegovina			Yes			Non-democratic
4 Brazil		Yes	Yes		.747	Semi-democracy
5 Bulgaria		Yes	Yes	Yes	.772	Newer democracy
6 Chile		Yes	Yes	Yes	.826	Newer democracy
7 Colombia			Yes		.764	Semi-democracy
8 Croatia			Yes	Yes	.795	Semi-democracy
9 Czech Republic		Yes	Yes	Yes	.843	Newer democracy
10 Estonia		Yes	Yes	Yes	.801	Newer democracy
11 Georgia			Yes		.762	Semi-democracy
12 Greece				Yes	.875	Older democracy
13 Hungary	Yes	Yes	Yes	Yes	.817	Newer democracy
14 Korea, Rep.	Yes	Yes	Yes		.854	Newer democracy
15 Latvia		Yes	Yes	Yes	.771	Newer democracy
16 Lithuania		Yes	Yes	Yes	.789	Newer democracy
17 Macedonia			Yes		.763	Semi-democracy
18 Malta				Yes	.865	Older democracy
19 Mexico	Yes	Yes	Yes	Yes	.784	Semi-democracy
20 Philippines				Yes	.744	Newer democracy
21 Poland		Yes	Yes	Yes	.814	Newer democracy
22 Portugal		Yes		Yes	.864	Older democracy
23 Romania		Yes	Yes	Yes	.770	Newer democracy
24 Russian Federation		Yes	Yes	Yes	.771	Semi-democracy
25 Slovakia		Yes	Yes	Yes	.825	Newer democracy
26 Slovenia		Yes	Yes	Yes	.861	Newer democracy
27 Taiwan			Yes			Newer democracy
28 Turkey		Yes	Yes	Yes	.732	Semi-democracy
29 Ukraine			Yes	Yes	.744	Semi-democracy
30 Uruguay			Yes		.825	Newer democracy

		Included in World Values Study				
Nation state (76 total)	*In 1980 Wave*	*In 1990 Wave*	*In 1995 Wave*	*In 2000 Wave*	*HDI 1998*	*Type of State*
31 Venezuela			Yes	Yes	.770	Semi-democracy
32 Yugoslavia, Fed. Rep.[a]			Yes			Non-democratic
Agrarian						
1 Albania			Yes		.713	Semi-democracy
2 Algeria				Yes	.704	Non-democratic
3 Armenia			Yes		.721	Semi-democracy
4 Azerbaijan			Yes		.722	Non-democratic
5 Bangladesh			Yes	Yes	.461	Semi-democracy
6 China		Yes	Yes		.706	Non-democratic
7 Dominican Rep.			Yes		.729	Newer democracy
8 Egypt				Yes	.623	Non-democratic
9 El Salvador				Yes	.696	Newer democracy
10 India		Yes	Yes		.563	Older democracy
11 Indonesia				Yes	.682	Semi-democracy
12 Iran				Yes	.709	Non-democratic
13 Jordan				Yes	.721	Semi-democracy
14 Moldova, Rep.				Yes	.700	Semi-democracy
15 Morocco				Yes	.589	Semi-democracy
16 Nigeria		Yes	Yes	Yes	.439	Semi-democracy
17 Pakistan			Yes		.522	Non-democratic
18 Peru			Yes		.737	Semi-democracy
19 South Africa	Yes	Yes	Yes	Yes	.697	Newer democracy
20 Tanzania				Yes	.415	Semi-democracy
21 Uganda				Yes	.409	Non-democratic
22 Viet Nam				Yes	.671	Non-democratic
23 Zimbabwe				Yes	.555	Non-democratic

NOTE: The classification of societies is based upon categorizing the UNDP Human Development Index (1998), based on longevity (as measured by life expectancy at birth); educational achievement; and standard of living (as measured by per capita GDP [PPP $US]). The classification of the type of democracy in each nation state is based on the Freedom House estimates of political rights and civil liberties (mean 1980–2000).

[a] It should be noted that certain independent nation states are subdivided into societies for analysis, due to their distinctive political legacies, historical traditions, and social cleavages, including Germany (subdividing West and East Germany), the United Kingdom (Northern Ireland and Great Britain), and the Federal Republic of Yugoslavia (Serbia and Montenegro after 1992). Therefore, in total there are 76 nation states, but 79 societies, compared within the study.

Source: UNDP: *UNDP Human Development Report 2000.* New York: UNDP/Oxford University Press.

Table A2. Type of Nation States Included in Any Wave of the World Values Surveys

	Total Number of Nation States in the World	Number of States in Any Wave of the WVS	% of States Included in the World Values Study
Size of State			
Small (population of 1 million or less)	41	2	5
Moderate (population from 1 million to 30 million)	116	45	39
Large (population over 30 million)	33	29	88
Type of society			
Postindustrial	21	21	100
Industrial	64	32	50
Agrarian	106	23	22
Type of Government Regime			
Older democracy	39	25	64
Newer democracy	43	19	44
Semi-democracy	47	20	43
Non-democracy	62	12	19
World Regions			
Asia-Pacific	38	13	34
Central and Eastern Europe	26	21	81
Middle East	19	6	32
North America	3	3	100
Scandinavia	5	5	100
South America	32	9	28
Sub-Saharan Africa	49	5	10
Western Europe	19	14	70
ALL	191	76	40

NOTE: For details of the classification of government regimes and types of societies, see Table A1.

Appendix B

Table B1. Concepts and Measures

Variable	Definitions, Coding, and Sources

HUMAN DEVELOPMENT INDICATORS

Human Development Index   The Human Development Index (HDI) is based on longevity, as measured by life expectancy at birth; educational achievement; and standard of living, as measured by per capita GDP (PPP $US). UNDP Human Development Report 2000.

Type of Society   "*Postindustrial societies*" were defined as the twenty most affluent states around the world, ranking with a HDI score over .900 and mean per capita GDP of $29,585. "*Industrial societies*" are classified as the 58 nations with a moderate HDI (ranging from .740 to .899) and a moderate per capita GDP of $6,314. Lastly, "*agrarian societies*" are the 97 nations with lower levels of development (HDI of 739 or below) and mean per capita GDP of $1,098.

Per Capita GDP   Measured in $US in Purchasing Power Parity, 1998. UNDP *Human Development Report 2000.*

Economic Equality   The GINI Index measures the extent to which the distribution of income within an economy deviates

(continued)

Table B1 (*continued*)

Variable	Definitions, Coding, and Sources
	from a perfectly equal distribution. The index has been reversed so that 1 represents perfect equality. *World Development Indicators 2001*, World Bank.
Lower Infant Mortality	The number of infants dying before the age of one year, per 1,000 live births, 1999. The indicator has been reversed so that a higher figure represents lower infant mortality. *World Development Indicators 2001*, World Bank.
Public Health Expenditure	Public health expenditure consists of recurrent and capital spending from government budgets, external borrowings, and grants as a percentage of GDP, 1997–99. *World Development Indicators 2001*, World Bank.
Life Expectancy	Life expectancy at birth (years) 1995–2000. UNDP *Human Development Report 2000*.
Adult Literacy Rate	Literacy as a percentage of adults (15 and above) 1998. UNDP *Human Development Report 2000*.
% Secondary Education	Secondary age group enrollment as a percentage of the relevant age group, 1997. UNDP *Human Development Report 2000*.
Contraceptive Prevalence Rate	The percentage of married women of childbearing age (16–44) who are using any form of contraception. UNDP *Human Development Report 2000*.
Dependency Ratio	The ratio of the population defined as dependent – those aged under 15 and over 64 – to the working age population. UNDP *Human Development Report 2000*.
Gender-Related Development Index	A composite index using the same variables as the human development index but adjusting life expectancy, educational attainment, and income in accordance with the disparity in achievement between women and men in each country. UNDP *Human Development Report 2000*.
Gender Empowerment Measure	A composite index combining indices for economic participation and decision-making, for political participation and decision-making, and for power over economic resources. UNDP *Human Development Report 2000*.

POLITICAL INDICATORS

Level of Democracy	The Gastil index, a 7-point scale used by Freedom House, measuring political rights and civil liberties every year. Available online at www.Freedomhouse.com.
Type of State	Based on the Freedom House Gastil index (1999–2000), we define *older democracies* as states with at least

Variable	Definitions, Coding, and Sources
	twenty years continuous experience of democracy from 1980–2000 and a Freedom House rating of 5.5 to 7.0. States classified as *newer democracies* have less than twenty years' experience with democracy and a Gastil index rating of 5.5 to 7.0. *Semi-democracies* have been democratic for less than twenty years and have current Gastil index ratings of 3.5 to 5.5. *Non-democracies* are the remaining states with a Gastil index score from 1.0 to 3.0; they include military-backed dictatorships, authoritarian states, elitist oligarchies, and absolute monarchies.
Civic Activism	*Belong*: "Please look carefully at the following list of voluntary organizations and activities and say which, if any, do you belong to?" *Active*: (If belong) "And for which, if any, are you currently doing unpaid voluntary work?" Political parties or groups; Sports or recreation; Peace movement; Professional associations; Labor unions; Local community action groups; Youth work (e.g., scouts, guides, youth clubs, etc.); Conservation, environmental or animal rights; Third World development or human rights; Education, arts, music, or cultural activities; Religious or church organizations; Voluntary organizations concerned with health; Social welfare for the elderly, handicapped or deprived people; Women's groups.
Left-Right Ideology Scale	V123: *"In political matters people talk of 'the left' and 'the right.' How would you place your views on this scale, generally speaking?"* The 10-point scale is coded from 1 = Most Left, 10 = Most Right. Source: World Values Surveys.

CULTURAL INDICATORS

Gender Equality Scale	The combined 100-pt gender equality scale is based on the following 5 items: MENPOL Q118: "On the whole, men make better political leaders than women do." (Agree coded low); MENJOBS Q78: "When jobs are scarce, men should have more right to a job than women." (Agree coded low); BOYEDUC Q.119: "A university education is more important for a boy than a girl." (Agree coded low); NEEDKID Q110: "Do you think that a woman has to have children in order to be fulfilled or is this not necessary?" (Agree coded low); SGLMUM Q112: "If a woman wants to have a child as a single parent but she doesn't want to have a stable relationship

(*continued*)

Table B1 (*continued*)

Variable	Definitions, Coding, and Sources
	with a man, do you approve or disapprove?" (disapprove coded low). Source: World Values Surveys, pooled 1995–2001.
Type of Religion	V184: "*Do you belong to a religious denomination?* [IF YES] *Which one?*" Coded: No, not a member; Roman Catholic; Protestant; Orthodox (Russian/Greek/etc.); Jewish; Muslim; Hindu; Buddhist; Other. Source: World Values Surveys, 1981–2001.
Type of Predominant Religion Worldwide	The classification of the major religion (adhered to by the largest population) in all 193 states around the world is based on the CIA. *The World Factbook, 2001.* (Washington, DC: Central Intelligence Agency). Available online at: http://www.cia.gov/cia/publications/factbook.
Traditional versus Secular-Rational Values	The Traditional Values scale is measured by support of the following items: God is very important in respondent's life; It is more important for a child to learn obedience and religious faith than independence and determination; Autonomy index; Abortion is never justifiable; Respondent has strong sense of national pride; Respondent favors respect for authority. In contrast, support for Secular-rational values is measured by the opposite position on all of above. Source: World Values Surveys.
Sexual Liberalization Scale	"Please tell me for each of the following statements whether you think it can always be justified (10), never justified (1), or somewhere in-between, using this card . . . abortion, homosexuality, prostitution, divorce." Source: World Values Surveys

DEMOGRAPHIC INDICATORS

Occupational Class	Coded for the respondent's occupation. "In which profession/occupation do you, or did you, work?" The 9-point scale is coded from Employer/manager with 10+ employees (1) to Unskilled Manual Worker (9). Source: World Values Surveys
Paid Work Status	V220: "Are you employed now or not?" Coded full-time, part-time, or self-employed (1), other (0). Source: World Values Surveys
Education	V217: "What is the highest educational level that you have ever attained?" Coded on a 9-point scale from no formal education (1) to university level with degree (9). Source: World Values Surveys

Variable	Definitions, Coding, and Sources
Age	Coded from date of birth in continuous years. Source: World Values Surveys
Age Group	Young = under 30 years old; Middle aged = 30–59 years old; Older = 60 years and above. Source: World Values Surveys
Cohort	Coded into 10-year cohorts by year of birth: 1900–1916, 1917–1926, 1927–1936, 1947–1956, 1957–1966, 1967–1976, 1977–1984. Source: World Values Surveys

NOTE: Full details of the World Values Survey codebooks and questionnaires are available online at: www.worldvaluessurvey.com.

Appendix C

Technical Note on the Freedom of Religion Scale

The new Freedom of Religion scale was developed based on the following twenty criteria. Countries were coded from information contained in the U.S. State Department report on *International Religious Freedom, 2002*. The report is available online at: http://www.state.gov/g/drl/rls/irf/. Each criterion was coded 0/1 and the total scale was standardized to 100 points, ranging from low to high religious freedom. The scale represents an expanded version of the 1992 Chaves and Cann scale used to measure state regulation in eighteen postindustrial societies.[1]

1. The constitution limits freedom of religion.
2. The constitution does not recognize freedom of religion. (Or the law does not recognize freedom of religion, in countries without a written constitution.)
3. A single official (established) state church exists.
4. The state favors one religion.
5. Religious organizations must register with the state or be designated by it to operate legally, or the government imposes restrictions on those organizations not registered or recognized.

6. The state issues legal permits for religious buildings.

7. The state appoints or approves church leaders, church leaders appoint or approve government officials, and/or church leaders have specific positions in the government.

8. The state pays church salaries directly.

9. The state subsidizes some/all churches.

10. The state provides tax exemptions for some/all churches.

11. The state bans clergy from all or some specified religions from holding public office.

12. The state owns some church property and buildings.

13. The state mandates some religious education in state schools, even though students can be exempted from this requirement with a parent's request.

14. There are reports of forced religious conversions.

15. The state restricts some denominations, cults, or sects.

16. The state restricts/bans some missionaries entering the country for proselytizing purposes.

17. The state restricts/censors some religious literature entering the country or being distributed.

18. The state imprisons or detains some religious groups or individuals.

19. The state fails to deter serious incidents of ethno-religious conflict and violence directed against some minority groups.

20. The state is designated a country of particular concern for freedom of religion by the U.S. State Department.

Notes

Chapter 1

1. For a discussion, see Steve Bruce. 1992. *Religion and Modernization*. Oxford: Clarendon Press, 170–194; Alan Aldridge. 2000. *Religion in the Contemporary World*. Cambridge, U.K.: Polity Press. Chapter 4.

2. C. Wright Mills. 1959. *The Sociological Imagination*. Oxford: Oxford University Press. Pp. 32–33.

3. It should be noted that in this book the term *fundamentalist* is used in a neutral way to refer to those with an absolute conviction in the fundamental principles of their faith, to the extent that they will not accept the validity of any other beliefs.

4. See, for example, Peter L. Berger. Ed. 1999. *The Desecularization of the World*. Washington, D.C.: Ethics and Public Policy Center. P. 2. Compare this statement with the arguments in Peter L. Berger. 1967. *The Sacred Canopy*. Garden City, NY: Doubleday.

5. Rodney Stark and Roger Finke. 2000. *Acts of Faith*. Berkeley, CA: University of California Press. P. 79. See also Rodney Stark. 1999. "Secularization, RIP." *Sociology of Religion*. 60(3): 249–273.

6. For example, Roger Finke claims: "The vibrancy and growth of American religious institutions presents the most open defiance of the secularization model." Roger Finke. 1992. "An unsecular America." In *Religion and Modernization*. Ed. Steve Bruce. Oxford: Clarendon Press: P. 148.

7. For a discussion seeking to integrate these two strands into a single "secularization paradigm," see Steve Bruce. 2002. *God is Dead: Secularization in the West*. Oxford: Blackwell. Chapter 1.

8. Max Weber. 1930 [1904]. *The Protestant Ethic and the Spirit of Capitalism*. New York: Scribner's; Max Weber. 1993 [1922]. *Sociology of Religion*. Boston: Beacon Press. See Mathieu M. W. Lemmen. 1990. *Max Weber's Sociology of Religion*. Heerlen, The Netherlands: UPT-Katernen 10.

9. Peter L. Berger. 1967. *The Sacred Canopy*. Garden City, NY: Doubleday; Brian R. Wilson. 1966. *Religion in Secular Society*. Harmondsworth, Middlesex, U.K.: Penguin Books, Ltd.; David Martin. 1978. *A General Theory of Secularization*. Oxford: Blackwell. It should be noted that Berger and Martin subsequently revised these claims.

10. For example, see E. J. Larson and L. Witham. 1998. "Leading scientists still reject God." *Nature*. 394(6691): 313.

11. This argument is emphasized by Brian R. Wilson. 1969. *Religion in Secular Society*. Harmondsworth, Middlesex, U.K.: Penguin Books, Ltd.

12. Daniel Bell. 1973. *The Coming of Post-Industrial Society*. New York: Basic Books.

13. Steve Bruce. 2002. *God is Dead: Secularization in the West*. Oxford: Blackwell. P. 36.

14. Émile Durkheim. 1995 [1912]. *The elementary forms of the religious life*. New York: The Free Press.

15. Thomas Luckmann. 1967. *The Invisible Religion*. New York: Macmillan; Karel Dobbelaere. 1985. "Secularization theories and sociological paradigms: A reformulation of the private-public dichotomy and the problem of social integration." *Sociological Analysis*. 46(4): 377–387; Karel Dobbelaere. 1987. "Some trends in European sociology of religion: The secularization debate." *Sociological Analysis*. 48(2): 107–137; Karel Dobbelaere. 1999. "Towards an integrated perspective of the processes related to the descriptive concept of secularization." *Sociology of Religion*. 60(3): 229–247; Steve Bruce. 2002. *God is Dead: Secularization in the West*. Oxford: Blackwell.

16. Wolfgang Jagodzinski and Karel Dobbelaere. 1995. "Secularization and church religiosity." In *The Impact of Values*. Eds. Jan W. van Deth and Elinor Scarbrough. Oxford: Oxford University Press. P. 115.

17. See J. Verweij, Peter Ester, and R. Nauta. 1997. "Secularization as an economic and cultural phenomenon: A cross-national analysis." *Journal for the Scientific Study of Religion*. 36(2): 309–324.

18. For a critique, see, for example, Fran Hagopian. 2000. "Political development, revisited." *Comparative Political Studies*. 33(6/7): 880–911.

19. See, for example, the Pew Research Center for the People and the Press. 2002. *Americans Struggle with Religion's Role at Home and Abroad*. News Release by the Pew Forum on Religion and Public Life, March 2002. Available online at: http://pewforum.org/publications/reports/poll2002.pdf.

20. O. Tschannen. 1991. "The secularization paradigm." *Journal for the Scientific Study of Religion*. 30(1): 395–415; Andrew M. Greeley. 2003. *Religion in Europe at the End of the Second Millennium*. New Brunswick, NJ: Transaction Publishers.

21. Rodney Stark. 1999. "Secularization, RIP." *Sociology of Religion*. 60(3): 249–273.

22. Jeffrey Hadden. 1987. "Toward desacralizing secularization theory." *Social Forces.* 65(3): 587–611.

23. R. Stephen Warner. 1993. "Work in progress toward a new paradigm in the sociology of religion." *American Journal of Sociology.* 98(5): 1044–1093.

24. Rodney Stark and William Sims Bainbridge. 1985. "A supply-side reinterpretation of the 'secularization' of Europe." *Journal for the Scientific Study of Religion.* 33: 230–252; Rodney Stark and William Sims Bainbridge. 1987. *A Theory of Religion.* New York: Peter Lang; Roger Finke and Rodney Stark. 1992. *The Churching of America, 1776–1990.* New Brunswick, NJ: The University of Rutgers Press; Roger Finke and Lawrence R. Iannaccone. 1993. "The illusion of shifting demand: Supply-side explanations for trends and change in the American religious market place." *Annals of the American Association of Political and Social Science.* 527: 27–39; R. S. Warner. 1993. "Work in progress toward a new paradigm in the sociology of religion." *American Journal of Sociology* 98(5): 1044–1093; Roger Finke and Rodney Stark. 2000. *Acts of Faith: Explaining the Human Side of Religion.* Berkeley, CA: University of California Press.

25. Émile Durkheim. 1995 [1912]. *The elementary forms of the religious life.* New York: The Free Press. P. 159. This point is also emphasized by Peter L. Berger. 1967. *The Sacred Canopy.* Garden City, NY: Doubleday. Pp. 112–113.

26. Roger Finke and Rodney Stark. 1992. *The Churching of America.* New Brunswick, NJ: The University of Rutgers Press; Roger Finke and Laurence R. Iannaccone. 1993. "The illusion of shifting demand: Supply-side explanations for trends and change in the American religious market place." *Annals of the American Association of Political and Social Science.* 527: 27–39.

27. Robert Wuthnow. 1988. *The Restructuring of American Religion.* Princeton, NJ: Princeton University Press; Tom Smith. 1992. "Are conservative churches really growing?" *Review of Religious Research.* 33: 305–329; Michael Hout, Andrew M. Greeley, and Melissa J. Wilde. 2001. "The demographic imperative in religious change in the United States." *American Journal of Sociology.* 107(2): 468–500.

28. Rodney Stark and Lawrence Iannaccone. 1994. "A supply-side reinterpretation of the 'secularization' of Europe." *Journal for the Scientific Study of Religion.* 33: 230–252; Roger Finke and Rodney Stark. 2000. *Acts of Faith: Explaining the Human Side of Religion.* Berkeley, CA: University of California Press.

29. J. Verweij, Peter Ester, and R. Nauta. 1997. "Secularization as an economic and cultural phenomenon: A cross-national analysis." *Journal for the Scientific Study of Religion.* 36(2): 309–324. Others, however, seek to rescue the supply-side thesis by arguing that the monopolistic position of the Catholic Church in Italy is prevented by internal competition. See L. Diotallevi. 2002. "Internal competition in a national religious monopoly: The Catholic effect and the Italian case." *Sociology of Religion.* 63(2): 137–155. See also Anthony M. Abela. 1993. "Post-secularisation: The social significance of religious values in four Catholic European countries." *Melita Theolgica.* XLIV: 39–58.

30. David Voas, Daniel V. A. Olson, and Alasdair Crockett. 2002. "Religious pluralism and participation: Why previous research is wrong." *American Sociological Review.* 67(2): 212–230.

31. Mark Chaves and Philip S. Gorski. 2001. "Religious pluralism and religious participation." *Annual Review of Sociology.* 27: 261–281.

32. Rodney Stark and Roger Finke. 2000. *Acts of Faith.* Berkeley, CA: University of California Press. P. 33. Others also argue that traditional secularization theory needs revising, proposing that it implies not the decline of religion per se, but rather, more narrowly, the declining scope of religious authority at the individual, organizational, and societal levels of analysis. See D. Yamane. 1997. "Secularization on trial: In defense of a neosecularization paradigm." *Journal for the Scientific Study of Religion.* 36(1): 109–122.

33. United Nations Development Program. 1994. *New Dimensions of Human Security.* New York: Oxford University Press; Gary King and Christopher J. L. Murray. 2001. "Rethinking human security." *Political Science Quarterly.* 116(4): 585–610.

34. *Oxford English Dictionary.*

35. For summaries, see the annual reports: United Nations. 2002. *Human Development Report 2002.* New York: United Nations/Oxford University Press; World Bank. 2002. *World Development Report, 2002.* Washington, D.C.: World Bank.

36. See the Pew Research Center for the People and the Press. 2002. *Americans Struggle with Religion's Role at Home and Abroad.* News Release by the Pew Forum on Religion and Public Life, March 2002. Available online at: http://pewforum.org/publications/reports/poll2002.pdf. See also Pippa Norris, Montague Kern, and Marion Just. Eds. 2003. *Framing Terrorism.* New York: Routledge.

37. Ronald Inglehart and Wayne E. Baker. 2000. "Modernization, globalization and the persistence of tradition: Empirical evidence from 65 societies." *American Sociological Review.* 65: 19–55.

38. Max Weber. 1930 [1904]. *The Protestant Ethic and the Spirit of Capitalism.* New York: Scribner's.

39. Samuel P. Huntington. 1996. *The Clash of Civilizations and the Remaking of World Order.* New York: Simon & Schuster.

40. For a full discussion, see Ronald Inglehart and Pippa Norris. 2003. *Rising Tide.* New York and Cambridge, U.K.: Cambridge University Press. Chapter 1.

41. Monty Marshall and Ted Robert Gurr. 2003. *Peace and Conflict 2003.* University of Maryland, Center for Systemic Peace/ Minorities At Risk. Available online at: http://www.cidcm.umd.edu/inscr/pc03web.pdf. See also the *Minorities at Risk* project website for updates at: http://www.cidcm. umd.edu/inscr/mar/.

42. For empirical studies of the socialization process, see J. Kelley and N. D. DeGraaf. 1997. "National context, parental socialization, and religious belief: Results from 15 nations." *American Sociological Review.* 62(4): 639–659; S. M. Myers. 1996. "An interactive model of religiosity inheritance: The importance of family context." *American Sociological Review.* 61(5): 858–866.

43. Samuel P. Huntington. 1996. *The Clash of Civilizations and the Remaking of World Order.* New York: Simon & Schuster.

44. See Robert Putnam. 2000. *Bowling Alone*. New York: Simon & Schuster; Robert Wuthnow. 1988. *The Restructuring of American Religion: Society and Faith since World War II*. Princeton, NJ: Princeton University Press; Robert Wuthnow. 1999. "Mobilizing civic engagement: The changing impact of religious involvement." In *Civic Engagement in American Democracy*. Eds. Theda Skocpol and Morris P. Fiorina. Washington, D.C.: Brookings Institution Press.

45. Paul Dekker and Peter Ester. 1996. "Depillarization, deconfessionalization, and de-ideologization: Empirical trends in Dutch society 1958–1992." *Review of Religious Research*. 37(4): 325–341; L. Laeyendecker. 1995. "The case of the Netherlands." In *The Post-War Generation and Establishment Religion*. Eds. W. C. Roof, J. W. Carroll, and D. A. Roozen. Boulder, CO: Westview Press. Pp. 131–150; F. J. Lechner. 1996. "Secularization in the Netherlands?" *Journal for the Scientific Study of Religion*. 35(3): 252–264.

46. For general trends in the strength of religious voting see Mark Franklin et al., 1992. *Electoral Change: Responses to Evolving Social and Attitudinal Structures in Western Countries*. Cambridge, U.K.: Cambridge University Press. For the persistence of religious partisan alignments in voting behavior in the United States, France, Germany, and Britain, however, see also Russell Dalton. 2002. *Citizen Politics*. Chatham, NJ: Chatham House. Pp. 154–162. For a broader cross-national comparison, see also Pippa Norris. 2004. *Electoral Engineering*. New York: Cambridge University Press. Chapter 5. Table 5.2.

47. Andrew Kohut et al. 2000. *The Diminishing Divide: Religion's Changing Role in American Politics*. Washington, D.C.: Brookings Institution Press.

Chapter 2

1. William H. Swatos, Jr. and Kevin J. Christiano. 1999. "Secularization theory: The course of a concept." *Sociology of Religion*. 60(3): 209–228.

2. Andrew M. Greeley. 2003. *Religion in Europe at the End of the Second Millennium*. New Brunswick, NJ: Transaction Publishers. P. xi.

3. See J. Kelley and N. D. DeGraaf. 1997. "National context, parental socialization, and religious belief: Results from 15 nations." *American Sociological Review*. 62(4): 639–659; N. D. De Graaf. 1999. "Event history data and making a history out of cross-sectional data – How to answer the question 'Why cohorts differ?'" *Quality & Quantity*. 33(3): 261–276.

4. For a discussion illustrating the difficulties in analyzing period, cohort, and life-cycle effects in churchgoing patterns using the American General Social Survey data, see Michael Hout and Andrew M. Greeley. 1987. "The center doesn't hold: Church attendance in the United States, 1940–1984." *American Sociological Review*. 52(3): 325–345; Mark Chaves. 1989. "Secularization and religious revival: Evidence from U.S. church attendance rates, 1972–1986." *Journal for the Scientific Study of Religion* 28: 464–477; Michael Hout and Andrew M. Greeley 1990. "The cohort doesn't hold: Comment on Chaves 1989." *Journal for the Scientific Study of Religion*. 29(4): 519–524; Amy Argue, David R. Johnson, and Lynn K. White. 1999. "Age and religiosity: Evidence from a three-wave panel analysis." *Journal for The Scientific Study of Religion*. 38(3): 423–435.

5. Adam Przeworski and Henry Teune. 1970. *The Logic of Comparative Social Inquiry*. New York: Wiley–Interscience.

6. Full methodological details about the World Values Surveys, including the questionnaires, sampling procedures, fieldwork procedures, principle investigators, and organization can be found online at: http://wvs.isr.umich.edu/wvs-samp.html. It should be noted that this study subdivides the independent nation states with distinctive historical and religious traditions into separate societies, including the United Kingdom (Northern Ireland and Great Britain), Germany (East and West), and the Federal Republic of Yugoslavia (Serbia and Montenegro). The study therefore compares 75 nation states but 78 societies in total using the pooled WVS 1981–2000.

7. Nations are often subdivided by the predominant religion within major regions, such as the classic distinction in Germany between the Protestant North and the Catholic South, or the dividing line in Nigeria between the Muslim North and Christian South. But for the purposes of this study, we focus the primary comparison at the national level, since this allowed us to match official statistics about the characteristics of each society collected at the level of the nation state. Future research disaggregated at regional level within each nation would also be valuable.

8. These countries are ranked as equally "free" according to the 2000–2001 Freedom House assessments of political rights and civil liberties. Freedom House. 2000. *Freedom in the World 2000–2001*. Available online at: www.freedomhouse.org.

9. This conceptualization relates to Dobbelaere's distinction between secularization of the whole society, of religious institutions and organizations, and of the individual. See Karel Dobbelaere. 1981. "Secularization: A multidimensional concept." *Current Sociology*. 29(2): 1–21. See also S. Hanson. 1997. "The secularization thesis: Talking at cross purposes." *Journal of Contemporary Religion*. 12: 159–179; William H. Swatos, Jr. and Kevin J. Christiano. 1999. "Secularization theory: The course of a concept." *Sociology of Religion*. 60(3): 209–228; L. Shiner. 1966. "The concept of secularization in empirical research." *Journal for the Scientific Study of Religion*. 6: 207–220.

10. See, for example, Anne Motley Hallum. 2002. "Looking for hope in Central America: The Pentecostal movement." In *Religion and Politics in Comparative Perspective*. Eds. Ted Gerard Jelen and Clyde Wilcox. Cambridge, U.K.: Cambridge University Press.

11. Wade Clark Roof. 2001. *Spiritual Marketplace: Baby Boomers and the Remaking of American Religion*. Princeton, NJ: Princeton University Press. See also Robert C. Fuller. 2002. *Spiritual, but Not Religious: Understanding Unchurched America*. New York: Oxford University Press.

12. See Karel Dobbelaere. 1999. "Towards an integrated perspective of the processes related to the descriptive concept of secularization." *Sociology of Religion*. 60(3): 229–247; Rodney Stark. 1999. "Secularization, RIP." *Sociology of Religion*. 60(3): 249–273.

13. See Andrew M. Greeley. 2003. *Religion in Europe at the End of the Second Millennium*. New Brunswick, NJ: Transaction Publishers.

14. Steve Bruce. 2002. *God is Dead: Secularization in the West*. Oxford: Blackwell. P. 73. See also Steve Bruce. 1995. "The truth about religion in Britain." *Journal for the Scientific Study of Religion*. 34(4): 417–430. Others confirm this erosion; see, for example, G. Davie. 1994. *Religion in Britain since 1945: Believing without Belonging*. Oxford: Blackwell.

15. For the institutional assets, see The Church of England. *The Year in Review, 2001–2002*. Available online at: http://www.cofe.anglican.org/COE 2002version2.pdf. For estimates from official church records of the substantial decline in the proportion of regular attendance, baptisms, and confirmations, see The Church of England website, available online at: http://www.cofe.anglican.org/about/churchstats2000.pdf.

16. Alberto Alesina et al. 2003. "Fractionalization." *Journal of Economic Growth*. 82: 219–258. The dataset is available online at: www.stanford.edu/~wacziarg/papersum.html.

17. David B. Barrett, George T. Kurian, and Todd M. Johnson. Eds. 2001. *World Christian Encyclopedia: A Comparative Survey of Churches and Religions in the Modern World*. 2nd ed. Oxford: Oxford University Press. For details, see Table 1.1. See also Philip M. Parker. 1997. *Religious Cultures of the World: A Statistical Reference*. Westport, CT: Greenwood Press; David B. Barrett and Todd M. Johnson. 2001. *World Christian Trends AD 30–2200*. Pasadena, CA: William Carey Library; Global Evangelization Movement. 2001. *Status of Global Mission 2001*. Available online at: www.gem-werc.org/.

18. CIA. *The World Factbook, 2002*. Available online at: http://www.cia.gov/cia/publications/factbook/.

19. For discussion of the theoretical and policy relevance of the Human Development Index, its validity and the reliability of the data used in constructing the index, see The UNDP. 1995. *UNDP Human Development Report 1995*. New York: Oxford University Press/UNDP; Mark McGillivray and Howard White. 1993. "Measuring development? The UNDP's Human Development Index." *Journal of International Development*. 5(2): 183–192.

20. See the Technical Appendix A at the end of the book for the detailed classification of all nations. Note that this classification is not that used by the UNDP, which draws a different distinction between "medium" and "low" levels of human development.

21. See Adam Przeworski et al. 2000. *Democracy and Development: Political Institutions and Well-Being in the World, 1950–1990*. New York: Cambridge University Press. For the World Bank indicators of good governance, see Daniel Kaufmann, Aart Kraay, and Massimo Mastruzzi. 2003. *Governance Matters III: Governance Indicators for 1996–2002*. Available online at: http://econ.worldbank.org/view.php?type=5&id=28791. For the "democratic audit" approach, see International IDEA. Available online at: www.IDEA.int.

22. See also Geraldo L. Munck and Jay Verkuilen. 2002. "Conceptualizing and measuring democracy – Evaluating alternative indices." *Comparative Political Studies*. 35(1): 5–34.

23. See, in particular, Ronald Inglehart and Pippa Norris. 2003. *Rising Tide: Gender Equality and Cultural Change Around the World*. New York: Cambridge University Press.

24. Societies are defined based on the annual ratings provided by Freedom House since 1972. *The level of freedom* is classified according to the combined mean score for political rights and civil liberties in Freedom House's 1972–2000 annual surveys, *Freedom in the World*. Available online at: www.freedomhouse.org.

25. U.S. State Department. *International Religious Freedom, 2002*. Washington, D.C. Available online at: http://www.state.gov/g/drl/rls/irf/. The report is produced due to the *International Religious Freedom Act of 1998* (U.S. Public Law 105–92) and is monitored by the U.S. Commission on International Religious Freedom. Available online at: http://www.uscirf.gov. It should be noted that the report is used to create an index comparing levels of religious freedom in 2002, for comparisons with levels of religious participation in the WVS Survey 1990–2001. This means that our study cannot monitor to what extent the previous history of religious repression and persecution played an important role in the past. The report by the U.S. State Department largely reflects the evaluations of the state of religious freedoms reported by human rights organizations such as Freedom House and Amnesty International and by comparative studies. See, for example, Kevin Boyle and Juliet Sheen. Eds. 1997. *Freedom of Religion and Belief: A World Report*. New York: Routledge; Paul Marshall. Ed. 2000. *Religious Freedom in the World: A Global Report on Freedom and Persecution*. Nashville, TN: Broadman and Holman.

26. Mark Chaves and David E. Cann. 1992. "Regulation, pluralism and religious market structure." *Rationality and Society*. 4: 272–290.

27. The correlations between the Religious Freedom Index and other indicators are as follows:

Religious Freedom Index, 2002	Corr. (R)	Sig.	N. of Nations
Level of democracy, 1999–2000 (Freedom House)	0.488**		188
Level of religious freedom, 2001 (Freedom House)	0.703**		70
Religious fractionalization/pluralism index (Alesina et al. 2003)	0.403**		187
State regulation of religion (Chaves and Cann 1992)	0.742**		18

* Significant at the .05 level. ** Significant at the .01 level.

Chapter 3

1. Clearly, it could be argued that the process of societal modernization is itself contingent on the predominant religious culture, as exemplified by Weber's claims that the Protestant ethic led to the rise of a capitalist economy in the

West. Hence, we acknowledge that there could well be an interaction effect between the two. See Chapter 7 for further discussion on this point.

2. For details, see Gallup International. 2000. *Religion in the World at the End of the Millennium*. Available online at: www.gallup-international.com.

3. See Bradley K. Hawkins. 2002. *Asian Religions*. New York: Seven Bridges; Donald S. Lopez. 1999. *Asian Religions in Practice: An Introduction*. Princeton, NJ: Princeton University Press; C. Scott Littleton. Ed. 1996. *The Sacred East*. London: Macmillan.

4. Stephen Sharot. 2002. "Beyond Christianity: A critique of the rational choice theory of religion from a Weberian and comparative religions perspective." *Sociology of Religion*. 63(4): 427–454.

5. Robert J. Kisala. 2003. "Japanese religiosity and morals." In *Religion in a Secularizing Society*. Eds. Loek Halman and Ole Riis. Leiden: Brill.

6. In the pooled WVS, the correlations between religious participation (the frequency of attending religious services) and the frequency of prayer (all proving significant at the .01 levels) for adherents of different faiths at individual level were as follows. Roman Catholic: .568, Protestant: .663, Orthodox: .454, Jewish: .443, Muslim: .344, Hindu: .251, Buddhist: .336, other religion: .249, and none: .441.

7. In the pooled WVS, the correlations between religious participation and the 10-point scale concerning the importance of God were all significant for adherents of different faiths at individual level in every group except Buddhists and Others, as follows. Roman Catholic: .357, Protestant: .467, Orthodox: .411, Jewish: .407, Muslim: .181, Hindu: .238, Buddhist: .107, other religion: .012, and none: .389.

8. This pattern was also found by Robert A. Campbell and James E. Curtis. 1994. "Religious involvement across societies: Analysis for alternative measures in national surveys." *Journal for the Scientific Study of Religion*. 33(3): 215–229.

9. The Pew Research Center for the People and the Press. December 19, 2002. Survey Report: *Among Wealthy Nations, U.S. Stands Alone in Its Embrace of Religion*. Available online at: http://people-press.org/reports/display.php3?ReportID=167.

10. This pattern was also confirmed in the comparison of churchgoing in the Gallup International Millennium Survey, where 82% of Africans reported attending religious services at least weekly. For details, see Gallup International. 2000. *Religion in the World at the End of the Millennium*. Available online at: www.gallup-international.com/survey15.htm.

11. The WVS estimated that about 44% of Americans attend church weekly. For comparison, it should be noted that similar estimates are produced by regular Gallup polls in the United States. For example, the March 14, 2003 Gallup–CNN/*USA Today* Poll asked: "*How often do you attend church or synagogue?*" The results were at least once a week (31%), almost every week (9%), about once a month (16%), seldom (28%), or never (16%). Yet, as discussed further in Chapter 4, the measures used by Gallup may produce a systematic bias. Gallup's procedures may systematically exaggerate attendance due to a lack of social

desirability filters in the measurement of churchgoing (thereby unintentionally "cueing" respondents) and also due to unrepresentative sample completion rates based on a limited number of random digit dialing callbacks and respondent substitution. See R. D. Woodberry. 1998. "When surveys lie and people tell the truth: How surveys over-sample church attenders." *American Sociological Review.* 63(1): 119–122.

12. For the long-term Scandinavian trends, see G. Gustafsson. 1994. "Religious change in the five Scandinavian countries, 1930–1980"; and also Ole Riis. 1994. "Patterns of secularization in Sandinavia." Both in *Scandinavian Values: Religion and Morality in the Nordic Countries.* Eds. Thorleif Pettersson and Ole Riis. Upssala: Acta Universitatis Upsaliensis.

13. Irena Borowik. 2002. "Between orthodoxy and eclecticism: On the religious transformations of Russia, Belarus and Ukraine." *Social Compass.* 49(4): 497–508; Andrew M. Greeley. 2003. *Religion in Europe at the End of the Second Millennium.* New Brunswick, NJ: Transaction Publishers. Chapter 6. "Russia: The biggest revival ever?"

14. For a fuller discussion, see R. Grier. 1997. "The effects of religion on economic development: A cross-national study of 63 former colonies." *Kyklos.* 50(1): 47–62; Robert J. Barro and Rachel M. McCleary. 2003. "Religion and economic growth." Unpublished paper. Available online at: http://post.economics.harvard.edu/faculty/barro/papers.

15. Many studies have found similar gender differences in religiosity; see, for example, David A. de Vaus and Ian McAllister. 1987. "Gender differences in religion: A test of the structural location theory." *American Sociological Review.* 52: 472–481; Alan S. Miller and Rodney Stark. 2002. "Gender and religiousness: Can socialization explanations be saved?" *American Journal of Sociology.* 107(6): 1399–1423.

16. For comparison, see B. C. Hayes. 2000. "Religious independents within Western industrialized nations: A socio-demographic profile." *Sociology of Religion.* 61(2): 191–207.

17. See J. Kelley and N. D. De Graaf. 1997. "National context, parental socialization, and religious belief: Results from 15 nations." *American Sociological Review.* 62(4): 639–659; A. Argue, D. R. Johnson, and L. K. White. 1999. "Age and religiosity: Evidence from a three-wave panel analysis." *Journal for the Scientific Study of Religion.* 38(3): 423–435.

18. For this approach, see N. D. De Graaf. 1999. "Event history data and making a history out of cross-sectional data – How to answer the question 'Why do cohorts differ?'" *Quality & Quantity.* 33(3): 261–276.

19. For example, a study using cross-sectional and panel survey data in Britain, drawing upon the series of British Election Studies and the British Household Panel Study, concluded that generational differences, not family formation factors such as marriage and childrearing, were responsible for age differences in church attendance. See J. R. Tilley. 2003. "Secularization and aging in Britain: Does family formation cause greater religiosity?" *Journal for the Scientific Study of Religion.* 42(2): 269–278.

20. Andrew M. Greeley. 1994. "A religious revival in Russia?" *Journal for the Scientific Study of Religion.* 33(3): 253–272.

Chapter 4

1. Peter L. Berger. Ed. 1999. *The Desecularization of the World.* Washington, D.C.: Ethics and Public Policy Center; Andrew M. Greeley. 2003. *Religion in Europe at the End of the Second Millennium.* New Brunswick, NJ: Transaction Publishers.

2. Postindustrial nation states are defined as those estimated by the UN Development Report to have a Human Development Index score over .900. These countries have a mean per capita GDP of $29,585. In this ranking, Malta, the other nation in Figure 3.1 with high religious participation, is classified an "industrial" state.

3. Peter L. Berger. Ed. 1999. *The Desecularization of the World.* Washington, D.C.: Ethics and Public Policy Center. See also discussions of American cultural exceptionalism in Louis Hartz. 1955. *The Liberal Tradition in America.* New York: Harcourt, Brace; Seymour Martin Lipset.1990. *Continental Divide: The Values and Institutions of Canada and the United States.* New York: Routledge; Edward A. Tiryakian. 1993. "American religious exceptionalism: A reconsideration." *The Annals of the American Academy of Political and Social Science.* 527: 40–54; Graham K. Wilson. 1998. *Only in America? The Politics of the United States in Comparative Perspective.* Chatham, NJ: Chatham House.

4. R. Currie, A. D. Gilbert, and L. Horsley. 1977. *Churches and Churchgoers: Patterns of Church Growth in the British Isles since 1700.* Oxford: Oxford University Press; Sabino Samele Acquaviva. 1979. *The Decline of the Sacred in Industrial Society.* Oxford: Basil Blackwell; Steve Bruce. 1996. *Religion in the Modern World: From Cathedrals to Cults.* Oxford: Oxford University Press; Sheena Ashford and Noel Timms. 1992. *What Europe Thinks: A Study of Western European Values.* Aldershot U.K.: Dartmouth; Wolfgang Jagodzinski and Karel Dobbelaere. 1995. "Secularization and church religiosity." In *The Impact of Values.* Eds. Jan W. van Deth and Elinor Scarbrough. Oxford: Oxford University Press; L. Voye. 1999. "Secularization in a context of advanced modernity." *Sociology of Religion.* 60(3): 275–288; Höllinger F. 1996. *Volksreligion und Herrschaftskirche. Die Würzeln Religiösen Verhaltens in Westlichen Gesellschaften.* Opladen: Leske und Budrich. For a challenge to this view, however, see Rodney Stark and William Sims Bainbridge. 1985. "A supply-side reinterpretation of the 'secularization' of Europe." *Journal for the Scientific Study of Religion.* 33: 230–252.

5. Wolfgang Jagodzinski and Karel Dobbelaere. 1995. "Secularization and church religiosity." In *The Impact of Values.* Eds. Jan W. van Deth and Elinor Scarbrough. Oxford: Oxford University Press. P. 105.

6. Steve Bruce. 2002. *God is Dead.* Oxford: Blackwell. Chapter 3; G. Gustafsson. 1994. "Religious change in the five Scandinavian countries, 1930–1980" and also O. Riis. "Patterns of secularization in Scndinavia." Both are in *Scandinavian Values: Religion and Morality in the Nordic Countries.* Eds. T. Pettersson and O. Riis. Upssala: Acta Universitatis Upsaliensis. Also see T. Pettersson and E. M. Hamberg. 1997. "Denominational pluralism and church membership in

contemporary Sweden: A longitudinal study of the period, 1974–1995." *Journal of Empirical Theology*. 10: 61–78. For a summary, see Table 1 in Steve Bruce. 2000. "The supply-side model of religion: The Nordic and Baltic states." *Journal for the Scientific Study of Religion*. 39(1): 32–46; V. Cesareo, et al. 1995. *La Religiosità in Italia*. 2nd ed. Milan: A. Mondadori; Reginald W. Bibby. 1979. "The state of collective religiosity in Canada: An empirical analysis." *Canadian Review of Sociology and Anthropology*. 16(1): 105–116; Alain Baril and George A. Mori. 1991. "Leaving the fold: Declining church attendance." *Canadian Social Trends*. Autumn: 21–24; Peter Beyer. 1997. "Religious vitality in Canada: The complimentarity of religious market and secularization perspectives." *Journal for the Scientific Study of Religion*. 36(2): 272–288; G. Michelat et al. 1991. *Les Français, Sont-ils Encore Catholiques?: Analyse d'un Sondage d'Opinion*. Paris: Editions du Cerf; G. Dekker, J. de Hart, and J. Peters. 1997. *God in Nederland 1966–1996*. Amsterdam: Anthos; F. J. Lechner. 1996. "Secularization in the Netherlands?" *Journal of the Scientific Study of Religion*. 35: 252–264.

7. As noted in Table 3.5, using regression analysis, the only European countries where the fall was not statistically significant (at the .10 level) was Italy (due to a slight recovery in the early 1990s). At the .05 level, Britain, Northern Ireland, and Greece also emerged as not significant. See also Anthony M. Abela. 1993. "Post-secularisation: The social significance of religious values in four Catholic European countries." *Melita Theolgica*. XLIV: 39–58.

8. Andrew M. Greeley. 2003. *Religion in Europe at the End of the Second Millennium*. New Brunswick, NJ: Transaction Publishers. P. xi.

9. Reginald W. Bibby. 1979. "The state of collective religiosity in Canada: An empirical analysis." *Canadian Review of Sociology and Anthropology*. 16(1): 105–116. Table III shows that in Canada church attendance fell from 67% in 1946 to 35% in 1978; Hans Mol. 1985. *The Faith of Australians*. Sydney: George, Allen, & Unwin; Ian McAllister. 1988. "Religious change and secularization: The transmission of religious values in Australia." *Sociological Analysis*. 49(3): 249–263.

10. Wade Clark Roof. 2001. *Spiritual Marketplace: Baby Boomers and the Remaking of American Religion*. Princeton, NJ: Princeton University Press. See also Robert C. Fuller. 2002. *Spiritual, but Not Religious: Understanding Unchurched America*. New York: Oxford University Press.

11. Grace Davie. 1994. *Religion in Britain since 1945: Believing without Belonging*. Oxford: Blackwell; D. Hervieu-Leger. 2003. "The case for a sociology of 'multiple religious modernities': A different approach to the 'invisible religion' of European societies." *Social Compass*. 50(3): 287–295.

12. Andrew M. Greeley. 2003. *Religion in Europe at the End of the Second Millennium*. New Brunswick, NJ: Transaction Publishers.

13. Andrew M. Greeley. 1980. *Religious Change in America*. Cambridge, MA: Harvard University Press; Andrew M. Greeley. 1985. *Unsecular Man: The Persistence of Religion*. New York: Schocken Books; M. Hout and Andrew M. Greeley. 1998. "What church officials' reports don't show: Another look at church

attendance data." *American Sociological Review.* 63(1): 113–119; M. Hout and Andrew M. Greeley. 1987. "The center doesn't hold: Church attendance in the United States, 1940–1984." *American Sociological Review.* 52(3): 325–345.

14. March 1939, Gallup poll–AIPO: *"Did you happen to go to church last Sunday?"* 40% yes, 60% no. March 14, 2003, Gallup-CNN/*USA Today* Poll: *"How often do you attend church or synagogue – at least once a week (31%), almost every week (9%), about once a month (16%), seldom (28%), or never (16%)?"* Hadaway points out that self-reported church attendance figures may well contain systematic bias toward over-reporting, compared with records of the actual size of congregations. C. Kirk Hadaway and P. L. Marler. 1998. "Did you really go to church this week? Behind the poll data." *Christian Century.* May 6: 472–475; Kirk Hadaway et al. 1993. "What the polls don't show: A closer look at church attendance." *American Sociological Review.* 58(6): 741–752. See also S. Presser and L. Stinson. 1998. "Data collection mode and social desirability bias in self-reported religious attendance." *American Sociological Review.* 63(1): 137–145. Although we accept this argument, this cannot explain the apparent discrepancy between reported churchgoing in the United States and Western Europe, unless some sort of "spiral of silence" claims about the social acceptability of churchgoing in America are brought into the argument. Other evidence based on cohort and period analysis of the General Social Survey suggests that the apparent long-term stability of the aggregate levels of churchgoing in the United States, in fact, disguises two simultaneous changes occurring since the early 1970s: a negative cohort effect *and* a positive period effect. Mark Chaves. 1989. "Secularization *and* religious revival: Evidence from U.S. church attendance rates, 1972–1986." *Journal for the Scientific Study of Religion.* 28(4): 464–477. For more details about the Gallup organization time-series tracking religion in America, see D. Michael Lindsay. 2000. *Surveying the Religious Landscape: Trends in U.S. Beliefs.* New York: Moorhouse Publishing.

15. R. D. Woodberry. 1996. *The Missing Fifty Percent: Accounting for the Gap Between Survey Estimates and Head-Counts of Church Attendance.* Nashville, TN: *Society for the Scientific Study of Religion.* R.D. Woodberry. 1998. "When surveys lie and people tell the truth: How surveys over-sample church attenders." *American Sociological Review* 63(1): 119–122; S. Presser and L. Stinson. 1998. "Data collection mode and social desirability bias in self-reported religious attendance." *American Sociological Review.* 63(1): 137–145.

16. Robert D. Woodberry. 1998. "When surveys lie and people tell the truth: How surveys oversample church attenders." *American Sociological Review.* 63(1): 119–122; C. Kirk Hadaway, P. L. Marler, and Mark Chaves. 1998. "Overreporting church attendance in America: Evidence that demands the same verdict." *American Sociological Review.* 63(1): 122–130; B. Steensland et al. 2000. "The measure of American religion: Toward improving the state of the art." *Social Forces.* 79(1): 291–318.

17. See details of the NES series online at: www.umich.edu/~NES.

18. See also C. Kirk Hadaway, P. L. Marler, and Mark Chaves. 1998. "Overreporting church attendance in America: Evidence that demands the same verdict." *American Sociological Review.* 63(1): 122–130.

19. Robert Wuthnow. 1988. *The Restructuring of American Religion*, Princeton, NJ: Princeton University Press; Tom Smith. 1992. "Are conservative churches really growing?" *Review of Religious Research*. 33:305–329; Michael Hout, Andrew M. Greeley, and Melissa J. Wilde. 2001. "The demographic imperative in religious change in the United States." *American Journal of Sociology*. 107(2): 468–500.

20. Brian R. Wilson. 1969. *Religion in Secular Society*. Harmondsworth, U.K.: Penguin Books, Ltd.

21. Pippa Norris. 2000. "U.S. campaign 2000: Of pregnant chads, butterfly ballots and partisan vitriol." *Government and Opposition*. 35(2): 1–24; VNS exit polls in "Who Voted." *New York Times*. November 12, 2000; Andrew Kohut et al. 2000. *The Diminishing Divide: Religion's Changing Role in American Politics*. Washington, D.C.: Brookings Institution Press.

22. Gertrude Himmelfarb. 1999. *One Nation: Two Cultures*. New York: Random House.

23. Rodney Stark and William Sims Bainbridge. 1985. "A supply-side reinterpretation of the 'secularization' of Europe." *Journal for the Scientific Study of Religion*. 33: 230–252; Rodney Stark and William Sims Bainbridge. 1987. *A Theory of Religion*. New York: Peter Lang; Roger Finke and Rodney Stark. 1992. *The Churching of America*. New Brunswick, NJ: Rutgers University Press; Roger Finke and Lawrence R. Iannaccone. 1993. "The illusion of shifting demand: Supply-side explanations for trends and change in the American religious market place." *Annals of the American Association of Political and Social Science*. 527: 27–39; R. S. Warner. 1993. "Work in progress toward a new paradigm in the sociology of religion." *American Journal of Sociology*. 98(5): 1044–1093; Roger Finke and Rodney Stark. 2000. *Acts of Faith: Explaining the Human Side of Religion*. Berkeley, CA: University of California Press.

24. Roger Finke and Rodney Stark. 2000. *Acts of Faith: Explaining the Human Side of Religion*. Berkeley, CA: University of California Press. P. 88. It should be noted that the assumed universal rationality in the supply-side theory has been criticized as inapplicable to religions, such as Confucianism and Judaism, that do not believe that behavior in this life generates otherworldly rewards in any after life. See Mark Chaves and P. S. Gorski. 2001. "Religious pluralism and religious participation." *Annual Review of Sociology*. 27: 261–281; S. Sharot. 2002. "Beyond Christianity: A critique of the rational choice theory of religion from a Weberian and comparative religions perspective." *Sociology of Religion*. 63(4): 427–454.

25. Mark Chaves. 1999. "The National Congregations Study: Background, methods and selected results." *Journal for the Scientific Study of Religion*. 38(4): 458–476.

26. Roger Finke and Rodney Stark. 2000. *Acts of Faith: Explaining the Human Side of Religion*. Berkeley, CA: University of California Press. P. 230.

27. Roger Finke and Rodney Stark. 2000. *Acts of Faith: Explaining the Human Side of Religion*. Berkeley, CA: University of California Press. Pp. 237–238.

28. Roger Finke and Rodney Stark. 2000. *Acts of Faith: Explaining the Human Side of Religion*. Berkeley, CA: University of California Press. P. 257.

29. Mark Chaves and P. S. Gorski. 2001. "Religious pluralism and religious participation." *Annual Review of Sociology*. 27: 261–281.

30. J. M. Bryant. 2000. "Cost-benefit accounting and the piety business: Is *homo religious*, at bottom, a *homo economicus*?" *Methods and Theory in the Study of Religion*. 12: 520–548. It should be noted that other popular commentators have gone even further with this analogy than Finke and Stark; for example, Cimino and Lattin argue that the U.S. consumer-driven culture has led Americans to go "shopping" for spiritual experiences. See Richard Cimino and Don Lattin. 2002. *Shopping for Faith: American Religion in the New Millennium*. New York: Jossey-Bass.

31. For example, the Herfindahl Index for religious fractionalization is computed as follows:

	Community A High Pluralism		Community B Moderate Pluralism		Community C Limited Pluralism	
	%	Squares	%	Squares	%	Squares
Anglican	.20	.0400	.30	.0900	90	.0810
Catholic	.20	.0400	.25	.0625	5	.0025
Methodist	.15	.0225	.20	.0400	3	.0090
Baptist	.09	.0081	.13	.0169	2	.0040
Mormons	.09	.0081	.05	.0025	0	.0000
Muslims	.09	.0081	.02	.0040	0	.0000
Jewish	.09	.0081	.02	.0040	0	.0000
Other	.09	.0081	.03	.0090	0	.0000
TOTAL %	100	0.1430	100	0.2136	100	0.8138
Index	$(1 - 0.1430) = 0.857$		$(1 - 0.2136) = 0.786$		$(1 - 0.8138) = 0.186$	

32. The ethno-religious fractionalization variable is computed as one minus the Herfindahl Index of ethno-linguistic group shares, representing the probability that two randomly selected individuals from a population belonged to different religious faiths. For a discussion, see Alberto Alesina, Arnaud Devleeschauwer, William Easterly, Sergio Kurlat, and Romain Wacziarg. 2003. "Fractionalization." *Journal of Economic Growth*. 82: 219–258. The dataset is available online at: www.stanford.edu/~wacziarg/papersum.html. The index is calculated as follows:

$$FRACT_j = 1 - \sum_{i=1}^{N} s_{ij}^2$$

where s_{ij} is the share of group i ($i = 1 \ldots N$) in country j.

33. Morgens Pedersen. 1979. "The dynamics of European party systems: Changing patterns of electoral volatility." *European Journal of Political Research*. 7: 1–27.

34. Mark Chaves and P. S. Gorski. 2001. "Religious pluralism and religious participation." *Annual Review of Sociology*. 27: 261–281.

35. In particular, irrespective of the effect of pluralism upon participation, non-zero correlations will occur that depend mathematically only upon the size distributions of the denominations in the dataset across geographical units. David Voas, Daviel V. A. Olson, and Alasdair Crockett. 2002. "Religious pluralism and participation: Why previous research is wrong." *American Sociological Review*. 67(2): 212–230.

36. See also Rodney Stark and Lawrence Iannaccone. 1994. "A supply-side reinterpretation of the 'secularization' of Europe." *Journal for the Scientific Study of Religion*. 33: 230–252.

37. For an attempt to explain the Italian case as the result of internal competition within Catholicism, see L. Diotallevi. 2002. "Internal competition in a national religious monopoly: The Catholic effect and the Italian case." *Sociology of Religion*. 63(2): 137–155.

38. Lawrence R. Iannaccone. 1991. "The consequences of religious market structure." *Rationality and Society*. 3: 156–177.

39. Ian Smith, John W. Sawkins, and Paul T. Seaman. 1998. "The economics of religious participation: A cross-country study." *Kyklos*. 51(1): 25–43.

40. Johan Verweij, Peter Ester, and Rein Nauta. 1997. "Secularization as an economic and cultural phenomenon: A cross-national analysis." *Journal for the Scientific Study of Religion*. 36(2): 309–324.

41. Steve Bruce. 2000. "The supply-side model of religion: The Nordic and Baltic states." *Journal for the Scientific Study of Religion*. 39(1): 32–46. See also Beyer's related argument that the privatization of religion in Canada led toward greater secularization. Peter Beyer. 1997. "Religious vitality in Canada: The complimentarity of religious market and secularization perspectives." *Journal for the Scientific Study of Religion*. 36(2): 272–288.

42. Mark Chaves and Philip S. Gorski. 2001. "Religious pluralism and religious participation." *Annual Review of Sociology*. 27: 261–281; David Voas, Daniel V. A. Olson, and Alasdair Crockett. 2002. "Religious pluralism and participation: Why previous research is wrong." *American Sociological Review*. 67(2): 212–230.

43. This argument finds parallels in the debate about the relative importance of changes in the mass political culture and in society, or in the strength of party organizations, for explaining patterns of social and partisan dealignment. See the discussion in Pippa Norris. 2003. *Electoral Engineering*. New York: Cambridge University Press.

44. Alberto Alesina et al. 2003. "Fractionalization." *Journal of Economic Growth*. 82: 219–258. The dataset is available online at: www.stanford.edu/~wacziarg/papersum.html.

45. It should be noted that the proportion of adherents to the majority religion in each country was also compared as an alternative measure of religious diversity or homogeneity, but this measure also proved an insignificant predictor of religious participation, whether the comparison was restricted to postindustrial societies or to all nations worldwide.

46. Seymour Martin Lipset. 1990. *Continental Divide: The Values and Institutions of Canada and the United States*. New York: Routledge.

47. Mark Chaves and David E. Cann. 1992. "Regulation, pluralism and religious market structure." *Rationality and Society*. 4: 272–290. The scale is reversed in this study, for ease of presentation, so that a low score represents greater regulation.

48. Paul Marshall. 2000. *Religious Freedom in the World*. Available online at: www.freedomhouse.org

49. F. J. Lechner. 1991. "The case against secularization: A rebuttal." *Social Forces*. 69: 1103–1119.

50. See J. Verweij, Peter Ester, and R. Nauta. 1997. "Secularization as an economic and cultural phenomenon: A cross-national analysis." *Journal for the Scientific Study of Religion*. 36(2): 309–324. The comparative study of sixteen nations, based on the 1990 European Values Survey, found that religiosity was significantly related to the percentage of GNP spent on social security in 1990, even controlling for per capita GNP.

51. For a discussion of the comparative evidence see, for example, Derek Bok. 1996. *The State of the Nation: Government and the Quest for a Better Society*. Cambridge, MA: Harvard University Press.

52. For example, a recent detailed study comparing the levels of household income after government redistribution through tax and welfare transfers, based on the Luxembourg Income Study (LIS) database, found that the GINI coefficient for income inequality was greatest in the United States compared with thirteen other advanced industrial democracies. See David Bradley et al. 2003. "Distribution and redistribution in postindustrial democracies." *World Politics*. 55(1): 193–228.

53. Katherine McFate, Roger Lawson, and William Julius Wilson. Eds. 1995. *Poverty, Inequality, and the Future of Social Policy: Western States in the New World Order*. New York: Russell Sage; Alexander Hicks. 1999. *Social Democracy and Welfare Capitalism: A Century of Income Security Policies*. Ithaca, NY: Cornell University Press; Gosta Esping-Andersen. 1999. *Social Foundations of Postindustrial Economies*. Oxford: Oxford University Press.

Chapter 5

1. Paul Froese. 2001. 'Hungary for Religion: "A supply-side interpretation of Hungarian religious revival." *Journal for the Scientific Study of Religion*. 40(2): 251–268.

2. In 1980, 31% of the relevant age group in Europe and Central Asia enrolled in tertiary (higher) education, compared with 36% in high-income nations. World Bank. 2001. *World Development Indicators 2001*. Washington, D.C.: World Bank.

3. Ariana Need and Geoffrey Evans. 2001. "Analyzing patterns of religious participation in post-communist Eastern Europe." *British Journal of Sociology*. 52(2): 229–248.

4. Irena Borowik. 2002. "Between orthodoxy and eclecticism: On the religious transformations of Russia, Belarus and Ukraine." *Social Compass*. 49(4): 497–508.

5. K. Kaariainen. 1999. "Religiousness in Russia after the collapse of communism." *Social Compass*. 46(1): 35–46.

6. D. Pollack. 2003. "Religiousness inside and outside the church in selected post-Communist countries of Central and Eastern Europe." *Social Compass*. 50(3): 321–334.

7. Grzegorz W. Kolodko. 2000. *From Shock to Therapy: The Political Economy of Socialist Transformations*. New York: Oxford University Press; Marie Lavigne. 2001. *The Economics of Transition: From Socialist Economy to Market Economy*. London: Palgrave; Anders Åsland. 2002. *Building Capitalism: The Transformation of the Former Soviet Bloc*. Cambridge, U.K.: Cambridge University Press.

8. John Anderson. 1994. *Religion, State and Politics in the Soviet Union and Successor States*. New York: Cambridge University Press; William B. Husband. 2000. *'Godless Communists': Atheism and Society in Soviet Russia, 1917–1932*. DeKalb: Northern Illinois Press.

9. B. R. Bociurkie and J. W. Strong. Eds. 1975. *Religion and Atheism in the USSR and Eastern Europe*. London: Macmillan; I. Troyanovsky. Ed. 1991. *Religion in the Soviet Republics*. San Francisco: HarperCollins; W. H. Swatos, Jr. Ed. 1994. *Politics and Religion in Central and Eastern Europe: Traditions and Transitions*. Westport, CT: Praeger; Miklós Tomka. 1998. "Coping with persecution: Religious change in communism and in post-communist reconstruction in Central Europe." *International Sociology*. 13(2): 229–248.

10. Andrew M. Greeley. 1994. "A religious revival in Russia?" *Journal for the Scientific Study of Religion*. 33(3): 253–272; Andrew M. Greeley. 2003. *Religion in Europe at the End of the Second Millennium*. New Brunswick, NJ: Transaction Publishers. Chapters 6 and 7.

11. See, however, Bruce's study of the role of religion in the Baltic nations after independence, which casts serious doubt on the claims in the supply-side thesis in these countries. Steve Bruce. 2000. "The supply-side model of religion: The Nordic and Baltic states." *Journal for the Scientific Study of Religion*. 39(1): 32–46.

12. Paul Froese. 2001. "Hungary for religion: A supply-side interpretation of Hungarian religious revival." *Journal for the Scientific Study of Religion* 40(2): 251–268; Paul Froese and S. Pfaff. 2001. "Replete and desolate markets: Poland, East Germany, and the new religious paradigm." *Social Forces*. 80(2): 481–507.

13. H. Johnston. 1994. "Religio-Nationalist subcultures under the Communists: Comparisons from the Baltics, Transcaucasia and Ukraine." In *Politics and Religion in Central and Eastern Europe: Traditions and Transitions*. Ed. W. H. Swatos, Jr. Westport, CT: Praeger.

14. Mary L. Gautier. 1997. "Church attendance and religious beliefs in post-communist societies." *Journal for the Scientific Study of Religion*. 36(2): 289–296; Barbara Strassberg. 1988. "Changes in religious culture in Post World War II Poland." *Sociological Analysis*. 48(4): 342–354; Miklós Tomka. 1998. "Coping

with persecution: Religious change in communism and in post-communist reconstruction in Central Europe." *International Sociology.* 13(2): 229–248.

15. Irena Borowik. 2002. "The Roman Catholic Church in the process of democratic transformation: The case of Poland." *Social Compass.* 49(2): 239–252.

16. Paul Froese. 2001. "Hungary for religion: A supply-side interpretation of Hungarian religious revival." *Journal for the Scientific Study of Religion.* 40(2): 251–268; Paul Froese and S. Pfaff. 2001. "Replete and desolate markets: Poland, East Germany, and the new religious paradigm." *Social Forces.* 80(2): 481–507.

17. S. Zrinscak. 2002. "Roles, expectation and conflicts: Religion and churches in societies undergoing transition." *Social Compass.* 49(4): 509–521.

18. Ariana Need and Geoffrey Evans. 2001. "Analyzing patterns of religious participation in post-communist Eastern Europe." *British Journal of Sociology.* 52(2): 229–248.

19. All the linear models measuring the effects of age on religiosity were significant at the .05 level, except for belief in the existence of a soul.

20. Roger Finke and Rodney Stark. 2000. *Acts of Faith: Explaining the Human Side of Religion.* Berkeley, CA: University of California Press. Pp. 237–238.

21. Alberto Alesina et al. 2003. "Fractionalization." *Journal of Economic Growth.* 82: 219–258. The dataset is available online at: www.stanford.edu/~wacziarg/papersum.html.

22. P. M. Thornton. 2002. "Framing dissent in contemporary China: Irony, ambiguity and metonymy." *China Quarterly.* 171: 661–681.

23. U.S. State Department. 2003. *International Religious Freedom, 2002.* Washington, DC. Available online at: http://www.state.gov/g/drl/rls/irf/. The report is produced due to the *International Religious Freedom Act of 1998* (U.S. Public Law 105–92) and is monitored by the U.S. Commission on International Religious Freedom (http://www.uscirf.gov). It should be noted that the report is used to create an index comparing levels of religious freedom in 2002, for comparisons with levels of religious participation in the WVS 1990–2001. This means that our study cannot monitor to what extent the previous history of religious repression and persecution played an important role in the past. The report by the U.S. State Department largely reflects the evaluations of the state of religious freedoms reported by human rights organizations such as Freedom House and Amnesty International and by comparative studies. See, for example, Kevin Boyle and Juliet Sheen. Eds. 1997. *Freedom of Religion and Belief: A world report.* New York: Routledge; Paul Marshall. Ed. 2000. *Religious Freedom in the World: A Global Report on Freedom and Persecution.* Nashville, TN: Broadman and Holman.

24. John Anderson. 1994. *Religion, State and Politics in the Soviet Union and Successor States.* New York: Cambridge University Press; Kevin Boyle and Juliet Sheen. Eds. 1997. *Freedom of Religion and Belief: A World Report.* New York: Routledge; Paul Marshall. Ed. 2000. *Religious Freedom in the World: A Global Report on Freedom and Persecution.* Nashville, TN: Broadman and Holman; William B. Husband. 2000. *'Godless Communists': Atheism and Society in Soviet Russia, 1917–1932.* DeKalb: Northern Illinois Press.

Chapter 6

1. Samuel P. Huntington. 1996. *The Clash of Civilizations and the Remaking of World Order*. New York: Simon & Schuster. P. 28.

2. Edward Said. 2001. "A clash of ignorance." *The Nation* 273(12): 1–13; B. M. Russett, J. R. O'Neal, and M. Cox. 2000. "Clash of civilizations, or realism and liberalism déjà vu? Some evidence." *Journal of Peace Research*. 37(5): 583–608; Tedd Gurr 2000. *Peoples versus States*. Washington, D.C.: U.S. Institute for Peace Press.

3. Niaz Faizi Kabuli. 1994. *Democracy according to Islam*. Pittsburgh, PA: Dorrance Publications; John L. Esposito and John O. Voll. 1996. *Democracy and Islam*, New York: Oxford University Press; Anthony Shadid. 2001. *Legacy of the Prophet: Despots, Democrats, and the New Politics of Islam*. Boulder, CO: Westview Press.

4. Samuel P. Huntington. 1996. *The Clash of Civilizations and the Remaking of World Order*. New York: Simon & Schuster. Pp. 41–43.

5. Samuel P. Huntington. 1996. *The Clash of Civilizations and the Remaking of World Order*. New York: Simon & Schuster. Pp. 70–71.

6. Ronald Inglehart and Pippa Norris. 2003. *Rising Tide: Gender Equality and Cultural Change Around the World*. New York: Cambridge University Press.

7. M. I. Midlarsky. 1998. "Democracy and Islam: Implications for civilizational conflict and the democratic process." *International Studies Quarterly*. 42(3): 485–511.

8. International relations scholars have strongly challenged the evidence for Huntington's claim that ethnic inter-state conflict has increased during the 1990s, although this body of work is not central to the argument presented here. See, for example, Tedd Gurr. 2000. *Peoples versus States*. Washington, D.C.: U.S. Institute for Peace Press; B. M. Russett, J. R. O'Neal, and M. Cox. 2000. "Clash of civilizations, or realism and liberalism déjà vu? Some evidence." *Journal of Peace Research*. 37(5): 583–608.

9. Shireen T. Hunter. 1998. *The Future of Islam and the West: Clash of Civilizations or Peaceful Coexistence?* Westport, CT: Praeger; John Esposito. Ed. 1997. *Political Islam: Revolution, Radicalism or Reform?* Boulder, CO: Lynne Reinner; Graham E. Fuller. 2002. "The future of political Islam." *Foreign Affairs*. 81(2): 48–60.

10. Niaz Faizi Kabuli. 1994. *Democracy according to Islam*. Pittsburgh, PA: Dorrance Publications; John L. Esposito and John O. Voll. 1996. *Democracy and Islam*. New York: Oxford University Press; Anthony Shadid. 2001. *Legacy of the Prophet: Despots, Democrats, and the New Politics of Islam*. Boulder, CO: Westview Press.

11. Edward Said. 2001. "A clash of ignorance." *The Nation* 273(12): 11–13.

12. D. Chirot. 2001. "A clash of civilizations or of paradigms? Theorizing progress and social change." *International Sociology*. 16(3): 341–360.

13. Ronald Inglehart and Pippa Norris. 2003. *Rising Tide: Gender Equality and Cultural Change Around the World*. New York: Cambridge University Press.

14. Ibid.

15. See Bernard Lewis. 2002. *What Went Wrong? Western Impact and Middle Eastern Response*. New York: Oxford University Press.

16. The main exceptions are the first-ever Gallup survey in nine predominately Islamic societies that was conducted to monitor reactions to the events of 9/11. Gallup surveyed 10,000 people in December 2001 and January 2002, with researchers conducting hour-long, in-person interviews in Saudi Arabia, Iran, Pakistan, Indonesia, Turkey, Lebanon, Kuwait, Jordan, and Morocco. For details, see online: http://www.gallup.com/poll/releases/pr020305.asp. In addition, Roper Reports Worldwide conducted an annual worldwide survey from October 2001 to January 2002 in 30 nations, including an urban sample of 1,000 residents in the metropolitan areas in Saudi Arabia. For details of the Roper results, see Thomas A. W. Miller and Geoffrey Feinberg. 2002. "Culture clash." *Public Perspective*. 13(2): 6–9.

17. The Gallup Poll. Available online at: http://www.gallup.com/poll/summits/islam.asp.

18. Thomas A. W. Miller and Geoffrey Feinberg. 2002. "Culture clash." *Public Perspective*. 13(2): 6–9.

19. Mark Tessler. 2002. "Islam and democracy in the Middle East: The impact of religious orientations on attitudes towards democracy in four Arab countries." *Comparative Politics*. 34(1): 337–254; Mark Tessler. 2003. "Do Islamic orientations influence attitudes toward democracy in the Arab world? Evidence from Egypt, Jordan, Morocco and Algeria." *International Journal of Comparative Sociology*. 43(3–5): 229–249.

20. Richard Rose. 2002. "How Muslims view democracy: Evidence from Central Asia." *Journal of Democracy*. 14(4): 102–111.

21. Although it should be noted that despite the centrality of the concept there are ambiguities in the definition, labeling, and classification of "civilizations" in Huntington's study, for example, it remains unclear whether Huntington believes that there is or is not a distinct African civilization, and the major discussion of types (pp. 45–47) excludes the Orthodox category altogether.

22. Ronald Inglehart. 1997. *Modernization and Postmodernization: Cultural, Economic and Political Change in 43 Societies*. Princeton, NJ: Princeton University Press.

23. These countries are ranked as equally "free" according to the 2000–2001 Freedom House assessments of political rights and civil liberties. Freedom House. 2001. *Freedom in the World 2000–2001*. Available online at: www.freedomhouse.org.

24. Pippa Norris. Ed. 1999. *Critical Citizens: Global Support for Democratic Governance*. Oxford: Oxford University Press; Robert D. Putnam and Susan Pharr. Eds. 2001. *Disaffected Democracies: What's Troubling the Trilateral Countries?* Princeton, NJ: Princeton University Press.

25. Hans Dieter Klingemann. 1999. "Mapping political support in the 1990s: A global analysis." In *Critical Citizens: Global Support for Democratic Governance*. Ed. Pippa Norris. Oxford: Oxford University Press.

26. Pippa Norris. Ed. 1999. *Critical Citizens: Global Support for Democratic Governance*. Oxford: Oxford University Press; Robert D. Putnam and Susan Pharr. Eds. 2001. *Disaffected Democracies: What's Troubling the Trilateral Countries?* Princeton, NJ: Princeton University Press.

27. The combined 100-point gender equality scale is based on the following five items: MENPOL Q118: "On the whole, men make better political leaders than women do." (Agree coded low); MENJOBS Q78: "When jobs are scarce, men should have more right to a job than women." (Agree coded low); BOYEDUC Q.119: "A university education is more important for a boy than a girl." (Agree coded low); NEEDKID Q110: "Do you think that a woman has to have children in order to be fulfilled or is this not necessary?" (Agree coded low); SGLMUM Q112: "If a woman wants to have a child as a single parent but she doesn't want to have a stable relationship with a man, do you approve or disapprove?" (disapprove coded low). Three items used statements with Likert-style 4-point agree-disagree responses, while two used dichotomies, and these items were all recoded so that higher values consistently represent greater support for gender equality. Principal component factor analysis revealed that all five items fell into a single consistent scale (not reproduced here), with a Cronbach's alpha of 0.54. For details of the construction, reliability, validity, and distribution of this scale, see Ronald Inglehart and Pippa Norris. 2003. *Rising Tide: Gender Equality and Cultural Change Around the World*. New York: Cambridge University Press.

Chapter 7

1. P. Scheepers, M. T. Grotenhuis, and F. Van Der Slik. 2002. "Education, religiosity and moral attitudes: Explaining cross-national effect differences." *Sociology of Religion*. 63(2): 157–176; Wolfgang Jagodzinski and Karel Dobbelaere. 1995. "Religious and ethical pluralism." In *The Impact of Values*. Eds. Jan W. van Deth and Elinor Scarbrough. Oxford: Oxford University Press.

2. Hartmut Lehman and Guenther Roth. Eds. 1993. *Weber's Protestant Ethic: Origins, Evidence, Contexts*. New York: Cambridge University Press; Michael H. Lessnoff. 1994. *The Spirit of Capitalism and the Protestant Ethic: An Enquiry into the Weber Thesis*. Aldershot, U.K.: Edward Elgar; David J. Chalcraft and Austin Harrington. 2001. *The Protestant Ethic Debate: Max Weber Replies to His Critics, 1907–1910*. Liverpool: Liverpool University Press; Harold B. Jones, Jr. 1997. "The Protestant ethic: Weber's model and the empirical literature." *Human Relations*. 50(7): 757–778; R. Swedburg. 1998. *Max Weber and the Idea of Economic Sociology*. Princeton, NJ: Princeton University Press.

3. Max Weber. 1992 [1904]. *The Protestant Ethic and the Spirit of Capitalism*. New York: Routledge. P. 19.

4. Ibid.

5. Ibid. P. 62.

6. Ibid. P. 52.

7. Ibid.

8. Laurence R. Iannaccone. 1998. "Introduction to the economics of religion." *Journal of Economic Literature*. 36(3): 1465–1496. For a summary of the many critiques made over the years, see Anthony Giddens. 1992. "Introduction." In Max Weber. *The Protestant Ethic and the Spirit of Capitalism*. New York: Routledge.

9. R. H. Tawney. 1926. *Religion and the Rise of Capitalism.* New York: Harper & Row; K. Samuelson. 1993. *Religion and Economic Action: The Protestant Ethic, the Rise of Capitalism and the Abuses of Scholarship.* Toronto: University of Toronto Press; U. Blum and L. Dudley. 2001. "Religion and economic growth: Was Weber right?" *Journal of Evolutionary Economics.* 11(2): 207–230. It should be noted that Max Weber anticipated this argument: "It is true that . . . religious affiliation is not a cause of the economic conditions, but to a certain extent appears to be a result of them." Max Weber. 1992 [1904]. *The Protestant Ethic and the Spirit of Capitalism.* New York: Routledge. Pp. 36–37.

10. M. Ter Voert. 1997. "The Protestant ethic in the Republic of the Seven United Netherlands: Fiction or fact?" *Netherlands Journal of Social Sciences.* 33(1): 1–10.

11. Luigi Guiso, Paola Sapienza, and Luigi Zingales. 2003. "People's opium? Religion and economic attitudes." *Journal of Monetary Economics.* 50: 225–282. See also Liah Greenfield. 2001. *The Spirit of Capitalism: Nationalism and Economic Growth.* Cambridge, MA: Harvard University Press; A. Furnham et al. 1993. "A Comparison of Protestant work-ethic beliefs in 13 nations." *Journal of Social Psychology.* 133(2): 185–197; Robert J. Barro and Rachel M. McCleary. 2003. "Religion and economic growth." Unpublished paper.

12. Ronald Inglehart. 1997. *Modernization and Postmodernization.* Princeton, NJ: Princeton University Press. Pp. 222–223. See also a study examining economic individualism and evangelicalism in the United States in D. C. Barker and C. J. Carman. 2000. "The spirit of capitalism? Religious doctrine, values, and economic attitude constructs." *Political Behavior.* 22(1): 1–27.

13. To explore further we also checked whether any patterns established at societal-level were also evident if we analyzed the type of faith held at individual-level, measured by whether respondents belong to different world religions. The results of the analysis replicated themselves with no significant difference to the major conclusions.

14. Ronald Inglehart. 1997. *Modernization and Postmodernization.* Princeton, NJ: Princeton University Press. Chapter 7.

15. Harold B. Jones, Jr. 1997. "The Protestant ethic: Weber's model and the empirical literature." *Human Relations.* 50(7): 757–778.

16. M. J. Miller, D. J. Woehr, and N. Hudspeth. 2002. "The meaning and measurement of work ethic: Construction and initial validation of a multidimensional inventory." *Journal of Vocational Behavior.* 60(3): 451–489.

17. K. Samuelson. 1993. *Religion and Economic Action: The Protestant Ethic, the Rise of Capitalism and the Abuses of Scholarship.* Toronto: University of Toronto Press.

18. Robert D. Putnam. 1995. *Making Democracy Work.* Princeton, NJ: Princeton University Press.

19. Louise Keely. 2003. "Comment on: People's opium? Religion and economic attitudes." *Journal of Monetary Economics.* 50(1): 283–287.

20. Luigi Guiso, Paola Sapienza, and Luigi Zingales. 2003. "People's opium? Religion and economic attitudes." *Journal of Monetary Economics* 50: 225–282. P. 228.

21. See Pippa Norris. Ed. 1999. *Critical Citizens: Global Support for Democratic Governance.* Oxford: Oxford University Press.

22. On the United States, see Clyde Wilcox. 1996. *Onward Christian Soldiers: The Religious Right in American Politics*. Boulder, CO: Westview; J. H. Evans. 2002. "Polarization in abortion attitudes in U.S. religious traditions, 1972–1998." *Sociological Forum*. 17(3): 397–422; J. Strickler and N. L. Danigelis. 2002. "Changing frameworks in attitudes toward abortion." *Sociological Forum*. 17(2): 187–201.

23. On comparisons of attitudes and policy in Western Europe, see Jacqueline Scott. 1998. "Generational changes in attitudes to abortion: A cross-national comparison." *European Sociological Review*. 14(2): 177–190; P. Scheepers and F. Van Der Slik. 1998. "Religion and attitudes on moral issues: Effects of individual, spouse and parental characteristics." *Journal for the Scientific Study of Religion*. 37(4): 678–691; M. Minkenberg. 2002. "Religion and public policy: Institutional, cultural, and political impact on the shaping of abortion policies in western democracies." *Comparative Political Studies*. 35(2): 221–247; M. Minkenberg. 2003. "The policy impact of church-state relations: Family policy and abortion in Britain, France, and Germany." *West European Politics*. 26(1): 195–206; P. Scheepers, M. T. Grotenhuis, and F. Van Der Slik. 2002. "Education, religiosity and moral attitudes: Explaining cross-national effect differences." *Sociology of Religion*. 63(2): 157–176; E. Arisi. 2003. "Changing attitudes towards abortion in Europe." *European Journal of Contraception and Reproductive Health Care*. 8(2): 109–121.

24. Karel Dobbelaere. 1999. "Towards an integrated perspective of the processes related to the descriptive concept of secularization." *Sociology of Religion*. 60(3): 229–247; L. Voye. 1999. "Secularization in a context of advanced modernity." *Sociology of Religion*. 603: 275–288.

Chapter 8

1. Robert Wuthnow. 1999. "Mobilizing Civic Engagement: The Changing Impact of Religious Involvement." In *Civic Engagement in American Democracy*. Eds. Theda Skocpol and Morris P. Fiorina. Washington, D.C.: Brookings Institution Press; Robert Wuthnow. 2002. "Religious involvement and status-bridging social capital." *Journal for the Scientific Study of Religion*. 41(4): 669–675; Robert Wuthnow and John H. Evans. Eds. 2002. *The Quiet Hand of God*. Berkeley, CA: University of California Press.

2. Pierre Bourdieu. 1970. *Reproduction in Education, Culture and Society*. London: Sage; James S. Coleman. 1988. "Social capital in the creation of human capital." *American Journal of Sociology*. 94: 95–120; James S. Coleman. 1990. *Foundations of Social Theory*. Cambridge: Belknap. For a discussion of the history of the concept, see also the introduction in Stephen Baron, John Field, and Tom Schuller. Eds. 2000. *Social Capital: Critical Perspectives*. Oxford: Oxford University Press.

3. The seminal works are Robert D. Putnam. 1993. *Making Democracy Work: Civic Traditions in Modern Italy*. Princeton, NJ: Princeton University Press; Robert D. Putnam. 1996. "The strange disappearance of civic America." *The American Prospect*. 7(24): 50–64; Robert D. Putnam. 2000. *Bowling Alone: The Collapse and Revival of American Community*. New York: Simon & Schuster. More recent comparative research is presented in Susan Pharr and Robert Putnam. Eds.

2001. *Disaffected Democracies: What's Troubling the Trilateral Countries?* Princeton, NJ: Princeton University Press; Robert D. Putnam. Ed. 2002. *Democracies in Flux*. Oxford: Oxford University Press.

4. Robert D. Putnam. 2000. *Bowling Alone: The Collapse and Revival of American Community*. New York: Simon & Schuster. P. 19. Putnam also offers a related definition: "By 'social capital' I mean features of social life – networks, norms and trust – that enable participants to act together more effectively to pursue shared objectives." Robert D. Putnam. 1996. "The Strange Disappearance of Civic America." *The American Prospect* 7(24): 56.

5. Robert Putnam. 2000. Ibid. P. 290. For details, see chapters 17–20.

6. Robert D. Putnam. 2000. *Bowling Alone: The Collapse and Revival of American Community*. New York: Simon & Schuster. P. 66.

7. Robert D. Putnam. 2000. *Bowling Alone: The Collapse and Revival of American Community*. New York: Simon & Schuster. P. 79.

8. Robert D. Putnam. Ed. 2002. *Democracies in Flux*. Oxford: Oxford University Press. P. 409.

9. Sidney Verba, Kay Lehman Schlozman, and Henry E. Brady. 1995. *Voice and Equality: Civic Volunteerism in American Politics*. Cambridge, MA: Harvard University Press. P. 389.

10. Steven J. Rosenstone and John Mark Hansen. 1995. *Mobilization, Participation and Democracy in America*. New York: Macmillan. See also C. A. Cassel. 1999. "Voluntary associations, churches and social participation theories of turnout." *Social Science Quarterly*. 80(3): 504–517.

11. Robert Putnam. 2000. Op Cit. P. 27.

12. See Carl Everett Ladd. 1996. "The data just don't show erosion of America's social capital." *The Public Perspective*. 7(4); Theda Skopol. 1996. "Unravelling from above." *The American Prospect*. 25: 20–25; Michael Schudson. 1996. "What if civic life didn't die?" *The American Prospect*. 25: 17–20; Pippa Norris. 2000. *A Virtuous Circle: Political Communications in Postindustrial Societies*. Cambridge, U.K.: Cambridge University Press. Chapter 13; Pippa Norris. 2002. *Democratic Phoenix: Political Activism Worldwide*. New York and Cambridge, U.K.: Cambridge University Press. Chapter 8.

13. Thomas Rotolo. 1999. "Trends in voluntary association participation." *Nonprofit and Voluntary Sector Quarterly*. 28(2): 199–212.

14. Robert Wuthnow. 2002. "The United States: Bridging the privileged and the marginalized?" In *Democracies in Flux*. Ed. Robert D. Putnam. Oxford: Oxford University Press.

15. For comparative work, see Jan Willem Van Deth. Ed. 1997. *Private Groups and Public Life: Social Participation, Voluntary Associations and Political Involvement in Representative Democracies*. London: Routledge; Jan Willem Van Deth and F. Kreuter. 1998. "Membership in voluntary associations." In *Comparative Politics: The Problem of Equivalence*. Ed. Jan.W. Van Deth. London: Routledge. Pp. 135–155; Jan Van Deth. 2000. "Interesting but irrelevant: Social capital and the saliency of politics in Western Europe." *European Journal of Political Research*. 37: 115–147.

16. Kees Aarts. 1995. "Intermediate organizations and interest representation." In *Citizens and the State*. Ed. Hans-Dieter Klingemann and Dieter Fuchs. Oxford: Oxford University Press.

17. Peter Hall. 2000. "Social Capital in Britain." In *The Dynamics of Social Capital*. Ed. Robert D. Putnam. Oxford: Oxford University Press; Peter Hall. 1999. "Social Capital in Britain." *British Journal of Political Science*. 29(3): 417–461. See also William L. Maloney, Graham Smith, and Gerry Stoker. 2000. "Social capital and associational life." In *Social Capital: Critical Perspectives*. Eds. Stephen Baron, John Field, and Tom Schuller. Oxford: Oxford University Press.

18. See Bo Rothstein. 2000. "Social capital in the social democratic state." In *Democracies in Flux*. Ed. Robert D. Putnam. Oxford: Oxford University Press.

19. Partha Dasgupta and Ismail Serageldin. Eds. 2000. *Social Capital: A Multifaceted Perspective*. The World Bank: Washington, D.C.; Richard Rose. 2000. "Uses of social capital in Russia: Modern, pre-modern, and anti-modern." *Post-Soviet Affairs*. 16(1): 33–57. See also Richard Rose, William Mishler, Christopher Haerpfer. 1997. "Social capital in civic and stressful societies." *Studies in Comparative International Development*. 32(3): 85–111.

20. Unfortunately, the wording of the questions used to monitor membership and activism in voluntary associations varied over different waves of the WVS survey, as follows:
    Wave I: Early 1980: *"Please look carefully at the following list of voluntary organizations and activities and say which, if any, do you belong to?"*
    Wave II and IV: Early 1990 and 1999–2001: *"Please look carefully at the following list of voluntary organizations and activities and say . . . (a) Which, if any, do you belong to? (b) Which, if any, are you currently doing unpaid voluntary work for?"*
    Wave III: Mid-1990s: *"Now I am going to read off a list of voluntary organizations; for each one, could you tell me whether you are an active member, an inactive member or not a member of that type of organization?"*
    This makes it difficult to compare *activism* among all waves, although we can use the identical items carried in Waves II and IV. The questions on voluntary associations were also excluded from the last wave of the survey conducted in many Muslim nations.

21. Robert Wuthnow. 1999. "Mobilizing civic engagement: The changing impact of religious involvement." In *Civic Engagement in American Democracy*. Eds. Theda Skocpol and Morris P. Fiorina. Washington, D.C.: Brookings Institution Press; Robert Wuthnow. 2002. "Religious involvement and status-bridging social capital." *Journal for the Scientific Study of Religion*. 41(4): 669–675.

22. For more details, see Pippa Norris. 2003. "Gendering social capital? Bowling in women's leagues?" Conference on Gender and Social Capital, St. John's College, University of Manitoba, May 2–3, 2003. See also Ronald Inglehart and Pippa Norris. 2003. *Rising Tide*. New York: Cambridge University Press; Gwen Moore. 1990. "Structural determinants of men's and women's personal networks." *American Sociological Review*. 55: 726–735; J. McPherson and Lynn Smith-Lovin. 1982. "Women and weak ties: Differences by sex in the size of voluntary organizations." *American Journal of Sociology*. 87: 883–904.

23. Variations among different sectors and the reason why people join are discussed in detailed elsewhere. See Pippa Norris. 2002. *Democratic Phoenix: Reinventing Political Activism*. New York and Cambridge, U.K.: Cambridge University Press. Chapter 8.

24. Sidney Verba, Norman Nie, and Jae-on Kim. 1978. *Participation and Political Equality: A Seven-Nation Comparison*. New York: Cambridge University Press; Sidney Verba, Kay Lehman Schlozman, and Henry E. Brady. 1995. *Voice and Equality: Civic Voluntarism in American Politics*. Cambridge, MA: Harvard University Press.

25. For a discussion, see Kenneth Newton and Pippa Norris. 2000. "Confidence in public institutions: Faith, culture or performance?" In *Disaffected Democracies: What's Troubling the Trilateral Countries?* Eds. Susan Pharr and Robert Putnam. Princeton, NJ: Princeton University Press; Kenneth Newton. 2001. "Trust, social capital, civic society, and democracy." *International Political Science Review*. 22(2): 201–214.

26. Francis Fukuyama. 1995. *Trust: The Social Virtuous and the Creation of Prosperity*. New York: The Free Press.

27. Pippa Norris. 2002. *Democratic Phoenix*. New York and Cambridge, U.K.: Cambridge University Press.

Chapter 9

1. David Broughton and Hans-Martien ten Napel. Eds. 2000. *Religion and Mass Electoral Behavior in Europe*. London: Routledge.

2. Pippa Norris. 2000. "U.S. campaign 2000: Of pregnant chads, butterfly ballots and partisan vitriol." *Government and Opposition*. 35(2): 1–24; VNS Exit Polls in "Who voted." *New York Times*. November 12, 2000; Andrew Kohut, John C. Green, Scott Keeter, and Robert C. Toth. 2000. *The Diminishing Divide: Religion's Changing Role in American Politics*. Washington, D.C.: Brookings Institution Press.

3. Seymour Martin Lipset and Stein Rokkan. 1967. *Party Systems and Voter Alignments*. New York: The Free Press. See also Robert R. Alford. 1967. "Class voting in the Anglo-American political systems." In *Party Systems and Voter Alignments: Cross National Perspectives*. Ed. Seymour M. Lipset and Stein Rokkan. New York: The Free Press; Richard Rose and Derek W. Urwin. 1970. "Persistence and change in western party systems since 1945." *Political Studies*. 18: 287–319; Richard Rose. 1974. *Electoral Behavior: A Comparative Handbook*. New York: The Free Press.

4. For Britain, see David Butler and Donald Stokes. 1974. *Political Change in Britain*. 2nd ed. London: Macmillan. On France, see Michael Lewis-Beck and Andrew Skalaban. "France." In *Electoral Change: Responses to Evolving Social and Attitudinal Structures in Western Countries*. Eds. Mark Franklin et al. Cambridge, U.K.: Cambridge University Press. On Belgium, see Anthony Mughan. 1983. "Accommodation or diffusion in the management of ethnic conflict in Belgium." *Political Studies*. 31: 431–451.

5. Angus Campbell, Philip Converse, Warren E. Miller, and Donald E. Stokes. 1960. *The American Voter*. New York: Wiley. For more recent analysis suggesting the decline of the religious cleavage but the continued stability of social alignments to explain American voting behavior, see C. Brooks and Jeff Manza. 1997. "Social cleavages and political alignments: U.S. presidential elections, 1960 to 1992." *American Sociological Review*. 62(6): 937–946; C. Brooks and Jeff Manza. 1997. 'The religious factor in U.S. presidential elections, 1960–1992." *American Journal of Sociology*. 103(1): 38–81.

6. Clyde Wilcox. 1992. *God's Warriors: The Christian Right in Twentieth Century America*. Baltimore: The Johns Hopkins University Press; David C. Leege and Lyman A. Kellstedt. Eds. 1993. *Rediscovering the Religious Factor in American Politics*. Armonk, NY: M. E. Sharpe.

7. Irena Borowik. 2002. "The Roman Catholic Church in the process of democratic transformation: The case of Poland." *Social Compass*. 49(2): 239–252.

8. Ted Gerard Jelen and Clyde Wilcox. Eds. 2002. *Religion and Politics in Comparative Perspective*. New York: Cambridge University Press.

9. For a more recent argument that these stable patterns have persisted with considerable continuity displayed within the major "left" and "right" blocks, see Stephano Bartolini and Peter Mair. 1990. *Identity, Competition, and Electoral Availability: The Stabilization of European Electorates, 1885–1985*. Cambridge, U.K.: Cambridge University Press.

10. Jerome M. Clubb, William H. Flanigan, and Nancy H. Zingale. 1990. *Partisan Realignment: Voters, Parties and Government in American History*. Boulder, CO: Westview Press.

11. John Madeley. 1991. "Politics and religion in Western Europe." In *Politics and Religion in the Modern World*. Ed. George Moyser. London: Routledge; David Hanley. Ed. 1996. *Christian Democracy in Europe: A Comparative Perspective*. New York: Pinter; Carolyn M. Warner. 2000. *Confessions of an Interest Group: The Catholic Church and Political Parties in Europe*. Princeton, NJ: Princeton University Press; Thomas Keslman and Joseph A. Buttigieg. Eds. 2003. *European Christian Democracy: Historical Legacies and Comparative Perspectives*. Notre Dame, IN: University of Notre Dame Press.

12. David Butler and Donald E. Stokes. 1974. *Political Change in Britain: The Evolution of Electoral Choice*. 2nd ed. London: Macmillan; Mark Franklin et al. 1992. *Electoral Change: Responses to Evolving Social and Attitudinal Structures in Western Countries*. Cambridge, U.K.: Cambridge University Press.

13. Paul Mitchell, Brendan O'Leary, and Geoffrey Evans. 2001. "Northern Ireland: Flanking extremists bite the moderates and emerge in their clothes." *Parliamentary Affairs*. 54(4): 725–742.

14. See, for example, George Moyser. Ed. 1991. *Politics and Religion in the Modern World*. London: Routledge; Scott Mainwaring and Timothy R. Scully. Eds. 2003. *Christian Democracy in Latin America: Electoral Competition and Regime Conflicts*. Stanford, CA: Stanford University Press.

15. Ivor Crewe, Jim Alt, and Bo Sarlvik. 1977. "Partisan dealignment in Britain 1964–1974." *British Journal of Political Science*. 7: 129–190; Norman Nie, Sidney

Verba, and John Petrocik. 1976. *The Changing American Voter*. Cambridge, MA: Harvard University Press; Ivor Crewe and David Denver. Eds. 1985. *Electoral Change in Western Democracies: Patterns and Sources of Electoral Volatility*. New York: St. Martin's Press; Mark Franklin, et al. 1992. *Electoral Change: Responses to Evolving Social and Attitudinal Structures in Western Countries*. Cambridge, U.K.: Cambridge University Press; Russell J. Dalton, Scott C. Flanagan, and Paul A. Beck. Eds. 1984. *Electoral Change in Advanced Industrial Democracies: Realignment or Dealignment?* Princeton, NJ: Princeton University Press; Mark Franklin 1985. *The Decline of Class Voting in Britain: Changes in the Basis of Electoral Choice, 1964–1983*. Oxford: Clarendon Press; Jeff Manza and Clem Brooks. 1999. *Social Cleavages and Political Change: Voter Alignments and U.S. Party Coalitions*. New York: Oxford University Press; Terry Nichols Clark and Seymour Martin Lipset. Eds. 2001. *The Breakdown of Class Politics*. Baltimore, MD: The Johns Hopkins University Press.

16. Russell J. Dalton, Scott C. Flanagan, and Paul A. Beck. Eds. 1984. *Electoral Change in Advanced Industrial Democracies: Realignment or Dealignment?* Princeton, NJ: Princeton University Press.

17. Hans Daalder and Peter Mair. Eds. 1985. *Western European Party Systems*. London: Sage; Morgens N. Pedersen. 1979. "The dynamics of European party systems: Changing patterns of electoral volatility." *European Journal of Political Research*. 7: 1–27; Herbert Kitschelt. Ed. 1995. *The Radical Right in Western Europe*. Ann Arbor, MI: The University of Michigan Press.

18. Pippa Norris. 2000. *A Virtuous Circle? Political Communications in Post-Industrial Democracies*. Cambridge, U.K.: Cambridge University Press; David Farrell and Rudiger Schmitt-Beck. Eds. 2002. *Do Political Campaigns Matter?* London: Routledge.

19. Pippa Norris. 2004. *Electoral Engineering*. New York: Cambridge University Press.

Chapter 10

1. Jeffrey K. Hadden. 1987. "Toward desacralizing secularization theory." *Social Forces*. 65(3): 587–611.

2. Rodney Stark and Roger Finke. 2000. *Acts of Faith*. Berkeley, CA: University of California Press. See also Rodney Stark. 1999. "Secularization, RIP." *Sociology of Religion*. 60(3): 270.

3. Peter L. Berger. Ed. 1999. *The Desecularization of the World*. Washington, D.C.: Ethics and Public Policy Center.

4. R. Stephen Warner. 1993. "Work in progress toward a new paradigm in the sociology of religion." *American Journal of Sociology*. 98(5): 1044–1093.

5. UNDP. 2003. *World Development Report*. New York: Oxford University Press. "Overview."

6. Grace Davie. 1994. *Religion in Britain since 1945: Believing without Belonging*. Oxford: Blackwell; Rodney Stark and W. S. Bainbridge. 1985. "A supply-side

reinterpretation of the 'secularization' of Europe." *Journal for the Scientific Study of Religion*. 33: 230–252.

7. Grace Davie. 1999. "Europe: The exception?" In *The Desecularization of the World*. Ed. Peter L. Berger. Washington, D.C.: Ethics and Public Policy Center. P. 68.

8. Clyde Wilcox and Ted G. Jelen. 2002. "Religion and politics in an open market: Religious mobilization in the United States." In *Religion and Politics in Comparative Perspective: The One, the Few and the Many*. Eds. Ted Gerard Jelen and Clyde Wilcox. New York: Cambridge University Press. P. 292.

9. Andrew Greeley. 1994. "A religious revival in Russia?" *Journal for the Scientific Study of Religion*. 33(3): 253–272; Andrew M. Greeley. 2003. *Religion in Europe at the End of the Second Millennium*. New Brunswick, NJ: Transaction Publishers. Chapter 6. "Russia: The biggest revival ever?" See also M. L. Gautier. 1997. "Church attendance and religious belief in post-Communist societies." *Journal for the Scientific Study of Religion*. 36(2): 289–296; Ariana Need and Geoffrey Evans. 2001. "Analyzing patterns of religious participation in post-communist Eastern Europe." *British Journal of Sociology*. 52(2): 229–248.

10. Peter L. Berger. Ed. 1999. *The Desecularization of the World*. Washington, D.C.: Ethics and Public Policy Center; W. H. Swatos, Jr. Ed. 1989. *Religious Politics in Global and Comparative Perspective*. New York: Greenwood Press; Alan Aldridge. 2000. *Religion in the Contemporary World: A Sociological Introduction*. Cambridge, U.K.: Polity Press; Martin Marty and R. Scott Appleby. Eds. 1991. *Fundamentalisms Observed*. Chicago: University of Chicago Press.

11. See, for example, Robert J. Kisala. 2003. "Japanese religiosity and morals." In *Religion in a Secularizing Society*. Eds. Loek Halman and Ole Riis. Leiden: Brill.

12. The 4-item scale of religious beliefs was tested for reliability. The Cronbach's alpha for the scale was as follows: Catholics (.789), Protestants (.804), Orthodox (.813), Jewish (.749), Muslim (.910), Hindu (.795), and Buddhist (.863). It should be noted that an additional item monitoring belief in God was carried in the WVS, but this was not included in the scale because exploratory factor analysis suggested that this item loaded on the values scale (along with the importance of religion) rather than the belief scale.

13. Michael Hout, Andrew M. Greeley, and Melissa J. Wilde. 2001. "The demographic imperative in religious change in the United States." *American Journal of Sociology*. 107(2): 468–500.

14. Pippa Norris. 2002. *Democratic Phoenix*. New York and Cambridge, U.K.: Cambridge University Press; Inglehart and Catterberg, 2003.

15. Ronald Inglehart and Pippa Norris. 2003. *Rising Tide*. New York: Cambridge University Press.

16. K. Mason and A-M. Jenson. Eds. 1995. *Gender and Family Change in Industrialized Countries*. Oxford: Clarendon Press; United Nations. 2000. *The World's Women 2000: Trends and Statistics*. New York: United Nations.

17. The Traditional values scale is measured by support of the following items: God is very important in respondent's life; It is more important for a child to learn obedience and religious faith than independence and determination;

Autonomy index; Abortion is never justifiable; Respondent has strong sense of national pride; Respondent favors respect for authority. By contrast support for Secular-rational values is measured by the opposite position on all of above. See Ronald Inglehart. 1997. *Modernization and Postmodernization: Cultural, Economic and Political Change in 43 Societies.* Princeton, NJ: Princeton University Press; Ronald Inglehart and Wayne E. Baker. 2000. "Modernization, globalization and the persistence of tradition: Empirical evidence from 65 societies." *American Sociological Review.* 65: 19–55.

18. Ronald S. Immerman and Wade C. Mackey. 2003. "Religion and fertility." *Mankind Quarterly.* 43(4): 377–403.

19. Ted Robert Gurr, Monty Marshall, and Deepa Khosla. 2000. "Global conflict trends." University of Maryland, Center for Systemic Peace/ Minorities At Risk. Available online at: http://members.aol.com/CSPmgm/cspframe.htm.

20. Robert Wuthnow. 1988. *The Restructuring of American Religion.* Princeton, NJ: Princeton University Press; Tom Smith. 1992. "Are conservative churches really growing?" *Review of Religious Research.* 33: 305–329; Martin Marty and R. Scott Appleby. Eds. 1991. *Fundamentalisms Comprehended.* Chicago: University of Chicago Press.

Appendix C

1. Mark Chaves and David E. Cann. 1992. "Regulation, pluralism and religious market structure." *Rationality and Society.* 4: 272–290.

Bibliography

Aarts, Kees. 1995. "Intermediate organizations and interest representation." In *Citizens and the State*. Eds. Hans-Dieter Klingemann and Dieter Fuchs. Oxford: Oxford University Press.

Abela, Anthony M. 1993. "Post-secularisation: The social significance of religious values in four Catholic European countries." *Melita Theolgica*. XLIV: 39–58.

Abramson, Paul R., and Ronald Inglehart. 1995. *Value Change in Global Perspective*. Ann Arbor, MI: University of Michigan Press.

Abu-Lughod, Lila. Ed. 1998. *Remaking Women: Feminism and Modernity in the Middle East*. Princeton, NJ: Princeton University Press.

Acquaviva, Sabino Samele. 1979. *The Decline of the Sacred in Industrial Society*. Oxford: Basil Blackwell.

Addi, L. 1992. "Islamicist utopia and democracy." *Annals of the American Academy of Political and Social Science*. 524: 120–130.

Akhavi, S. 1992. "The clergy's concepts of rule in Egypt and Iran." *Annals of the American Academy of Political and Social Science*. 524: 92–102.

al-Braizat, Fares. 2003. "Muslims and democracy: An empirical critique of Fukuyama's culturalist approach." *International Journal of Comparative Sociology*.

Aldridge, Alan. 2000. *Religion in the Contemporary World: A Sociological Introduction*. Cambridge, U.K.: Polity Press.

Alesina, Alberto, Arnaud Devleeschauwer, William Easterly, Sergio Kurlat, and Romain Wacziarg. 2003. "Fractionalization." *Journal of Economic Growth*. 82: 219–258.

Alex-Assensoh, Y., and A. B. Assensoh. 2001. "Inner-city contexts, church attendance, and African-American political participation." *Journal of Politics*. 63(3): 886–901.

Alford, Robert R. 1967. "Class voting in the Anglo-American political systems." In *Party Systems and Voter Alignments: Cross National Perspectives*. Eds. Seymour M. Lipset and Stein Rokkan. New York: The Free Press.

Almond, Gabriel A., and Sidney Verba. 1963. *The Civic Culture: Political Attitudes and Democracy in Five Nations*. Princeton, NJ: Princeton University Press.

Anderson, John. 1994. *Religion, State and Politics in the Soviet Union and Successor States*. New York: Cambridge University Press.

Arat, Y. 2000. "Feminists, Islamists, and political change in Turkey." *Political Psychology*. 19(1): 117–131.

Argue, Amy, David R. Johnson, and Lynn K. White. 1999. "Age and religiosity: Evidence from a three-wave panel analysis." *Journal for the Scientific Study of Religion*. 38(3): 423–435.

Argyle M., and Benjamin Beit-Hallahmi. 1975. *The Social Psychology of Religion*. London: Routledge & Kegan Paul.

Arisi, E. 2003. "Changing attitudes towards abortion in Europe." *European Journal of Contraception and Reproductive Health Care*. 8(2): 109–121.

Asghar, Ali Engineer. Ed. 2001. *Islam, Women and Gender Justice*. New Delhi: Gyan Pub. House.

Ashford, Sheena, and Noel Timms. 1992. *What Europe Thinks: A Study of Western European Values*. Aldershot, U.K.: Dartmouth.

Åsland, Anders. 2002. *Building Capitalism: The Transformation of the Former Soviet Bloc*. Cambridge, U.K.: Cambridge University Press.

Ayubi, N. 1992. "State Islam and communal plurality." *Annals of the American Academy of Political and Social Science*. 524: 79–91.

Azzi, Corry, and Ronald Ehrenberg. 1975. "Household allocation of time and church attendance." *Journal of Political Economy*. 83: 27–56.

Bainbridge, William Simms. 1997. *The Sociology of Religious Movements*. New York: Routledge.

Baril, Alain, and George A. Mori. 1991. "Leaving the fold: Declining church attendance." *Canadian Social Trends*. Autumn: 21–24.

Barker, D. C., and C. J. Carman. 2000. "The spirit of capitalism? Religious doctrine, values, and economic attitude constructs." *Political Behavior*. 22(1): 1–27.

Barker, E., J. Beckford, and Karel Dobbelaere. Eds. 1993. *Secularization, Rationalism, and Sectarianism: Essays in Honour of Bryan R. Wilson*. New York: Oxford University Press.

Barnes, Samuel, and Max Kaase. 1979. *Political Action: Mass Participation in Five Western Democracies*. Beverly Hills, CA: Sage.

Baron, Stephen, John Field, and Tom Schuller. Eds. 2000. *Social Capital: Critical Perspectives*. Oxford: Oxford University Press.

Barrett, David B. Ed. 1982. *World Christian Encyclopedia*. Nairobi: Oxford University Press.

Barrett, David B., and Todd M. Johnson. 2001. *World Christian Trends AD 30–2200*. Pasedena, CA: William Carey Library.

Barrett, David B., George T. Kurian, and Todd M. Johnson. Eds. 2001. *World Christian Encyclopedia: A Comparative Survey of Churches and Religions in the Modern World*. 2nd ed. Oxford: Oxford University Press.

Barrett, David V. 1996. *Sects, "Cults," and Alternative Religions: A World Survey and Sourcebook*. London: Blandford.

Barro, Robert J., and Rachel M. McCleary. 2003. "Religion and economic growth." Unpublished paper. Available online at: http://post.economics.harvard.edu/faculty/barro/papers/.

Bartolini, Stephano, and Peter Mair. 1990. *Identity, Competition, and Electoral Availability: The Stabilization of European Electorates, 1885–1985*. Cambridge, U.K.: Cambridge University Press.

Becker, P. E., and P. H. Dhingra. 2001. "Religious involvement and volunteering: Implications for civil society." *Sociology of Religion*. 62:315–336.

Beit-Hallahmi, Benjamin. 1997. *The Psychology of Religious Behavior, Belief and Experience*. New York: Routledge.

Bell, Daniel. 1973. *The Coming of Post-Industrial Society: A Venture in Social Forecasting*. New York: Basic Books.

Bensen, Peter L., Michael J. Donahue, and Joseph A. Erickson. 1989. "Adolescence and religion: A review of the literature from 1970–1986." *Research in the Social Scientific Study of Religion*. 1:153–181.

Berger, Peter L. 1967. *The Sacred Canopy*. Garden City, NY: Doubleday.

———. 1979. *The Heretical Imperative: Contemporary Possibilities of Religious Affirmation*. Garden City, NY: Anchor Books.

———. Ed. 1999. *The Desecularization of the World*. Washington, D.C.: Ethics and Public Policy Center.

Berkovitch, N., and V. M. Moghadam. 1999. "Middle East politics and women's collective action: Challenging the status quo." *Social Politics*. 6(3): 273–291.

Beyer, P. 1997. "Religious vitality in Canada: The complementarity of religious market and secularization perspectives." *Journal for the Scientific Study of Religion*. 36(2): 272–288.

———. "Secularization from the perspective of globalization: A response to Dobbelaere." *Sociology of Religion*. 60(3): 289–301.

Bibby, Reginald W. 1979. "The state of collective religiosity in Canada: An empirical analysis." *Canadian Review of Sociology and Anthropology*. 16(1): 105–116.

Blancarte, R. J. 2000. "Popular religion, Catholicism and socioreligious dissent in Latin America – Facing the modernity paradigm." *International Sociology*. 15(4): 591–603.

Blondel, Jean. 1970. *Votes, Parties and Leaders*. London: Penguin.

Blum, U., and L. Dudley. 2001. "Religion and economic growth: Was Weber right?" *Journal of Evolutionary Economics.* 11(2): 207–230.

Bociurkie, B. R., and J. W. Strong. Eds. 1975. *Religion and Atheism in the USSR and Eastern Europe.* London: Macmillan.

Bok, Derek. 1996. *The State of the Nation: Government and the Quest for a Better Society.* Cambridge, MA: Harvard University Press.

Borowik, Irena. 2002. "Between orthodoxy and eclecticism: On the religious transformations of Russia, Belarus and Ukraine." *Social Compass.* 49(4): 497–508.

_____. 2002. "The Roman Catholic Church in the process of democratic transformation: The case of Poland." *Social Compass.* 49(2): 239–252.

Bourdieu, Pierre. 1970. *Reproduction in Education, Culture and Society.* London: Sage.

Boyle, Kevin, and Juliet Sheen. Eds. 1997. *Freedom of Religion and Belief: A World Report.* New York: Routledge.

Bradley, David, Evelyn Huber, Stephanie Moller, Francois Nielsen, and John D. Stephens. 2003. "Distribution and redistribution in postindustrial democracies." *World Politics* 55(1): 193–228.

Brechon, Pierre. 1997. *Religions et politique en Europe.* Paris: Presses de la Fondation nationale des sciences politiques.

Brehm, J., and Wendy Rahn. 1997. "Individual-level evidence for the causes and consequences of social capital." *American Journal of Political Science.* 41: 999–1024.

Bromley, David G., and Jeffrey K. Hadden. Eds. 1993. *The Handbook of Cults and Sects in America.* Greenwich, CT, and London: Association for the Sociology of Religion and JAI Press.

Brooks, C., and Jeff Manza. 1997. "Social cleavages and political alignments: U.S. presidential elections, 1960 to 1992." *American Sociological Review.* 62(6): 937–946.

_____. 1997. "The religious factor in U.S. presidential elections, 1960–1992." *American Journal of Sociology.* 103(1): 38–81.

Broughton, David, and Hans-Martien ten Napel. Eds. 2000. *Religion and Mass Electoral Behavior in Europe.* London: Routledge.

Bruce, Steve. 1992. *Religion and Modernization: Sociologists and Historians Debate the Secularization Thesis.* Oxford: Clarendon Press.

_____. 1995. "The truth about religion in Britain." *Journal for the Scientific Study of Religion.* 34(4): 417–430.

_____. 1996. *Religion in the Modern World: From Cathedrals to Cults.* Oxford: Oxford University Press.

_____. 2000. "The supply-side model of religion: The Nordic and Baltic states." *Journal for the Scientific Study of Religion.* 39(1): 32–46.

_____. 2002. *God is Dead: Secularization in the West.* Oxford: Blackwell.

Bryant, J. M. 2000. "Cost-benefit accounting and the piety business: Is *homo religious,* at bottom, a *homo economicus?*" *Methods and Theory in the Study of Religion.* 12: 520–548.

Buncak, J. 2001. "Religiosity in Slovakia and its European context." *Sociologia.* 33(1): 47–69.

Burn, Shawn Meghan. 2000. *Women across Cultures: A Global Perspective.* Mountain View, CA: Mayfield Pub.

Burns, Nancy, Kay Lehman Schlozman, and Sidney Verba. 2001. *The Private Roots of Public Action.* Cambridge, MA: Harvard University Press.

Butler, David, and Donald E. Stokes. 1974. *Political Change in Britain: The Evolution of Electoral Choice.* 2nd ed. London: Macmillan.

Campbell, Angus, Philip Converse, Warren E. Miller, and Donald E. Stokes. 1960. *The American Voter.* New York: Wiley.

Campbell, Robert A., and James E. Curtis. 1994. "Religious involvement across societies: Analysis for alternative measures in national surveys." *Journal for the Scientific Study of Religion.* 33(3): 215–229.

———. 1996. "The public's views on the future of religion and science: Cross-national survey results." *Review of Religious Research.* 37(3): 260–267.

Caplow, T. 1998. "The case of the phantom Episcopalians." *American Sociological Review.* 63(1): 112–113.

Carone, D. A., and D. F. Barone. 2001. "A social cognitive perspective on religious beliefs: Their functions and impact on coping and psychotherapy." *Clinical Psychology Review.* 21(7): 989–1003.

Carroll, Jackson W., Barbara Hargrove, and Adair Lummis. 1983. *Women of the Cloth.* San Francisco: Harper & Row.

Casanova, Jose. 1994. *Public Religions in the Modern World.* Chicago: University of Chicago Press.

Cassel, C. A. 1999. "Voluntary associations, churches, and social participation theories of turnout." *Social Science Quarterly.* 80(3): 504–517.

Castles, Francis G. 1994. "On religion and public policy: Does Catholicism make a difference?" *European Journal of Political Research.* 25(1): 19–40.

Cesareo, V., et al. 1995. *La Religiosità in Italia.* 2nd ed. Milan: A. Mondadori.

Chalcraft, David J., and Austin Harrington. 2001. *The Protestant Ethic Debate: Max Weber Replies to His Critics, 1907–1910.* Liverpool: Liverpool University Press.

Chalfant, H. Paul, Robert E. Beckley, and C. Eddie Palmer. 1994. *Religion in Contemporary Society.* Itasca, IL: F. E. Peacock.

Chaves, Mark. 1989. "Secularization and religious revival: Evidence from U.S. church attendance rates, 1972–1986." *Journal for the Scientific Study of Religion.* 28: 464–477.

———. 1999. "The National Congregations Study: Background, Methods and Selected Results." *Journal for the Scientific Study of Religion.* 38(4): 458–476.

Chaves, Mark, and David E. Cann. 1992. "Regulation, pluralism and religious market structure." *Rationality and Society.* 4: 272–290.

Chaves, Mark, and Philip S. Gorski. 2001. "Religious pluralism and religious participation." *Annual Review of Sociology.* 27: 261–281.

Chirot, D. 2001. "A clash of civilizations or of paradigms? Theorizing progress and social change." *International Sociology.* 16(3): 341–360.

Church of England, The. *The Year in Review, 2001–2002*. Available online at: http://www.cofe.anglican.org/COE2002version2.pdf.

CIA. *The World Factbook, 2002*. Available online at: http://www.cia.gov/cia/publications/factbook/.

Cimino, Richard, and Don Lattin. 2002. *Shopping for Faith: American Religion in the New Millennium*. New York: Jossey-Bass.

Cipriani, R. 1994. "Religiosity, religious secularism and secular religions." *International Social Science Journal*. 46(2): 277–284.

Clubb, Jerome M., William H. Flanigan, and Nancy H. Zingale. 1990. *Partisan Realignment: Voters, Parties and Government in American History*. Boulder, CO: Westview Press.

Coleman, James S. 1988. "Social capital in the creation of human capital." *American Journal of Sociology*. 94: 95–120.

———. 1990. *Foundations of Social Theory*. Cambridge: Belknap.

Conover, Pamela Johnston. 1988. "Feminists and the gender gap." *Journal of Politics*. 50: 985–1010.

Conquest, Robert. Ed. 1968. *Religion in the U.S.S.R.* New York: Praeger.

Conway, Margaret, Gertrude A. Steuernagel, and David Ahern. 1997. *Women and Political Participation*. Washington, D.C.: CQ Press.

Crewe, Ivor, Jim Alt, and Bo Sarlvik. 1977. "Partisan dealignment in Britain 1964–1974." *British Journal of Political Science*. 7: 129–190.

Crewe, Ivor, and D. T. Denver. Eds. 1985. *Electoral Change in Western Democracies: Patterns and Sources of Electoral Volatility*. New York: St. Martin's Press.

Currie, R., A. D. Gilbert, and L. Horsley. 1977. *Churches and Churchgoers: Patterns of Church Growth in the British Isles since 1700*. Oxford: Oxford University Press.

Curtis J. E., D. E. Baer, and E. G. Grabb. 2001. "Nations of joiners: Explaining voluntary association membership in democratic societies." *American Sociological Review*. 66(6): 783–805.

Dahrendorf, Ralph. 1959. *Class and Class Conflict in Industrial Society*. Stanford, CA: Stanford University Press.

Dalton, Russell J. 1999. "Political support in advanced industrialized democracies." In *Critical Citizens: Global Support for Democratic Governance*. Ed. Pippa Norris. Oxford: Oxford University Press.

———. 2002. *Citizen Politics*. Chatham, NJ: Chatham House.

Dalton, Russell J., Scott C. Flanagan, and Paul A. Beck. Eds. 1984. *Electoral Change in Advanced Industrial Democracies: Realignment or Dealignment?* Princeton, NJ: Princeton University Press.

Dasgupta, Partha, and Ismail Serageldin. Eds. 2000. *Social Capital: A Multifaceted Perspective*. Washington, D.C.: The World Bank.

Davie, Grace. 1994. *Religion in Britain since 1945: Believing without Belonging*. Oxford: Blackwell.

Davis N. J., and R. V. Robinson. 1999. "Their brothers' keepers? Orthodox religionists, modernists, and economic justice in Europe." *American Journal of Sociology.* 104(6): 1631–1665.

De Graaf, N. D. 1999. "Event history data and making a history out of cross-sectional data – How to answer the question 'Why cohorts differ?'" *Quality & Quantity.* 33(3): 261–276.

de Vaus, David A. 1984. "Workforce participation and sex differences in church attendance." *Review of Religious Research.* 25: 247–258.

de Vaus, David A., and Ian McAllister. 1987. "Gender differences in religion: A test of the structural location theory." *American Sociological Review.* 52: 472–481.

Deeb, M. J. 1992. "Militant Islam and the politics of redemption." *Annals of the American Academy of Political and Social Science.* 524: 52–65.

Dekker, G., J. de Hart, and J. Peters. 1997. *God in Nederland 1966–1996.* Amsterdam: Anthos.

Dekker, Paul, and Peter Ester. 1996. "Depillarization, deconfessionalization, and de-ideologization: Empirical trends in Dutch society 1958–1992." *Review of Religious Research.* 37(4): 325–341.

Dhruvarajan, Vanaja. 1988. "Religious ideology and interpersonal relationships within the family." *Journal of Comparative Family Studies.* 19: 273–285.

Diotallevi, Luca. 2002. "Internal competition in a national religious monopoly: The Catholic effect and the Italian case." *Sociology of Religion.* 63(2): 137–155.

Djupe, P. A., and J. T. Grant. 2001. "Religious institutions and political participation in America." *Journal for the Scientific Study of Religion.* 40(2): 303–314.

Dobbelaere, Karel. 1981. "Secularization: A multidimensional concept." *Current Sociology.* 29(2): 1–21.

––––––. 1985. "Secularization theories and sociological paradigms: A reformulation of the private-public dichotomy and the problem of social integration." *Sociological Analysis.* 46: 377–387.

––––––. 1987. "Some trends in European sociology of religion: The secularization debate." *Sociological Analysis.* 48: 107–137.

––––––. 1993. "Church involvement and secularization: Making sense of the European case." In *Secularization, Rationalism and Sectarianism.* Eds. E. Barker, J. A. Beckford, and Karel Dobbelaere. Oxford: Clarendon Press.

––––––. 1995. "Religion in Europe and North America." In *Values in Western Societies.* Ed. Ruud de Moor. Tilburg, Netherlands: Tilburg University Press.

––––––. 1999. "Towards an integrated perspective of the processes related to the descriptive concept of secularization." *Sociology of Religion.* 60(3): 229–247.

Dobbelaere, Karel, and Wolfgang Jagodzinski. 1995. "Religious cognitions and beliefs." In *The Impact of Values.* Eds. Jan W. van Deth and Elinor Scarbrough. Oxford: Oxford University Press.

Dogan, Mattei, and Richard Rose. Eds. 1971. *European Politics: A Reader.* London: Macmillan.

Douglas, Ann. 1977. *The Feminization of American Culture*. New York: Knopf.

Durant, Henry W. 1949. *Political Opinion*. London: Allen and Unwin.

———. 1969. "Voting behavior in Britain 1945–1966." In *Studies in British Politics*. Ed. Richard Rose. London: Macmillan.

Durkheim, Émile. 1984 [1893]. *The Division of Labor in Society*. New York: The Free Press. Trans. W. D. Haus.

———. 1995 [1912]. *The Elementary Forms of Religious Life*. New York: The Free Press. Trans. Karen E. Fields.

Duverger, Maurice. 1955. *The Political Role of Women*. Paris: UNESCO.

Ebaugh, Helen Rose, Jon Lorence, and Janet Saltzman Chafetz. 1996. "The growth and decline of the population of Catholic nuns cross-nationally, 1960–1990: A case of secularization as social structural change." *Journal for the Scientific Study of Religion*. 35: 171–183.

Eisenstadt, S. *Comparative Perspectives in Social Change*. Boston: Little, Brown.

Esmer, Yilmaz. 2003. "Is there an Islamic civilization?" In *Culture and Social Change: Findings from the Values Surveys*. Ed. Ronald Inglehart. Leiden: Brill Academic Publishers.

Esping-Andersen, Gosta. 1999. *Social Foundations of Postindustrial Economies*. Oxford: Oxford University Press.

Esposito, John. Ed. 1997. *Political Islam: Revolution, Radicalism or Reform?* Boulder, CO: Lynne Reinner.

Esposito, John L., and John O. Voll. 1996. *Democracy and Islam*. New York: Oxford University Press.

Evans, J. H. 2002. "Polarization in abortion attitudes in U.S. religious traditions, 1972–1998." *Sociological Forum* 17(3): 397–422.

Farrell, David, and Rudiger Schmitt-Beck. Eds. 2002. *Do Political Campaigns Matter?* London: Routledge.

Ferraro, Kenneth F., and Jessica A. Kelley-Moore. 2000. "Religious consolation among men and women: Do health problems spur seeing?" *Journal for the Scientific Study of Religion*. 39: 220–234.

Fichter, Joseph H. 1952. "The profile of Catholic religious life." *American Journal of Sociology*. 58: 145–149.

Finke, Roger. 1992. "An unsecular America." In *Religion and Modernization*. Ed. Steve Bruce. Oxford: Clarendon Press.

Finke, Roger, and Lawrence R. Iannaccone. 1993. "The illusion of shifting demand: Supply-side explanations for trends and change in the American religious market place." *Annals of the American Association of Political and Social Science*. 527: 27–39.

Finke, Roger, and Rodney Stark. 1992. *The Churching of America, 1776–1990: Winners and Losers in Our Religious Economy*. New Brunswick, NJ: Rutgers University Press.

Finke, Roger, and Rodney Stark. 2000. *Acts of Faith: Explaining the Human Side of Religion*. Berkeley, CA: University of California Press.

Firebaugh, Glenn. 1992. "Where does social change come from? Estimating the relative contributions of individual change and population turnover." *Population Research and Policy Review.* 11: 1–20.

Flere, S. 2001. "The impact of religiosity upon political stands: Survey findings from seven central European countries." *East European Quarterly.* 35(2): 183–199.

Fox, J. 1999. "The influence of religious legitimacy on grievance formation by ethno-religious minorities." *Journal of Peace Research.* 36(3): 289–307.

———. "Two civilizations and ethnic conflict: Islam and the West." *Journal of Peace Research.* 38(4): 459–472.

Franklin, Mark, Thomas T. Mackie, Henry Valen, and Clive Bean. 1992. *Electoral Change: Responses to Evolving Social and Attitudinal Structures in Western Countries.* Cambridge, U.K.: Cambridge University Press.

Freedom House. 2000. *Freedom in the World 2000–2001.* Available online at: www.freedomhouse.org.

———. 2002. *Freedom in the World 2002: The Democracy Gap.* New York: Freedom House. Available online at: www.freedomhouse.org.

Froese, Paul. 2001. "Hungary for religion: A supply-side interpretation of Hungarian religious revival." *Journal for the Scientific Study of Religion.* 40(2): 251–268.

Froese, Paul, and S. Pfaff. 2001. "Replete and desolate markets: Poland, East Germany, and the new religious paradigm." *Social Forces.* 80(2): 481–507.

Fukuyama, Francis. 1995. *Trust: The Social Virtuous and the Creation of Prosperity.* New York: The Free Press.

Fuller, Graham E. 2002. "The future of political Islam." *Foreign Affairs.* 81(2): 48–60.

Fuller, Robert C. 2002. *Spiritual, but Not Religious: Understanding Unchurched America.* New York: Oxford University Press.

Funkhouser, G. R. 2000. "A world ethos and the clash of civilizations: A cross-cultural comparison of attitudes." *International Journal of Public Opinion Research.* 12(1): 73–79.

Furnham, A., et al. 1993. "A comparison of Protestant work-ethic beliefs in 13 nations." *Journal of Social Psychology.* 133 (2): 185–197.

Gallup International. 2000. *Religion in the World at the End of the Millennium.* Available online at: www.gallup.international.com.

Gautier, M. L. 1997. "Church attendance and religious Belief in post-Communist societies." *Journal for The Scientific Study of Religion.* 36(2): 289–296.

Giddens, Anthony. 1981. *The Class Structure of the Advanced Societies.* 2nd ed. London: Hutchinson.

Gill, Anthony James. 1998. *Rendering unto Caesar: The Catholic Church and the State in Latin America.* Chicago: University of Chicago Press.

Gill, Anthony James. 1999. "Government regulation, social anomie and Protestant growth in Latin America – A cross-national analysis." *Rationality and Society.* 11(3): 287–316.

Gill, Anthony James, and Erik Lundsgaarde. 2005. "State Welfare Spending and Religiosity." *Rationality and Society* (forthcoming).

Gill, R., et al. 1998. "Is religious belief declining in Britain?" *Journal for the Scientific Study of Religion.* 37(3): 507–516.

Giner, S., and M. Archer. Eds. 1978. *Contemporary Europe: Social Structures and Cultural Patterns.* London: Routledge.

Global Evangelization Movement. 2001. *Status of Global Mission 2001.* Available online at: www.gem-werc.org/.

Greeley, Andrew M. 1980. *Religious Change in America.* Cambridge, MA: Harvard University Press.

———. 1985. *Unsecular Man: The Persistence of Religion.* New York: Schocken Books.

———. 1994. "A religious revival in Russia?" *Journal for the Scientific Study of Religion.* 33(3): 253–272.

———. 1995. "The persistence of religion." *Cross Currents.* 45(Spring): 24–41.

———. 2003. *Religion in Europe at the End of the Second Millennium.* New Brunswick, NJ: Transaction Publishers.

Greenfield, Liah. 2001. *The Spirit of Capitalism: Nationalism and Economic Growth.* Cambridge, MA: Harvard University Press.

Grier, R. 1997. "The effects of religion on economic development: A cross-national study of 63 former colonies." *Kyklos.* 50(1): 47–62.

Guiso, Luigi, Paola Sapienza, and Luigi Zingales. 2003. "People's opium? Religion and economic attitudes." *Journal of Monetary Economics.* 50: 225–282.

Gurr, Ted. 2000. *Peoples versus States.* Washington, D.C.: U.S. Institute for Peace Press.

Gustafsson, G. 1994. "Religious change in the five Scandinavian countries, 1930–1980." In *Scandinavian Values: Religion and Morality in the Nordic Countries.* Eds. Thorleif Pettersson and Ole Riis. Upssala: Acta Universitatis Upsaliensis.

Hadaway, Kirk, et al. 1993. "What the polls don't show: A closer look at church attendance." *American Sociological Review.* 58(6): 741–752.

Hadaway, Kirk, and P. L. Marler. 1998. "Did you really go to church this week? Behind the poll data." *Christian Century.* May 6: 472–475.

Hadaway, Kirk, P. L. Marler, and Mark Chaves. 1998. "Overreporting church attendance in America: Evidence that demands the same verdict." *American Sociological Review.* 63(1): 122–130.

Hadden, J. K. 1987. "Toward desacralizing secularization theory." *Social Forces.* 65(3): 587–611.

Hagopian, Fran. 2000. "Political development, revisited." *Comparative Political Studies.* 33(6/7): 880–911.

Hall, Peter. 1999. "Social capital in Britain." *British Journal of Political Science.* 29(3): 417–461.

———. 2000. "Social Capital in Britain." In *The Dynamics of Social Capital.* Ed. Robert D. Putnam. Oxford: Oxford University Press.

Haller, M. 2002. "Theory and method in the comparative study of values: Critique and alternative to Inglehart." *European Sociological Review.* 18(2): 139–158.

Hallum, Anne Motley. 2002. "Looking for hope in Central America: The Pentecostal movement." In *Religion and Politics in Comparative Perspective.* Eds. Ted Gerard Jelen and Clyde Wilcox. Cambridge, U.K.: Cambridge University Press.

Halman L., T. Pettersson, and J. Verweij. 1999. "The religious factor in contemporary society – The differential impact of religion on the private and public sphere in comparative perspective." *International Journal of Comparative Sociology.* 40(1): 141–160.

Halman, Loek, and Ole Reis. Eds. 2003. *Religion in a Secularizing Society.* Leiden: Brill.

Hamilton, Malcolm. 1998. *Sociology and the World's Religions.* New York: St. Martins.

––––––. Ed. 2001. *The Sociology of Religion: Theoretical and Comparative Perspectives.* 2nd edition. New York: Routledge.

Hanley, David. Ed. 1996. *Christian Democracy in Europe: A Comparative Perspective.* New York: Pinter.

Hanson, S. 1997. "The secularization thesis: Talking at cross purposes." *Journal of Contemporary Religion.* 12: 159–179.

Hartz, Louis. 1955. *The Liberal Tradition in America.* New York: Harcourt, Brace.

Hawkins, Bradley K. 2002. *Asian Religions.* New York: Seven Bridges.

Hayes, B. C. 2000. "Religious independents within Western industrialized nations: A socio-demographic profile." *Sociology of Religion.* 61(2): 191–207.

Hefner, R. W. 1998. "Multiple modernities: Christianity, Islam, and Hinduism in a globalizing age." *Annual Review of Anthropology.* 27: 83–104.

Henderson, R. A., and R. Tucker. 2001. "Clear and present strangers: The clash of civilizations and international politics." *International Studies Quarterly.* 45(2): 317–338.

Hervieu-Leger, D. 2003. "The case for a sociology of 'multiple religious modernities': A different approach to the 'invisible religion' of European societies." *Social Compass.* 50(3): 287–295.

Hicks, Alexander. 1999. *Social Democracy and Welfare Capitalism: A Century of Income Security Policies.* Ithaca, NY: Cornell University Press.

Himmelfarb, Gertrude. 1999. *One Nation: Two Cultures.* New York: Random House.

Hoffmann, J. P. 1998. "Confidence in religious institutions and secularization: Trends and implications." *Review of Religious Research.* 39(4): 321–343.

Höllinger F. 1996. *Volksreligion und Herrschaftskirche. Die Würzeln Religiösen Verhaltens in Westlichen Gesellschaften.* Opladen: Leske und Budrich.

Hout, Michael. 2001. "The decline of the mainline: Demography, doctrine and attachment." *American Journal of Sociology.* 107: 468–500.

Hout, Michael, and Andrew M. Greeley 1987. "The center doesn't hold: Church attendance in the United States, 1940–1984." *American Sociological Review.* 52(3): 325–345.

———. 1990. "The cohort doesn't hold: Comment on Chaves 1989." *Journal for the Scientific Study of Religion.* 29(4): 519–524.

———. 1998. "What church officials' reports don't show: Another look at church attendance data." *American Sociological Review.* 63(1): 113–119.

Hout, Michael, and C. S. Fischer. 2002. "Why more Americans have no religious preference: Politics and generations." *American Sociological Review.* 67(2): 165–190.

Hout, Michael, Andrew M. Greeley, and Melissa J. Wilde. 2001. "The demographic imperative in religious change in the United States." *American Journal of Sociology.* 107(2): 468–500.

Houtman, Dick, and Peter Mascini. 2002. "Why do churches become empty, while New Age grows? Secularization and religious change in the Netherlands." *Journal for the Scientific Study of Religion.* 41(3): 455–473.

Huber, Jon, and Ronald Inglehart. 1995. "Expert interpretations of party space and party locations in 42 societies." *Party Politics.* 11: 71–111.

Hunter, Shireen T. 1998. *The Future of Islam and the West: Clash of Civilizations or Peaceful Coexistence?* Westport, CT: Praeger.

Huntington, Samuel P. 1993. "If not civilizations, what? Paradigms of the post-Cold War world." *Foreign Affairs.* 72(5): 186–194.

———. 1993. "The clash of civilizations?" *Foreign Affairs.* 72(3): 22–49.

———. 1996. "The West unique, not universal." *Foreign Affairs.* 75(6): 28–34.

———. 1996. *The Clash of Civilizations and the Remaking of World Order.* New York: Simon & Schuster.

———. 1997. "The clash of civilizations – response." *Millennium – Journal of International Studies.* 26(1): 141–142.

Hunwick, J. 1992. "An African case study of political Islam: Nigeria." *Annals of the American Academy of Political and Social Science.* 524: 143–155.

Husband, William B. 2000. *"Godless Communists": Atheism and Society in Soviet Russia, 1917–1932.* DeKalb: Northern Illinois Press.

Iannaccone, Laurence R. 1990. "Religious practice: A human capital approach." *Journal for the Scientific Study of Religion.* 29: 297–314.

———. 1991. "The consequences of religious market structure." *Rationality and Society.* 3: 156–177.

———. 1998. "Introduction to the economics of religion." *Journal of Economic Literature.* 36(3): 1465–1496.

Iannaccone, Lawrence R., and Roger Finke. 1993. "Supply-side explanations for religious change." *The Annals.* 527: 27–39.

Immerman, Ronald S., and Wade C. Mackey. 2003. "Religion and fertility." *Mankind Quarterly.* 43(4): 377–403.

Inglehart, Ronald. 1977. *The Silent Revolution: Changing Values and Political Styles among Western Publics.* Princeton, NJ: Princeton University Press.

———. 1990. *Culture Shift in Advanced Industrial Society.* Princeton, NJ: Princeton University Press.

———. 1997. *Modernization and Postmodernization: Cultural, Economic and Political Change in 43 Societies.* Princeton, NJ: Princeton University Press.

———. 1997. "The trend toward Postmaterialist values continues." In *Citizen Politics in Post-Industrial Societies.* Eds. Terry Clark and Michael Rempel. Boulder, CO: Westview Press.

———. 1999. "Trust, well-being and democracy." In *Democracy and Trust.* Ed. Mark Warren. Cambridge, U.K.: Cambridge University Press.

———. 2000. "Culture and democracy." In *Culture Matters.* Eds. Samuel Huntington and Lawrence Harrison. New York: Basic Books.

———. 2000. "Globalization and postmodern values." *Washington Quarterly.* 232: 215–228.

———. 2003. "How solid is mass support for democracy and how do we measure it?" *PS: Political Science and Politics.*

Inglehart, Ronald, and Paul Abramson. 1999. "Measuring post-materialism." *American Political Science Review.* 93(3): 665–677.

Inglehart, Ronald, and Pippa Norris. 2000. "The developmental theory of the gender gap: Women's and men's voting behavior in global perspective." *International Political Science Review.* 214: 441–462.

———. 2003. "Muslims and the West: A clash of civilizations?" *Foreign Policy.* March/April: 63–70.

———. 2003. *Rising Tide: Gender Equality and Cultural Change Around the World.* New York and Cambridge, U.K.: Cambridge University Press.

Inglehart, Ronald, and Wayne E. Baker. 2000. "Modernization, globalization and the persistence of tradition: Empirical evidence from 65 societies." *American Sociological Review.* 65: 19–55.

———. 2001. "Modernization's challenge to traditional values: Who's afraid of Ronald McDonald?" *Futurist.* 35(2): 16–21.

Inkeles, A., and David Smith. 1974. *Becoming Modern.* Cambridge, MA: Harvard University Press.

Ivekovic, I. 2002. "Nationalism and the political use and abuse of religion: The politicization of Orthodoxy, Catholicism and Islam in Yugoslav successor states." *Social Compass.* 49(4): 523–536.

Jagodzinski, Wolfgang, and Karel Dobbelaere. 1995. "Religious and ethical pluralism." In *The Impact of Values.* Eds. Jan W. van Deth and Elinor Scarbrough. Oxford: Oxford University Press.

———. 1995. "Secularization and church religiosity." In *The Impact of Values.* Eds. Jan W. van Deth and Elinor Scarbrough. Oxford: Oxford University Press.

Jelen, Ted Gerard. 1987. "The effect of religious separatism on white Protestants in the 1984 presidential election." *Sociological Analysis.* 48(1): 30–45.

Jelen, Ted Gerard, and Clyde Wilcox. 1995. *Public Attitudes towards Church and State.* Armonk, NY: M. E. Sharpe.

———. 1998. "Context and conscience: The Catholic Church as an agent of political socialization in Western Europe." *Journal for the Scientific Study of Religion.* 37(1): 28–40.

_____. Eds. 2002. *Religion and Politics in Comparative Perspective: The One, the Few and the Many.* New York: Cambridge University Press.

Jensen, T., and Mikael Rothstein. Eds. 2000. *Secular Theories on Religion: Current Perspectives.* Copenhagen: Museum Tusculanum Press.

Johnston, H. 1994. "Religio-Nationalist subcultures under the Communists: Comparisons from the Baltics, Transcaucasia and Ukraine." In *Politics and Religion in Central and Eastern Europe: Traditions and Transitions.* Ed. W. H. Swatos, Jr. Westport, CT: Praeger.

Johnstone, R. 1997. *Religion in Society: A Sociology of Religion.* Upper Saddle River, NJ: Prentice Hall.

Jones, Harold B., Jr. 1997. "The Protestant ethic: Weber's model and the empirical literature." *Human Relations* 50(7): 757–778.

Kaariainen, K. 1999. "Religiousness in Russia after the collapse of communism." *Social Compass.* 46 (1): 35–46.

Kabuli, Niaz Faizi. 1994. *Democracy according to Islam.* Pittsburgh, PA: Dorrance Publications.

Karawan, I. 1992. "Monarchs, mullahs and marshals: Islamic regimes?" *Annals of the American Academy of Political and Social Science.* 524: 103–119.

Kaufmann, Daniel, Aart Kraay, and Massimo Mastruzzi. 2003. *Governance Matters III: Governance Indicators for 1996–2002.* Available online at: http://econ.worldbank.org/view.php?type=5&id=28791.

Kazemi F. 2000. "Gender, Islam and politics." *Social Research.* 67(2): 453–474.

Keely, Louise. 2003. "Comment on: People's opium? Religion and economic attitudes." *Journal of Monetary Economics.* 50(1): 283–287.

Kelley, J., and N. D. DeGraaf. 1997. "National context, parental socialization, and religious belief: Results from 15 nations." *American Sociological Review.* 62(4): 639–659.

Keslman, Thomas, and Joseph A. Buttigieg. Eds. 2003. *European Christian Democracy: Historical Legacies and Comparative Perspectives.* Notre Dame, IN: University of Notre Dame Press.

Khan, S. 1998. "Muslim women: Negotiations in the third space." *Signs.* 23(2): 463–494.

Kim, A. E. 2002. "Characteristics of religious life in South Korea: A sociological survey." *Review of Religious Research.* 43(4): 291–310.

King, Gary, and Christopher J. L. Murray. 2001. "Rethinking Human Security." *Political Science Quarterly* 116(4): 585–610.

Kisala, Robert J. 2003. "Japanese religiosity and morals." In *Religion in a Secularizing Society.* Eds. Loek Halman and Ole Reis. Leiden: Brill.

Kitagawa, Joseph M. 1987. *On Understanding Japanese Religion.* Princeton, NJ: Princeton University Press.

Klingemann, Hans Dieter. 1999. "Mapping political support in the 1990s: A global analysis." In *Critical Citizens: Global Support for Democratic Governance.* Ed. Pippa Norris. Oxford: Oxford University Press.

Kohut, Andrew, John C. Green, Scott Keeter, and Robert C. Toth. 2000. *The Diminishing Divide: Religion's Changing Role in American Politics*. Washington, D.C.: Brookings Institution Press.

Kolodko, Grzegorz W. 2000. *From Shock to Therapy: The Political Economy of Socialist Transformations*. New York: Oxford University Press.

Kotler-Berkowitz, L. A. 2001. "Religion and voting behaviour in Great Britain: A reassessment." *British Journal of Political Science*. 31(3): 523–554.

Kutz, Lester. 1995. *Gods in the Global Village: The World's Religions in Sociological Perspective*. Thousand Oaks, CA: Sage.

Ladd, Carl Everett. 1996. "The data just don't show erosion of America's social capital." *The Public Perspective* 7(4).

Laeyendecker, L. 1995. "The case of the Netherlands." In *The Post-War Generation and Establishment Religion*. W. C. Roof, J. W. Carroll, and D. A. Roozen. Boulder, CO: Westview Press.

Lambert, Y. 1999. "Religion in modernity as a new axial age: Secularization or new religious forms?" *Sociology of Religion*. 60(3): 303–333.

Larson, E. J., and L. Witham. 1998. "Leading scientists still reject God." *Nature*. 394(6691): 313.

Lavigne, Marie. 2001. *The Economics of Transition: From Socialist Economy to Market Economy*. London: Palgrave.

Laznjak, J. 1997. "Traditional and new religiosity in post-communism: The changes in student religiosity 1990–1994." *Drustvena Istrazivanja*. 6(1): 49–70.

Lechner, F. J. 1991. "The case against secularization: A rebuttal." *Social Forces* 69: 1103–1119.

———. 1996. "Secularization in the Netherlands?" *Journal for the Scientific Study of Religion*. 35(3): 252–264.

Leege, David, and Lyman A. Kellstedt. Eds. 1993. *Rediscovering the Religious Factor in American Politics*. Armonk, NY: M. E. Sharpe.

Lehman, Hartmut, and Guenther Roth. Eds. 1993. *Weber's Protestant Ethic: Origins, Evidence, Contexts*. New York: Cambridge University Press.

Lemmen, M. M. W. 1990. *Max Weber's Sociology of Religion: Its Method and Content in the Light of the Concept of Rationality*. Heevlen, The Netherlands: GPT-Katernen 10.

Lerner, Daniel. 1958. *The Passing of Traditional Society: Modernizing the Middle East*. New York: The Free Press.

Lessnoff, Michael H. 1994. *The spirit of capitalism and the Protestant ethic: An enquiry into the Weber thesis*. Aldershot, U.K.: Edward Elgar.

Lewis, Bernard. 2002. *What Went Wrong? Western Impact and Middle Eastern Response*. New York: Oxford University Press.

Lewis-Beck, Michael, and Andrew Skalaban. "France." In *Electoral Change: Responses to Evolving Social and Attitudinal Structures in Western Countries*. Eds. Mark Franklin et al. Cambridge, U.K.: Cambridge University Press.

Lindsay, D. Michael. 2000. *Surveying the Religious Landscape: Trends in U.S. Beliefs.* New York: Moorhouse Publishing.

Lipset, Seymour Martin. 1959. "Some social requisites of democracy: Economic development and political legitimacy." *American Political Science Review.* 53: 69–105.

————. 1960. *Political Man: The Social Bases of Politics.* Garden City, NY: Doubleday.

————. 1990. *Continental Divide: The Values and Institutions of Canada and the United States.* New York: Routledge.

Lipset, Seymour Martin, and Stein Rokkan. 1967. *Party Systems and Voter Alignments.* New York: The Free Press.

Lipset, Seymour Martin, Kyoung-Ryung Seong, and John Charles Torres. 1993. "A comparative analysis of the social requisites of democracy." *International Social Science Journal.* 452: 154–175.

Littleton, C. Scott. Ed. 1996. *The Sacred East.* London: Macmillan.

Lopez, Donald S. 1999. *Asian Religions in Practice: An Introduction.* Princeton, NJ: Princeton University Press.

Lovenduski, Joni. 1986. *Women and European Politics.* Sussex, U.K.: Wheatsheaf.

Luckmann, Thomas. 1967. *The Invisible Religion: The Problem of Religion in Modern Society.* New York: Macmillan.

Madeley, John. 1991. "Politics and religion in Western Europe." In *Politics and Religion in the Modern World.* Ed. George Moyser. London: Routledge.

Mainwaring, Scott, and Timothy R. Scully. Eds. 2003. *Christian Democracy in Latin America: Electoral Competition and Regime Conflicts.* Stanford, CA: Stanford University Press.

Majid, A. 2000. "The politics of feminism in Islam." *Signs.* 23(2): 321–361.

Maloney, William L., Graham Smith, and Gerry Stoker. 2000. "Social capital and associational life." In *Social Capital: Critical Perspectives.* Eds. Stephen Baron, John Field, and Tom Schuller. Oxford: Oxford University Press.

Manza, Jeff, and Clem Brooks. 1997. "The religious factor in U.S. presidential elections, 1960–1992." *American Journal of Sociology.* 103(1): 38–81.

————. 1998. "The gender gap in U.S. presidential elections: When? Why? Implications?" *American Journal of Sociology.* 103(5): 1235–1266.

Marshall, Monty, and Ted Robert Gurr. 2003. *Peace and Conflict 2003.* University of Maryland, Center for Systemic Peace/Minorities At Risk. Available online at: http://www.cidcm.umd.edu/inscr/pc03web.pdf.

Marshall, Paul. 2000. *Religious Freedom in the World.* Available online at: www.freedomhouse.org.

Marshall, Paul. Ed. 2000. *Religious Freedom in the World: A Global Report on Freedom and Persecution.* Nashville, TN: Broadman and Holman.

Martin, David. 1967. *A Sociology of English Religion.* London: SCM Press.

————. 1978. *A General Theory of Secularization.* Oxford: Blackwell.

Marty, Martin, and R. Scott Appleby. Eds. 1991. *Fundamentalisms Comprehended.* Chicago: University of Chicago Press.

_____. Eds. 1991. *Fundamentalisms Observed*. Chicago: University of Chicago Press.

_____. Eds. 1993. *Fundamentalisms and Society*. Chicago: University of Chicago Press.

_____. Eds. 1993. *Fundamentalisms and the State*. Chicago: University of Chicago Press.

_____. Eds. 1994. *Accounting for Fundamentalisms*. Chicago: University of Chicago Press.

Mayer, Lawrence, and Roland E. Smith. 1985. "Feminism and Religiosity: Female Electoral Behavior in Western Europe." In *Women and Politics in Western Europe*. Ed. Sylia Bashekin. London: Frank Cass.

McAllister, Ian. 1988. "Religious change and secularization: The transmission of religious values in Australia." *Sociological Analysis*. 49(3): 249–263.

McAllister, R. J. 2000. "Religious identity and the future of Northern Ireland." *Policy Studies Journal*. 28(4): 843–857.

McCready, William, and Nancy McCready. 1973. "Socialization and the persistence of religion." In *The Persistence of Religion*. Eds. Andrew Greeley and Gregory Baum. New York: Herder & Herder.

McFate, Katherine, Roger Lawson, and William Julius Wilson. Eds. 1995. *Poverty, Inequality, and the Future of Social Policy: Western States in the New World Order*. New York: Russell Sage.

McGillivray, Mark, and Howard White. 1993. "Measuring development? The UNDP's Human Development Index." *Journal of International Development*. 5(2): 183–192.

McKenzie, B. D. 2001. "Self-selection, church attendance, and local civic participation." *Journal for the Scientific Study of Religion*. 40(3): 479–488.

McPherson, J., and Lynn Smith-Lovin. 1982. "Women and weak ties: Differences by sex in the size of voluntary organizations." *American Journal of Sociology*. 87: 883–904.

McVeigh, R., and D. Sikkink. 2001. "God, politics, and protest: Religious beliefs and the legitimation of contentious tactics." *Social Forces*. 79(4): 1425–1458.

Meadows, D., et al. 1972. *The Limits to Growth*. New York: Universe Books.

Meriwether, Margaret L., and Judith E. Tucker. Eds. 2000. *Social History of Women and Gender in the Modern Middle East*. Boulder, CO: Westview Press.

Meyer K., H. Rizzo, and Y. Ali. 1998. "Islam and the extension of citizenship rights to women in Kuwait." *Journal for the Scientific Study of Religion*. 37(1): 131–144.

Michelat, G., et al. 1991. *Les Français, Sont-ils Encore Catholiques?: Analyse d'un Sondage d'Opinion*. Paris: Editions du Cerf.

Midlarsky, M. I. 1998. "Democracy and Islam: Implications for civilizational conflict and the democratic process." *International Studies Quarterly*. 42(3): 485–511.

Miller, Alan S. 1992. "Conventional religious behavior in modern Japan: A service industry perspective." *Journal for the Scientific Study of Religion*. 31: 207–214.

———. 1995. "A rational choice model for religious behavior in Japan." *Journal for the Scientific Study of Religion.* 34: 234–244.

———. 1998. "Why Japanese religions look different: The social role of religious organizations in Japan." *Review of Religious Research.* 39: 379–389.

———. 2000. "Going to hell in Asia: The relationship between risk and religion in a cross cultural setting." *Review of Religious Research.* 42: 5–18.

Miller, Alan S., and John P. Hoffmann. 1995. "Risk and religion: An explanation of gender differences in religiosity." *Journal for the Scientific Study of Religion.* 34: 63–75.

Miller Alan S., and Rodney Stark. 2002. "Gender and religiousness: Can socialization explanations be saved?" *American Journal of Sociology.* 107(6): 1399–1423.

Miller, Alan S., and Satoshi Kanazawa. 2000. *Order by Accident: The Origins and Consequences of Conformity in Contemporary Japan.* Boulder, CO: Westview.

Miller, Alan S., and T. Nakamura 1996. "On the stability of church attendance patterns: 1965–1988." *Journal for the Scientific Study of Religion.* 35(3): 275–284.

Miller, K. D. 2002. "Competitive strategies of religious organizations." *Strategic Management Journal.* 23(5): 435–456.

Miller, M. J., D. J. Woehr, and N. Hudspeth. 2002. "The meaning and measurement of work ethic: Construction and initial validation of a multidimensional inventory." *Journal of Vocational Behavior.* 60(3): 451–489.

Miller, Thomas W., and Geoffrey Feinberg. 2002. "Culture clash." *Public Perspective.* 13(2): 6–9.

Miller, Warren, and Merrill Shanks. 1996. *The New American Voter.* Ann Arbor, MI: University of Michigan Press.

Minkenberg, M. 2002. "Religion and public policy: Institutional, cultural, and political impact on the shaping of abortion policies in Western democracies." *Comparative Political Studies.* 35(2): 221–247.

———. 2003. "The policy impact of church-state relations: Family policy and abortion in Britain, France, and Germany." *West European Politics.* 26(1): 195–206.

Mitchell, Paul, Brendan O'Leary, and Geoffrey Evans. 2001. "Northern Ireland: Flanking extremists bite the moderates and emerge in their clothes." *Parliamentary Affairs* 54(4): 725–742.

Moaddel, M. 2002. "The study of Islamic culture and politics: An overview and assessment." *Annual Review of Sociology.* 28: 359–386.

Moaddel, Mansoor, and Taghi Azadarmaki. 2003. "The worldview of Islamic publics: The cases of Egypt, Iran and Jordan." In *Culture and Social Change: Findings from the Values Surveys.* Ed. Ronald Inglehart. Leiden: Brill Academic Publishers.

Moen, Matthew C., and Lowell Gustafson. Eds. *The Religious Challenge to the State.* Philadelphia: Temple University Press.

Mol, Hans. 1985. *The Faith of Australians.* Sydney: George Allen & Unwin.

Monsma, Steven V., and J. Chrisopher Soper. 1997. *The Challenge of Pluralism: Church and State in Five Democracies.* Lanham, MD: Rowman & Littlefield.

Moore, Gwen. 1990. "Structural determinants of men's and women's personal networks." *American Sociological Review* 55: 726–735.

Moyser, George. Ed. 1991. *Politics and Religion in the Modern World*. London: Routledge.

Mughan, Anthony. 1983. "Accommodation or diffusion in the management of ethnic conflict in Belgium." *Political Studies*. 31: 431–451.

Munck, Geraldo L., and Jay Verkuilen. 2002. "Conceptualizing and measuring democracy – Evaluating alternative indices." *Comparative Political Studies*. 35(1): 5–34.

Myers, S. M. 1996. "An interactive model of religiosity inheritance: The importance of family context." *American Sociological Review*. 61(5): 858–866.

Naumkin, V. 1992. "Islam in the states of the Former USSR." *Annals of the American Academy of Political and Social Science*. 524: 131–142.

Need, Ariana, and Geoffrey Evans. 2001. "Analysing patterns of religious participation in post-communist Eastern Europe." *British Journal of Sociology*. 52(2): 229–248.

Neitz, Mary Jo. 1990. "In goddess we trust." In *In Gods We Trust: New Patterns of Religious Pluralism in America*. Ed. Thomas Robbins and Dick Anthony. New Brunswick, NJ: Transaction Books.

Newton, Kenneth. 2001. "Trust, social capital, civic society, and democracy." *International Political Science Review*. 22(2): 201–214.

Newton, Kenneth, and Pippa Norris. 2000. "Confidence in public institutions: Faith, culture or performance?" In *Disaffected Democracies: What's Troubling the Trilateral Countries?* Eds. Susan Pharr and Robert Putnam. Princeton, NJ: Princeton University Press.

Nie, Norman, Sidney Verba, and John Petrocik. 1976. *The Changing American Voter*. Cambridge, MA: Harvard University Press.

Norris, Pippa. 1985. "Women in European legislative elites." *West European Politics*. 84: 90–101.

———. 1988. "The gender gap: A cross national trend?" In *The Politics of the Gender Gap*. Ed. Carol Mueller. Beverley Hills, CA: Sage.

———. 1996. "Gender realignment in comparative perspective." In *The Paradox of Parties*. Ed. Marian Simms. Sydney, Australia: Allen & Unwin.

———. Ed. 1999. *Critical Citizens: Global Support for Democratic Governance*. Oxford: Oxford University Press.

———. 2000. *A Virtuous Circle: Political Communications in Postindustrial Societies*. Cambridge: Cambridge University Press.

———. 2001. "US Campaign 2000: Of pregnant chads, butterfly ballots and partisan vitriol." *Government and Opposition*. January 35(2): 1–24.

———. 2002. *Democratic Phoenix: Political Activism Worldwide*. New York and Cambridge, U.K.: Cambridge University Press.

———. 2003. *Electoral Engineering: Voting Rules and Political Behavior*. New York: Cambridge University Press.

———. 2003. "Gendering social capital? Bowling in women's leagues?" Conference on Gender and Social Capital, St. John's College, University of Manitoba, 2–3 May 2003.

Norris, Pippa, Montague Kern, and Marion Just. Eds. 2003. *Framing Terrorism*. New York: Routledge.

Norris, Pippa, and Ronald Inglehart. 2001. "Cultural obstacles to equal representation." *The Journal of Democracy*. 123: 126–140.

Norris, Pippa, and Joni Lovenduski. 1995. *Political Recruitment: Gender, Race and Class in the British Parliament*. Cambridge, U.K.: Cambridge University Press.

Norton, A. R. 1997. "Gender, politics and the state: What do Middle Eastern women want?" *Middle East Policy*. 5(3): 155–165.

Ntambue, R. 2000. "Secularism and religion in Africa: Sphere of humanization." *Social Compass*. 47(3): 329–341.

Page, Benjamin I., and Robert Y. Shapiro. 1993. *The Rational Public*. Chicago: University of Chicago Press.

Parker, Philip M. 1997. *Religious Cultures of the World: A Statistical Reference*. Westport, CT: Greenwood Press.

Pedersen, Morgens. 1979. "The Dynamics of European Party Systems: Changing Patterns of Electoral Volatility." *European Journal of Political Research*. 7: 1–27.

Petersen, Larry R., and Gregory V. Donnenwerth. 1998. "Religion and declining support for traditional beliefs and gender roles and homosexual rights." *Sociology of Religion*. 59: 353–371.

Pettersson, Thorleif, and E. M. Hamberg. 1997. "Denominational pluralism and church membership in contemporary Sweden: A longitudinal study of the period, 1974–1995." *Journal of Empirical Theology*. 10: 61–78.

Pew Research Center for the People and the Press. 2002. *"Americans Struggle with Religion's Role at Home and Abroad."* News Release by the Pew Forum on Religion.

Polanyi, K. 1944. *The Great Transformation*. New York: Farrar and Rinehart.

Pollack, D. 2003. "Religiousness inside and outside the church in selected post-Communist countries of Central and Eastern Europe." *Social Compass*. 50(3): 321–334.

Presser, S., and L. Stinson 1998. "Data collection mode and social desirability bias in self-reported religious attendance." *American Sociological Review*. 63(1): 137–145.

Przeworski, Adam, Michael Alvarez, Jose Antonio Cheibub, and Fernando Limongi. 2000. *Democracy and Development: Political Institutions and Well-Being in the World, 1950–1990*. New York: Cambridge University Press.

Przeworski, Adam, and Henry Teune. 1970. *The Logic of Comparative Social Inquiry*. New York: Wiley–Interscience.

Pulzer, Peter, G. J. 1967. *Political Representation and Elections in Britain*. London: Allen & Unwin.

Putnam, Robert D. 1995. *Making Democracy Work: Civic Traditions in Modern Italy*. Princeton, NJ: Princeton University Press.

———. 1995. "Tuning in, tuning out: The strange disappearance of social capital in America." *P.S.: Political Science and Politics.* XXVIII (4): 664–683.

———. 1996. "The strange disappearance of civic America." *The American Prospect.* 7(24): 50–64.

———. 2000. *Bowling Alone: The Collapse and Revival of American Community.* New York: Simon & Schuster.

———. Ed. 2002. *The Dynamics of Social Capital.* Oxford: Oxford University Press.

Putnam, Robert D., and Susan Pharr. Eds. 2001. *Disaffected Democracies: What's Troubling the Trilateral Countries?* Princeton, NJ: Princeton University Press.

Putnam, Robert D. Ed. 2002. *Democracies in Flux.* Oxford: Oxford University Press.

Reader, I. 1991. *Religion in Contemporary Japan.* London: Macmillan.

Regan, D. 1993. "Islamic resurgence – Characteristics, causes, consequences and implications." *Journal of Political & Military Sociology.* 21(2): 259–266.

Riis, Ole. 1994. "Patterns of secularization in Scandinavia." In *Scandinavian Values: Religion and Morality in the Nordic Countries.* Eds. Thorleif Pettersson and Ole Riis. Upssala: Acta Universitatis Upsaliensis.

———. 1998. "Religion re-emerging: The role of religion in legitimating integration and power in modern societies." *International Sociology.* 13(2): 249–272.

Roberts, K. A. 1990. *Religion in Sociological Perspective.* Belmont, CA: Wadsworth.

Rokkan, Stein. 1970. *Citizens, Elections, Parties. Approaches to the Comparative Study of the Processes of Development.* Oslo: Universitetsforlaget.

Roof, Wade Clark. 2001. *Spiritual Marketplace: Baby Boomers and the Remaking of American Religion.* Princeton, NJ: Princeton University Press.

Rose, Richard. 1974. *Electoral Behavior: A Comparative Handbook.* New York: The Free Press.

Rose, Richard. 2000. "Uses of social capital in Russia: Modern, pre-modern, and anti-modern." *Post-Soviet Affairs.* 16(1): 33–57.

———. 2002. "How Muslims view democracy: Evidence from Central Asia." *Journal of Democracy.* 14(4): 102–111.

Rose, Richard, William Mishler, and Christopher Haerpfer. 1997. "Social capital in civic and stressful societies." *Studies in Comparative International Development.* 32(3): 85–111.

Rose, Richard, and Derek W. Urwin. 1970. "Persistence and change in Western party systems since 1945." *Political Studies.* 18: 287–319.

Rosenstone, Steven J., and John Mark Hansen. 1995. *Mobilization, Participation and Democracy in America.* New York: Macmillan.

Rostow, Walt Whitman. 1952. *The Process of Economic Growth.* New York: Norton.

———. 1960. *The Stages of Economic Growth.* Cambridge, U.K.: Cambridge University Press.

Rothstein, Bo. 2000. "Social capital in the social democratic state." In *Democracies in Flux.* Ed. Robert D. Putnam. Oxford: Oxford University Press.

Rotolo, Thomas. 1999. "Trends in voluntary association participation." *Nonprofit and Voluntary Sector Quarterly.* 28(2): 199–212.

Rothstein, Bo, and Dieter Stolle. 2003. "Introduction: Social capital in Scandinavia." *Scandinavian Political Studies.* 26(1): 1–26.

Russett B. M., J. R. O'Neal, and M. Cox. 2000. "Clash of civilizations, or realism and liberalism déjà vu? Some evidence." *Journal of Peace Research.* 37(5): 583–608.

Said, Edward. 2001. "A Clash of Ignorance." *The Nation.* 273(12): 11–13.

Saliba, T. 2000. "Arab feminism at the millennium." *Signs.* 25(4): 1087–1092.

Samuelson, K. 1993. *Religion and Economic Action: The Protestant Ethic, the Rise of Capitalism and the Abuses of Scholarship.* Toronto: University of Toronto Press.

Sasaki, M., and T. Suzuki 1987. "Change in religious commitment in the United States, Holland, and Japan." *American Journal of Sociology.* 92(5): 1055–1076.

Scheepers, P., and F. Van Der Slik. 1998. "Religion and attitudes on moral issues: Effects of individual, spouse and parental characteristics." *Journal for the Scientific Study of Religion.* 37(4): 678–691.

Scheepers, P., M. Gijsberts, and E. Hello. 2002. "Religiosity and prejudice against ethnic minorities in Europe: Cross-national tests on a controversial relationship." *Review of Religious Research.* 43(3): 242–265.

Scheepers, P., M. T. Grotenhuis, and F. Van Der Slik. 2002. "Education, religiosity and moral attitudes: Explaining cross-national effect differences." *Sociology of Religion.* 63(2): 157–176.

Schoenfeld, Eugen, and Stjepan G. Mestrovic. 1991. "With justice and mercy: Instrumental-masculine and expressive-feminine elements in religion." *Journal for the Scientific Study of Religion.* 30: 363–380.

Schudson, Michael. 1996. "What if civic life didn't die?" *The American Prospect.* 25: 17–20.

Schumpeter, Joseph. 1947. *Capitalism, Socialism and Democracy.* New York: Harper Brothers.

Scott, Jacqueline. 1998. "Generational changes in attitudes to abortion: A cross-national comparison." *European Sociological Review.* 14(2): 177–190.

Seltzer, Richard A., Jody Newman, and Melissa V. Leighton. 1997. *Sex As a Political Variable.* Boulder, CO: Lynne Reinner.

Sen, Amartya. 1999. *Development as Freedom.* New York: Anchor Books.

Sengers, E. 2001. *We Want Our Part! The Dutch Catholic Church from Sect to Church as Explanation for its Growth and Decline: A Rational Choice Perspective.* Amsterdam: University of Amsterdam Press.

Shadid, Anthony. 2001. *Legacy of the Prophet: Despots, Democrats, and the New Politics of Islam.* Boulder, CO: Westview Press.

Sharma, Arvind, and Katherine K. Young. Eds. 1999. *Feminism and World Religions.* Albany, NY: State University of New York Press.

Sharot, Stephen. 2001. *A Comparative Sociology of World Religions.* New York: New York University Press.

———. 2002. "Beyond Christianity: A critique of the rational choice theory of religion from a Weberian and comparative religions perspective." *Sociology of Religion.* 63(4): 427–454.

Sherkat, Darren E. 2002. "Sexuality and religious commitment in the United States: An empirical examination." *Journal for the Scientific Study of Religion.* 41: 313–323.

Sherkat, Darren E., and Christopher G. Ellison. 1999. "Recent developments and current controversies in the sociology of religion." *Annual Review of Sociology.* 25: 363–394.

Shiner, L. 1966. "The concept of secularization in empirical research." *Journal for the Scientific Study of Religion.* 6: 207–220.

Siaroff, A. 2000. "Women's representation in legislatures and cabinets in industrial democracies." *International Political Science Review.* 21(2): 197–215.

Sigelman, Lee. 1977. "Multi-nation surveys of religious beliefs." *Journal for the Scientific Study of Religion.* 16: 289–294.

Skopol, Theda. 1996. "Unravelling from above." *The American Prospect.* 25: 20–25.

Smith, Christian. 1998. *American Evangelicalism: Embattled and thriving.* Chicago: University of Chicago Press.

———. 2003. *The Secular Revolution.* Berkeley, CA: University of California Press.

Smith, Ian. 1993. "The economics of church decline in Scotland." *International Journal of Social Economics.* 20(12): 27–36.

Smith, Ian, John W. Sawkins, and Paul T. Seaman. 1998. "The economics of religious participation: A cross-country study." *Kyklos.* 51(1): 25–43.

Smith, Tom. 1992. "Are conservative churches really growing?" *Review of Religious Research.* 33: 305–329.

Snow, D. A., and C. L. Phillips. 1980. "The Lofland-Stark conversion model: A critical reassessment." *Social Problems.* 27: 430–437.

Spier, F. 1996. *The Structure of Big History.* Amsterdam: Amsterdam University Press.

Stark, Rodney. 1997. "German and German American religiousness: Approximating a crucial experiment." *Journal for the Scientific Study of Religion.* 36(2): 182–193.

———. 1999. "Secularization, RIP." *Sociology of Religion.* 60(3): 249–273.

———. 2002. "Physiology and faith: Addressing the 'universal' gender difference in religious commitment." *Journal for the Scientific Study of Religion.* 41: 495–507.

Stark, Rodney, and William Sims Bainbridge. 1985. *The Future of Religion: Secularization, Revival and Cult Formation.* Berkeley, CA: University of California Press.

———. 1985. "A supply-side reinterpretation of the 'secularization' of Europe." *Journal for the Scientific Study of Religion.* 33: 230–252.

———. 1987. *A Theory of Religion.* New York: Peter Lang.

Stark, Rodney, and Roger Finke. 2000. *Acts of Faith: Explaining the Human Side of Religion.* Berkeley, CA: University of California Press.

Stark, Rodney, and Lawrence Iannaccone. 1994. "A supply-side reinterpretation of the 'secularization' of Europe." *Journal for the Scientific Study of Religion.* 33: 230–252.

Steensland, B, J. Z. Park, M. D. Regnerus, L. D. Robinson, W. B. Wilcox, and Robert D. Woodberry. 2000. "The measure of American religion: Toward improving the state of the art." *Social Forces.* 79(1): 291–318.

Steggarda, M. 1993. "Religion and the social positions of men and women." *Social Compass.* 40: 65–73.

Strassberg, Barbara. 1988. "Changes in religious culture in post World War II Poland." *Sociological Analysis.* 48(4): 342–354.

Strickler, J., and N. L. Danigelis. 2002. "Changing frameworks in attitudes toward abortion." *Sociological Forum.* 17(2): 187–201.

Suziedelis, Antanas, and Raymond H. Potvin. 1981. "Sex differences in factors affecting religiousness among Catholic adolescents." *Journal for the Scientific Study of Religion.* 20: 38–50.

Swatos, Jr. W. H. Ed. 1989. *Religious Politics in Global and Comparative Perspective.* New York: Greenwood Press.

———. Ed. 1994. *Politics and Religion in Central and Eastern Europe: Traditions and Transitions.* Westport, CT: Praeger.

Swatos, Jr. W. H., and K. J. Christiano. 1999. "Secularization theory: The course of a concept." *Sociology of Religion.* 60(3): 209–228.

Swedburg, R. 1998. *Max Weber and the Idea of Economic Sociology.* Princeton, NJ: Princeton University Press.

Takayama, K. 1988. "Revitalization movement of modern Japanese civil religion." *Sociological Analysis.* 48(4): 328–341.

Tanwir, Farooq. 2003. "Religious parties and politics in Pakistan." *International Journal of Comparative Sociology.*

Tawney, R. H. 1926. *Religion and the Rise of Capitalism.* New York: Harper & Row.

Tessler, Mark. 2002. "Islam and democracy in the Middle East: The impact of religious orientations on attitudes towards democracy in four Arab Countries." *Comparative Politics.* 34(1): 337–254.

———. 2003. "Do Islamic orientations influence attitudes toward democracy in the Arab world? Evidence from Egypt, Jordan, Morocco and Algeria." *International Journal of Comparative Sociology.* 43(3–5): 229–249.

Thompson, Edward H. 1991. "Beneath the status characteristic: Gender variations in religiousness." *Journal for the Scientific Study of Religion.* 30: 381–394.

Thornton, P. M. 2002. "Framing dissent in contemporary China: Irony, ambiguity and metonymy." *China Quarterly.* 171: 661–681.

Tilley, J. R. 2003. "Secularization and aging in Britain: Does family formation cause greater religiosity?" *Journal for the Scientific Study of Religion.* 42(2): 269–278.

Tingsten, Herbert L. G. 1937. *Political Behavior: Studies in Election Statistics.* London: P. S. King.

Tiryakian, Edward A. 1993. "American religious exceptionalism: A reconsideration." *The Annals of the American Academy of Political and Social Science.* 527: 40–54.

Tomka, Miklós. 1998. "Coping with persecution: Religious change in communism and in post-communist reconstruction in Central Europe." *International Sociology.* 13(2): 229–248.

Troyanovsky, I. Ed. 1991. *Religion in the Soviet Republics.* San Francisco: Harper-Collins.

Tschannen, O. 1991. "The secularization paradigm." *Journal for the Scientific Study of Religion.* 30(1): 395–415.

Turner, Bryan S. 1991. *Religion and Social Theory.* London: Sage.

Tversky, A., and D. Kahneman. 1974. "Judgment under uncertainty: Heuristics and biases." *Science.* 185: 1124–1131.

Uhlaner, Carole. 1989. "Rational turnout: The neglected role of groups." *American Journal of Political Science.* 33: 390–422.

United Nations. 2000. *The World's Women 2000: Trends and Statistics.* New York: United Nations.

———. 2002. *Human Development Report 2002.* New York: United Nations/Oxford University Press.

UNDP. 1995. *UNDP Human Development Report 1995.* New York: Oxford University Press/UNDP.

United Nations Development Program. 1994. *New Dimensions of Human Security.* New York: Oxford University Press.

United States Census Bureau. 2000. *Statistical Abstract of the United States, 1999.* Available online at: www.census.gov.

Van Deth, Jan Willem. Ed. 1997. *Private Groups and Public Life: Social Participation, Voluntary Associations and Political Involvement in Representative Democracies.* London: Routledge.

———. 2000. "Interesting but irrelevant: Social capital and the saliency of politics in Western Europe." *European Journal of Political Research.* 37:115–147.

van Deth, Jan Willem, and F. Kreuter. 1998. "Membership in voluntary associations." In *Comparative Politics: The Problem of Equivalence.* Ed. Jan W. van Deth. London: Routledge.

Verba, Sidney, and Norman Nie. 1972. *Participation in America: Political Democracy and Social Equality.* New York: Harper & Row.

Verba, Sidney, Kay Lehman Schlozman, and Henry E. Brady. 1995. *Voice and Equality: Civic Voluntarism in American Politics.* Cambridge, MA: Harvard University Press.

Verba, Sidney, Norman Nie, and Jae-on Kim. 1978. *Participation and Political Equality: A Seven-Nation Comparison.* New York: Cambridge University Press.

Vertigans, S., and P. Sutton. 2001. "Back to the future: 'Islamic terrorism' and interpretations of past and present." *Sociological Research Online.* 6(3): U55–U60.

Verweij, J., Peter Ester, and R. Nauta. 1997. "Secularization as an economic and cultural phenomenon: A cross-national analysis." *Journal for the Scientific Study of Religion.* 36(2): 309–324.

Voas, David, Daniel V. A. Olson, and Alasdair Crockett. 2002. "Religious pluralism and participation: Why previous research is wrong." *American Sociological Review.* 67(2): 212–230.

Voert, M. Ter. 1997. "The Protestant ethic in the Republic of the Seven United Netherlands: Fiction or fact?" *Netherlands Journal of Social Sciences.* 33(1): 1–10.

Voye, L. 1999. "Secularization in a context of advanced modernity." *Sociology of Religion*. 603: 275–288.

Wallis, R. 1988. "Paradoxes of freedom and regulation: The case of new religious movements in Britain and America." *Sociological Analysis*. 48(4): 355–371.

Walter, Tony, and Grace Davie. 1998. "The religiosity of women in the modern West." *British Journal of Sociology*. 49: 640–660.

Warner, Carolyn M. 2000. *Confessions of an Interest Group: The Catholic Church and Political Parties in Europe*. Princeton, NJ: Princeton University Press.

Warner, R. S. 1993. "Work in progress toward a new paradigm in the sociology of religion." *American Journal of Sociology*. 98(5): 1044–1093.

Weber, Max. 1930 [1904]. *The Protestant Ethic and the Spirit of Capitalism*. Trans. by T. Parsons. New York: Scribner's.

———. 1993 [1922]. *The Sociology of Religion*. Boston: Beacon Press.

Welzel, Christopher, Ronald Inglehart, and Hans-Dieter Klingemann. 2003. "The theory of human development: A cross-cultural analysis." *European Journal of Political Research*. 42(3): 341–379.

Wilcox, Clyde. 1991. "The causes and consequences of feminist consciousness among Western European women." *Comparative Political Studies*. 23(4): 519–545.

———. 1992. *God's Warriors: The Christian Right in Twentieth Century America*. Baltimore: The Johns Hopkins University Press.

———. 1996. *Onward Christian Soldiers: The Religious Right in American Politics*. Boulder, CO: Westview.

Wilcox, Clyde, and Lee Sigelman. 2001. "Political mobilization in the pews: Religious contacting and electoral turnout." *Social Science Quarterly*. 82(3): 524–535.

Wilson, Brian R. 1969. *Religion in Secular Society*. Harmondsworth, Middlesex, U.K.: Penguin Books, Ltd.

Wilson, Graham K. 1998. *Only in America? The Politics of the United States in Comparative Perspective*. Chatham, NJ: Chatham House.

Woodberry, R. D. 1996. *The Missing Fifty Percent: Accounting for the Gap Between Survey Estimates and Head-Counts of Church Attendance*. Nashville, TN: Society for the Scientific Study of Religion.

———. 1998. "When surveys lie and people tell the truth: How surveys over-sample church attenders." *American Sociological Review*. 63(1): 119–122.

World Bank. 2001. *World Development Indicators 2001*. Washington, D.C.: World Bank.

———. 2002. *World Development Report, 2002*. Washington, D.C.: World Bank.

Wuthnow, Robert. 1988. *The Restructuring of American Religion: Society and Faith since World War II*. Princeton, NJ: Princeton University Press.

———. 1994. *Sharing the Journey: Support Groups and America's New Quest for Community*. New York: The Free Press.

———. 1998. *Loose Connections: Joining Together in America's Fragmented Communities*. Cambridge, MA: Harvard University Press.

————. 1999. "Mobilizing civic engagement: The changing impact of religious involvement." In *Civic Engagement in American Democracy*. Eds. Theda Skocpol and Morris P. Fiorina. Washington, D.C.: Brookings Institution Press.

————. 2002. "Religious involvement and status-bridging social capital." *Journal for the Scientific Study of Religion*. 41(4): 669–675.

————. 2002. "The United States: Bridging the Privileged and the Marginalized?" In *Democracies in Flux*. Ed. Robert D. Putnam. Oxford: Oxford University Press.

Wuthnow, Robert, and John H. Evans. Eds. 2002. *The Quiet Hand of God*. Berkeley, CA: University of California Press.

Yamane, D. 1997. "Secularization on trial: In defense of a neosecularization paradigm." *Journal for the Scientific Study of Religion*. 36(1): 109–122.

Zrinscak, S. 2002. "Roles, expectation and conflicts: Religion and churches in societies undergoing transition." *Social Compass*. 49(4): 509–521.

Zubaida, S. 1995. "Is there a Muslim society? Ernest Gellner's sociology of Islam." *Economy and Society*. 24(2): 151–188.

Index